# Payroll Administration
# Technical Units 71 to 73

AAT Level 2 Certificate in
Payroll Administration (QCF)
(Finance Act 2009)

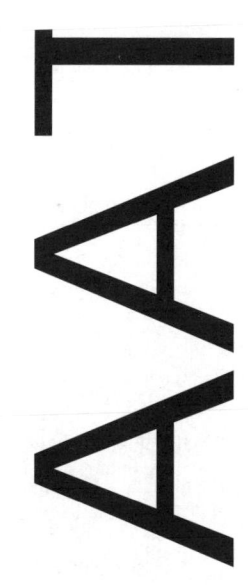

**Revision Companion**

### In this August 2009 edition

- Geared to the 2003 standards, as revised in November 2006
- Material up to date at 1 August 2009 taking into account changes in the Finance Act 2009

**FOR JUNE AND DECEMBER 2010 EXAMS AND SKILLS TESTS**

First edition September 2003
Seventh edition August 2009

ISBN 9780 7517 6776 6
(Previous edition 9780 7517 4650 1)

**British Library Cataloguing-in-Publication Data**
A catalogue record for this book
is available from the British Library

Published by

BPP Learning Media Ltd
BPP House, Aldine Place
London W12 8AA

www.bpp.com/learningmedia

Printed in the United Kingdom

Your learning materials, published by BPP Learning Media Ltd, are printed on paper sourced from sustainable, managed forests.

All our rights reserved. No part of this publication may be reproduced, stored in a retrieval system or transmitted, in any form or by any means, electronic, mechanical, photocopying, recording or otherwise, without the prior written permission of BPP Learning Media Ltd.

We are grateful to the QCA for permission to reproduce extracts from the Standards of Competence for Accounting, and to the AAT for permission to reproduce extracts from the mapping and Guidance Notes.

©
BPP Learning Media Ltd
2009

# Contents

## Introduction

How to use this Revision Companion – Level 2 Standards of competence – Exam technique – Assessment strategy – Building your portfolio – Extracts of tax tables

|  | Page | Answers to activities |
|---|---|---|
| **Practice activities** | 7 | 251 |

Practice activities are activities directly related to the actual content of the BPP Course Companion.

## AAT Sample Simulations

| | | |
|---|---|---|
| Unit 71 | 83 | 309 |
| Unit 72 | 149 | 337 |

## AAT Exams

Unit 73

| | | |
|---|---|---|
| 1. June 2008 | 185 | 355 |
| 2. December 2007 | 205 | 371 |
| 3. June 2007 | 225 | 383 |

**Appendices – tax tables** ........................................ 399

## Review form & free prize draw

# Introduction

## How to use this Revision Companion

### Aims of this Revision Companion

> To provide the knowledge and practice to help you succeed in the exam and skills testing for the Level 2 Certificate in Payroll Administration.

To pass the assessment successfully you need a thorough understanding in all areas covered by the standards of competence.

> To tie in with the other components of the BPP Learning Media Effective Study Package to ensure you have the best possible chance of success.

### Course Companion

This covers all you need to know for the exam and skills testing for Level 2. Numerous activities throughout the text help you practise what you have just learnt.

### Revision Companion

When you have understood and practised the material in the Course Companion, you will have the knowledge and experience to tackle this Revision Companion for Level 2. This aims to get you through the exam and skills testing, whether in the form of a simulation or a workplace assessment. It contains the AAT's Sample Simulations for Units 71 and 72, and the June 2007, December 2007 and June 2008 exams for Unit 73.

## Recommended approach to this Revision Companion

(a) To achieve competence in all units, you need to be able to do **everything** specified by the standards. Study the Course Companion very carefully and do not skip any of it.

(b) Learning is an **active** process. Do **all** the activities as you work through the Course Companion so you can be sure you really understand what you have read.

(c) After you have covered the material in the Course Companion, work through this **Revision Companion**.

(d) **Try the Practice Activities**. These are linked into each chapter of the Course Companion, and are designed to reinforce your learning and consolidate the practice that you have had doing the activities in the Course Companion. There is an activity checklist at the start of each chapter, which shows which performance criteria, range statement and knowledge and understanding point is covered by each activity.

(e) Next do the AAT's **Sample Simulations**.

(f) **Try the AAT's Exams**. It is probably best to leave these until the last stage of your revision, and then attempt them as 'mocks' under 'exam conditions'. This will help you develop techniques in approaching the assessment and allocating time correctly. For guidance on this, please see Exam Technique on page (xvi).

(g) This approach is only a suggestion. Your college may well adapt it to suit your needs.

Remember this is a **practical** course.

(a) Try to relate the material to your experience in the workplace or any other work experience you may have had.

(b) Try to make as many links as you can to your study of the other units at this level.

# Level 2 Standards of competence

## The structure of the Standards for Level 2

Each Unit commences with a statement of the **knowledge and understanding** which underpin competence in the Unit's elements.

The Unit of Competence is then divided into **elements of competence** describing activities which the individual should be able to perform.

Each element includes:

(a) A set of **performance criteria.** This defines what constitutes competent performance.

(b) A **range statement.** This defines the situations, contexts, methods etc in which competence should be displayed.

(c) **Evidence requirements.** These state that competence must be demonstrated consistently, over an appropriate time scale with evidence of performance being provided from the appropriate sources.

(d) **Sources of evidence.** These are suggestions of ways in which you can find evidence to demonstrate that competence. These fall under the headings: 'observed performance; work produced by the candidate; authenticated testimonies from relevant witnesses; personal account of competence; other sources of evidence.'

The elements of competence for Level 2 are set out below. Knowledge and understanding required for the unit as a whole are listed first, followed by the performance criteria and range statements for each element.

## Important note

The revised 2006 standards still refer to tax credits. These are no longer dealt with through the payroll and are not examinable from the 2006 exams and skills tests.

# Unit 71 Maintaining Employee Records

## Knowledge and understanding

**The Statutory framework**

1. Income tax and Social Security legislation affecting:

   Starters and leavers (Element 71.1)
   Tax code changes (Element 71.2)
   Student Loan Deductions (Element 71.2)
   Tax Credits (Element 71.2)
   National Insurance category letters (Elements 71.1 & 71.2)

2. Employment Rights legislation (Elements 71.1, 71.2 & 71.3)

3. Data Protection legislation (Element 71.1)

4. Asylum and Immigration legislation (Element 71.1)

5. Legislation relating to attachments of earnings

**The organisation**

6. Procedures for keeping data confidential and secure (Elements 71.1, 71.2 & 71.3)

7. Dealing with instructions from external agencies (71.2)

8. Who to refer discrepancies to (Elements 71.1, 71.2 & 71.3)

9. How to record and store data (Element 71.1, 71.2 & 71.3)

10. Types of information input from external agencies (Element 71.2)

11. Signatories and authorisations (Element 71.1, 71.2 and 71.3)

12. Timescales and schedules for updating, presenting and despatching data (Elements 71.1, 71.2 & 71.3)

13. Information flows within the organisation (Elements 71.1, 71.2 & 71.3)

## INTRODUCTION

### Element 71.1 Verify and process personal data for starters and leavers

**Performance criteria**

A  Ensure proper authorised **documentation** of every appointment and cessation of employment is obtained before payroll is amended

B  Input accurately statutory and **non-statutory** personal and contract details, including allowances and deductions, onto new employee records

C  Amend leavers' records to ensure that leavers will not be paid in future pay runs

D  Accurately complete and despatch **statutory documentation.**

E  Identify and document all discrepancies and either resolve directly or by reference to the appropriate organisation or person

F  Comply with all organisational and statutory timescales

G  File source **documentation** in accordance with statutory and organisational requirements and in a logical and orderly manner

H  Maintain confidentiality and security of data at all times

**Range statement**

1  **Non-statutory data:** marital status; employee number; rates of variable elements of pay; details of fixed deductions; bank or building society details; pay frequency; eligibility for occupational payments for adoption, maternity, paternity and sickness; duration of contract

2  **Source documentation:** form P45; form P38S; certificates of reduced liability and age exemption; form P46; evidence of appointment; evidence of termination of employment; communications in relation to queries

### Element 71.2 Implement instructions from external agencies

**Performance criteria**

A  Verify all payment and deduction instructions for accuracy, completeness and correct **documentation**

B  Process instructions from **statutory agencies** or **non-statutory bodies** in accordance with statutory and organisational requirements and within the timescale specified

C  Ensure all non-statutory deductions are authorised by the employee concerned

D  Identify and resolve all discrepancies directly or by reference to the appropriate organisation or person

**Range statement**

1  **Documentation:** court orders; HM Revenue and Customs documentation; Child Support Agency instructions; local authority attachment of earnings; individual mandates

2  **Statutory agencies:** Inland Revenue*; National Insurance Contributions Office*; Child Support Agency; courts; local authorities; student loans office

3  **Non-statutory bodies:** pension funds; trades unions and associations; financial institutions; charities

*Now known as HM Revenue and Customs

## Element 71.3 Evaluate and process permanent organisational variations to payroll

**Performance criteria**

A  Evaluate all data relating to **permanent variations** for accuracy and reasonableness
B  Check all data and documentation received for proper **authorisation**
C  Identify and resolve all discrepancies directly or by reference to the appropriate person
D  Process permanent variations accurately and in a timely manner

**Range statement**

1  **Permanent variations:** changes of grade; changes of employment status; variation in voluntary deductions; changes to pay rates for fixed and variable pay; changes in personal details

2  **Authorisation:** authorised signatory list; authority from the employee; organisational instructions

# Unit 72 Ascertaining gross pay

## Knowledge and understanding

**General information**

1. Positive payrolls (those payrolls where employees will not get paid unless input is submitted such as hourly paid employees)
2. Negative payrolls (those payrolls where employees will be paid automatically unless action is taken to prevent payment such as salaried employees)

**The statutory framework**

3. Employment Rights legislation (Elements 72.1 & 72.2)
4. Statutory Maternity Pay – including the rules relating to entitlement, earnings, evidence of pregnancy, start date for payment, stopping payments (Element 72.2)
5. Statutory Sick Pay – including the rules relating to period of incapacity for work, qualifying days, waiting days, linking, earnings test, changeover to state responsibility, stopping payments (Element 72.2)
6. Statutory Adoption Pay – including the rules relating to entitlement, earnings, evidence of adoption, start date for payment, stopping payments (Element 72.2)
7. Statutory Paternity Pay including the rules relating to entitlement, earnings, evidence of parenthood, start date for payment, stopping payments (Element 72.2)
8. Parental Leave including the rules relating to entitlement, earnings, evidence of parental responsibility, payment (Element 72.2)
9. Time off for Dependents including the rules relating to entitlement, evidence of emergency, payment and their interaction with occupational schemes (Element 72.2)

**The organisation**

10. The security and confidentiality of information (Elements 72.1 & 72.2)
11. Dealing with instructions from external agencies (Element 72.2)
12. The resolution of discrepancies (Elements 72.1 & 72.2)
13. How to record and store data (Elements 72.1 & 72.2)
14. Types of information input from external agencies (Element 72.2)
15. Signatories and authorisations (Elements 72.1 & 72.2)
16. Timescales and schedules for updating, presenting and despatching data (Elements 72.1 & 72.2)
17. Information flows within the organisation (Elements 72.1 & 72.2)

**Techniques and methods**

18. The use of statutory tables and values to perform manual calculations of payments with regard to adoption, maternity, paternity and sickness.
19. How to set up and use spreadsheets for the manual calculation of gross pay

### Element 72.1 Determine entitlements

**Performance criteria**

A  Evaluate all data relating to **temporary variations** for accuracy and reasonableness

B  Ensure **documentation** relating to temporary variations is verified for authorisation

C  Identify employees where input is required in order to ensure payment and ensure relevant details are correctly inserted

D  Check rates for overtime payments against agreed scales for each type of employee affected

E  Identify all payments in respect of their tax, National Insurance and pension liability

F  Take appropriate action when employees are absent and apply the correct payment schemes, with regard to adoption, maternity, paternity and sickness.

G  Identify and resolve all discrepancies directly or by reference to the appropriate person

H  Process temporary payments and deductions accurately

I  File source **documentation** in accordance with statutory and organisational requirements and in a logical and orderly manner

J  Maintain security and confidentiality of sensitive information at all times

**Range statement**

1  **Temporary variations:** payments; deductions

2  **Documentation:** authorised time recording documentation; authorised instructions from management; approved external instructions on payments

# INTRODUCTION

## Element 72.2 Determine statutory pay entitlements

**Performance criteria**

A     Determine entitlement to Statutory Sick Pay when entitlement to occupational sick pay expires or is not paid

B     Process Statutory Sick Pay payments accurately on receipt of regulatory forms

C     Determine entitlement to Statutory Maternity Pay, Statutory Adoption Pay, Statutory Paternity Pay, when entitlement to occupational payments are not made.

D     Process Statutory Maternity Pay, Statutory Adoption Pay, Statutory Paternity Pay payments accurately on receipt of regulatory forms

E     Process Tax Credit payments on receipt of regulatory forms

F     Contribute to the resolution of individual employees' queries by checking statutory pay entitlements manually, using the appropriate tables

G     Identify and resolve all discrepancies directly or by reference to the appropriate person

H     Issue the correct **regulatory documentation** where entitlement to statutory payments does not arise or ceases

**Range statement**

1     **Regulatory documentation:** SSP1; SMP1; stop notice and certificates of payment; other routine forms relating to the specified statutory entitlements.

# Unit 73 Determining Net Pay

## Knowledge and understanding

**The statutory framework**

1. Data Protection legislation (Elements 73.1 & 73.2)
2. PAYE regulations in respect of the manual calculation of gross to net pay (Element 73.1)
3. PAYE regulations in respect of charitable giving (Element 73.1)
4. Social Security regulations governing contributions in particular the manual calculation of gross to net pay (Element 73.1)
5. Pension legislation in respect of tax relief (Element 73.1)
6. Attachment and Arrestment of Earnings assessment and deduction (where single orders apply to the employee)
7. Income tax regulations as they apply to the recovery of student loans

**The organisation**

8. Checking validity of all employees (Element 73.1)
9. Timescales and schedules for despatching payslips (Element 73.1)
10. Information flows within the organisation (Element 73.2)
11. Procedures for the security and confidentiality of information (Elements 73.1 & 73.2)
12. Procedures for initiating and monitoring payments (Element 73.1)
13. Methods of disbursement (Element 73.2)
14. Information and timescale requirements of systems for transmission of disbursements to employees (Element 73.1)

**Techniques and methods**

15. How to use tax and National Insurance tables to perform manual calculations of net pay
16. How to set up and use spreadsheets for reconciliations and the manual calculation of net pay

## INTRODUCTION

### Element 73.1 Calculate and verify net pay

**Performance criteria**

A  Check the payroll status of all employees for validity for the pay period

B  Input any applicable **pre-tax deductions**

C  Input all relevant **statutory** and **non-statutory deductions**

D  Produce and distribute accurate and legible payslips in accordance with statutory and organisational requirements

E  Contribute to the resolution of individual employees' queries by checking net pay calculations manually, using the appropriate tax and National Insurance tables

F  Check net pay totals to ensure that the full range of applicable allowances and deductions has been made

G  Check net pay figures against the parameters for the payroll concerned and resolve any discrepancies or refer them to the appropriate person for resolution

**Range statement**

1  **Pre-tax deductions:** contributions to occupational pension schemes; charitable giving

2  **Statutory deductions:** attachment and arrestment of earnings; student loans; income tax; National Insurance contributions

3  **Non-statutory deductions:** pensions contributions; recovery of overpayments; repayment of loans and advances; voluntary deductions

## Element 73.2 Ascertain and reconcile aggregate payroll totals

**Performance criteria**

A  Reconcile actual payroll totals against authorised totals for all pay periods

B  Reconcile the number of no pays and actual pays promptly with the number of employees on the payroll

C  Ensure that aggregate **statutory payments** and **non-statutory deductions** are correctly calculated and reconciled against control totals.

D  Check aggregate **statutory payments** against control totals

E  Calculate sums recoverable from the National Insurance Contributions Office in respect of **statutory payments** and net them off against payments due

F  Calculate and reconcile aggregate amounts payable to **statutory and non-statutory bodies,** in respect of **statutory and non-statutory deductions** against control totals

G  Resolve discrepancies and where they cannot be resolved, refer them to the appropriate supervisor(s)

H  Meet all organisational and statutory timescales

**Range statement**

1  **Statutory payments:** Statutory Sick Pay; Statutory Maternity Pay; Statutory Adoption Pay; Statutory Paternity Pay

2  **Non-statutory deductions:** employee and employer pension contributions; charitable giving; recovery of overpayments; repayment of loans and advances; voluntary deductions

3  **Statutory bodies:** Inland Revenue\*; courts; Child Support Agency; local authorities

4  **Non-statutory bodies:** pension provider; bodies responsible for miscellaneous deductions; trade unions; social clubs

5  **Statutory deductions:** tax; Employee and Employer National Insurance contributions; student loan deductions; earnings attachments; Scottish arrestments of earnings; child support orders and attachment of earnings orders

\*Now known as HM Revenue and Customs

**INTRODUCTION**

# Exam technique

Completing exams successfully at this level is half about having the knowledge, and half about doing yourself full justice on the day. You must have the right **technique**.

## The day of the exam

1. Set at least one **alarm** (or get an alarm call) for a morning exam.

2. Have **something to eat** but beware of eating too much; you may feel sleepy if your system is digesting a large meal.

3. Allow plenty of **time to get to where you are sitting the exam**; have your route worked out in advance and listen to news bulletins to check for potential travel problems.

4. **Don't forget** pens, pencils, rulers, erasers.

5. Put **new batteries** into your calculator and take a spare set (or a spare calculator).

6. **Avoid discussion** about the exam with other candidates outside the venue.

## Technique in the exam

1. **Read the instructions (the 'rubric') on the front of the exam carefully**

   Check that the format hasn't changed. It is surprising how often assessors' reports remark on the number of students who do not attempt all the tasks.

2. **Read the paper twice**

   **Read through the paper twice** – don't forget that you are given 15 minutes' reading time. Check carefully that you have got the right end of the stick before putting pen to paper. Use your 15 minutes' reading time wisely.

3. **Check the time allocation for each section of the exam**

   Time allocations are given for each section of the exam. When the time for a section is up, you should go on to the next section.

4. **Read the task carefully and plan your answer**

   Read through the task again very carefully when you come to answer it. Plan your answer to ensure that you **keep to the point**. Two minutes of planning plus eight minutes of writing is virtually certain to produce a better answer than ten minutes of writing. Planning will also help you answer the exam efficiently, for example by identifying workings that can be used for more than one task.

5. **Produce relevant answers**

   Particularly with written answers, make sure you **answer what has been set**, and not what you would have preferred to have been set. Do not, for example, answer a question on **why** something is done with an explanation of **how** it is done.

6. **Work your way steadily through the exam**

   **Don't get bogged do**wn in one task. If you are having problems with something, the chances are that everyone else is too.

**INTRODUCTION**

7 **Produce an answer in the correct format**

The assessor will state **in the requirements** the format which should be used, for example in a report or memorandum.

8 **Do what the assessor wants**

You should ask yourself what the assessor is expecting in an answer; many tasks will demand a combination of technical knowledge and business commonsense. Be careful if you are required to give a decision or make a recommendation; you cannot just list the criteria you will use, but you will also have to say whether those criteria have been fulfilled.

9 **Lay out your numerical computations and use workings correctly**

Make sure the layout is in a style the assessor likes.

Show all your **workings** clearly and explain what they mean. Cross reference them to your answer. This will help the assessor to follow your method (this is of particular importance where there may be several possible answers).

10 **Present a tidy paper**

You are a professional, and it should show in the **presentation of your work**. You should make sure that you write legibly, label diagrams clearly and lay out your work neatly.

11 **Stay until the end of the exam**

Use any spare time **checking and rechecking** your script. Check that you have answered all the requirements of the task and that you have clearly labelled your work. Consider also whether your answer appears reasonable in the light of the information given in the question.

12 **Don't worry if you feel you have performed badly in the exam**

It is more than likely that the other candidates will have found the exam difficult too. As soon as you get up to leave the venue, **forget** that exam and think about the next – or, if it is the last one, celebrate!

13 **Don't discuss an exam with other candidates**

This is particularly the case if you **still have other exams to sit**. Even if you have finished, you should put it out of your mind until the day of the results. Forget about exams and relax!

# INTRODUCTION

# Assessment strategy

The Units at Level 2 are assessed by **skills testing only**, except for Unit 73 which is assessed by both **exam and skills testing**.

An assessment is a means of collecting evidence that you have the **essential knowledge and understanding** that underpins competence. It is also a means of collecting evidence across the **range of contexts** for the standards and evidence of your ability to transfer skills, knowledge and understanding to different situations. Thus, although assessments will contain practical tasks linked to the performance criteria, they will also focus on the underpinning knowledge and understanding. You should in addition expect each assessment to contain tasks taken from across a broad range of the Standards.

## Exam

The exam will last three hours plus 15 minutes' reading time and will be divided into 2 sections:

- Operational Tasks
- Short Answer Questions

The Operational tasks contain exercises that require candidates to focus on issues surrounding payroll preparation. Candidates will be expected to know about various aspects of preparing payrolls including manual calculations in a series of different contexts. They can also expect to deal with simple reconciliations and/or communication exercises (eg memos) testing their understanding of payroll procedures.

The Short Answer Questions are designed to explore the candidates' understanding of a miscellany of different issues relating to general payroll. Some questions require only yes/no answers and most a straightforward one or two sentence response will be required. However some questions will require the completion of a short task.

## Operational tasks

This unit has a far reaching scope and candidates are expected to be prepared to deal with a variety of tasks.

**Example tasks**

- Tax allowance codes and how they should be used
- The tax calendar including payments in weeks 53, 54 and 56
- Tax and NI treatment of advanced holiday pay
- Use of tax tables and National Insurance rates and earnings limits
- Regulations relating to statutory payments (SSP, SMP, SAP and SPP) and statutory deductions (student loans)
- National Insurance letters and all the rules relating to them as regards UK employees (excluding mariners)
- Pre and post tax deductions
- Identification of taxable and NICable pay
- Deductions and effect of the Employment Rights Act (no unauthorised deductions)
- Principles of attachment of earnings orders (particularly Child Support DEOs)
- Principles of an itemised payslip

Candidates will be advised on the exam paper how long to take on this section (June 2008: 130 minutes).

## Short answer questions

This section will always contain a mixture of 10 questions and short tasks.

**Example tasks**

- National Insurance table letters to be used in different cases
- Tax codes
- Operation of student loans
- Legislation regarding what may be deducted from an employee's pay, including correction of errors
- Attachment of earnings
- The tax calendar
- Revenue forms
- Revenue and other organisation's deadlines
- Data protection as it impacts on payroll

Candidates will be advised on the exam paper how long to take on this section (June 2008: 50 minutes).

## Skills testing

Skills testing is a means of collecting evidence of your ability to **carry out practical activities** and to **operate effectively in the conditions of the workplace** to the standards required. Evidence may be collected at your place of work, or at an Approved Assessment Centre by means of simulations of workplace activity, or by a combination of these methods.

If the Approved Assessment Centre is a **workplace**, you may be observed carrying out payroll activities as part of your normal work routine. You should collect documentary evidence of the work you have done, or contributed to, in an **payroll portfolio**. Evidence collected in a portfolio can be assessed in addition to observed performance or where it is not possible to assess by observation.

Where the Approved Assessment Centre is a **college or training organisation**, skills testing will be by means of a combination of the following.

- Documentary evidence of activities carried out at the workplace, collected by you in an **payroll portfolio**.
- Realistic **simulations** of workplace activities. These simulations may take the form of case studies and in-tray exercises and involve the use of primary documents and reference sources.
- **Projects and assignments** designed to assess the Standards of Competence.

If you are unable to provide workplace evidence you will be able to complete the assessment requirements by the alternative methods listed above.

## Possible assessment methods

Where possible, evidence should be collected in the workplace, but this may not be a practical prospect for you. Equally, where workplace evidence can be gathered it may not cover all elements.

The AAT regards performance evidence from simulations, case studies, projects and assignments as an acceptable substitute for performance at work, provided that they are based on the Standards and, as far as possible, on workplace practice.

There are a number of methods of assessing competence in the payroll field. The list below is not exhaustive, nor is it prescriptive. Some indication is given on the suitability of each method for assessing particular aspects of payroll competence, such as analysing information, giving advice, or dealing with contingencies. Some methods have limited applicability, but others are capable of being expanded to provide challenging tests of competence.

## INTRODUCTION

| Assessment method | Suitable for assessing |
|---|---|
| **Performance of a payroll task either in the workplace or by simulation:** eg preparing the input for a small payroll that involves a few new starters, leavers and changes to the core detail for individual employees; calculating an employee's entitlement to a statutory payment; calculating the deductions to be made under an attachment of earnings; reconciling the payroll; processing instructions from external agencies. | **Basic task competence.** Adding supplementary oral questioning may help to draw out underpinning knowledge and understanding and highlight your ability to deal with contingencies and unexpected occurrences |
| **General case studies.** These are broader than simulations. They include more background information about the system and business environment | Ability to **analyse a system** and suggest ways of modifying it. It could take the form of a written report, with or without the addition of oral or written questions |
| **Payroll problems/cases:** eg a series of 'what if?' questions | Understanding of the **general principles of payroll** as applied to a particular case or topic |
| **Preparation of flowcharts/diagrams.** To illustrate an actual (or simulated) payroll procedure | **Understanding of the logic** behind a procedure, of controls, and of relationships between departments and procedures. Questions on the flow chart or diagram can provide evidence of underpinning knowledge and understanding |
| **Interpretation of payroll information** from an actual or simulated situation. The assessment could include non-payroll information and written or oral questioning | **Interpretative competence** |
| **Preparation of written reports on an actual or simulated situation** | **Written communication skills** as well as your understanding of the subject material. |
| **Analysis of critical incidents, problems encountered, achievements** | Your ability to handle **contingencies** |
| **Listing of likely errors** eg preparing a list of the main types of errors likely to occur in an actual or simulated procedure | Appreciation of the range of **contingencies** likely to be encountered. Oral or written questioning would be a useful supplement to the list |
| **Outlining the organisation's policies, guidelines and regulations** | Performance criteria relating to these aspects of competence. It also provides evidence of competence in **researching information** |
| **Objective tests and short-answer questions** | **Specific knowledge** |
| **In-tray exercises** | Your **task-management ability** as well as technical competence |
| **Supervisors' reports** | **General job competence**, personal effectiveness, reliability, accuracy, and time management. Reports need to be related specifically to the Standards of Competence |
| **Analysis of work logbooks/diaries** | **Personal effectiveness**, time management etc. It may usefully be supplemented with oral questioning |
| **Formal written answers to questions** | Knowledge and understanding of the **general payroll environment** and its impact on particular units of competence |
| **Oral questioning** | **Knowledge and understanding** across the range of competence including organisational procedures, methods of dealing with unusual cases, contingencies and so on. It is often used in conjunction with other methods |

# Building your portfolio

## What is a portfolio?

A portfolio is a collection of work that demonstrates what the owner can do. In AAT language the portfolio demonstrates **competence**.

A painter will have a collection of his paintings to exhibit in a gallery, an advertising executive will have a range of advertisements and ideas that she has produced to show to a prospective client. Both the collection of paintings and the advertisements form the portfolio of that artist or advertising executive.

Your portfolio will be unique to you just as the portfolio of the artist will be unique because no one will paint the same range of pictures in the same way. It is a very personal collection of your work and should be treated as a **confidential** record.

## What evidence should a portfolio include?

No two portfolios will be the same but by following some simple guidelines you can decide which of the following suggestions will be appropriate in your case.

(a) **Your current CV**

This should be at the front. It will give your personal details as well as brief descriptions of posts you have held with the most recent one shown first.

(b) **References and testimonials**

References from previous employers may be included especially those of which you are particularly proud.

(c) **Your current job description**

You should emphasise financial **responsibilities and duties**.

(d) **Your student record sheets**

These should be supplied by AAT when you begin your studies, and your training provider should also have some if necessary.

(e) **Evidence from your current workplace**

This could take many forms including **letters, memos, reports** you have written, **copies of accounts** or **reconciliations** you have prepared, **discrepancies** you have investigated etc. Remember to obtain permission to include the evidence from your line manager because some records may be sensitive. Discuss the performance criteria that are listed in your Student Record Sheets with your training provider and employer, and think of other evidence that could be appropriate to you.

(f) **Evidence from your social activities**

For example you may be the treasurer of a club in which case examples of your cash and banking records could be appropriate.

(g) **Evidence from your studies**

Few students are able to satisfy all the requirements of competence by workplace evidence alone. They therefore rely on simulations to provide the remaining evidence to complete a unit. If you are not working or not working in a relevant post, then you may need to rely more heavily on simulations as a source of evidence.

(h) **Additional work**

Your training provider may give you work that specifically targets one or a group of performance criteria in order to complete a unit. It could take the form of questions, presentations or demonstrations. Each training provider will approach this in a different way.

(i) **Evidence from a previous workplace**

This evidence may be difficult to obtain and should be used with caution because it must satisfy the 'rules' of evidence, that is it must be current. Only rely on this as evidence if you have changed jobs recently.

(j) **Prior achievements**

For example you may have already completed the health and safety unit during a previous course of study, and therefore there is no need to repeat this work. Advise your training provider who will check to ensure that it is the same unit and record it as complete if appropriate.

## How should it be presented?

As you assemble the evidence remember to **make a note** of it on your Student Record Sheet in the space provided and **cross reference** it. In this way it is easy to check to see if your evidence is **appropriate**. Remember one piece of evidence may satisfy a number of performance criteria so remember to check this thoroughly and discuss it with your training provider if in doubt.

To keep all your evidence together a ring binder or lever arch file is a good means of storage.

## When should evidence be assembled?

You should begin to assemble evidence **as soon as you have registered as a student**. **Don't leave it all** until the last few weeks of your studies, because you may miss vital deadlines and your resulting certificate sent by the AAT may not include all the units you have completed. Give yourself and your training provider time to examine your portfolio and report your results to AAT at regular intervals. In this way the task of assembling the portfolio will be spread out over a longer period of time and will be presented in a more professional manner.

## What are the key criteria that the portfolio must fulfil?

As you assemble your evidence bear in mind that it must be:

- **Valid**. It must relate to the Standards.
- **Authentic**. It must be your own work.
- **Current**. It must refer to your current or most recent job.
- **Sufficient**. It must meet all the performance criteria by the time you have completed your portfolio.

## Confidentiality

Payroll is an extremely sensitive area and you must be aware of your responsibilities under data protection legislation at all times.

Therefore portfolio evidence relating to **real employees** must be adjusted to remove individual identifiers (eg removing names, addresses, works numbers).

So you should include a declaration, signed by your supervisor, that the portfolio evidence is your own work and that personal details have been amended to stop the possibility of individuals being identified. However, the original work was correctly prepared.

## Finally

Remember that the portfolio is **your property** and **your responsibility**. Not only could it be presented to the external verifier before your award can be confirmed; it could be used when you are seeking **promotion** or applying for a more senior and better paid post elsewhere. How your portfolio is presented can say as much about you as the evidence inside.

> For further information on portfolio building, see the BPP Text Learning Media *Building Your Portfolio*. This can be ordered via the Internet: www.bpp.com/aat

# Extracts of tax tables

The following extracts of Tax Tables are provided in the Appendices at the end of this Revision Companion. You will need to refer to these extracts as you work through the activities and assessments. Due to the volume of the Tables, it would be impractical to reproduce them all in this Kit.

## Taxable pay tables

| | |
|---|---|
| Tables A | 399 |
| Which tax table should I use? | 410 |
| Table B | 412 |
| Table C | 414 |
| Table D | 416 |
| Student Loan Deductions | 417 |

## National Insurance tables

### Not contracted out

| | |
|---|---|
| Table A earnings limits and National Insurance Contribution rates | 424 |
| Table A not contracted out (weekly) extracts | 425 |
| Table A not contracted out (monthly) extracts | 426 |
| Tables B and C earnings limit and National Insurance Contribution rates | 429 |
| Table C (weekly) Not contracted out extracts | 430 |
| Table C (monthly) Not contracted out extracts | 431 |

### Contracted out: salary related schemes

| | |
|---|---|
| Earnings limits and National Insurance Contribution rates | 434 |

### Contracted out: money purchase schemes

| | |
|---|---|
| Earnings limits and National Insurance Contribution rates | 436 |

# Practice Activities

Practice activities are short activities directly related to the actual content of Parts A to C of the BPP Course Companion.

| | | Page | Answers to activities | Done |
|---|---|---|---|---|
| **Chapter 1 Starters and leavers** | | | | |
| 1 | Retention | 8 | 251 | |
| 2 | Paula Mell | 8 | 251 | |
| 3 | Statutory data | 8 | 251 | |
| 4 | Change of name | 8 | 251 | |
| 5 | Filing | 8 | 252 | |
| 6 | Freelance | 8 | 252 | |
| 7 | Alan Wilson | 9 | 253 | |
| 8 | David Ricketts | 11 | 254 | |
| 9 | Deceased | 14 | 256 | |
| 10 | Joiners | 16 | 257 | |
| 11 | Graduate | 19 | 260 | |
| 12 | Bonus after leaving | 22 | 263 | |
| **Chapter 2 Instructions from external agencies** | | | | |
| 13 | Verification | 24 | 264 | |
| 14 | CSA 1 | 24 | 264 | |
| 15 | CSA 2 | 24 | 264 | |
| 16 | Trade union subs | 24 | 264 | |
| **Chapter 3 Recording permanent payroll variations** | | | | |
| 17 | Promotion | 26 | 265 | |
| 18 | Overtime | 26 | 265 | |
| 19 | Change of conditions | 26 | 265 | |
| **Chapter 4 Calculation of gross pay** | | | | |
| 20 | Agreed rate | 28 | 266 | |
| 21 | Contract of employment | 28 | 266 | |
| 22 | Coding | 28 | 266 | |
| 23 | Commission | 28 | 266 | |
| 24 | Payment changes | 29 | 266 | |
| 25 | Payroll processing | 29 | 267 | |
| 26 | Hourly pay | 29 | 267 | |
| 27 | Piecework | 29 | 267 | |
| 28 | Bonus and commisson | 29 | 268 | |
| 29 | Annual | 30 | 268 | |
| 30 | Back pay | 30 | 268 | |
| 31 | Mary Down | 30 | 269 | |
| 32 | Gosplan plc 1 | 31 | 269 | |

|  | Page | Answers to activities | Done |
|---|---|---|---|
| **Chapter 4 Calculation of gross pay (continued)** | | | |
| 33 Gosplan plc 2 | 34 | 272 | |
| 34 Design | 38 | 273 | |
| **Chapter 5 Statutory pay entitlements** | | | |
| 35 Sick pay | 40 | 274 | |
| 36 SSP | 40 | 274 | |
| 37 SMP | 40 | 274 | |
| 38 SPP | 40 | 274 | |
| 39 SAP | 40 | 274 | |
| **Chapter 6 Income tax: simple cases** | | | |
| 40 Ghost | 42 | 275 | |
| 41 Tax code | 42 | 275 | |
| 42 Emergency code | 42 | 275 | |
| 43 Tax calculations | 42 | 275 | |
| 44 Ralph Thomas | 42 | 276 | |
| 45 Barbara Walton | 43 | 277 | |
| 46 Burnham Peters Ltd | 44 | 277 | |
| **Chapter 7 Income tax: more complex cases** | | | |
| 47 Code and pay changes | 46 | 279 | |
| 48 Philip Phantom | 47 | 279 | |
| 49 John David Rose | 48 | 281 | |
| 50 Week 53 | 49 | 282 | |
| 51 Trade dispute | 50 | 283 | |
| 52 K codes | 51 | 284 | |
| 53 Mushtaq Ahmed | 52 | 285 | |
| 54 Martin Carr | 52 | 286 | |
| **Chapter 8 National Insurance: basic NICs** | | | |
| 55 NI tables | 55 | 287 | |
| 56 NICs | 55 | 287 | |
| 57 Earnings | 55 | 287 | |
| 58 Knowledge | 55 | 287 | |
| 59 Water babies | 55 | 287 | |
| 60 Harold Childe 1 | 56 | 287 | |
| 61 Harold Childe 2 | 56 | 288 | |
| 62 Churne Orvill | 56 | 288 | |
| **Chapter 9 National Insurance: advanced NICs** | | | |
| 63 Exact percentage | 62 | 293 | |
| 64 COSRS | 62 | 294 | |

|  | Page | Answers to activities | Done |
|---|---|---|---|

**Chapter 10 Other deductions**

| 65 | Gilberta Sullivan | 65 | 296 | |
| 66 | Groddy Ltd | 65 | 296 | |
| 67 | Gill Tee Ltd | 65 | 297 | |
| 68 | Sandy Shore | 67 | 298 | |
| 69 | Pension scheme | 69 | 300 | |
| 70 | Panther Ltd | 69 | 300 | |
| 71 | Harris Ltd | 71 | 302 | |
| 72 | Holmes plc | 72 | 304 | |

**Chapter 11 Net pay and aggregate payroll**

| 73 | Cash wages | 74 | 305 | |
| 74 | Cash reconciliation | 76 | 305 | |
| 75 | Direct credit | 77 | 306 | |

PRACTICE ACTIVITIES

chapter 1

# Starters and leavers

## Activity checklist

This checklist shows which performance criteria, range statement or knowledge and understanding point is covered by each activity in this chapter. Tick off each activity as you complete it.

**Activity**

1. ☐ This activity covers performance criteria 71.1.G.

2. ☐ This activity covers performance criteria 71.1.E.

3. ☐ This activity covers performance criteria 71.1.B.

4. ☐ This activity covers performance criteria 71.1.B.

5. ☐ This activity covers performance criteria 71.1.G and knowledge and understanding point 9.

6. ☐ This activity covers performance criteria 71.1.E.

7. ☐ This activity covers performance criteria 71.1.A and 71.1.D and range statement 2: form P45.

8. ☐ This activity covers performance criteria 71.1.A and 71.1.D and arrange statement 2: form P45.

9. ☐ This activity covers performance criteria 71.1. A and 71.1.D and arrange statement 2: form P45.

| | | |
|---|---|---|
| 10 | | This activity covers performance criteria 71.1. A and 71.1.D and arrange statement 2: form P45. |
| 11 | | This activity covers performance criteria 71.1. A and 71.1.D and arrange statement 2: form P46. |
| 12 | | This activity covers knowledge and understanding point 1. |

## 1 Retention

(a) What is the minimum period that PAYE documentation must be kept after the end of the tax year?

(b) How far back can a PAYE audit go?

## 2 Paula Mell

Paula Mell works Mondays to Wednesdays for White Elephant Ltd, and Thursdays and Fridays for Budgie Wharf Ltd. She wants to be a freelance worker and asks you about her status.

(a) What are the relative pros and cons of self-employed status as opposed to employed status?

(b) How would you assess Paula's case?

## 3 Statutory data

What data must be kept on each employee by law?

## 4 Change of name

An employee tells you that he has changed his name and wants all his records altered. What evidence do you need to see?

## 5 Filing

Your supervisor asks you to sort out a filing system for employees. There are only fifteen employees. In what order would you choose to file them?

## 6 Freelance

An employee come up to you and says 'I'm sick of PAYE. Can't I go self-employed or freelance?'

What do you say to her? What do you do?

# 7 Alan Wilson

This activity requires the correct completion of a P45 for a leaver.

You are the payroll officer of Shepherds Brushes Ltd, 3 Long Road, Dutton, Worcs DT2 3BP. You receive notification that Alan Wilson, an employee, will be leaving the company on 26 September 2009 (Week 25).

You check his P11 and find the following information.

Starting date 1.8.91
National Insurance no          AB225518C
Date of birth          8/7/73
Tax code          547L
Week 25

| | |
|---|---|
| Total pay to date | £3,550.00 |
| Total free pay to date | £2,634.50 |
| Total taxable pay to date | £915.50 |
| Total tax due | £183.00 |

His address is 5 River Street, Dutton, Worcs DT13 9XX.

You have already calculated the final wage payable on 26 September and this is included above. Your company's Tax Office reference is 123/B1234.

**Task**

Prepare a P45 (blank Part 1 provided) for Alan Wilson.

## PRACTICE ACTIVITIES

**P45 Part 1**
**Details of employee leaving work**
Copy for HM Revenue & Customs

**HM Revenue & Customs**

File your employee's P45 online at www.hmrc.gov.uk

Use capital letters when completing this form

1. **Employer PAYE reference**
   Office number   Reference number

2. **Employee's National Insurance number**

3. **Title** - enter MR, MRS, MISS, MS or other title

   Surname or family name

   First or given name(s)

4. **Leaving date** DD MM YYYY

5. **Student Loan deductions**
   Enter 'Y' if Student Loan deduction is due to be made

6. **Tax Code at leaving date**

   If week 1 or month 1 applies, enter 'X' in the box below.
   Week 1/Month 1

7. Last entries on P11 *Deductions Working Sheet*.
   **Complete only if Tax Code is cumulative.** Make no entry if week 1 or month 1 applies, go straight to box 8.
   Week number     Month number
   Total pay to date
   £                                          .
   Total tax to date
   £                                          .

8. This employment pay and tax. Leave blank if the Tax Code is cumulative and the amounts are the same as box 7.
   Total pay in this employment
   £                                          .
   Total tax in this employment
   £                                          .

9. Works number/Payroll number and Department or branch (if any)

10. **Gender.** Enter 'X' in the appropriate box
    Male         Female

11. **Date of birth** DD MM YYYY

12. **Employee's private address**

    Postcode

13. I certify that the details entered in items 1 to 11 on this form are correct.
    Employer name and address

    Postcode

    Date DD MM YYYY

14. **When an employee dies.** If the employee has died enter 'D' in the box and send all four parts of this form to your HMRC office immediately.

*For information only*

**Instructions for the employer**
- Complete this form following the 'What to do when an employee leaves' instructions in the Employer Helpbook E13 *Day-to-day payroll*. Make sure the details are clear on all four parts of this form and that your name and address is shown on Parts 1 and 1A.
- Send Part 1 to your HM Revenue & Customs office immediately.
- Hand Parts 1A, 2 and 3 to your employee when they leave.

P45(Manual) Part 1                                                                 HMRC 04/08

# 8 David Ricketts

You are the payroll officer of Gumm Boots Ltd of 7 Worple Street, Haderton, Lancs HA1 2FT (PAYE ref 011/C2334). You receive notification on 24 July that an employee, David Ricketts, having been paid his weekly wage on 21 July 2009, walked out of his job after an argument with his supervisor and has not returned to work. He has therefore been dismissed.

From the P11 for David Ricketts you obtain the following information.

At 21 July (Week 16):

| | |
|---|---|
| National Insurance no | DC986721B |
| Date of birth | 30/3/70 |
| Tax code | 350T |
| Total pay to date | £2,420.50 |
| Total free pay to date | £1,079.84 |
| Total taxable pay to date | £1,340.66 |
| Total tax due | £268.00 |

The last known address you have for Mr Ricketts is 17 River Mansions, Haderton, Lancs HA12 1YP.

You also notice on the P11 that Mr Ricketts only joined your company in May 2009, and you find Part 2 of the P45 from his previous employment, which shows the following information.

# PRACTICE ACTIVITIES

## HM Revenue & Customs

**P45 Part 2**
**Details of employee leaving work**
Copy for new employer

**1 Employer PAYE reference**
Office number / Reference number
621 / BM1223

**2 Employee's National Insurance number**
DC 98 67 21 B

**3 Title** - enter MR, MRS, MISS, MS or other title
MR

Surname or family name
RICKETTS

First or given name(s)
DAVID

**4 Leaving date** DD MM YYYY
28 05 2009

**5 Student Loan deductions**
☐ Student Loan deductions to continue

**6 Tax Code at leaving date**
300T

If week 1 or month 1 applies, enter 'X' in the box below.
Week 1/Month 1 ☐

**7** Last entries on P11 Deductions Working Sheet. Complete only if Tax Code is cumulative. If there is an 'X' at box 6, there will be no entries here.

Week number 08    Month number ☐☐

Total pay to date
£ 1145 · 00

Total tax to date
£ 136 · 40

*For information only*

### To the employee
This form is important to you. Take good care of it and keep it safe. Copies are not available. Please keep Parts 2 and 3 of the form together and do not alter them in any way.

**Going to a new job**
Give Parts 2 and 3 of this form to your new employer, or you will have tax deducted using the emergency code and may pay too much tax. If you do not want your new employer to know the details on this form, send it to your HM Revenue & Customs (HMRC) office immediately with a letter saying so and giving the name and address of your new employer. HMRC can make special arrangements, but you may pay too much tax for a while as a result of this.

**Going abroad**
If you are going abroad or returning to a country outside the UK ask for form P85 *Leaving the United Kingdom* from any HMRC office or Enquiry Centre.

**Becoming self-employed**
You must register with HMRC within three months of becoming self-employed or you could incur a penalty. To register as newly self-employed see The Phone Book under HM Revenue & Customs or go to www.hmrc.gov.uk to get a copy of the booklet SE1 *Are you thinking of working for yourself?*

**Claiming Jobseeker's Allowance or Employment and Support Allowance (ESA)**
Take this form to your Jobcentre Plus office. They will pay you any tax refund you may be entitled to when your claim ends, or at 5 April if this is earlier.

**Not working and not claiming Jobseeker's Allowance or Employment and Support Allowance (ESA)**
If you have paid tax and wish to claim a refund ask for form P50 *Claiming Tax back when you have stopped working* from any HMRC office or Enquiry Centre.

### Help
If you need further help you can contact any HMRC office or Enquiry Centre. You can find us in The Phone Book under HM Revenue & Customs or go to www.hmrc.gov.uk

### To the new employer
Check this form and complete boxes 8 to 18 in Part 3 and prepare a form P11 *Deductions Working Sheet*. Follow the instructions in the Employer Helpbook E13 *Day-to-day payroll*, for how to prepare a P11 *Deductions Working Sheet*. Send Part 3 of this form to your HMRC office immediately. Keep Part 2.

P45(Manual) Part 2                                          HMRC 04/08

## Task

If you think that you should prepare a P45 for Mr Ricketts, prepare Part 1 of this form using the blank sheet provided, and explain what you would do with it. If you do not think you should prepare a P45 explain why.

**P45 Part 1**
**Details of employee leaving work**
Copy for HM Revenue & Customs

HM Revenue & Customs

*For information only*

File your employee's P45 online at www.hmrc.gov.uk — Use capital letters when completing this form

1. Employer PAYE reference — Office number / Reference number
2. Employee's National Insurance number
3. Title - enter MR, MRS, MISS, MS or other title
   - Surname or family name
   - First or given name(s)
4. Leaving date DD MM YYYY
5. Student Loan deductions — Enter 'Y' if Student Loan deduction is due to be made
6. Tax Code at leaving date
   - If week 1 or month 1 applies, enter 'X' in the box below.
   - Week 1/Month 1
7. Last entries on P11 *Deductions Working Sheet*. **Complete only if Tax Code is cumulative.** Make no entry if week 1 or month 1 applies, go straight to box 8.
   - Week number — Month number
   - Total pay to date £
   - Total tax to date £
8. This employment pay and tax. Leave blank if the Tax Code is cumulative and the amounts are the same as box 7.
   - Total pay in this employment £
   - Total tax in this employment £
9. Works number/Payroll number and Department or branch (if any)
10. Gender. Enter 'X' in the appropriate box — Male / Female
11. Date of birth DD MM YYYY
12. Employee's private address — Postcode
13. I certify that the details entered in items 1 to 11 on this form are correct. Employer name and address — Postcode — Date DD MM YYYY
14. **When an employee dies.** If the employee has died enter 'D' in the box and send all four parts of this form to your HMRC office immediately.

**Instructions for the employer**
- Complete this form following the 'What to do when an employee leaves' instructions in the Employer Helpbook E13 *Day-to-day payroll.* Make sure the details are clear on all four parts of this form and that your name and address is shown on Parts 1 and 1A.
- Send Part 1 to your HM Revenue & Customs office immediately.
- Hand Parts 1A, 2 and 3 to your employee when they leave.

P45(Manual) Part 1 — HMRC 04/08

# 9 Deceased

You are the payroll officer of Larks Ltd. On 11 November 2009 one of your company's salesmen, Gerald Anthony Wallet, died.

Details from his P11 are as follows.

| | | Tax code | | Amended | | | | K codes | | | K codes |
|---|---|---|---|---|---|---|---|---|---|---|---|
| | | 640T | | WK/mnth | | | | | | | |
| | | | | | K codes | | | | | | Tax not deducted owing to the regulatory limit |
| Month | Week | Pay in the week | Total pay to date | Total free pay to date | Total additional pay to date | Total taxable pay to date | Total tax due to date | Tax due at end of current period | Regulatory limit | Tax deducted in the week | |
| | | 2 | 3 | 4a | 4b | 5 | 6 | 6a | 6b | 7 | 8 |
| 7 | 27 | | | | | | | | | | |
| | 28 | | | | | | | | | | |
| | 29 | | | | | | | | | | |
| | 30 | 3,000.00 | 21,000.00 | 3,738.63 | | 17,261.37 | 3,452.20 | | | 493.17 | |
| | 31 | | | | | | | | | | |
| | 32 | | | | | | | | | | |
| 8 | 33 | | | | | | | | | | |
| | 34 | | | | | | | | | | |

A P45 was completed and sent to the Tax Office on 13 November 2009. Mr Wallet's NI number is FG 23 32 45A and his payroll number is 622. His date of birth is 4 November 1946.

Mr Wallet's earnings from 1 to 11 November were not confirmed at that stage, as the Sales Director was at a conference. On her return, it was agreed that £1,600 was the gross pay due for the period. You have been authorised by your supervisor to make a payment on 28 November of the unpaid earnings to his widow, Mrs Mary Wallet (address 17 Cedar Avenue, Top Village, Herts HE2 4TP) as she is the beneficiary of her husband's estate.

Your company's address is Larks House, 5 High Street, Borton, Herts, HE17 1JK, and the PAYE reference for the company is 333/C2468.

**Tasks**

(a) Complete the P45 for Mr Wallet (below) on 13 November 2009.
(b) Following the payment to Mrs Wallet, do you prepare a further P45? Give reasons for your answer.

PRACTICE ACTIVITIES

**P45 Part 1
Details of employee leaving work**
Copy for HM Revenue & Customs

**HM Revenue & Customs**

File your employee's P45 online at www.hmrc.gov.uk          Use capital letters when completing this form

**1** Employer PAYE reference
*Office number   Reference number*
☐☐☐ / ☐☐☐☐☐☐☐☐☐☐

**2** Employee's National Insurance number
☐☐ ☐☐ ☐☐ ☐☐ ☐

**3** Title - enter MR, MRS, MISS, MS or other title

Surname or family name

First or given name(s)

**4** Leaving date *DD MM YYYY*
☐☐ ☐☐ ☐☐☐☐

**5** Student Loan deductions
☐ Enter 'Y' if Student Loan deduction is due to be made

**6** Tax Code at leaving date
☐ ☐☐☐☐☐☐☐

If week 1 or month 1 applies, enter 'X' in the box below.
Week 1/Month 1 ☐

**7** Last entries on P11 *Deductions Working Sheet*.
**Complete only if Tax Code is cumulative.** Make no entry if week 1 or month 1 applies, go straight to box 8.
Week number ☐☐   Month number ☐☐
Total pay to date
£ ☐☐☐☐☐☐☐☐ . ☐☐
Total tax to date
£ ☐☐☐☐☐☐☐☐ . ☐☐

*For information only*

**8** This employment pay and tax. Leave blank if the Tax Code is cumulative and the amounts are the same as box 7.
Total pay in this employment
£ ☐☐☐☐☐☐☐ . ☐☐
Total tax in this employment
£ ☐☐☐☐☐☐☐ . ☐☐

**9** Works number/Payroll number and Department or branch (if any)

**10** Gender. Enter 'X' in the appropriate box
Male ☐   Female ☐

**11** Date of birth *DD MM YYYY*
☐☐ ☐☐ ☐☐☐☐

**12** Employee's private address

Postcode
☐☐☐☐ ☐☐☐☐

**13** I certify that the details entered in items 1 to 11 on this form are correct.
Employer name and address

Postcode
☐☐☐☐ ☐☐☐☐
Date *DD MM YYYY*
☐☐ ☐☐ ☐☐☐☐

**14 When an employee dies.** If the employee has died enter 'D' in the box and send all four parts of this form to your HMRC office immediately. ☐

**Instructions for the employer**
- Complete this form following the 'What to do when an employee leaves' instructions in the Employer Helpbook E13 *Day-to-day payroll*. Make sure the details are clear on all four parts of this form and that your name and address is shown on Parts 1 and 1A.
- Send Part 1 to your HM Revenue & Customs office immediately.
- Hand Parts 1A, 2 and 3 to your employee when they leave.

P45(Manual) Part 1                                                                                                   HMRC 04/08

PRACTICE ACTIVITIES

## 10 Joiners

You are the payroll officer of Fry and Dice Ltd. Your company's tax reference number is 146/B1323. Its address is Home Works, Rudderton Estate, Gloucester, G99 1YY.

You ask to see two employees who have joined your company on 1 May 2009, and you obtain their P45s. Part 3 of each P45 is shown on the next pages.

Ms Williams supplies you with her personal details, as follows:

Address: 113A Town St, Little Smelting, Gloucs, G35 2HU

Date of birth: 12.12.1973

Mr Smith's address is 4 Constable Drive, Gloucester G22 4PQ. His date of birth is 29 May 1980.

Ms Williams, a quality controller, has works number 351 and Mr Smith, a personnel assistant, has works number 724. Both are weekly paid.

Upon checking the tax tables you find that Ms Williams' tax due to week 4 is £69.40 and Mr Smith's £86.60.

**Tasks**

(a) Complete Part 3 of each P45, for despatch to your Tax Office.
(b) Complete the following extract from the tax side of a P11 for Mr Smith.

|  | Tax code |  | Amended |  |  |  |  |  |  |  |
|---|---|---|---|---|---|---|---|---|---|---|
|  |  |  | WK/mnth |  |  |  |  |  |  |  |
|  |  |  |  | K codes |  |  | K codes |  |  | K codes |
| W e e k | Pay in the week | Total pay to date | Total free pay to date | Total additional pay to date | Total taxable pay to date | Total tax due to date | Tax due at end of current period | Regulatory limit | Tax deducted in the week | Tax not deducted owing to the regulatory limit |
|  | 2 | 3 | 4a | 4b | 5 | 6 | 6a | 6b | 7 | 8 |
| 1 |  |  |  |  |  |  |  |  |  |  |
| 2 |  |  |  |  |  |  |  |  |  |  |
| 3 |  |  |  |  |  |  |  |  |  |  |
| 4 |  |  |  |  |  |  |  |  |  |  |

(Note free pay for code 379L for week 4 is £292.24 and for code 502T for week 4 is £386.88.)

## PRACTICE ACTIVITIES

**HM Revenue & Customs**

**P45 Part 3**
**New employee details**
For completion by new employer

File your employee's P45 online at www.hmrc.gov.uk                Use capital letters when completing this form

**1** Employer PAYE reference
Office number  Reference number
1 5 2 / C 3 1 2 4

**2** Employee's National Insurance number
A B 2 3 4 5 6 7 C

**3** Title - enter MR, MRS, MISS, MS or other title
MS

Surname or family name
WILLIAMS

First or given name(s)
KAREN ALICE

**4** Leaving date DD MM YYYY
3 0 0 4 2 0 0 9

**5** Student Loan deductions
☐ Student Loan deductions to continue

**6** Tax Code at leaving date
3 7 9 L
If week 1 or month 1 applies, enter 'X' in the box below.
Week 1/Month 1 ☐

**7** Last entries on P11 *Deductions Working Sheet*.
Complete only if Tax Code is cumulative. If there is an 'X' at box 6, there will be no entries here.
Week number  0 4     Month number ☐
Total pay to date
£ 6 4 0 . 0 0
Total tax to date
£ 6 9 . 4 0

**To the new employer** Complete boxes 8 to 18 and send P45 Part 3 only to your HMRC office immediately.

**8** New employer PAYE reference
Office number  Reference number
☐ ☐ ☐ / ☐ ☐ ☐ ☐ ☐ ☐ ☐

**9** Date new employment started DD MM YYYY

**10** Works number/Payroll number and Department or branch (if any)

**11** Enter 'P' here if employee will not be paid by you between the date employment began and the next 5 April. ☐

**12** Enter Tax Code in use if different to the Tax Code at box 6

If week 1 or month 1 applies, enter 'X' in the box below.
Week 1/Month 1 ☐

**13** If the tax figure you are entering on P11 *Deductions Working Sheet* differs from box 7 (see the E13 Employer Helpbook *Day-to-day payroll*) please enter the figure here.
£

**14** New employee's job title or job description

**15** Employee's private address

Postcode

**16** Gender. Enter 'X' in the appropriate box
Male ☐   Female ☐

**17** Date of birth DD MM YYYY

**Declaration**

**18** I have prepared a P11 *Deductions Working Sheet* in accordance with the details above.
Employer name and address

Postcode

Date DD MM YYYY

P45(Manual) Part 3                                HMRC 04/08

**PRACTICE ACTIVITIES**

---

## HM Revenue & Customs

### P45 Part 3
### New employee details
For completion by new employer

File your employee's P45 online at www.hmrc.gov.uk

Use capital letters when completing this form

**1 Employer PAYE reference**
Office number  Reference number
1 8 1 / B 2 6 9 7

**2 Employee's National Insurance number**
L D 1 4 9 4 3 8 A

**3 Title** – enter MR, MRS, MISS, MS or other title
MR

Surname or family name
SMITH

First or given name(s)
PETER BENJAMIN

**4 Leaving date** DD MM YYYY
3 0 0 4 2 0 0 9

**5 Student Loan deductions**
☐ Student Loan deductions to continue

**6 Tax Code at leaving date**
5 0 2 T
If week 1 or month 1 applies, enter 'X' in the box below.
Week 1/Month 1 ☐

**7 Last entries on P11** *Deductions Working Sheet.*
Complete only if Tax Code is cumulative. If there is an 'X' at box 6, there will be no entries here.
Week number 0 4    Month number ☐☐

Total pay to date
£ 8 2 0 . 0 0

Total tax to date
£ 8 9 . 9 0

*For information only*

**To the new employer** Complete boxes 8 to 18 and send P45 Part 3 only to your HMRC office immediately.

**8 New employer PAYE reference**
Office number  Reference number
☐☐ / ☐☐☐☐☐☐☐

**9 Date new employment started** DD MM YYYY
☐☐ ☐☐ ☐☐☐☐

**10 Works number/Payroll number and Department or branch** (if any)
☐

**11** Enter 'P' here if employee will not be paid by you between the date employment began and the next 5 April. ☐

**12 Enter Tax Code in use if different to the Tax Code at box 6**
☐☐☐☐☐☐☐
If week 1 or month 1 applies, enter 'X' in the box below.
Week 1/Month 1 ☐

**13** If the tax figure you are entering on P11 *Deductions Working Sheet* differs from box 7 (see the E13 Employer Helpbook *Day-to-day payroll*) please enter the figure here.
£ ☐☐☐☐☐☐ . ☐☐

**14 New employee's job title or job description**
☐

**15 Employee's private address**
☐

Postcode
☐☐☐☐ ☐☐☐☐

**16 Gender.** Enter 'X' in the appropriate box
Male ☐    Female ☐

**17 Date of birth** DD MM YYYY
☐☐ ☐☐ ☐☐☐☐

**Declaration**

**18** I have prepared a P11 *Deductions Working Sheet* in accordance with the details above.
Employer name and address
☐

Postcode
☐☐☐☐ ☐☐☐☐

Date DD MM YYYY
☐☐ ☐☐ ☐☐☐☐

P45(Manual) Part 3

HMRC 04/08

# 11 Graduate

You are the payroll officer of Health Audit Agency, a government agency. On 15 September 2009, you are visited by a new employee, a university graduate, who has just joined your organisation as a research officer. She has brought her National Insurance number, which is YC657899B. As she does not have a Form P45, she has signed the attached Form P46.

You have already received the following information about her from personnel. For coding purposes, the research department is department 19.

| | |
|---|---|
| Surname | Carlyle |
| First names | Roberta Jane |
| Address | 15 Crescent Lane |
| | Willowby |
| | Bucks WL5 2TT |
| Date of birth | 19 August 1986 |
| Employment commenced | 8 September 2009 |
| Starting salary | £13,500 pa |

Your company's PAYE reference is 186/D5432 and its address is Mussel House, Lymm Road, London EC5V 6ZP.

**Task**

Complete the attached Form P46. What information needs to be entered in the employee records?

PRACTICE ACTIVITIES

## HM Revenue & Customs
## P46: Employee without a Form P45

**Section one** To be completed by the employee

Please complete section one and then hand the form back to your present employer. If you later receive a form P45 from your previous employer, hand it to your present employer.
Use capital letters when completing this form.

### Your details

**National Insurance number**
This is very important in getting your tax and benefits right

Y C 6 5 7 8 9 9 B

**Title** - enter MR, MRS, MISS, MS or other title

MS

**Surname or family name**

C A R L Y L E

**First or given name(s)**

R O B E R T A

**Gender.** Enter 'X' in the appropriate box

Male ☐    Female X

**Date of birth** DD MM YYYY

1 9 0 8 1 9 8 6

**Address**
House or flat number

1 5

Rest of address including house name or flat name

C R E S C E N T   L A N E
W I L L O W B Y
B U C K S

**Postcode**

W L 5   2 T T

### Your present circumstances
Read all the following statements carefully and enter 'X' in **the one** box that applies to you.

**A** - This is my first job since last 6 April and **I have not** been receiving taxable Jobseeker's Allowance or taxable Incapacity Benefit or a state or occupational pension.   A X

OR

**B** - This is now my only job, but since last 6 April **I have** had another job, or have received taxable Jobseeker's Allowance or Incapacity Benefit. I do not receive a state or occupational pension.   B ☐

OR

**C** - I have another job or receive a state or occupational pension.   C ☐

### Student Loans
If you left a course of Higher Education before last 6 April and received your first Student Loan instalment on or after 1 September 1998 and you have not fully repaid your Student Loan, enter 'X' in box D. *(If you are required to repay your Student Loan through your bank or building society account do **not** enter an 'X' in box D.)*   D X

### Signature and date
I can confirm that this information is correct

Signature

*R. Carlyle*

Date DD MM YYYY

1 5   0 9   2 0 0 9

P46                Page 1                HMRC 02/08

20

## PRACTICE ACTIVITIES

### Section two  To be completed by the employer

File your employee's P46 online at **www.hmrc.gov.uk/employers/doitonline**
Use capital letters when completing this form. Guidance on how to fill it in, including what to do if your employee has not entered their National Insurance number on page 1, is at **www.hmrc.gov.uk/employers/working_out.htm** and in the E13 Employer Helpbook *Day-to-day payroll*.

#### Employee's details

Date employment started  *DD MM YYYY*

Works/payroll number and department or branch (if any)

Job title

#### Employer's details

Employer PAYE reference
*Office number   Reference number*

Address
Building number

Employer name

Rest of address

Postcode

#### Tax code used

If you do not know the tax code to use or the current National Insurance contributions (NICs) lower earnings limit, go to **www.hmrc.gov.uk/employers/rates_and_limits.htm**

Enter 'X' in the appropriate box

**Box A**
Emergency code on a **cumulative** basis     A ☐

**Box B**
Emergency code on a **non-cumulative**
Week 1/Month 1 basis     B ☐

**Box C**
Code BR     C ☐

Tax code used

If week 1 or month 1 applies, enter 'X' in this box ☐

**Send this form to your HM Revenue & Customs office on the first pay day.**
If the employee has entered 'X' in box A or box B, on page 1, and their earnings are below the NICs lower earnings limit, **do not send the form until their earnings reach the NICs lower earnings limit.**

## 12 Bonus after leaving

Olly Whalley, a monthly paid employee assessed to NICs under Table D, left at the end of June, but was paid a regular bonus on July 15th, two weeks after he had left. What is the NIC treatment?

chapter 2

# Instructions from external agencies

## Activity checklist

This checklist shows which performance criteria, range statement or knowledge and understanding point is covered by each activity in this chapter. Tick off each activity as you complete it.

**Activity**

| | | |
|---|---|---|
| 13 | ☐ | This activity covers performance criteria 71.2.A and 71.2.C. |
| 14 | ☐ | This activity covers performance criteria 71.2.A and 71.2.B. |
| 15 | ☐ | This activity covers performance criteria 71.2.B. |
| 16 | ☐ | This activity covers performance criteria 71.2.C and 71.2.D. |

PRACTICE ACTIVITIES

## 13 Verification

How can you verify that a deduction for pension contributions is correct?

## 14 CSA 1

You receive an attachment of earnings order from the Child Support Agency. This orders you to deduct £130 per month from Joe Johnson's pay, subject to a minimum protected rate of £350 per month.

What records do you need to make?

## 15 CSA 2

The Child Support Agency has heard that Joe Johnson has had a pay rise. Joe comes to tell you that he doesn't want the CSA to be given details of his pay rise. Just after his visit, you receive a letter from the CSA demanding details of his pay rise. What do you do?

## 16 Trade union subs

You receive a letter from the local trade union, advising subscriptions have increased to £2 per month from £1.50 per month. Your employer operates the 'check off' system and so you automatically deduct £2.00 pm from all employees who are trade union members. Marlene Ramsay complains that she has not authorised the increase in the deductions from her pay. What do you do?

PRACTICE ACTIVITIES

chapter 3

# Recording permanent payroll variations

## Activity checklist

This checklist shows which performance criteria, range statement or knowledge and understanding point is covered by each activity in this chapter. Tick off each activity as you complete it.

**Activity**

17 ☐ This activity covers performance criteria 71.3.A, 71.3.B and 71.3.C.

18 ☐ This activity covers performance criteria 71.3.A and 71.3.B.

19 ☐ This activity covers performance criteria 71.3.A and 71.3.B and knowledge and understanding point 13.

PRACTICE ACTIVITIES

## 17 Promotion

Joe Johnson tells you that he has been promoted and that his new salary rate is £20,000 pa. However, you receive a memorandum from personnel confirming the promotion, but stating that the new salary rate is £19,500 pa.

**Tasks**

(a) Which rate do you pay?
(b) Do you contact Joe Johnson about the pay rise?

## 18 Overtime

Marlene Ramsay's contract of employment states that Sunday overtime is to be paid at time and a half. However, personnel have recently issued a memo stating that grade D employees' overtime rate for Sundays will increase to double time.

Which overtime rate do you use if Marlene is a grade D employee?

## 19 Change of conditions

Personnel inform you that the factory workers' basic working week has been reduced to 35 hours from 40 hours and that hourly pay has increased to £5.50 per hour from £4.75.

**Tasks**

(a) Calculate basic pay before the change.
(b) Calculate basic pay after the change.

**Note.** Ignore the national minimum wage for the purpose of this activity.

chapter 4

# Calculation of gross pay

## Activity checklist

This checklist shows which performance criteria, range statement or knowledge and understanding point is covered by each activity in this chapter. Tick off each activity as you complete it.

**Activity**

| Activity | | |
|---|---|---|
| 20 | ☐ | This activity covers performance criteria 72.1.B and 72.1.D. |
| 21 | ☐ | This activity covers knowledge and understanding point 3. |
| 22 | ☐ | This activity covers performance criteria 72.1.I and knowledge and understanding point 13. |
| 23 | ☐ | This activity covers performance criteria 72.1.G. |
| 24 | ☐ | This activity covers performance criteria 72.1.G. |
| 25 | ☐ | This activity covers performance criteria 72.1.J and knowledge and understanding points 10 and 16. |
| 26 | ☐ | This activity covers performance criteria 72.1.A, 72.1.C, 72.1.D and 72.1.H. |
| 27 | ☐ | This activity covers performance criteria 72.1.A, 72.1.C, 72.1.D and 72.1.H. |
| 28 | ☐ | This activity covers performance criteria 72.1.A, 72.1.C and 72.1.H. |

# PRACTICE ACTIVITIES

| Activity | | |
|---|---|---|
| 29 | | This activity covers performance criteria 72.1.H. |
| 30 | | This activity covers performance criteria 72.1.A, 72.1.D and 72.1.H. |
| 31 | | This activity covers performance criteria 72.1.E. |
| 32 | | This activity covers performance criteria 72.1.A, 72.1.B, 72.1.C, 72.1.D and 72.1.H. |
| 33 | | This activity covers performance criteria 72.1.A, 72.1.B, 72.1.C, 72.1.D and 72.1.H. |
| 34 | | This activity covers knowledge and understanding point 13. |

## 20 Agreed rate

How would you ensure that you are paying an employee the agreed rate?

## 21 Contract of employment

What would you expect to see in a contract of employment?

## 22 Coding

Joe Johnson has just moved from sales to the accounts department. Your organisation uses the following codes:

Sales           S01
Purchases       P01
Financial       F01
Administration  A01

Which department code should be used for Joe's new department?

## 23 Commission

Joe Johnson queries his first pay received after moving to the accounts department. When in sales, his pay was increased by commission. He wants to know why he is no longer receiving this. You are paying an increased basic salary but no commission in accordance with instructions received from personnel. Explain the situation to Joe.

PRACTICE ACTIVITIES

## 24 Payment changes

You have been on holiday. On your return you notice that Joe Johnson's salary has been paid into a different bank account. However, there is no change of account noted in the employee records. What do you do?

## 25 Payroll processing

What are the four main requirements for payroll processing?

## 26 Hourly pay

Alphonse is an hourly paid employee. His basic rate is £6.50 per hour for daytime shifts and £7.50 per hour for night shifts, £7.50 per hour for overtime (ie hours worked in excess of 40 hours a week) except weekends when the rate is always £10 per hour.

How much would he earn in the following cases, assuming an 8-hour day.

(a) For a 40 hour week of daytime shifts with no overtime?
(b) For a 40 hour week of daytime shifts, if one day is worked on Saturday?
(c) For a 40 hour week of nightshifts and an additional four hours overtime on weekdays?

## 27 Piecework

Boris is a pieceworker, and is paid £5 for each of the first 60 widgets produced per week. However, he gets a guaranteed minimum wage of £235, and if he works more than 40 hours a week he gets £4 per hour as overtime. If he produces over 60 widgets per week he gets £6 per widget for the 61st and each subsequent widget. How much would he earn in each of the following weeks?

(a) In the week ending 13/3/X1 Boris made 50 widgets and did 4 hours of overtime.
(b) In the week ending 20/3/X1 he produced 10 widgets.
(c) In the week ending 27/3/X1 he produced 34 widgets.
(d) In the week ending 3/4/X1, Boris produced 70 widgets, and worked 6 hours overtime.

**Note:** Assume the NMW rate for Boris is £5.80 per hour.

## 28 Bonus and commission

Cassandra works for a company which pays bonuses and commission. Her basic pay is £900 per month, but at the end of the month she receives commission of 5% of the sales she made in the previous month (so that at the end of May she will be paid the commission for April for example). If her sales exceed £10,000 in any quarter (ie three month period from 1 January to 31 March, 1 April to 30 June, 1 July to 30 September, 1 October to 31 December) she gets a one-off bonus of £1,000. These are paid in the month after the quarter.

PRACTICE ACTIVITIES

Here are her sales figures for the first six months of 20X2.

| Month | £ |
|---|---|
| Jan | 5,000 |
| Feb | 4,000 |
| March | 3,000 |
| April | 2,000 |
| May | 3,000 |
| June | 4,000 |

Her sales in December 20X1 were £5,000. Sales in the quarter to December 20X1 did not exceed £10,000.

What will be included in her gross pay at the end of each month from January to June inclusive?

# 29 Annual

Dana is paid an annual salary of £30,000 pa. This is paid monthly in arrears on the last day of the month. Dana is leaving the firm on 15th September 20X1. What is her final period's basic pay? Assume that there are 10 working days in the period from 1 to 15 September 20X1. State any other assumptions that you make in your calculations.

# 30 Back pay

Dilys is a salaried worker, who also receives overtime of £10 per hour for hours worked over 156 a month, and a productivity bonus of 5% of her basic monthly salary if the quality of her work exceeds expectations.

Her salary was £12,000 per year, payable in equal monthly instalments. This has been increased to £15,000 by agreement on 1 May, backdated to 1 January.

In May she worked 175 hours, and produced work of better quality than standard. For January to April the quality of her work exactly matched expectations.

What was her total gross pay for May?

# 31 Mary Down

The following information relates to Mary Down, an employee. She had a pay advance of £20, which needs to be deducted this week.

| | £ |
|---|---|
| Employee's National Insurance contribution | 10 |
| Overtime | 20 |
| Back pay | 15 |
| Basic pay | 150 |
| Bonus | 30 |
| Award for staff suggestion | 20 |
| Income tax | 25 |

**Tasks**

(a) What is Mary's gross pay?
(b) What is Mary's net pay?

Which would you expect to see on her pay cheque?

# 32 Gosplan plc 1

You administer the payroll for Gosplan plc. The company runs two payrolls.

(a) A production payroll, for production workers.
(b) An administration payroll for all others.

The production payroll contains 20 employees.

You are provided with the following information, which applies to 20X1.

(a) A memorandum from the Board detailing wage rates, hours and overtime rates for 20X1.
(b) Timesheet summaries for Week 13 in 20X1 showing **authorised** overtime.
(c) A list of employee names and job titles.
(d) A proforma payroll.

**Task**

Complete the proforma payroll for the week (see page 34) differentiating between basic pay and overtime/Saturday pay.

**Note**: for the purposes of this activity, ignore the national minimum wage legislation.

## GOSPLAN PLC INTERNAL MEMORANDUM

To: Personnel Department
Finance Department
From: Board of directors

cc: Payroll Department
Date: 16/12/20X0

**Settlement of wages claim for 20X1**

The Board, after negotiations with the General and Provision Production Union, and with the Skilled Artisan Syndicalist Association, announce that the pay for production staff will be fixed at the following rates. Overall there has been a 10.6% rise since 20X0.

| *Grade title* | *Hourly rate effective 1 January 20X1* |
|---|---|
| Foreman | £7.50 |
| Underforeman | £6.50 |
| Boiler maintenance | £5.75 |
| Chargehand | £5.00 |
| Templateer | £5.10 |
| Hopper steerer | £5.20 |
| Optical fibre twister | £7.00 |

Overtime remains at time and a half. It will be paid after 40 hours, as opposed to 41 hours. *All* Saturday working is paid at double time, irrespective as to how many hours have been worked previously.

By order of the Board

*Anthony Paratchik*

Anthony Paratchik
Company secretary

Timesheet summary

| 20X1 Week 13 | Timesheet summary (hours) | | | | | | |
|---|---|---|---|---|---|---|---|
| Employee | Staff no | Mon | Tues | Wed | Th | Fri | Sat | Total |
| Ashdown P | 071 | – | 8 | 8 | 8 | 8 | 8 | 40 |
| Baker K | 659 | 8 | 8 | 8 | 8 | 7 | – | 39 |
| Blair T | 660 | – | 8 | 8 | 8 | 8 | 8 | 40 |
| Callaghan J | 661 | 12 | 12 | 12 | 4 | – | – | 40 |
| Clarke K | 624 | 7 | 7 | 7 | 7 | 7 | – | 35 |
| Delors J | 010 | 9 | 9 | 11 | 10 | 9 | – | 48 |
| Heath E | 970 | 8 | 8 | 9 | 9 | – | – | 34 |
| Heseltine M | 664 | 10 | 10 | 7 | 7 | 7 | – | 41 |
| Hurd D | 663 | 9 | 9 | 9 | 9 | 9 | – | 45 |
| King T | 662 | – | – | 10 | 10 | 10 | 10 | 40 |
| Kinnock N | 992 | 8 | 8 | 8 | 8 | 9 | 4 | 45 |
| Lamont N | 666 | – | 8 | 8 | 8 | 8 | – | 32 |
| Lilley P | 665 | 8 | 8 | 8 | 8 | 8 | – | 40 |
| Major J | 990 | – | 9 | 9 | 9 | 8 | 8 | 43 |
| Patten C | 696 | 9 | 8 | 8 | 8 | - | – | 33 |
| Rifkind M | 621 | – | 8 | 8 | 8 | 8 | 8 | 40 |
| Scargill A | 917 | 8 | 9 | 8 | 9 | 8 | – | 42 |
| Thatcher M | 999 | 8 | 8 | 8 | 8 | 8 | 8 | 48 |
| Waldegrave W | 721 | 8 | 8 | 8 | 8 | 8 | – | 40 |
| Wilson H | 964 | – | – | 8 | 8 | 12 | 12 | 40 |

**Note.** All overtime and Saturday working has been properly authorised.

| Employee | Staff number | Job title |
|---|---|---|
| Ashdown P | 071 | Underforeman |
| Baker K | 659 | Templateer |
| Blair T | 660 | Boiler maintenance |
| Callaghan J | 661 | Optical Fibre Twister |
| Clarke K | 624 | Hopper steerer |
| Delors J | 010 | Foreman |
| Heath E | 970 | Chargehand |
| Heseltine M | 664 | Hopper Steerer |
| Hurd D | 663 | Boiler maintenance |
| King T | 662 | Templateer |
| Kinnock N | 992 | Underforeman |
| Lamont N | 666 | Hopper Steerer |
| Lilley P | 665 | Hopper Steerer |
| Major J | 990 | Chargehand |
| Patten C | 696 | Templateer |
| Rifkind M | 621 | Templateer |
| Scargill A | 917 | Boiler maintenance |
| Thatcher M | 999 | Chargehand |
| Waldegrave W | 721 | Templateer |
| Wilson H | 964 | Optical Fibre Twister |

PRACTICE ACTIVITIES

Payroll Proforma (please fill in)

| PAYROLL – 20X1 WEEK 13<br>Employee | Staff number | Basic<br>£ p | Saturday & overtime<br>£ p | Total<br>£ p |
|---|---|---|---|---|
| Ashdown P | 071 | | | |
| Baker K | 659 | | | |
| Blair T | 660 | | | |
| Callaghan J | 661 | | | |
| Clarke K | 624 | | | |
| Delors J | 010 | | | |
| Heath E | 970 | | | |
| Heseltine M | 664 | | | |
| Hurd D | 663 | | | |
| King T | 662 | | | |
| Kinnock N | 992 | | | |
| Lamont N | 666 | | | |
| Lilley P | 665 | | | |
| Major J | 990 | | | |
| Patten C | 696 | | | |
| Rifkind M | 621 | | | |
| Scargill A | 917 | | | |
| Thatcher M | 999 | | | |
| Waldegrave W | 721 | | | |
| Wilson H | 964 | | | |
| TOTAL | | | | |

## 33 Gosplan plc 2

It is now 20X2. You, and all the production workforce, are still employed by Gosplan plc, even though Gosplan plc has been taken over by another company.

The new management are changing the pay and staff grading structure, and, after negotiating with the Trades Unions, have come up with an agreement.

It is Week 20 and you are required to work out the wages.

You have been given the following documents.

(a) A timesheet summary for Week 20, with details of good production.
(b) The new grades with payment details, and overtime details.
(c) Details of the productivity and quality bonus scheme.
(d) A note from the production director.
(e) A list of the employees and their job titles in the old system (see activity 32).
(f) A proforma payroll.

## PRACTICE ACTIVITIES

**Task**

Complete the payroll for Week 20 20X2.

| 20X2 Week 20 | | Timesheet summary (Hours) | | | | | | |
|---|---|---|---|---|---|---|---|---|
| Employee | Staff no | Mon | Tues | Wed | Th | Fri | Sat | Total |
| Ashdown P | 071 | 8 | 8 | 7 | 7 | 7 | - | 37 |
| Baker K | 659 | 9 | 7 | 7 | 7 | 9 | - | 39 |
| Blair T | 660 | 8 | 8 | 8 | 8 | 8 | - | 40 |
| Callaghan J | 661 | 10 | 10 | - | 10 | 10 | - | 40 |
| Clarke K | 624 | - | 8 | 10 | 8 | - | 10 | 36 |
| Delors J | 010 | 8 | 8 | 8 | 8 | 8 | 8 | 48 |
| Heath E | 970 | - | - | 9 | 9 | 9 | 9 | 36 |
| Heseltine M | 664 | 7 | 7 | 7 | 7 | 7 | 7 | 42 |
| Hurd D | 663 | - | 9 | 9 | 9 | 9 | 9 | 45 |
| King T | 662 | 9 | 9 | 8 | 8 | 8 | - | 42 |
| Kinnock N | 992 | 4 | 10 | 8 | 9 | 8 | 8 | 47 |
| Lamont N | 666 | 8 | 8 | 8 | 7 | 7 | - | 38 |
| Lilley P | 665 | - | 9 | 7 | 7 | 7 | 10 | 40 |
| Major J | 990 | - | 8 | 8 | 8 | 8 | 8 | 40 |
| Patten C | 696 | 7 | 6 | 6 | 9 | 9 | - | 37 |
| Rifkind M | 621 | - | 7 | 7 | 7 | 7 | 7 | 35 |
| Scargill A | 917 | - | 10 | 8 | 9 | 8 | 8 | 43 |
| Thatcher M | 999 | 9 | 7 | 7 | 9 | 9 | - | 41 |
| Waldegrave W | 721 | 6 | 7 | 7 | 7 | 7 | 7 | 41 |
| Wilson H | 964 | 9 | 9 | 9 | 9 | - | - | 36 |
| TOTAL | | | | | | | | 803 |

| | |
|---|---:|
| Total number of units produced | 1,273 |
| Units rejected by quality control | 153 |
| Good units of production | 1,120 |

**Note.** All overtime and Saturday work has been authorised. Once again, for the purposes of this activity, please ignore the national minimum wage legislation.

## PRACTICE ACTIVITIES

**GOSPLAN PLC INTERNAL MEMORANDUM**

To: Payroll Department
From: Yashuhiro Tokugawa, Personnel Director
Date: 15/12/20X1

Before formal announcement of the deal, you might like to know the following grading structure is to be introduced from 1 January 20X2.

| Old grade | New grade | Basic pay per week £ | Overtime per hour £ p |
|---|---|---|---|
| Foreman | A | 285 | 9.30 |
| Underforeman | B | 230 | 7.75 |
| Boiler maintenance | B | 230 | 7.75 |
| Chargehand | C | 180 | 6.30 |
| Templateer | C | 180 | 6.30 |
| Hopper steerer | C | 180 | 6.30 |
| Optical fibre twister | A | 285 | 9.30 |

**Overtime**

This will be paid at the rate per hour above for the first ten hours worked over 35 hours. Overtime hours over and above 10 hours should be paid at the above rate × 1.25.

There is no special rate for weekend working.

All employees are expected to work a standard 35 hours a week.

## PRACTICE ACTIVITIES

---

**GOSPLAN PLC INTERNAL MEMORANDUM**

To: Payroll Department
From: Yashuhiro Tokugawa, Personnel Director
Date: 16/12/20X1

**Staff incentives**

(1) PRODUCTIVITY AND QUALITY BONUS

Production workers will be eligible for a group bonus each week. The scheme will commence on 1 January 20X2.

For every good unit produced over 1,000 units a £5 bonus will be paid. Units rejected by Quality Control are excluded from the calculation. The bonus is allocated equally between production employees.

(2) STAFF SUGGESTION SCHEME

A reward of up to £5,000 will be offered for any idea to improve productivity or quality which is implemented. Amounts under £100 will be paid through the payroll. The rest will be paid by separate cheque.

---

**GOSPLAN PLC INTERNAL MEMORANDUM**

To: Payroll Department
cc: Payroll Department
From: Toshiro Mifune, Production Director
Date: 2/5/20X2

**Staff incentives**

The following employees are to be rewarded as follows for suggestions leading to increases in productivity or quality. Please pay in Week 20.

J Delors is to receive £30.
A Scargill is to receive £50.

---

PAYROLL PROFORMA (please fill in)

| PAYROLL – 20X2 WEEK 120<br>Employee | Staff number | Basic<br>£ p | Overtime<br>£ p | Bonus<br>£ p | Other<br>£ p | Total<br>£ p |
|---|---|---|---|---|---|---|
| Ashdown P | 071 | | | | | |
| Baker K | 659 | | | | | |
| Blair T | 660 | | | | | |
| Callaghan J | 661 | | | | | |
| Clarke K | 624 | | | | | |
| Delors J | 010 | | | | | |
| Heath E | 970 | | | | | |
| Heseltine M | 664 | | | | | |
| Hurd D | 663 | | | | | |
| King T | 662 | | | | | |
| Kinnock N | 992 | | | | | |
| Lamont N | 666 | | | | | |
| Lilley P | 665 | | | | | |
| Major J | 990 | | | | | |
| Patten C | 696 | | | | | |
| Rifkind M | 621 | | | | | |
| Scargill A | 917 | | | | | |
| Thatcher M | 999 | | | | | |
| Waldegrave W | 721 | | | | | |
| Wilson H | 964 | | | | | |
| TOTAL | | | | | | |

# 34 Design

How could the documentation with which you were provided for activities 32 and 33 have been better designed so as to make your calculations easier?

chapter 5

# Statutory pay entitlements

## Activity checklist

This checklist shows which performance criteria, range statement or knowledge and understanding point is covered by each activity in this chapter. Tick off each activity as you complete it.

**Activity**

| | | |
|---|---|---|
| 35 | | This activity covers performance criteria 72.1.F, 72.2.A and 72.2.B. |
| 36 | | This activity covers performance criteria 72.1.F, 72.2.A and 72.2.B and knowledge and understanding point 5. |
| 37 | | This activity covers performance criteria 72.1.F, 72.2.C and 72.2.D and knowledge and understanding point 4. |
| 38 | | This activity covers performance criteria 72.1.F, 72.2.C and 72.2.D and knowledge and understanding point 7. |
| 39 | | This activity covers performance criteria 72.1.F, 72.2.C and 72.2.D and knowledge and understanding point 6. |

PRACTICE ACTIVITIES

## 35 Sick pay

It is your firm's policy that all employees who are sick need to supply a doctor's certificate after 7 working days' absence. Joe Johnson has been off sick for two weeks and has sent in self certification certificates for both weeks. The firm's rules state that occupational sick pay can only be paid if the correct certificates are sent in. Can you pay Joe occupational sick pay for either week? If you can not, what action should you take?

## 36 SSP

In week 20 of 2009, K Baker was sick for 3 days. He had previously been sick for the whole of week 19. His normal working week is 5 days and he earns an average of £95 per week. How much SSP is due for week 20? (The weekly rate of SSP for 2009/10 is £79.15.)

## 37 SMP

In week 21 of 2009, H Maranthawalla starts approved maternity leave. Her pay in week 20 was £324.30. Assume pay in week 20 is the same as the average over the last eight weeks. What is the amount of SMP due to her? After six weeks of maternity leave, how much SMP will she receive?

## 38 SPP

Joe Johnson is going to be a father again. He has provided all the appropriate paper work and is entitled to SPP. He elects to take two weeks leave. His annual salary is currently £20,000 pa. How much SPP is he due?

## 39 SAP

Mary Gillespie has obtained a court adoption order for Felicity, who she is currently fostering. She earns an average of £95 per week. She applies for Statutory Adoption Pay, how much will she receive?

chapter 6

# Income tax: simple cases

## Activity checklist

This checklist shows which performance criteria, range statement or knowledge and understanding point is covered by each activity in this chapter. Tick off each activity as you complete it.

**Activity**

| | | |
|---|---|---|
| 40 | ☐ | This activity covers performance criteria 73.1.E and knowledge and understanding point 15. |
| 41 | ☐ | This activity covers performance criteria 73.1.E and knowledge and understanding point 15 |
| 42 | ☐ | This activity covers performance criteria 73.1.E and knowledge and understanding point 15 |
| 43 | ☐ | This activity covers performance criteria 73.1.E and knowledge and understanding point 15 |
| 44 | ☐ | This activity covers performance criteria 73.1.E and knowledge and understanding point 15 |
| 45 | ☐ | This activity covers performance criteria 73.1.E and knowledge and understanding point 15 |
| 46 | ☐ | This activity covers performance criteria 73.1.E and knowledge and understanding point 15 |

PRACTICE ACTIVITIES

## 40 Ghost

In Month 4 of the 2009/10 tax year, George Ghost earns £1,500 in gross pay. He earned £1,000 in each of Months 1, 2 and 3. His free pay to date is £603 (in Month 3 it was £452.25).

(a)  What is his taxable pay to date?
(b)  If, by the end of Month 3, George had paid £509.40 in tax, how much would he pay in Month 4?

## 41 Tax code

What is the significance of a person's tax code, and how is it notified to the payroll department?

## 42 Emergency code

What is the emergency code?

## 43 Tax calculations

If an employee is taxable on Tables C and D, what do you do about the Basic Rate band?

## 44 Ralph Thomas

The purpose of this activity is to test your ability to calculate correctly the PAYE income tax deductions for an employee who is paid weekly and taxed on a cumulative basis, and to fill in a P11 for him.

Ralph Thomas is a weekly paid worker with your company. Details about him are as follows.

| | |
|---|---|
| National Insurance number | YY223344Y |
| Date of birth | 3.9.71 |
| Works number | 626 |
| Tax code | 472T |

On 8 April 2009, his total pay was £240.60.

On 15 April 2009, his total pay was £290.30, which includes an overtime payment of £49.70.

On 22 April 2009, his total pay was £260.00.

Tables A give the following free pay for code 472.

| Week | Free pay £ |
|---|---|
| 1 | 90.95 |
| 2 | 181.90 |
| 3 | 272.85 |

Taxable pay tables are given in Appendix I at the end of this text.

**Tasks**

(a) Using the appropriate Tax Tables, calculate the total tax due in each of these three weeks.

(b) Fill in the following extract from the deductions working sheet for his PAYE income tax, as it should be as at 22 April 2009.

| Week | | Tax code | | Amended WK/mnth | | | | | | | |
|---|---|---|---|---|---|---|---|---|---|---|---|
| | | | | | K codes | | | | K codes | | K codes |
| | Pay in the week | Total pay to date | Total free pay to date | Total additional pay to date | Total taxable pay to date | Total tax due to date | Tax due at end of current period | Regulatory limit | Tax deducted in the week | Tax not deducted owing to the regulatory limit |
| | 2 | 3 | 4a | 4b | 5 | 6 | 6a | 6b | 7 | 8 |
| 1 | | | | | | | | | | |
| 2 | | | | | | | | | | |
| 3 | | | | | | | | | | |

# 45 Barbara Walton

This activity is similar to number 44 except that it deals with a monthly-paid employee.

Barbara Walton is an employee of your company. Her monthly pay is £3,600 and her tax code is 505T. Staff are paid on the 22nd of each month.

Tables A give the following free pay.

| | Month | |
|---|---|---|
| Code | 1 | 2 |
| | £ | £ |
| 5 | 4.92 | 9.84 |
| 500 | 417.42 | 834.84 |
| Boxed 500 | 416.67 | 833.34 |

**Tasks**

(a) Calculate the tax payable or refundable on the 22nd of (i) April 2009 and (ii) May 2009.

(b) Fill in the following extract from a P11 for this employee up to the end of May 2009.

PRACTICE ACTIVITIES

|  | Tax code |  | Amended WK/mnth |  |  |  |  |  |  |  |
|---|---|---|---|---|---|---|---|---|---|---|
|  |  |  |  | K codes |  |  | K codes |  |  | K codes |
| M o n t h | Pay in the month | Total pay to date | Total free pay to date | Total additional pay to date | Total taxable pay to date | Total tax due to date | Tax due at end of current period | Regulatory limit | Tax deducted in the month | Tax not deducted owing to the regulatory limit |
|  | 2 | 3 | 4a | 4b | 5 | 6 | 6a | 6b | 7 | 8 |
| 1 |  |  |  |  |  |  |  |  |  |  |
| 2 |  |  |  |  |  |  |  |  |  |  |
|  |  |  |  |  |  |  |  |  |  |  |

## 46 Burnham Peters Ltd

You are the payroll officer of Burnham Peters Ltd. During the course of a week in your job, you receive several queries from employees.

(a) Ellen Priestley is a pensioner, who now works for the company part time. She tells you that because she is now old enough for a state pension, and is only a part time worker, you shouldn't deduct any tax from her pay.

(b) Tina Gonzalez is a temporary switchboard operator, who has been sent to your company by the Bright Sounds Employment Agency Ltd, an employment agency for temporary secretarial staff. She has been with your company for over three months, and has come to tell you that she would now like to be paid directly by you instead of by the agency. This is because the agency has been very slow recently to pay her weekly wages.

(c) Bob Harkins is a warehouse worker, who telephones you to say that his Tax Office has given him a code BR. He wants to know what it means.

(d) Simone Michel is a manager of your company who has just been posted to the overseas branch in Germany, where she expects to be (almost full time) for the next two to three years. She asks you whether her monthly salary will be subject to PAYE.

(e) Ali Shah is a part-time worker in your company warehouse. He telephones you to say that he wants to become self-employed and that you shouldn't deduct any income tax from his pay.

(f) Goran Ivanov tells you that he is on emergency code, and asks you what it means.

How would you deal with each of these queries?

PRACTICE ACTIVITIES

chapter 7

# Income tax: more complex cases

## Activity checklist

This checklist shows which performance criteria, range statement or knowledge and understanding point is covered by each activity in this chapter. Tick off each activity as you complete it.

**Activity**

| | | |
|---|---|---|
| 47 | ☐ | This activity covers performance criteria 73.1.E and knowledge and understanding point 15 |
| 48 | ☐ | This activity covers performance criteria 73.1.E and knowledge and understanding point 15 |
| 49 | ☐ | This activity covers performance criteria 73.1.E and knowledge and understanding point 15 |
| 50 | ☐ | This activity covers performance criteria 73.1.E and knowledge and understanding point 15 |
| 51 | ☐ | This activity covers performance criteria 73.1.E and knowledge and understanding point 15 |
| 52 | ☐ | This activity covers performance criteria 73.1.E and knowledge and understanding point 15 |
| 53 | ☐ | This activity covers performance criteria 73.1.E and knowledge and understanding point 15 |
| 54 | ☐ | This activity covers performance criteria 73.1.E and knowledge and understanding point 15 |

PRACTICE ACTIVITIES

## 47 Code and pay changes

Maria Pfeffer's salary as at 1 January 2009 was £15,000 per annum. On 1 January 2010 she received a pay rise of 5%. Her tax code at 6 April 2009 was 433L. On 22 July 2009 her employer received a P6(T) from the Tax Office notifying a change in Maria's tax code to 130L, to be used as soon as possible.

Tables A give the following figures.

| Month | Code 130 Free pay £ | Code 433 Free pay £ |
|---|---|---|
| 1 | 109.09 | 361.59 |
| 2 | 218.18 | 723.18 |
| 3 | 327.27 | 1,084.77 |
| 4 | 436.36 | 1,446.36 |
| 5 | 545.45 | 1,807.95 |
| 6 | 654.54 | 2,169.54 |
| 7 | 763.63 | 2,531.13 |
| 8 | 872.72 | 2,892.72 |
| 9 | 981.81 | 3,254.31 |
| 10 | 1,090.90 | 3,615.90 |
| 11 | 1,199.99 | 3,977.49 |
| 12 | 1,309.08 | 4,339.08 |

**Task**

Complete the extract from Maria's P11 for 2009/10 shown below, making (and stating) any further assumptions you think are necessary.

| Month | Tax code | | Amended WK/mnth | | | | | | | | |
|---|---|---|---|---|---|---|---|---|---|---|---|
| | | | | K codes | | | K codes | | | | K codes |
| | Pay in the month 2 | Total pay to date 3 | Total free pay to date 4a | Total additional pay to date 4b | Total taxable pay to date 5 | Total tax due to date 6 | Tax due at end of current period 6a | Regulatory limit 6b | Tax deducted in the month 7 | Tax not deducted owing to the regulatory limit 8 |
| 1 | | | | | | | | | | | |
| 2 | | | | | | | | | | | |
| 3 | | | | | | | | | | | |
| 4 | | | | | | | | | | | |
| 5 | | | | | | | | | | | |
| 6 | | | | | | | | | | | |
| 7 | | | | | | | | | | | |
| 8 | | | | | | | | | | | |
| 9 | | | | | | | | | | | |
| 10 | | | | | | | | | | | |
| 11 | | | | | | | | | | | |
| 12 | | | | | | | | | | | |

# 48 Philip Phantom

Philip Phantom earns £1,500 in Month 1 and £2,000 in Month 2. Free pay for his tax code (498L) in Month 1 is £415.75 and in Month 2 is £831.50.

(a) What is his taxable pay to date in Month 1, and Month 2:

    (i) on a Week 1/Month 1 basis?
    (ii) on the normal cumulative basis?

(b) How much tax will he pay in Month 1 and 2:

    (i) on a Week 1/Month 1 basis?
    (ii) on a cumulative basis?

(c) How much tax would he pay in Month 1 and Month 2, if Philip were on the following four codes.

    (i) D0
    (ii) BR
    (iii) NT
    (iv) 0T

(d) What would be the tax payable in Month 1 and Month 2, if Philip earned £3,500 and was on the following codes?

    (i) BR
    (ii) 0T

PRACTICE ACTIVITIES

## 49 John David Rose

This activity is designed to test your awareness of taxation on a Week 1/Month 1 basis.

John David Rose is an employee of your company. He is paid a monthly salary of £3,000 before deductions on the 25th of each month. You receive the following P6(T) from your Tax Office.

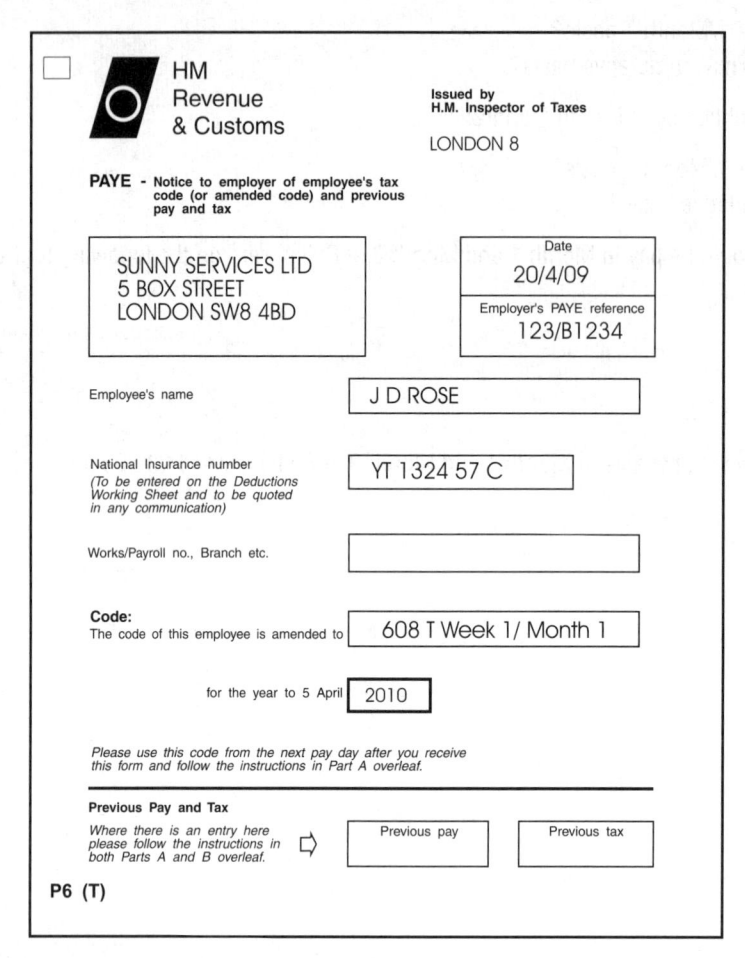

```
                    HM                      Issued by
                    Revenue                 H.M. Inspector of Taxes
                    & Customs
                                            LONDON 8

PAYE - Notice to employer of employee's tax
       code (or amended code) and previous
       pay and tax

       SUNNY SERVICES LTD              Date
       5 BOX STREET                    20/4/09
       LONDON SW8 4BD
                                       Employer's PAYE reference
                                       123/B1234

Employee's name            J D ROSE

National Insurance number  YT 1324 57 C
(To be entered on the Deductions
Working Sheet and to be quoted
in any communication)

Works/Payroll no., Branch etc.

Code:
The code of this employee is amended to    608 T Week 1/ Month 1

            for the year to 5 April     2010

Please use this code from the next pay day after you receive
this form and follow the instructions in Part A overleaf.

Previous Pay and Tax
Where there is an entry here
please follow the instructions in     Previous pay       Previous tax
both Parts A and B overleaf.

P6 (T)
```

Tables A give the following figures.

| Month | Code 108 £ | Code 120 £ | Code 500 £ | Boxed 500 £ |
|---|---|---|---|---|
| 1 | 90.75 | 100.75 | 417.42 | 416.67 |
| 2 | 181.50 | 201.50 | 834.84 | 833.34 |
| 3 | 272.25 | 302.25 | 1,252.26 | 1,250.01 |

**Tasks**

(a) Complete the following extract from a P11 for this employee for his April and May salary payments, to show his PAYE income tax deductions.

(b) Complete the extract from the P11 for his June salary, after you have received a notice from the Tax Office in June of a change in his tax code to 620T (cumulative basis).

|   | Tax code |   | Amended WK/mnth |   |   |   | K codes |   |   | K codes |
|---|---|---|---|---|---|---|---|---|---|---|
| M o n t h | Pay in the month 2 | Total pay to date 3 | Total free pay to date 4a | Total additional pay to date 4b | Total taxable pay to date 5 | Total tax due to date 6 | Tax due at end of current period 6a | Regulatory limit 6b | Tax deducted in the month 7 | Tax not deducted owing to the regulatory limit 8 |
| 1 |   |   |   |   |   |   |   |   |   |   |
| 2 |   |   |   |   |   |   |   |   |   |   |
| 3 |   |   |   |   |   |   |   |   |   |   |

# 50 Week 53

One of the unusual features of a tax year is a Week 53 payment, which will occasionally occur. This activity tests your ability to compute the PAYE income tax payable, and to fill in a P11 in this situation.

An employee is paid £300.00 every week, and in this particular year (2009/10), there are wage payments on (a) 29 March 2010 - Week 52 and (b) 5 April 2010 - Week 53.

His tax code, 329T, gives him free pay as follows.

| Week | Free pay £ |
|---|---|
| 1 | 63.45 |
| 47 | 2,982.15 |
| 48 | 3,045.60 |
| 49 | 3,109.05 |
| 50 | 3,172.50 |
| 51 | 3,235.95 |
| 52 | 3,299.40 |

**Task**

Complete the following extract from a P11 for Weeks 47 to 53. Total pay to and including week 47 is £300 × 47 = £14,100 and total tax to and including week 46 is £2,176.20.

PRACTICE ACTIVITIES

|  | Tax code |  | Amended |  |  |  |  |  |  |  |  |
|---|---|---|---|---|---|---|---|---|---|---|---|
|  |  |  | WK/mnth |  |  |  |  |  |  |  |  |
|  |  |  |  | K codes |  |  |  | K codes |  |  | K codes |
| W e e k | Pay in the month 2 | Total pay to date 3 | Total free pay to date 4a | Total additional pay to date 4b | Total taxable pay to date 5 | Total tax due to date 6 | Tax due at end of current period 6a | Regulatory limit 6b | Tax deducted in the month 7 | Tax not deducted owing to the regulatory limit 8 |
| 47 |  |  |  |  |  |  |  |  |  |  |
| 48 |  |  |  |  |  |  |  |  |  |  |
| 49 |  |  |  |  |  |  |  |  |  |  |
| 50 |  |  |  |  |  |  |  |  |  |  |
| 51 |  |  |  |  |  |  |  |  |  |  |
| 52 |  |  |  |  |  |  |  |  |  |  |
| 53 |  |  |  |  |  |  |  |  |  |  |

## 51 Trade dispute

This activity deals with another unusual feature of a payroll system, which is what to do when there is a strike or a lay-off of staff in your organisation.

Grade A staff at your company went on strike at the end of Week 1 of the 2009/10 tax year. Grade A each get £250 a week gross when not on strike. As a result of the strike, your company's management have had to lay off all Grade B staff immediately. Grade B staff are paid 25% of their normal basic wage of £200 per week during their lay-off (£50 per week per Grade B employee).

Blank extracts from the P11s of two of your employees are shown below.

(a)     Paul Rodgers is a Grade A employee, who is on strike from Week 2.
(b)     Richard Stout is a Grade B employee, who is paid £50 in Week 2.

## PRACTICE ACTIVITIES

(a) **Paul Rodgers**

|  | Tax code |  | Amended WK/mnth |  |  |  |  |  |  |  |  |
|---|---|---|---|---|---|---|---|---|---|---|---|
|  |  |  |  | K codes |  |  | K codes |  |  | K codes |  |
| W e e k | Pay in the month 2 | Total pay to date 3 | Total free pay to date 4a | Total additional pay to date 4b | Total taxable pay to date 5 | Total tax due to date 6 | Tax due at end of current period 6a | Regulatory limit 6b | Tax deducted in the month 7 | Tax not deducted owing to the regulatory limit 8 |
| 1 |  |  |  |  |  |  |  |  |  |  |
| 2 |  |  |  |  |  |  |  |  |  |  |

(b) **Richard Stout**

|  | Tax code |  | Amended WK/mnth |  |  |  |  |  |  |  |  |
|---|---|---|---|---|---|---|---|---|---|---|---|
|  |  |  |  | K codes |  |  | K codes |  |  | K codes |  |
| W e e k | Pay in the month 2 | Total pay to date 3 | Total free pay to date 4a | Total additional pay to date 4b | Total taxable pay to date 5 | Total tax due to date 6 | Tax due at end of current period 6a | Regulatory limit 6b | Tax deducted in the month 7 | Tax not deducted owing to the regulatory limit 8 |
| 1 |  |  |  |  |  |  |  |  |  |  |
| 2 |  |  |  |  |  |  |  |  |  |  |

Each employee has a tax code of 300T, giving free pay of £57.87 for Week 1 and £115.74 for week 2.

**Tasks**

(a) Complete the P11s for Weeks 1 and 2 for each of these employees.
(b) What would you do about any tax refunds due to Paul Rodgers and Richard Stout?

## 52 K codes

(a) Why are some people given K codes?
(b) Carol Lewis, a senior manager in your company has just phoned to query the amount of PAYE income tax deducted from her salary last month. You promise to look into it and on checking you find that her code was changed from 94T to K321 last month. You call back but her assistant explains that she is out of the office for the rest of the day.

**Task**

Write Miss Lewis a memo explaining what has happened. Judging from your conversation she has no understanding of the PAYE system and you will need to explain about tax codes generally.

PRACTICE ACTIVITIES

(c) Miss Lewis's office is only a few seconds walk away. Should you leave the memo on her desk?

(d) Since Miss Lewis is away for the day, could this matter not be dealt with tomorrow?

## 53 Mushtaq Ahmed

Mushtaq Ahmed earns a salary of £38,400 per annum. His tax code is K149. Tables A give the following figures for code 149.

| Month | Amount £ |
|---|---|
| 1 | 124.92 |
| 2 | 249.84 |
| 3 | 374.76 |

Complete the following extract from his P11 for Months 1 to 3.

| Month | Tax code | Amended WK/mnth | | | | | | | | |
|---|---|---|---|---|---|---|---|---|---|---|
| | | | K codes | | | | K codes | | | K codes |
| | Pay in the month 2 | Total pay to date 3 | Total free pay to date 4a | Total additional pay to date 4b | Total taxable pay to date 5 | Total tax due to date 6 | Tax due at end of current period 6a | Regulatory limit 6b | Tax deducted in the month 7 | Tax not deducted owing to the regulatory limit 8 |
| 1 | | | | | | | | | | |
| 2 | | | | | | | | | | |
| 3 | | | | | | | | | | |

## 54 Martin Carr

Martin Carr's tax code is K491. Tables A give £409.92 for Month 1 and £819.84 for Month 2. He is still a director of MC Ltd although he has almost retired. He receives fees of £1,500 per annum for attending monthly meetings, drives a company car and receives other benefits.

# PRACTICE ACTIVITIES

**Task**

(a) Complete Martin Carr's P11 for Months 1 and 2.

| | Tax code | | Amended WK/mnth | | | | | | | | |
|---|---|---|---|---|---|---|---|---|---|---|---|
| | | | | K codes | | | | K codes | | | K codes |
| Month | Pay in the month 2 | Total pay to date 3 | Total free pay to date 4a | Total additional pay to date 4b | Total taxable pay to date 5 | Total tax due to date 6 | Tax due at end of current period 6a | Regulatory limit 6b | Tax deducted in the month 7 | Tax not deducted owing to the regulatory limit 8 |
| 1 | | | | | | | | | | |
| 2 | | | | | | | | | | |

(b) Complete Martin Carr's P11 for Months 1 and 2 assuming that the K code operates on Month 1 basis.

| | Tax code | | Amended WK/mnth | | | | | | | | |
|---|---|---|---|---|---|---|---|---|---|---|---|
| | | | | K codes | | | | K codes | | | K codes |
| Month | Pay in the month 2 | Total pay to date 3 | Total free pay to date 4a | Total additional pay to date 4b | Total taxable pay to date 5 | Total tax due to date 6 | Tax due at end of current period 6a | Regulatory limit 6b | Tax deducted in the month 7 | Tax not deducted owing to the regulatory limit 8 |
| 1 | | | | | | | | | | |
| 2 | | | | | | | | | | |

PRACTICE ACTIVITIES

chapter 8

# National Insurance: basic NICs

## Activity checklist

This checklist shows which performance criteria, range statement or knowledge and understanding point is covered by each activity in this chapter. Tick off each activity as you complete it.

Activity

| | | |
|---|---|---|
| 55 | ☐ | This activity covers performance criteria 73.1.E and knowledge and understanding point 15. |
| 56 | ☐ | This activity covers performance criteria 73.1.E and knowledge and understanding point 15. |
| 57 | ☐ | This activity covers performance criteria 73.1.E and knowledge and understanding point 15. |
| 58 | ☐ | This activity covers performance criteria 73.1.E and knowledge and understanding point 15. |
| 59 | ☐ | This activity covers performance criteria 73.1.E and knowledge and understanding point 15. |
| 60 | ☐ | This activity covers performance criteria 73.1.E and knowledge and understanding point 15. |
| 61 | ☐ | This activity covers performance criteria 73.1.E and knowledge and understanding point 15. |
| 62 | ☐ | This activity covers performance criteria 73.1.E and knowledge and understanding point 15. |

## 55 NI tables

Which of the NI tables would you use for:

(a) an employee under 16?
(b) a not contracted out man over 65 who has given you a certificate of age exemption?
(c) a married woman, aged 25, who had contracted out in a salary-related scheme?
(d) a man of 40 who had taken out a personal pension plan with his bank?

## 56 NICs

You earn £850 a week. How much is assessable to NICs payable by:

(a) you?
(b) your employer?

Assume that Letter A applies.

## 57 Earnings

Earnings for NICs is the same amount as pay in the week or month for PAYE purposes.

True ☐    False ☐

## 58 Knowledge

When do employees normally pay NICs? Why doesn't form P45 include details of NICs?

## 59 Water babies

You are a payroll clerk for Water Babies plc, a company which manufactures educational toys for children.

One of the employees is Harold Childe. He has just recently joined the company as Office Factotum. Harold joined on 27 July 2009, the day after he left school for good. Harold has been paid £120 a week for his services.

He is 16 years old on 25 August 2009.

**Task**

What is the significance of Harold's sixteenth birthday as far as NICs and income tax are concerned?

PRACTICE ACTIVITIES

## 60 Harold Childe 1

Harold writes you a note asking why his pay is lower after his 16th birthday and how you worked it out.

Write a simple reply to him, stating how you arrived at the figure, and the reasons for the deduction.

## 61 Harold Childe 2

Harold Childe asks you another question. 'I don't see why I have to pay NICs. Some of my friends say that they have contracted out, and pay less. Can't I do the same?'

Draft a memorandum in reply.

## 62 Churne Orvill

Churne Orvill Ltd is a company which has two main activities.

(a) The manufacture of fireworks for sale.
(b) The arrangement of firework displays for local authorities and other bodies on days of celebration.

Staff employed in the manufacturing department are paid weekly. Staff who arrange the displays receive both a salary and a bonus based on each successful display, and are paid on a monthly basis.

The company does not run a contracted out pension scheme.

The following information relates to four members of staff in Months 1, 2 and 3 of the year 2009/10.

### Tasks

Complete the following extracts from the NIC side of the P11s provided for Months 1 to 3/Weeks 1 to 13.

(a) Diane Geness, aged 34, is a monthly paid employee, who has been responsible for many of the company's most innovative experiments.

Her basic salary is £1,577.33 per month, but in Month 2 her pay rises to £2,200 a month basic (and stays at that level).

(b) Horace Inkley is a weekly paid employee, earning £180 per week, without variation. Horace reaches retirement age at the beginning of Week 7, and provides you with a certificate of age exemption. Although he is past retirement age, he continues to work for Churne Orvill Ltd.

(c) Maggie Knox earns £380 a month. She works three days a week, but has no other employment.

(d) Silas Izewell has been with the company since it was founded. He will be 70 on 4 May 2008. He is retained as his skill and artistry in designing displays is famed throughout the industry.

His monthly salary is £2,000.

In Month 1 he also earned a bonus of £300 which, as is the case with all his bonus payments, he gives to charity. In Month 3 he received a further bonus, of £700, although the bonus related to a display he gave on 1 June.

He has also given you a certificate of age exemption.

National Insurance tables are in the Appendix.

## PRACTICE ACTIVITIES

**Diane Geness**

**National Insurance contributions**

|  |  |  | Earnings details ||||  Contribution details || Statutory payments ||||  |
|---|---|---|---|---|---|---|---|---|---|---|---|---|---|
| M O N T H N O | W E E K N O | For employer's use only | Earnings at the LEL (where earnings are equal to or exceed the LEL) 1a £ p | Earnings above the LEL, up to and including the ET 1b £ p | Earnings above the ET, up to and including the UAP 1c £ p | Earnings above the UAP, up to and including the UEL 1d £ p | Total of employee's and employer's contributions 1e £ p | Employee's contribution due on all earnings above the ET 1f £ p | SSP 1g £ p | SMP 1h £ p | SPP 1i £ p | SAP 1j £ p | Student Loan Deductions 1k £ |
| 1 | 1 |  |  |  |  |  |  |  |  |  |  |  |  |
| 1 | 2 |  |  |  |  |  |  |  |  |  |  |  |  |
| 1 | 3 |  |  |  |  |  |  |  |  |  |  |  |  |
| 1 | 4 |  |  |  |  |  |  |  |  |  |  |  |  |
| 2 | 5 |  |  |  |  |  |  |  |  |  |  |  |  |
| 2 | 6 |  |  |  |  |  |  |  |  |  |  |  |  |
| 2 | 7 |  |  |  |  |  |  |  |  |  |  |  |  |
| 2 | 8 |  |  |  |  |  |  |  |  |  |  |  |  |
| 3 | 9 |  |  |  |  |  |  |  |  |  |  |  |  |
| 3 | 10 |  |  |  |  |  |  |  |  |  |  |  |  |
| 3 | 11 |  |  |  |  |  |  |  |  |  |  |  |  |
| 3 | 12 |  |  |  |  |  |  |  |  |  |  |  |  |
| 3 | 13 |  |  |  |  |  |  |  |  |  |  |  |  |

*Enter NIC Contribution Table letter here*

**End of Year Summary**

| 1a £ p | 1b £ p | 1c £ p | 1d £ p | 1e £ p | 1f £ p |
|---|---|---|---|---|---|
|  |  |  |  |  |  |
|  |  |  |  |  |  |
|  |  |  |  |  |  |

P11(1999)    BMSD 11/98

## PRACTICE ACTIVITIES

**Horace Inkley**

**National Insurance contributions**

| MONTH NO | WEEK NO | For employer's use only | Earnings details ||||| Contribution details || Statutory payments |||| Student Loan Deductions 1k £ |
|---|---|---|---|---|---|---|---|---|---|---|---|---|---|
| | | | Earnings at the LEL (where earnings are equal to or exceed the LEL) 1a £ p | Earnings above the LEL, up to and including the ET 1b £ p | Earnings above the ET, up to and including the UAP 1c £ p | Earnings above the UAP, up to and including the UEL 1d £ p | Total of employee's and employer's contributions 1e £ p | Employee's contribution due on all earnings above the ET 1f £ p | SSP 1g £ p | SMP 1h £ p | SPP 1i £ p | SAP 1j £ p | |
| 1 | 1 | | | | | | | | | | | | |
| | 2 | | | | | | | | | | | | |
| | 3 | | | | | | | | | | | | |
| | 4 | | | | | | | | | | | | |
| 2 | 5 | | | | | | | | | | | | |
| | 6 | | | | | | | | | | | | |
| | 7 | | | | | | | | | | | | |
| | 8 | | | | | | | | | | | | |
| 3 | 9 | | | | | | | | | | | | |
| | 10 | | | | | | | | | | | | |
| | 11 | | | | | | | | | | | | |
| | 12 | | | | | | | | | | | | |
| | 13 | | | | | | | | | | | | |

*Enter NIC Contribution Table letter here*  **End of Year Summary**

| 1a £ p | 1b £ p | 1c £ p | 1d £ p | 1e £ p | 1f £ p |
|---|---|---|---|---|---|
| | | | | | |
| | | | | | |
| | | | | | |

P11(1999)   BMSD 11/98

## PRACTICE ACTIVITIES

**Maggie Knox**

**National Insurance contributions**

| Month No | Week No | For employer's use only | Earnings details ||||  Contribution details || Statutory payments |||| |
|---|---|---|---|---|---|---|---|---|---|---|---|---|---|
| | | | Earnings at the LEL (where earnings are equal to or exceed the LEL) 1a £ p | Earnings above the LEL, up to and including the ET 1b £ p | Earnings above the ET, up to and including the UAP 1c £ p | Earnings above the UAP, up to and including the UEL 1d £ p | Total of employee's and employer's contributions 1e £ p | Employee's contribution due on all earnings above the ET 1f £ p | SSP 1g £ p | SMP 1h £ p | SPP 1i £ p | SAP 1j £ p | Student Loan Deductions 1k £ |
| 1 | 1 | | | | | | | | | | | | |
| | 2 | | | | | | | | | | | | |
| | 3 | | | | | | | | | | | | |
| | 4 | | | | | | | | | | | | |
| 2 | 5 | | | | | | | | | | | | |
| | 6 | | | | | | | | | | | | |
| | 7 | | | | | | | | | | | | |
| | 8 | | | | | | | | | | | | |
| 3 | 9 | | | | | | | | | | | | |
| | 10 | | | | | | | | | | | | |
| | 11 | | | | | | | | | | | | |
| | 12 | | | | | | | | | | | | |
| | 13 | | | | | | | | | | | | |

*Enter NIC Contribution Table letter here*   **End of Year Summary**

| 1a £ p | 1b £ p | 1c £ p | 1d £ p | 1e £ p | 1f £ p |
|---|---|---|---|---|---|
| | | | | | |
| | | | | | |
| | | | | | |

P11(1999)   BMSD 11/98

## PRACTICE ACTIVITIES

### Silas Izewell
### National Insurance contributions

| MONTH NO | WEEK NO | For employer's use only | Earnings at the LEL (where earnings are equal to or exceed the LEL) 1a £ p | Earnings above the LEL, up to and including the ET 1b £ p | Earnings above the ET, up to and including the UAP 1c £ p | Earnings above the UAP, up to and including the UEL 1d £ p | Total of employee's and employer's contributions 1e £ p | Employee's contribution due on all earnings above the ET 1f £ p | SSP 1g £ p | SMP 1h £ p | SPP 1i £ p | SAP 1j £ p | Student Loan Deductions 1k £ |
|---|---|---|---|---|---|---|---|---|---|---|---|---|---|
| 1 | 1 | | | | | | | | | | | | |
| | 2 | | | | | | | | | | | | |
| | 3 | | | | | | | | | | | | |
| | 4 | | | | | | | | | | | | |
| 2 | 5 | | | | | | | | | | | | |
| | 6 | | | | | | | | | | | | |
| | 7 | | | | | | | | | | | | |
| | 8 | | | | | | | | | | | | |
| 3 | 9 | | | | | | | | | | | | |
| | 10 | | | | | | | | | | | | |
| | 11 | | | | | | | | | | | | |
| | 12 | | | | | | | | | | | | |
| | 13 | | | | | | | | | | | | |

*Enter NIC Contribution Table letter here*   **End of Year Summary**

| 1a £ p | 1b £ p | 1c £ p | 1d £ p | 1e £ p | 1f £ p |
|---|---|---|---|---|---|
| | | | | | |
| | | | | | |
| | | | | | |

P11(1999)                                           BMSD 11/98

chapter 9

# National Insurance: advanced NICs

## Activity checklist

This checklist shows which performance criteria, range statement or knowledge and understanding point is covered by each activity in this chapter. Tick off each activity as you complete it.

**Activity**

63 ☐ This activity covers performance criteria 73.1.E and knowledge and understanding point 15.

64 ☐ This activity covers performance criteria 73.1.E and knowledge and understanding point 15.

PRACTICE ACTIVITIES

## 63 Exact percentage

The payroll department of Revolution-Art Ltd uses the exact percentage method of calculating NI contributions.

(a) Use the exact percentage tables given in Appendix II to calculate how much in NICs would be paid for and by the following employees in a month or week. All are below pension age.

   (i) P Morris earns £2,000 a month and is not contracted out.
   (ii) B Jones earns £150 a week and is not contracted out.
   (iii) F Sanders earns £98 a week and is not contracted out.
   (iv) J Jellicoe earns £880 a week and is not contracted out.
   (v) F Majid, who pays NICs under Table B at a reduced rate, earns £115 a week.

(b) Complete the following table, showing the entries to be made on each of the employees' P11s.

| Name | Column 1a | Column 1b | Column 1c | Column 1d | Column 1e | Column 1f |
|------|-----------|-----------|-----------|-----------|-----------|-----------|
| P Morris | | | | | | |
| B Jones | | | | | | |
| F Sanders | | | | | | |
| J Jellicoe | | | | | | |
| F Majid | | | | | | |

## 64 COSRS

In Month 1, Penny Shaw earns £3,700 gross. Her employer, Executive Perks Ltd, runs a salary related occupational pension scheme which has the contracted out number S4 AB12CD3.

Penny contributes to the occupational pension scheme, which means that she is contracted out of S2P, and the employer's and employee's contributions for Table D apply. As a result, the contribution rates are reduced for earnings between the earnings threshold and the UAP by 1.6% for employees and 3.7% for employers.

Penny makes pension contributions of £100 per month.

**Task**

Complete the following extract from Penny Shaw's P11. Use the exact percentage method to calculate NICs.

PRACTICE ACTIVITIES

**National Insurance contributions**

|   |   |   | Earnings details |||| Contribution details || Statutory payments |||| |
|---|---|---|---|---|---|---|---|---|---|---|---|---|---|
| M O N T H N O | W E E K N O | For employer's use only | Earnings at the LEL (where earnings are equal to or exceed the LEL) 1a £ p | Earnings above the LEL, up to and including the ET 1b £ p | Earnings above the ET, up to and including the UAP 1c £ p | Earnings above the UAP, up to and including the UEL 1d £ p | Total of employee's and employer's contributions 1e £ p | Employee's contribution due on all earnings above the ET 1f £ p | SSP 1g £ p | SMP 1h £ p | SPP 1i £ p | SAP 1j £ p | Student Loan Deductions 1k £ |
| 1 | 1 |  |  |  |  |  |  |  |  |  |  |  |  |
|   | 2 |  |  |  |  |  |  |  |  |  |  |  |  |
|   | 3 |  |  |  |  |  |  |  |  |  |  |  |  |
|   | 4 |  |  |  |  |  |  |  |  |  |  |  |  |
| 2 | 5 |  |  |  |  |  |  |  |  |  |  |  |  |
|   | 6 |  |  |  |  |  |  |  |  |  |  |  |  |
|   | 7 |  |  |  |  |  |  |  |  |  |  |  |  |
|   | 8 |  |  |  |  |  |  |  |  |  |  |  |  |
| 3 | 9 |  |  |  |  |  |  |  |  |  |  |  |  |
|   | 10 |  |  |  |  |  |  |  |  |  |  |  |  |
|   | 11 |  |  |  |  |  |  |  |  |  |  |  |  |
|   | 12 |  |  |  |  |  |  |  |  |  |  |  |  |
|   | 13 |  |  |  |  |  |  |  |  |  |  |  |  |

PRACTICE ACTIVITIES

# chapter 10

# Other deductions

## Activity checklist

This checklist shows which performance criteria, range statement or knowledge and understanding point is covered by each activity in this chapter. Tick off each activity as you complete it.

**Activity**

| | | |
|---|---|---|
| 65 | ☐ | This activity covers performance criteria 72.1.E and 73.1.B. |
| 66 | ☐ | This activity covers performance criteria 73.1.A and 73.1.E. |
| 67 | ☐ | This activity covers performance criteria 72.1.E and 73.1.B. |
| 68 | ☐ | This activity covers performance criteria 72.1.E and 73.1.E. |
| 69 | ☐ | This activity covers performance criteria 73.1.B and 73.1.C. |
| 70 | ☐ | This activity covers performance criteria 73.1.B. |
| 71 | ☐ | This activity covers performance criteria 73.1.B. |
| 72 | ☐ | This activity covers performance criteria 73.1.B. |

**Tutorial note.** This section also contains some activities relating to earlier Chapters, as revision.

PRACTICE ACTIVITIES

# 65 Gilberta Sullivan

Gilberta Sullivan has looked at her payslip. She doesn't understand why some deductions like income tax are deductions from gross pay and some aren't. Write a memo explaining the difference.

# 66 Groddy Ltd

You work for Groddy Ltd, a company which sells recycled male cosmetics cheaply in the town of Bophinton. The town has a number of institutions of higher education. Your boss is thus never short of staff who can be paid a small sum for working a few hours a week.

At the beginning of the week you have three new employees to deal with. It is just after the end of the summer term.

(a) Charles Kingsley is nearly 16 years old, and has just left Dotheboys Hall, a local school. Mrs Groddy has written you a note saying that he is to be employed at £98 per week.

(b) Freddie Scullion is 19 and has just finished his first year at Porterhouse College, one of the local universities. He has run up an overdraft, and wants to go on holiday in August. He has done no paid work during term time, nor in the Christmas or Easter vacations.

Mrs Groddy has agreed to employ Freddie Scullion at a salary of £98 a week for eight weeks.

(c) Oliver Spend, a 17 year old student at the Ned Ludd Technical College, works one evening a week from 6pm to 9.30pm for Mrs Groddy during term time, at £10 an evening.

What should you do in each case, with regard to tax and NICs?

# 67 Gill Tee Ltd

Gill Tee Ltd of Workhouse Buildings, Almshouse Lane, Workington runs a payroll giving scheme for its employees. Each employee gives between £14 and £20 a month out of gross income to charities. Gill Tee Ltd does not charge for administration of the scheme. It is March 2010.

Gill Tee Ltd has a contract with the Charities Aid Foundation. The number of the contract is 9752. The following employees contribute to GAYE.

(a) Elizabeth Windsor (payroll number 02, NI number QE 201649 C) contributes £15 a month.
(b) Melani Ayre (payroll number 07, NI number AJ 999999 D) contributes £15 a month.
(c) R S I Croesus (payroll number 03, NI number KE 777777 B) gives £20 a month.
(d) Benedict Pope (payroll number 33, NI number ON 222222 A) gives £20 a month.

**Tasks**

(a) Fill in the GAYE listing form.

(b) These donations are made gross.

Assuming that Elizabeth Windsor has taxable income of £10,000 per month:

(i) how much is she saving in tax by participating in the payroll giving scheme?

## PRACTICE ACTIVITIES

(ii) how much is she saving in NICs?

---

### INSTRUCTIONS FOR SUBMITTING DONATIONS

1. Quote your CONTRACT NUMBER and PAYROLL NAME on all documentation.
2. Check that the Employee identification number on each Charity Choice Form is correct.
3. Check that the Employee identification number which you quote on your monthly deduction list is also the same on the Charity Choice form.
4. Send us the completed TOP SECTION of the Charity Choice form AND keep a copy or the yellow carbonated copy on your file for future reference.
5. Please arrange for your monthly lists to be in this format or PHOTOCOPY FREELY and write or type the information required.
6. Please arrange for your monthly lists to show the MONTH OF DEDUCTION where possible.
7. Please submit donations by cheque. Other means of payment should be agreed with Give As You Earn prior to any change.
8. Please arrange for all Give As You Earn documentation to come to us in one monthly packet.
9. Use this as an example of the format needed for computer printouts.
10. It will help us if we could have both these numbers. If this poses a problem, please submit one or the other (see * overleaf).

GIVE AS YOU EARN EMPLOYEE DONATIONS              PAYLISTING/DEDUCTION STATEMENT

CONTRACT NUMBER: _____               EMPLOYER NAME: _____
MONTH OF DEDUCTION: _____               EMPLOYER ADDRESS: _____
PAYROLL NAME/ID/CODE: _____

| *NI NUMBER AND *PAYROLL NUMBER | DONATION | NAME | STARTER/ LEAVER |
|---|---|---|---|
|  |  |  |  |

PAGE TOTAL
OPTIONAL 5% ADMIN
REMITTANCE ENCLOSED        MUST AGREE WITH ENCLOSED CHEQUE

PRACTICE ACTIVITIES

# 68 Sandy Shore

Sandy Shore is a weekly paid employee, whose basic weekly wage is £125, although she frequently does overtime. She is going on holiday.

At the end of Week 1, she asks for her pay for that week, which comprises basic of £125 plus £42 overtime, together with her basic pay of £125 for both Weeks 2 and 3. Sandy pays NICs based on Table A.

Her tax code is 419T, giving free pay as follows.

| Week | Free pay £ |
|---|---|
| 1 | 80.75 |
| 2 | 161.50 |
| 3 | 242.25 |

Use the exact percentage method to calculate NICs – table A rates are given in the Appendix 11.

**Tasks**

(a) Fill in the weeks 1, 2 and 3 on the P11 provided.
(b) What would she receive in her pay cheque at the end of Week 1?

PRACTICE ACTIVITIES

**National Insurance contributions**

| MONTH NO | WEEK NO | For employer's use only | Earnings details ||||  Contribution details || Statutory payments ||||  |
|---|---|---|---|---|---|---|---|---|---|---|---|---|---|
| | | | Earnings at the LEL (where earnings are equal to or exceed the LEL) 1a £ p | Earnings above the LEL, up to and including the ET 1b £ p | Earnings above the ET, up to and including the UAP 1c £ p | Earnings above the UAP, up to and including the UEL 1d £ p | Total of employee's and employer's contributions 1e £ p | Employee's contribution due on all earnings above the ET 1f £ p | SSP 1g £ p | SMP 1h £ p | SPP 1i £ p | SAP 1j £ p | Student Loan Deductions 1k £ |
| 1 | 1 | | | | | | | | | | | | |
| | 2 | | | | | | | | | | | | |
| | 3 | | | | | | | | | | | | |
| | 4 | | | | | | | | | | | | |
| 2 | 5 | | | | | | | | | | | | |
| | 6 | | | | | | | | | | | | |
| | 7 | | | | | | | | | | | | |
| | 8 | | | | | | | | | | | | |
| 3 | 9 | | | | | | | | | | | | |
| | 10 | | | | | | | | | | | | |
| | 11 | | | | | | | | | | | | |
| | 12 | | | | | | | | | | | | |
| | 13 | | | | | | | | | | | | |

*Enter NIC Contribution Table letter here*  **End of Year Summary**

| 1a £ p | 1b £ p | 1c £ p | 1d £ p | 1e £ p | 1f £ p |
|---|---|---|---|---|---|
| | | | | | |
| | | | | | |
| | | | | | |

P11(1999)        BMSD 11/98

|   | Tax code | Amended WK/mnth |   |   |   |   |   |   |   |   |
|---|---|---|---|---|---|---|---|---|---|---|
| W e e k | Pay in the month 2 | Total pay to date 3 | Total free pay to date 4a | K codes Total additional pay to date 4b | Total taxable pay to date 5 | Total tax due to date 6 | Tax due at end of current period 6a | K codes Regulatory limit 6b | Tax deducted in the month 7 | K codes Tax not deducted owing to the regulatory limit 8 |
| 1 |   |   |   |   |   |   |   |   |   |   |
| 2 |   |   |   |   |   |   |   |   |   |   |
| 3 |   |   |   |   |   |   |   |   |   |   |

# 69 Pension scheme

Your procedures manual states:

'All employees who have been in permanent paid employment with the company for 6 months or more are eligible to join the company pension scheme.'

You have been asked to go through the personnel records of non-members of the scheme to assess whether to send out letters inviting them to join.

The date is 1 July 2009. You extract the following personnel details.

| Name | Date joined company | Comments |
|---|---|---|
| R Dworkin | 31/3/79 | Personal pension plan from April 1991 |
| A Foot | 1/1/09 | Temporary, first 3 months, then permanent since 1/4/09 |
| Ian Grave | 23/12/00 | Director |
| R Hare | 15/10/00 | Aged 59 |
| V Toombes | 13/10/00 | Working mother |
| B Quiet | 4/2/09 | Payroll clerk |

**Task**

Which of them are eligible to join the pension scheme?

# 70 Panther Ltd

The employees of Panther Ltd are invited to join the company pension scheme. The pension fund trustees maintain two types of record:

(a) a service record
(b) a contribution record

for each member or prior member of the scheme. The pension scheme is only open to employees with over 6 months service. It only accepts joiners on 1 January of each year. Employee contributions are 6% of pensionable earnings per month and the company itself contributes 10%.

# PRACTICE ACTIVITIES

## Tasks

(a) What details are necessary to keep a record of pensionable service?

(b) An employee, A Hopeful, decides to join the Panther Ltd pension scheme. Using the information below complete the proforma service record.

(c) How much would the employee's contributions to the scheme be in 2009?

(d) How much would the employer's contributions to the scheme be in 2010?

(e) How much would have been contributed to the scheme by A Hopeful, by Panther Ltd, and in total by 31 December 2010?

Pensionable earnings are basic salary at 1 January for most employees. For employees who earn a substantial amount of income as commission, this is added up for the year and added to the next year's basic to give an approximation (so that 2009's pensionable earnings will be basic pay at 1 January 2009 plus the commission earned in 2008). Bonuses do not count as pensionable earnings.

A Hopeful joined Panther Ltd on 15 June 2008, at a salary of £20,000 pa. On 15 September 2008 his annual salary was increased to £22,000 pa. He joined the pension scheme on 1 January 2009.

On 3 January 2009 he changed jobs within the company, and his actual pay for the year was £12,000 basic plus £13,000 commission. On 1 January 2010 his basic salary increased to £14,500. His commission in 2010 was £15,000.

His NI number is WC963123X, and he was born on 3 June 1965. He intends to retire on his 65th birthday. His pension account number is H0943.

| NAME: | NI NO: | A/C: |
|---|---|---|
| SEX: M/F | | |

| DATE JOINED COMPANY: | DATE JOINED SCHEME: |
|---|---|
| ESTIMATED DATE OF RETIREMENT: | DATE LEFT SCHEME: |

YEARS (cross off) 1,2,3,4,5,6,7,8,9,10,11,12,13,14,15,16,17,18,19,20,21,22,23,24,25,26,27,28,29,30,31,32,33,34,35,36,37,38,39,40

| YEAR | PENSIONABLE EARNINGS (from 1/1) | YEAR | PENSIONABLE EARNINGS (from 1/1) | YEAR | PENSIONABLE EARNINGS (from 1/1) | YEAR | PENSIONABLE EARNINGS (from 1/1) |
|---|---|---|---|---|---|---|---|
| 1 | | 11 | | 21 | | 31 | |
| 2 | | 12 | | 22 | | 32 | |
| 3 | | 13 | | 23 | | 33 | |
| 4 | | 14 | | 24 | | 34 | |
| 5 | | 15 | | 25 | | 35 | |
| 6 | | 16 | | 26 | | 36 | |
| 7 | | 17 | | 27 | | 37 | |
| 8 | | 18 | | 28 | | 38 | |
| 9 | | 19 | | 29 | | 39 | |
| 10 | | 20 | | 30 | | 40 | |

Pensionable earnings are earnings at 1 January of each year

# 71 Harris Ltd

The occupational pensions scheme run for Harris Ltd takes 5% of the employee's pensionable earnings each month, and the company itself contributes 10% of the employee's pensionable earnings. 'Pensionable earnings' are the same as total pay in the month for PAYE purposes.

Jill Kernot earned a basic salary of £15,000 pa when she joined the scheme in January 2009. This rose to £17,000 pa from September 2009 and to £21,000 pa from September 2010. The standard working week is a 35 hour week. Occasionally she worked overtime and this was paid at time and a half.

| Month | Overtime hours |
|---|---|
| March 2009 | 10 |
| September 2009 | 5 |
| October 2009 | 12 |
| October 2010 | 14 |

**Tasks**

(a) Complete the contribution record for Jill Kernot for years 1 and 2 of her membership of the scheme.

(b) If Jill were to leave the scheme at the end of Year 1 what would she receive with regard to her pension contribution?

(c) If she left after two years what would happen?

(d) Jill has said she wants to make some extra provision for the future. Draft a brief memo explaining what she can do.

PRACTICE ACTIVITIES

## 72 Holmes plc

Holmes plc contributes to an occupational pension scheme run on behalf of its employees who contribute up to retirement age. Not every employee is a member of the scheme, however, as some have opted out to invest in a personal pension plan instead.

Holmes plc pays its employees every month, using one payroll system. At the end of the report, a summary is printed of all the entries.

This totals up to the following for November 20X1.

|  | £ |
|---|---|
| Gross pay | 300,000 |
| Income tax | 50,000 |
| NICs – employees | 20,000 |
| NICs – employer | 30,000 |
| Pension contributions – employees | 18,000 |
| Pension contributions – employer | 30,000 |

£47,950 was eventually credited to the pension fund for contributions.

During November 20X1 the following occurred.

(a) One employee, Dr H Watson, reached 65 years old the day before pay day. His pension contributions were £100 a month. These had been deducted in error.

(b) The pension fund deducted 10 pence from every employee's contribution from the payroll as part of its statutory registration levy. There are 500 employees at Holmes plc.

(c) One employee made separately from the payroll an additional voluntary contribution of £80. It will form part of the payroll system next month. The employee pays tax at basic rate. The employee also makes FSAVCs of £50 per month to Piranha Funds Management Ltd. Holmes plc agreed to pay the tax relief of £20 on the AVC to the pension fund.

**Task**

Reconcile the pension deductions per the payroll with the amount actually credited to the pension fund at the end of November 20X1.

PRACTICE ACTIVITIES

chapter 11

# Net pay and aggregate payroll totals

## Activity checklist

This checklist shows which performance criteria, range statement or knowledge and understanding point is covered by each activity in this chapter. Tick off each activity as you complete it.

**Activity**

| | | |
|---|---|---|
| 73 | | This activity covers knowledge and understanding point 13. |
| 74 | | This activity covers knowledge and understanding point 13. |
| 75 | | This activity covers knowledge and understanding point 13. |

PRACTICE ACTIVITIES

## 73 Cash wages

Some employees in your organisation are paid in cash, every Friday afternoon.

Your procedures manual states the following.

> 'Uncollected wage packets should be kept in the safe. Employees who do not, for whatever reason, collect their wage packets at the defined time should collect them before starting work on the next working day.
>
> If the employee does not collect the wage packet then, he or she should be contacted over the public address system. The employee should then be contacted at home.
>
> If the employee sends a representative to collect the wage, then the employee must provide a signed letter saying who the representative is, and the representative's address. The employee's signature on the letter should be checked against a specimen signature held by personnel department. The representative should bring evidence of identity so that the name and address can both be checked.'

(a) It is Friday 8 August, and you have been distributing wage packets to employees who still have the right to be paid in cash, and who insist on receiving wages this way.

One employee, Lolita Humbert, has not turned up to collect her wage by the appointed time.

What do you do?

(b) It is now Monday morning. You have come in early expecting to see Lolita Humbert. She is not there, so now what do you do?

(c) She does not appear to have turned up to work. Now what do you do?

(d) Suddenly, there is a knock on the door and a man walks in claiming to be Lolita's boyfriend. He tells you Lolita has been a bit out of sorts over the weekend and is ill. Could you give him the money? What should be your reply?

(e) He produces a letter from Lolita as follows.

> 13 James Mason St
> Cambridge CB2
> Mon 11 August
>
> To: Payroll Dept
>
> I authorise Vladimir Nabokov of 51 Russian Drive, Cambridge CB2, to collect my pay packet, which I should have picked up last Friday afternoon.
>
> Yours faithfully
>
>
> Lolita Humbert

He also produces the following driving licence.

```
Full Licence  (issued by DVLC, Swansea)

Valid
from    01 09 1984      to      30 04 2029

This is your Driver Number              Issue No.

| NABOK | 808019 | VL9YY |         | 91 |                A6912795

Summary of entitlement
              A,D,E ONLY


              VLADIMIR NABOKOV
              99 BOGARDE PARADE
              LONDON   NE15



Usual signature        V NABOKOV
  (IN INK)
```

What do you do?

# 74 Cash reconciliation

Greater London Supplies Ltd has fifteen employees.

The net pay owing to each employee is listed on the payroll extract below.

| | Net pay £ | Payment method |
|---|---|---|
| Mr Barnet | 175.91 | Cash |
| Mrs Bromley | 213.43 | Cash |
| Mr Camden | 141.32 | Cheque 10855 |
| Mr Ealing | 132.10 | Cash |
| Mrs Enfield | 241.53 | Cheque 10856 |
| Mr Hackney | 113.95 | Cheque 10857 |
| Mrs Hammersmith | 204.11 | Cheque 10858 |
| Mr Haringey | 123.45 | Cheque 10859 |
| Mrs Islington | 67.89 | Cheque 10860 |
| Mr Kensington | 232.91 | Cash |
| Mrs Lambeth | 184.32 | Cheque 10861 |
| Mr Redditch | 166.66 | Cheque 10862 |
| Mr Southwark | 297.43 | Cheque 10863 |
| Mrs Wandsworth | 148.04 | Cash |
| Mr Westminster | 159.91 | Cash |
| Total | 2,602.96 | |

## Tasks

(a) Complete the form below to order the right amount of notes and coins from the bank, analysed by employee. Use the largest denomination notes and coins possible. Fill in how many of each denomination you will need.

(b) Reconcile your cash and cheque payments to the total on the payroll.

| Denomination | Mr Barnet (no) | Mrs Bromley (no) | Mr Ealing (no) | Mr Kensington (no) | Mrs Wandsworth (no) | Mr Westminster (no) | Total (no) | Total (£) |
|---|---|---|---|---|---|---|---|---|
| £50 | 3 | 4 | 2 | 4 | 2 | 3 | 18 | 900.00 |
| £20 | 1 | 0 | 1 | 1 | 2 | 0 | 5 | 100.00 |
| £10 | 0 | 1 | 1 | 1 | 0 | 0 | 3 | 30.00 |
| £5 | 1 | 0 | 0 | 0 | 1 | 1 | 3 | 15.00 |
| £2 | 0 | 1 | 1 | 1 | 1 | 2 | 6 | 12.00 |
| £1 | 0 | 1 | 0 | 0 | 1 | 0 | 2 | 2.00 |
| 50p | 1 | 0 | 0 | 1 | 0 | 1 | 3 | 1.50 |
| 20p | 2 | 2 | 0 | 2 | 0 | 2 | 8 | 1.60 |
| 10p | 0 | 0 | 1 | 0 | 0 | 0 | 1 | 0.10 |
| 5p | 0 | 0 | 0 | 0 | 0 | 0 | 0 | 0.00 |
| 2p | 0 | 1 | 0 | 0 | 2 | 0 | 3 | 0.06 |
| 1p | 1 | 1 | 0 | 1 | 0 | 1 | 4 | 0.04 |
| Total (£) | 175.91 | 213.43 | 132.10 | 232.91 | 148.04 | 159.91 | | 1,062.30 |

**Reconciliation (b):**

| | £ |
|---|---|
| Total cash | 1,062.30 |
| Total cheques (10855–10863) | 1,540.66 |
| Total payments | 2,602.96 |
| Per payroll | 2,602.96 |

## 75 Direct credit

Your employer has decided to cease payment by cash or cheque, and use Direct Credit instead.

An employee who has heard about the plan through the 'grapevine' phones you up protesting that he does not understand what Direct Credit is. He says he does not have a bank account.

Draft a memorandum explaining to the employee what Direct Credit is, and its advantages. Your employer is prepared to give a one-off payment of £50 to every employee for accepting payment this way, and is prepared to help employees open bank or building society accounts if they so choose.

# AAT Sample Simulations

# Unit 71

# AAT SAMPLE SIMULATION – 2003 STANDARDS

# LEVEL 2 CERTIFICATE IN PAYROLL ADMINISTRATION (QCF)

UNIT 71

MAINTAINING EMPLOYEE RECORDS
(REVISED FOR FINANCE ACT 2009)

## COVERAGE OF PERFORMANCE CRITERIA AND RANGE STATEMENTS

All performance criteria are covered in this simulation.

| Element | PC Coverage |
|---|---|
| **71.1** | **Verify and process personal data for starters and leavers** |
| (a) | Ensure proper authorised **documentation** of every appointment and cessation of employment is obtained before payroll is amended. |
| (b) | Input accurately statutory and **non-statutory** personal and contract details, including allowances and deductions, onto new employee records. |
| (c) | Amend leavers' records to ensure that leavers will not be paid in future pay runs. |
| (d) | Accurately complete and despatch **statutory documentation.** |
| (e) | Identify and document all discrepancies and either resolve directly or by reference to the appropriate organisation or person. |
| (f) | Comply with all organisational and statutory timescales. |
| (g) | File source **documentation** in accordance with statutory and organisational requirements and in a logical and orderly manner |
| (h) | Maintain confidentiality and security of data at all times. |
| **71.2** | **Implement instructions from external agencies** |
| (a) | Verify all payment and deduction instructions for accuracy, completeness and correct **documentation.** |
| (b) | Process instructions from **statutory agencies** or **non-statutory bodies** in accordance with statutory and organisational requirements and within the timescale specified. |
| (c) | Ensure all non-statutory deductions are authorised by the employee concerned. |
| (d) | Identify and resolve all discrepancies directly or by reference to the appropriate organisation or person. |
| **71.3** | **Evaluate and process permanent organisational variations to payroll** |
| (a) | Evaluate all data relating to **permanent variations** for accuracy and reasonableness. |
| (b) | Check all data and documentation received for proper **authorisation.** |
| (c) | Identify and resolve all discrepancies directly or by reference to the appropriate person. |
| (d) | Process permanent variations accurately and in a timely manner. |

Any missing range statements should be assessed separately.

ASSOCIATION OF ACCOUNTING TECHNICIANS

# DATA AND TASKS

## INSTRUCTIONS

This simulation is designed to let you show your ability to:

- set up employees on the payroll;
- process instructions from statutory and non-statutory bodies;
- process permanent variations to the payroll;
- ensure leavers are processed.

**You should read the whole simulation before you start work, so that you are fully aware of you will have to do**.

You are allowed **three hours plus 15 minutes' reading time** to complete your work.

Write your answers in the answer booklet provided. Use a blue or black pen, not pencil. If you need more paper for your answers, ask the person in charge.

You may pull apart and rearrange your booklets if you wish to do so, but you must put them back in their original order before handing them in.

You may use correcting fluid, but in moderation. You should cross out your errors neatly and clearly.

Your work must be accurate, so check your work carefully before handing it in.

You are not allowed to refer to any unauthorised material, such as books or notes, while you are working on the simulation. If you have any such material with you, you must hand it to the person in charge before you start work.

Any instances of misconduct will be reported to the AAT, and disciplinary action may be taken.

*Coverage of performance criteria and range statements*

It is not always possible to cover all performance criteria and range statements in a single simulation. Any performance criteria and range statements not covered must be assessed by other means by the assessor before a candidate can be considered competent.

Performance criteria and range statement coverage for this simulation is shown on page 84.

# THE SITUATION

Advent Systems Ltd is a medium sized company providing website design services. They employ 230 staff and have 5 directors.

Their address is Advent House, Central Avenue, Midchester, MD4 6AF.

There are two payrolls with the same tax office, which is Midchester (reference 054 - ASL001):

- Directors: monthly paid on the last working day of the month via BACS. Non executive directors are paid quarterly in June, September, December and March. All directors are entitled to occupational sick pay on joining.

- Employees: monthly paid on the last working day of each month via BACS. Employees are only entitled to occupational sick pay when they have two years' service.

You are employed as Payroll Assistant reporting to Pamela Palmer, Human Resources Manager.

New employees are approved by Pamela Palmer.

**Directors**

Directors are not allocated payroll reference numbers. Their reference on the payroll system is their full initials.

**Employees**

Employees are allocated payroll reference numbers based on joining date on a sequential number basis. The last number used was 00582.

**Payment basis**

All employees are paid 1/12th of their annual salary each month.

Employees starting or leaving part way through a month are paid 1/260th of their annual salary for each working day remaining in the month unless the month is a complete whole month.

Hourly rates at the flat hourly rate are set at 1/260th of their salary divided by 7.

Hourly rates, when increased are always rounded according to the following rules:

- 0.5p or less rounded down;
- 0.51p or more rounded up.

Overtime is only paid to supervisors and below on submission of an authority signed by Jerry Jackson the Operations Manager.

Premium rates for overtime are only entered on the system for employees of supervisor level and below.

Salary increases for all staff except directors can be authorised by Pamela Palmer, Human Resources Manager. Director's salaries can only be authorised by Sally Jenkins the Managing Director.

### Pension scheme

The company have two pension schemes:

- Revenue approved contracted-out salary related pension scheme: only available to directors. Employee contributions are 5% of gross pay, employer contributions are 7% of gross pay. Directors may pay AVCs if they wish.

- Revenue approved contracted-out money purchase pension scheme: available to all employees. Employee contributions are 3% of basic pay, employer contributions are 3% of basic pay. There are no provisions for employees to pay AVCs.

### Holiday entitlement

Employees are entitled to 25 days paid annual leave plus public holidays. Employees joining part way through the holiday year are entitled to their full entitlement calculated pro rata to the days remaining in the leave year divided by 365 rounded up to the nearest whole day, plus any remaining public holidays.

Directors are entitled to 30 days paid annual leave plus public holidays. Directors joining part way through the holiday year are entitled to their full entitlement calculated pro rata to the days remaining in the leave year divided by 365 rounded up to the nearest whole day, plus any remaining public holidays.

For example, an employee joining part way through the year with 200 days remaining is entitled to $25 \times 200 / 365 = 13.698$, rounded up to 14 days.

The same method of calculation is used to determine any outstanding holiday entitlement on leaving.

Holidays may only be taken once a signed authority has been produced.

### Occupational Sick Pay

The occupational sick pay scheme is only open to employees with the title 'manager' or 'director'. All other employees are entitled to Statutory Sick Pay

### Maternity, Adoption and Paternity Pay

The company does not pay occupational maternity pay, adoption pay or paternity pay. All employees are, however, entitled to the statutory payments.

### Other Benefits

The company offers the following facilities and benefits which are entirely at the discretion of the individual employee.

- Subsidised health and fitness facilities: the company wishes to encourage employees to keep fit, and has reached an arrangement whereby employee can join the local fitness club at half the normal fee of £50 per month. Employees signify their intent by signing an individual mandate that is given directly to the Payroll Assistant.

- Charitable giving: the company has an arrangement with the CAF, an approved agency, and employees can pay into the charity of their choice through this arrangement. Employees signify their intent by signing an individual mandate that is given directly to the Payroll Assistant.

- Trade Union: Employees may have their trade union fees deducted from their pay and the company will pay it over to the union concerned. Employees signify their intent by signing an individual mandate that is given directly to the Payroll Assistant.

# THE TASKS TO BE COMPLETED

It is 10 September 2009 and you are preparing input for the two payrolls for September. Please complete the tasks below. **Page references are to pages in this Revision Companion.**

### Task 1

Refer to the new starter forms on page 90 of this booklet, given to you by your manager, and to the documentation on pages 91 to 111 of this booklet.

- Complete the record cards on pages 122, 124, 126, 128 and 130 of the answer booklet for each of the new employees and one director.
- Use the space provided on pages 123, 125, 127, 129 and 131 of the answer booklet to detail any issues or queries which require clarification, and state the name of the person with whom you will raise the query.
- Use the memo on page 142 of the answer booklet to highlight any issues you need to raise with the Human Resources Manager

You will need to ensure the correct tax codes and N.I. category letters are input into the system to ensure that employees are paid correctly in September.

### Task 2

Refer to the new starter information on pages 90 to 111 of this booklet.

- Complete the forms P45 and P46, on pages 132 to 138 of the answer booklet, for despatch to the Revenue. Assume the tax recorded on the P45 is correct in all cases.

### Task 3

Refer to the memo from Pamela Palmer on page 112 of this booklet, concerning leavers, and the calendar on page 113 of this booklet.

- Complete the relevant parts of the employee input sheet for the three leavers on page 139 of the answer booklet.

### Task 4

Refer to the memo from Pamela Palmer, on page 114 of this booklet, concerning salary reviews.

- Complete the salary adjustment sheet on page 140 of the answer booklet.
- Use the memo on page 142 of the answer booklet to identify any queries you have concerning the changes.

### Task 5

Refer to the memo from Pamela Palmer, on page 115 of this booklet, concerning miscellaneous issues.

- Complete the Miscellaneous Payroll Amendment/Change Sheet on page 141 of the answer booklet.
- Use the memo on page 142 of the answer booklet to identify any queries you have concerning the changes.

**Task 6**

Refer to the memo from Simon Callow, the Chief Accountant, on page 118 of this booklet, regarding data protection.

- Reply using the memo on page 144 of the answer booklet.

**Task 7**

Refer to the memo from Simon Callow, on page 119 of this booklet, regarding court orders.

- Reply using the memo on page 145 of the answer booklet.

# MEMO

**To:** Payroll Assistant
**From:** Pam Palmer
**Subject:** New starters – September 2009
**Date:** 8th September 2009

Please ensure the five new employees listed below are included on the payroll for this month. I enclose copies of the following documents:

- Offer letters;
- Voluntary deduction approval forms;
- P45 or P46 information as relevant.

| Name | James W Mason | Jenny P Smith | Michael B Jackson |
|---|---|---|---|
| Marital status | Single | Divorced | Single |
| Nationality | British | British | British |
| Date of birth | 27-08-1980 | 02-01-1949 | 17-11-1963 |
| Bank details<br><br>Sort code<br>Account number | Lloyds TSB<br>Middle Path<br>Midchester<br>45-07-96<br>1856920 | NatWest<br>West Bank<br>Midchester<br>60-08-18<br>16378942 | NatWest<br>North Street<br>Midchester<br>61-45-32 |
| Cost Code | S0056 | W0114 | D0010 |
| Permanent Contract | Yes | Yes | No |
| Grade | SA001 | WD003 | DIR002 |
| Employee Number | 00583 | 00584 | MBJ |
| Name | Clint Eastwood | Dorothy Lamour | |
| Marital status | Single | Married | |
| Nationality | British | British | |
| Date of birth | 20-02-1981 | 02-08-1957 | |
| Bank details<br><br>Sort code<br>Account number | Lloyds TSB<br>Middle Path<br>Midchester<br>45-07-96<br>1469482 | NatWest<br>West Bank<br>Midchester<br>60-08-18<br>16938285 | |
| Cost Code | W0114 | A0004 | |
| Permanent Contract | Yes | Yes | |
| Grade | SA001 | AD001 | |
| Employee Number | 00585 | 00586 | |

# Advent Systems Ltd
### Advent House, Central Avenue, Midchester, MD4 6AF

2 August 2009

James Mason
3 Ulverston Road
Midchester
MI6 7SF

Dear James

I am writing to confirm your appointment as Sales Assistant with our organisation commencing on 1 September 2009.

**Salary**

Your salary will be £18,000 per annum. Company policy is that you will be paid 1/12th of your annual salary on the last working day of each month. Should it be necessary to pay a part month at any time, pay will be calculated at 1/260th of your annual salary for each working day in the month.

Overtime is paid at time and third of your hourly rate during the week, time and half for Saturdays and double time for Sundays and public holidays.

**Hours of work**

Your hours of work will be 9.00am to 5.00pm Monday to Friday with one hour for lunch. We comply with the Working Time Regulations and whilst you may be required to work overtime, you are not obliged to work more than 48 hours per week unless you specifically opt out by signing the waiver.

**Annual leave**

You will be entitled to 20 days annual leave plus public holidays. Our holiday year runs from 1 January to 31 December each year. No holiday may be carried forward from one year to the next.

**Pension**

You are entitled to join the Revenue approved contracted-out money purchase pension scheme, available to all employees. Employee contributions are 3% of basic pay, and employer contributions are 3% of basic pay. There are no provisions for employees to pay AVCs.

If you wish to join, you must complete the form attached to this letter.

**Occupational Sick Pay**

You are not entitled to join the occupational sick pay scheme. However, you will be entitled to the statutory payment.

*continued*

**Maternity, Paternity and Adoption**

We have no occupational scheme. However, you are entitled to statutory payments and leave. Full details are contained in our company handbook which will be given to you when you join.

**Other benefits**

The company offers the following facilities and benefits which are entirely at the discretion of the individual employee.

- Subsidised health and fitness facilities: the company wishes to encourage employees to keep fit and have reached an arrangement whereby employee can join the local fitness club at half the normal fee of £50 per month. Employees signify their intent by signing an individual mandate that is given directly to the Payroll Assistant.

- Charitable giving: the company has an arrangement with the CAF, an approved agency, and employees can pay into the charity of their choice through this arrangement. Employees signify their intent by signing an individual mandate that is given directly to the Payroll Assistant.

- Trade Union: employees may have their trade union fees deducted from their pay and the company will pay it over to the union concerned. Employees signify their intent by signing an individual mandate that is given directly to the Payroll Assistant.

I look forward to seeing you again on 1 September.

Yours sincerely


*Pam Palmer*


Pam Palmer

# Advent Systems Ltd
## Advent House, Central Avenue, Midchester, MD4 6AF

2 August 2009

Jenny Smith
Bluebell Cottage
Midchester
MI5 8RE

Dear Jenny

I am writing to confirm your appointment as Web Design Manager with our organisation commencing on 8 September 2009.

**Salary**

Your salary will be £29,600 per annum. Company policy is that you will be paid 1/12th of your annual salary on the last working day of each month. Should it be necessary to pay a part month at any time, pay will be calculated at 1/260th of your annual salary for each working day in the month.

Overtime is not payable in this position.

**Hours of work**

Your hours of work will be 9.00am to 5.00pm Monday to Friday with one hour for lunch. We comply with the Working Time Regulations and whilst you may be required to work overtime, you are not obliged to work more than 48 hours per week unless you specifically opt out by signing the waiver.

**Annual leave**

You will be entitled to 25 days annual leave plus public holidays. Our holiday year runs from 1 January to 31 December each year. No holiday may be carried forward from one year to the next.

**Pension**

You are entitled to join the Revenue approved contracted-out salary related pension scheme. Employee contributions are 5% of gross pay, and employer contributions are 7% of gross pay. Directors may pay AVCs if they wish.

If you wish to join, you must complete the form attached to this letter.

**Occupational Sick Pay**

You are entitled to join the occupational sick pay scheme. Details will be given to you when you join the firm.

*continued*

**Maternity, Paternity and Adoption**

We have no occupational scheme. However you are entitled to statutory payment and leave. Full details are contained in our company handbook which we will give you when you join.

**Other benefits**

The company offers the following facilities and benefits which are entirely at the discretion of the individual employee.

- Subsidised health and fitness facilities: the company wishes to encourage employees to keep fit and have reached an arrangement whereby employee can join the local fitness club at half the normal fee of £50 per month. Employees signify their intent by signing an individual mandate that is given directly to the Payroll Assistant.

- Charitable giving: the company has an arrangement with the CAF, an approved agency, and employees can pay into the charity of their choice through this arrangement. Employees signify their intent by signing an individual mandate that is given directly to the Payroll Assistant.

- Trade Union: employees may have their trade union fees deducted from their pay and the company will pay it over to the union concerned. Employees signify their intent by signing an individual mandate that is given directly to the Payroll Assistant.

I look forward to seeing you again on 8 September.

Yours sincerely

**Pam Palmer**

Pam Palmer

# Advent Systems Ltd
### Advent House, Central Avenue, Midchester, MD4 6AF

2 August 2009

Michael B Jackson
Grey Gables
Southchester
MI8 7EW

Dear Michael

I am writing to confirm your appointment as Non Executive Director with our organisation commencing on 8 September 2009. Your employment is until 31 December 2011.

**Salary**

Your salary will be £36,000 per annum. Company policy is that you will be paid 1/12th of your annual salary on the last working day of each month. Should it be necessary to pay a part month at any time, pay will be calculated at 1/260th of your annual salary for each working day in the month.

Overtime is not payable in your position.

**Hours of work**

Your role does not require you to work specific hours. However, you are required, under this contract, to attend the monthly board meetings, a schedule will be provided to you within the next two weeks.

We comply with the Working Time Regulations and whilst you may be required to work overtime, you are not obliged to work more than 48 hours per week unless you specifically opt out by signing the waiver.

**Annual leave**

You will be entitled to 30 days annual leave plus public holidays. Our holiday year runs from 1 January to 31 December each year. No holiday may be carried forward from one year to the next.

**Pension**

You are entitled to join the Revenue approved contracted-out salary related pension scheme, which is only available to directors. Your contributions will be 5% of gross pay, and employer contributions are 7% of gross pay. You may pay AVCs if you wish.

If you wish to join, you must complete the form attached to this letter.

**Occupational Sick Pay**

You are entitled to join the occupational sick pay scheme. Details will be given to you when you join the firm.

*continued*

**Maternity, Paternity and Adoption**

We do not have an occupational scheme. However you may be entitled to statutory payment and leave. Full details are contained in our company handbook which will be given to you when you join.

**Other benefits**

The company offers the following facilities and benefits which are entirely at the discretion of the individual employee.

- Subsidised health and fitness facilities: the company wishes to encourage employees to keep fit and have reached an arrangement whereby employee can join the local fitness club at half the normal fee of £50 per month. Employees signify their intent by signing an individual mandate that is given directly to the Payroll Assistant.

- Charitable giving: the company has an arrangement with the CAF, an approved agency, and employees can pay into the charity of their choice through this arrangement. Employees signify their intent by signing an individual mandate that is given directly to the Payroll Assistant.

- Trade Union: employees may have their trade union fees deducted from their pay and the company will pay it over to the union concerned. Employees signify their intent by signing an individual mandate that is given directly to the Payroll Assistant.

I look forward to seeing you again on 8 September.

Yours sincerely

*Pam Palmer*

Pam Palmer

# Advent Systems Ltd
**Advent House, Central Avenue, Midchester, MD4 6AF**

2 August 2009

Clint Eastwood
Cuddlers Cottage
Southchester
SO21 5RT

Dear Clint

I am writing to confirm your appointment as Account Manager with our organisation commencing on 15 September 2009.

**Salary**

Your salary will be £25,700 per annum. Company policy is that you will be paid 1/12th of your annual salary on the last working day of each month. Should it be necessary to pay a part month at any time, pay will be calculated at 1/260th of your annual salary for each working day in the month.

You will also be paid commission on all sales made at 5% of the invoice value. This will be paid to you with your normal pay the month after we have received payment from the client.

Overtime is not payable in your position.

**Hours of work**

Your hours of work will be 9.00am to 5.00pm Monday to Friday with one hour for lunch. We comply with the Working Time Regulations and whilst you may be required to work overtime, you are not obliged to work more than 48 hours per week unless you specifically opt out by signing the waiver.

**Annual leave**

You will be entitled to 25 days annual leave plus public holidays. Our holiday year runs from 1 January to 31 December each year. No holiday may be carried forward from one year to the next.

**Pension**

You are entitled to join the Revenue approved contracted-out money purchase pension scheme, which is available to all employees. Employee contributions are 3% of basic pay, and employer contributions are 3% of basic pay. There are no provisions for employees to pay AVCs.

If you wish to join, you must complete the form attached to this letter.

*continued*

**Occupational Sick Pay**

You are entitled to join the occupational sick pay scheme. Details will be given to you when you join the firm.

**Maternity, Paternity and Adoption**

We do not have an occupational scheme. However you may be entitled to statutory payments and leave. Full details are contained in our company handbook which will be given to you when you join.

**Other benefits**

The company offers the following facilities and benefits which are entirely at the discretion of the individual employee.

- Subsidised health and fitness facilities: the company wishes to encourage employees to keep fit and have reached an arrangement whereby employee can join the local fitness club at half the normal fee of £50 per month. Employees signify their intent by signing an individual mandate that is given directly to the Payroll Assistant.

- Charitable giving: the company has an arrangement with the CAF, an approved agency, and employees can pay into the charity of their choice through this arrangement. Employees signify their intent by signing an individual mandate that is given directly to the Payroll Assistant.

- Trade Union: employees may have their trade union fees deducted from their pay and the company will pay it over to the union concerned. Employees signify their intent by signing an individual mandate that is given directly to the Payroll Assistant.

I look forward to seeing you again on 15 September.

Yours sincerely


Pam Palmer


Pam Palmer

# Advent Systems Ltd
### Advent House, Central Avenue, Midchester, MD4 6AF

2 August 2009

Dorothy Lamour
15A Court House
Midchester
MI4 7WD


Dear Dorothy

I am writing to confirm your appointment as Administration Clerk with our organisation commencing on 22 September 2009.

**Salary**

Your salary will be £14,000 per annum. Company policy is that you will be paid 1/12th of your annual salary on the last working day of each month. Should it be necessary to pay a part month at any time, pay will be calculated at 1/260th of your annual salary for each working day in the month.

Overtime is paid at time and third of your hourly rate during the week, time and half for Saturdays and double time for Sundays and public holidays.

**Hours of work**

Your hours of work will be 9.00am to 5.00pm Monday to Friday with one hour for lunch. We comply with the Working Time Regulations and whilst you may be required to work overtime, you are not obliged to work more than 48 hours per week unless you specifically opt out by signing the waiver.

**Annual leave**

You will be entitled to 25 days annual leave plus public holidays. Our holiday year runs from 1 January to 31 December each year. No holiday may be carried forward from one year to the next.

**Pension**

You are entitled to join the Revenue approved contracted-out money purchase pension scheme, which is available to all employees. Employee contributions are 3% of basic pay, and employer contributions are 3% of basic pay. There are no provisions for employees to pay AVCs.

If you wish to join, you must complete the form attached to this letter.

**Occupational Sick Pay**

You are not entitled to join the occupational sick pay scheme. However you may be entitled to statutory payments. Details will be given to you when you join the firm.

*continued*

**Maternity, Paternity and Adoption**

We do not have an occupational scheme. However you may be entitled to statutory payments and leave. Full details are contained in our company handbook which will be given to you when you join.

**Other benefits**

The company offers the following facilities and benefits which are entirely at the discretion of the individual employee.

- Subsidised health and fitness facilities: the company wishes to encourage employees to keep fit and have reached an arrangement whereby employee can join the local fitness club at half the normal fee of £50 per month. Employees signify their intent by signing an individual mandate that is given directly to the Payroll Assistant.

- Charitable giving: the company has an arrangement with the CAF, an approved agency, and employees can pay into the charity of their choice through this arrangement. Employees signify their intent by signing an individual mandate that is given directly to the Payroll Assistant.

- Trade Union: employees may have their trade union fees deducted from their pay and the company will pay it over to the union concerned. Employees signify their intent by signing an individual mandate that is given directly to the Payroll Assistant.

I look forward to seeing you again on 22 September.

Yours sincerely


*Pam Palmer*


Pam Palmer

AAT SAMPLE SIMULATION

# HM Revenue & Customs

**P45 Part 2**
**Details of employee leaving work**
Copy for new employer

**1 Employer PAYE reference**
Office number   Reference number
044 / DGW00195

**2 Employee's National Insurance number**
YB 38 57 20 A

**3 Title - enter MR, MRS, MISS, MS or other title**
MR

Surname or family name
MASON

First or given name(s)
JAMES

**4 Leaving date** DD MM YYYY
27 08 2009

**5 Student Loan deductions**
Y   Student Loan deductions to continue

**6 Tax Code at leaving date**
461 L
If week 1 or month 1 applies, enter 'X' in the box below.
Week 1/Month 1

**7 Last entries on P11** *Deductions Working Sheet.*
**Complete only if Tax Code is cumulative. If there is an 'X' at box 6, there will be no entries here.**
Week number   Month number 05
Total pay to date
£ 4863 · 96
Total tax to date
£ 587 · 80

*For information only*

### To the employee
This form is important to you. Take good care of it and keep it safe. Copies are not available. Please keep Parts 2 and 3 of the form together and do not alter them in any way.

**Going to a new job**
Give Parts 2 and 3 of this form to your new employer, or you will have tax deducted using the emergency code and may pay too much tax. If you do not want your new employer to know the details on this form, send it to your HM Revenue & Customs (HMRC) office immediately with a letter saying so and giving the name and address of your new employer. HMRC can make special arrangements, but you may pay too much tax for a while as a result of this.

**Going abroad**
If you are going abroad or returning to a country outside the UK ask for form P85 *Leaving the United Kingdom* from any HMRC office or Enquiry Centre.

**Becoming self-employed**
You must register with HMRC within three months of becoming self-employed or you could incur a penalty. To register as newly self-employed see The Phone Book under HM Revenue & Customs or go to **www.hmrc.gov.uk** to get a copy of the booklet SE1 *Are you thinking of working for yourself?*

**Claiming Jobseeker's Allowance or Employment and Support Allowance (ESA)**
Take this form to your Jobcentre Plus office. They will pay you any tax refund you may be entitled to when your claim ends, or at 5 April if this is earlier.

**Not working and not claiming Jobseeker's Allowance or Employment and Support Allowance (ESA)**
If you have paid tax and wish to claim a refund ask for form P50 *Claiming Tax back when you have stopped working* from any HMRC office or Enquiry Centre.

**Help**
If you need further help you can contact any HMRC office or Enquiry Centre. You can find us in The Phone Book under HM Revenue & Customs or go to **www.hmrc.gov.uk**

### To the new employer
Check this form and complete boxes 8 to 18 in Part 3 and prepare a form P11 *Deductions Working Sheet.* Follow the instructions in the Employer Helpbook E13 *Day-to-day payroll,* for how to prepare a P11 *Deductions Working Sheet.* Send Part 3 of this form to your HMRC office immediately. Keep Part 2.

P45(Manual) Part 2                               HMRC 04/08

# P45 Part 2
## Details of employee leaving work
### Copy for new employer

**HM Revenue & Customs**

**1** Employer PAYE reference
Office number   Reference number
0 2 5 / A K E 0 0 1 9 4 8 5

**2** Employee's National Insurance number
B A 6 8 2 0 4 9 C

**3** Title - enter MR, MRS, MISS, MS or other title
MS

Surname or family name
SMITH

First or given name(s)
JENNY

**4** Leaving date DD MM YYYY
2 7 0 8 2 0 0 9

**5** Student Loan deductions
☐ Student Loan deductions to continue

**6** Tax Code at leaving date
5 8 6 T
If week 1 or month 1 applies, enter 'X' in the box below.
Week 1/Month 1 ☐

**7** Last entries on P11 Deductions Working Sheet.
Complete only if Tax Code is cumulative. If there is an 'X' at box 6, there will be no entries here.

Week number ☐☐   Month number 0 5

Total pay to date
£ 1 1 8 8 0 . 8 3

Total tax to date
£ 1 8 8 7 . 0 0

*For information only*

### To the employee
This form is important to you. Take good care of it and keep it safe. Copies are not available. Please keep Parts 2 and 3 of the form together and do not alter them in any way.

**Going to a new job**
Give Parts 2 and 3 of this form to your new employer, or you will have tax deducted using the emergency code and may pay too much tax. If you do not want your new employer to know the details on this form, send it to your HM Revenue & Customs (HMRC) office immediately with a letter saying so and giving the name and address of your new employer. HMRC can make special arrangements, but you may pay too much tax for a while as a result of this.

**Going abroad**
If you are going abroad or returning to a country outside the UK ask for form P85 *Leaving the United Kingdom* from any HMRC office or Enquiry Centre.

**Becoming self-employed**
You must register with HMRC within three months of becoming self-employed or you could incur a penalty. To register as newly self-employed see The Phone Book under HM Revenue & Customs or go to www.hmrc.gov.uk to get a copy of the booklet SE1 *Are you thinking of working for yourself?*

**Claiming Jobseeker's Allowance or Employment and Support Allowance (ESA)**
Take this form to your Jobcentre Plus office. They will pay you any tax refund you may be entitled to when your claim ends, or at 5 April if this is earlier.

**Not working and not claiming Jobseeker's Allowance or Employment and Support Allowance (ESA)**
If you have paid tax and wish to claim a refund ask for form P50 *Claiming Tax back when you have stopped working* from any HMRC office or Enquiry Centre.

**Help**
If you need further help you can contact any HMRC office or Enquiry Centre. You can find us in The Phone Book under HM Revenue & Customs or go to www.hmrc.gov.uk

### To the new employer
Check this form and complete boxes 8 to 18 in Part 3 and prepare a form P11 *Deductions Working Sheet*. Follow the instructions in the Employer Helpbook E13 *Day-to-day payroll*, for how to prepare a P11 *Deductions Working Sheet*. Send Part 3 of this form to your HMRC office immediately. Keep Part 2.

P45(Manual) Part 2                              HMRC 04/08

**AAT SAMPLE SIMULATION**

**HM Revenue & Customs**

**P45 Part 2**
**Details of employee leaving work**
Copy for new employer

**1** Employer PAYE reference
Office number  Reference number
0 4 1 / P D A 6 8 3 5

**2** Employee's National Insurance number
F W 2 6 6 8 9 2 A

**3** Title - enter MR, MRS, MISS, MS or other title
MR

Surname or family name
EASTWOOD

First or given name(s)
CLINT

**4** Leaving date DD MM YYYY
2 9 0 8 2 0 0 9

**5** Student Loan deductions
Student Loan deductions to continue

**6** Tax Code at leaving date
K 4 2
If week 1 or month 1 applies, enter 'X' in the box below.
Week 1/Month 1  X

**7** Last entries on P11 *Deductions Working Sheet*.
Complete only if Tax Code is cumulative. If there is an 'X' at box 6, there will be no entries here.
Week number        Month number
Total pay to date
£
Total tax to date
£

*For information only*

**To the employee**
This form is important to you. Take good care of it and keep it safe. Copies are not available. Please keep Parts 2 and 3 of the form together and do not alter them in any way.

**Going to a new job**
Give Parts 2 and 3 of this form to your new employer, or you will have tax deducted using the emergency code and may pay too much tax. If you do not want your new employer to know the details on this form, send it to your HM Revenue & Customs (HMRC) office immediately with a letter saying so and giving the name and address of your new employer. HMRC can make special arrangements, but you may pay too much tax for a while as a result of this.

**Going abroad**
If you are going abroad or returning to a country outside the UK ask for form P85 *Leaving the United Kingdom* from any HMRC office or Enquiry Centre.

**Becoming self-employed**
You must register with HMRC within three months of becoming self-employed or you could incur a penalty. To register as newly self-employed see The Phone Book under HM Revenue & Customs or go to www.hmrc.gov.uk to get a copy of the booklet SE1 *Are you thinking of working for yourself?*

**Claiming Jobseeker's Allowance or Employment and Support Allowance (ESA)**
Take this form to your Jobcentre Plus office. They will pay you any tax refund you may be entitled to when your claim ends, or at 5 April if this is earlier.

**Not working and not claiming Jobseeker's Allowance or Employment and Support Allowance (ESA)**
If you have paid tax and wish to claim a refund ask for form P50 *Claiming Tax back when you have stopped working* from any HMRC office or Enquiry Centre.

**Help**
If you need further help you can contact any HMRC office or Enquiry Centre. You can find us in The Phone Book under HM Revenue & Customs or go to www.hmrc.gov.uk

**To the new employer**
Check this form and complete boxes 8 to 18 in Part 3 and prepare a form P11 *Deductions Working Sheet*. Follow the instructions in the Employer Helpbook E13 *Day-to-day payroll*, for how to prepare a P11 *Deductions Working Sheet*. Send Part 3 of this form to your HMRC office immediately. Keep Part 2.

P45(Manual) Part 2                                       HMRC 04/08

## P45 Part 2
### Details of employee leaving work
### Copy for new employer

**HM Revenue & Customs**

**1 Employer PAYE reference**
Office number   Reference number
D 3 3 / C D C 2 2 9 4 7 A

**2 Employee's National Insurance number**
K S 3 7 6 8 5 4 D

**3 Title** - enter MR, MRS, MISS, MS or other title
MRS

Surname or family name
LAMOUR

First or given name(s)
DOROTHY

**4 Leaving date** DD MM YYYY
3 0 0 1 2 0 0 9

**5 Student Loan deductions**
☐ Student Loan deductions to continue

**6 Tax Code at leaving date**
3 4 5 L
If week 1 or month 1 applies, enter 'X' in the box below.
Week 1/Month 1  X

**7 Last entries on P11** *Deductions Working Sheet*.
Complete only if Tax Code is cumulative. If there is an 'X' at box 6, there will be no entries here.

Week number ☐☐   Month number ☐☐

Total pay to date
£

Total tax to date
£

*For information only*

### To the employee
This form is important to you. Take good care of it and keep it safe. Copies are not available. Please keep Parts 2 and 3 of the form together and do not alter them in any way.

**Going to a new job**
Give Parts 2 and 3 of this form to your new employer, or you will have tax deducted using the emergency code and may pay too much tax. If you do not want your new employer to know the details on this form, send it to your HM Revenue & Customs (HMRC) office immediately with a letter saying so and giving the name and address of your new employer. HMRC can make special arrangements, but you may pay too much tax for a while as a result of this.

**Going abroad**
If you are going abroad or returning to a country outside the UK ask for form P85 *Leaving the United Kingdom* from any HMRC office or Enquiry Centre.

**Becoming self-employed**
You must register with HMRC within three months of becoming self-employed or you could incur a penalty. To register as newly self-employed see The Phone Book under HM Revenue & Customs or go to www.hmrc.gov.uk to get a copy of the booklet SE1 *Are you thinking of working for yourself?*

**Claiming Jobseeker's Allowance or Employment and Support Allowance (ESA)**
Take this form to your Jobcentre Plus office. They will pay you any tax refund you may be entitled to when your claim ends, or at 5 April if this is earlier.

**Not working and not claiming Jobseeker's Allowance or Employment and Support Allowance (ESA)**
If you have paid tax and wish to claim a refund ask for form P50 *Claiming Tax back when you have stopped working* from any HMRC office or Enquiry Centre.

**Help**
If you need further help you can contact any HMRC office or Enquiry Centre. You can find us in The Phone Book under HM Revenue & Customs or go to www.hmrc.gov.uk

### To the new employer
Check this form and complete boxes 8 to 18 in Part 3 and prepare a form P11 *Deductions Working Sheet*. Follow the instructions in the Employer Helpbook E13 *Day-to-day payroll*, for how to prepare a P11 *Deductions Working Sheet*. Send Part 3 of this form to your HMRC office immediately. Keep Part 2.

P45(Manual) Part 2   HMRC 04/08

**HM Revenue & Customs**

# P46: Employee without a Form P45

**Section one** To be completed by the employee

Please complete section one and then hand the form back to your present employer. If you later receive a form P45 from your previous employer, hand it to your present employer.
Use capital letters when completing this form.

## Your details

**National Insurance number**
This is very important in getting your tax and benefits right

**Title** - enter MR, MRS, MISS, MS or other title
MR

**Surname or family name**
JACKSON

**First or given name(s)**
MICHAEL

**Gender.** Enter 'X' in the appropriate box
Male [X]   Female [ ]

**Date of birth** DD MM YYYY
10  11  1963

**Address**
House or flat number

**Rest of address including house name or flat name**
GREY GABLES
SOUTHCHESTER

**Postcode**
M18  7EW

### Your present circumstances
Read all the following statements carefully and enter 'X' in **the one** box that applies to you.

**A** - This is my first job since last 6 April and **I have not** been receiving taxable Jobseeker's Allowance or taxable Incapacity Benefit or a state or occupational pension.  A [ ]

OR

**B** - This is now my only job, but since last 6 April **I have** had another job, or have received taxable Jobseeker's Allowance or Incapacity Benefit. I do not receive a state or occupational pension.  B [ ]

OR

**C** - I have another job or receive a state or occupational pension.  C [X]

### Student Loans
If you left a course of Higher Education before last 6 April and received your first Student Loan instalment on or after 1 September 1998 and you have not fully repaid your Student Loan, enter 'X' in box D. *(If you are required to repay your Student Loan through your bank or building society account do **not** enter an 'X' in box D.)*  D [ ]

### Signature and date
I can confirm that this information is correct

Signature
*Michael Jackson*

Date DD MM YYYY
08  09  2009

P46                Page 1                HMRC 02/08

AAT SAMPLE SIMULATION

## Section two To be completed by the employer

File your employee's P46 online at **www.hmrc.gov.uk/employers/doitonline**
Use capital letters when completing this form. Guidance on how to fill it in, including what to do if your employee has not entered their National Insurance number on page 1, is at **www.hmrc.gov.uk/employers/working_out.htm** and in the E13 Employer Helpbook *Day-to-day payroll*.

### Employee's details

Date employment started  DD MM YYYY

Works/payroll number and department or branch (if any)

Job title

### Employer's details

Employer PAYE reference
Office number   Reference number

Address
Building number

Employer name

Rest of address

Postcode

### Tax code used

If you do not know the tax code to use or the current National Insurance contributions (NICs) lower earnings limit, go to **www.hmrc.gov.uk/employers/rates_and_limits.htm**

Enter 'X' in the appropriate box

**Box A**
Emergency code on a **cumulative** basis    A

**Box B**
Emergency code on a **non-cumulative**
Week 1/Month 1 basis    B

**Box C**
Code BR    C

Tax code used

If week 1 or
month 1 applies,
enter 'X' in this box

**Send this form to your HM Revenue & Customs office on the first pay day.**
If the employee has entered 'X' in box A or box B, on page 1, and their earnings are below the NICs lower earnings limit, **do not send the form until their earnings reach the NICs lower earnings limit.**

Page 2

# MEMO

To: Payroll Assistant
From: Jenny Smith
Subject: Miscellaneous Deductions
Date: 1 September 2009

Thank you for your letter of 2 August.

I would like to confirm that I would like deductions to be made from my pay as follows.

| Deduction | Signature | Amount (£) |
|---|---|---|
| C/O salary related pension scheme | *Jenny Smith* | As per pension scheme rules |
| C/O money purchase pension scheme | | As per pension scheme rules |
| Trade Union | | |
| Charitable Giving | *Jenny Smith* | £25.00 |
| Health and Fitness Club | *Jenny Smith* | £25.00 |
| Additional Voluntary Contributions (pension fund) | | |

I hereby give authority that deductions from pay may be made as soon as possible against those items where I have put my signature.

*Jenny Smith.*

Jenny Smith

# MEMO

To: Payroll Assistant
From: James Mason
Subject: Pension and health club
Date: 29 August 2009

Thank you for your letter of 2 August.

I would like to confirm that I would like deductions to be made from my pay as follows.

| Deduction | Signature | Amount (£) |
|---|---|---|
| C/O salary related pension scheme |  | As per pension scheme rules |
| C/O money purchase pension scheme | James Mason | As per pension scheme rules |
| Trade Union | James Mason | £5.00 |
| Charitable Giving |  |  |
| Health and Fitness Club |  |  |
| Additional Voluntary Contributions (pension fund) | James Mason | £50.00 |

I hereby give authority that deductions from pay may be made as soon as possible against those items where I have put my signature.

*James Mason*

James Mason

## MEMO

To: Payroll Assistant
From: Michael Jackson
Subject: Miscellaneous Deductions
Date: 1 September 2009

Thank you for your letter of 2 August.

I would like to confirm that I would like deductions to be made from my pay as follows.

| Deduction | Signature | Amount (£) |
|---|---|---|
| C/O salary related pension scheme | *Michael Jackson* | As per pension scheme rules |
| C/O money purchase pension scheme | | As per pension scheme rules |
| Trade Union | | |
| Charitable Giving | *Michael Jackson* | £100.00 |
| Health and Fitness Club | *Michael Jackson* | £25.00 |
| Additional Voluntary Contributions (pension fund) | *Michael Jackson* | £200.00 |

I hereby give authority that deductions from pay may be made as soon as possible against those items where I have put my signature.

*Michael Jackson*

Michael Jackson

# MEMO

To: Payroll Assistant
From: Pam Palmer
Subject: Miscellaneous Deductions for Dorothy Lamour
Date: 1 September 2009

Dorothy is due to be starting work with us on 22 September.

She rang me to tell me that she has lost her Deduction Authorisation form and that she would like us to deduct the £25 Health and Fitness Club payment from her pay. Can you please take this as authorisation.

| Deduction | Signature | Amount (£) |
|---|---|---|
| C/O salary related pension scheme | | As per pension scheme rules |
| C/O money purchase pension scheme | | As per pension scheme rules |
| Trade Union | | |
| Charitable Giving | | |
| Health and Fitness Club | | £25.00 |
| Additional Voluntary Contributions (pension fund) | | |

I hereby give authority that deductions from pay may be made as soon as possible against those items where I have put my signature.

Pam Palmer

# MEMO

To: Payroll Assistant
From: Clint Eastwood
Subject: Miscellaneous Deductions
Date: 1 September 2009

Thank you for your letter of 2 August.

I would like to confirm that I would like deductions to be made from my pay as follows.

| Deduction | Signature | Amount (£) |
|---|---|---|
| C/O salary related pension scheme | | As per pension scheme rules |
| C/O money purchase pension scheme | *Clint Eastwood* | As per pension scheme rules |
| Trade Union | | |
| Charitable Giving | | |
| Health and Fitness Club | *Clint Eastwood* | £25.00 |
| Additional Voluntary Contributions (pension fund) | | |

I hereby give authority that deductions from pay may be made as soon as possible against those items where I have put my signature.

*Clint Eastwood*

Clint Eastwood

## MEMO

To: Payroll Assistant
From: Pam Palmer
Subject: Leavers: September 2009
Date: 8 September 2009

The following employees are leaving the company.
Can you please ensure they are paid for the last time in September.

| Name | Employee number | Salary (£) | Leaving Date |
|---|---|---|---|
| Jane Seymour | 00035 | 18,480.00 | 10 September |
| Donald Sinden | 00136 | 16,582.00 | 17 September |
| Jerry Springer | 00078 | 21,748.00 | 30 September |

Please note that Donald and Jerry have taken their full holiday entitlement, but Jane is still owed three days which needs to be added to her final pay.

Donald is to be paid his commission of £865.00.

Pam Palmer

AAT SAMPLE SIMULATION

## 2009 Calendar

### 2009

| January 2009 | | | | | | |
|---|---|---|---|---|---|---|
| S | M | T | W | T | F | S |
| | | | | 1 | 2 | 3 |
| 4 | 5 | 6 | 7 | 8 | 9 | 10 |
| 11 | 12 | 13 | 14 | 15 | 16 | 17 |
| 18 | 19 | 20 | 21 | 22 | 23 | 24 |
| 25 | 26 | 27 | 28 | 29 | 30 | 31 |

| February 2009 | | | | | | |
|---|---|---|---|---|---|---|
| S | M | T | W | T | F | S |
| 1 | 2 | 3 | 4 | 5 | 6 | 7 |
| 8 | 9 | 10 | 11 | 12 | 13 | 14 |
| 15 | 16 | 17 | 18 | 19 | 20 | 21 |
| 22 | 23 | 24 | 25 | 26 | 27 | 28 |

| March 2009 | | | | | | |
|---|---|---|---|---|---|---|
| S | M | T | W | T | F | S |
| 1 | 2 | 3 | 4 | 5 | 6 | 7 |
| 8 | 9 | 10 | 11 | 12 | 13 | 14 |
| 15 | 16 | 17 | 18 | 19 | 20 | 21 |
| 22 | 23 | 24 | 25 | 26 | 27 | 28 |
| 29 | 30 | 31 | | | | |

| April 2009 | | | | | | |
|---|---|---|---|---|---|---|
| S | M | T | W | T | F | S |
| | | | 1 | 2 | 3 | 4 |
| 5 | 6 | 7 | 8 | 9 | 10 | 11 |
| 12 | 13 | 14 | 15 | 16 | 17 | 18 |
| 19 | 20 | 21 | 22 | 23 | 24 | 25 |
| 26 | 27 | 28 | 29 | 30 | | |

| May 2009 | | | | | | |
|---|---|---|---|---|---|---|
| S | M | T | W | T | F | S |
| | | | | | 1 | 2 |
| 3 | 4 | 5 | 6 | 7 | 8 | 9 |
| 10 | 11 | 12 | 13 | 14 | 15 | 16 |
| 17 | 18 | 19 | 20 | 21 | 22 | 23 |
| 24 | 25 | 26 | 27 | 28 | 29 | 30 |
| 31 | | | | | | |

| June 2009 | | | | | | |
|---|---|---|---|---|---|---|
| S | M | T | W | T | F | S |
| | 1 | 2 | 3 | 4 | 5 | 6 |
| 7 | 8 | 9 | 10 | 11 | 12 | 13 |
| 14 | 15 | 16 | 17 | 18 | 19 | 20 |
| 21 | 22 | 23 | 24 | 25 | 26 | 27 |
| 28 | 29 | 30 | | | | |

| July 2009 | | | | | | |
|---|---|---|---|---|---|---|
| S | M | T | W | T | F | S |
| | | | 1 | 2 | 3 | 4 |
| 5 | 6 | 7 | 8 | 9 | 10 | 11 |
| 12 | 13 | 14 | 15 | 16 | 17 | 18 |
| 19 | 20 | 21 | 22 | 23 | 24 | 25 |
| 26 | 27 | 28 | 29 | 30 | 31 | |

| August 2009 | | | | | | |
|---|---|---|---|---|---|---|
| S | M | T | W | T | F | S |
| | | | | | | 1 |
| 2 | 3 | 4 | 5 | 6 | 7 | 8 |
| 9 | 10 | 11 | 12 | 13 | 14 | 15 |
| 16 | 17 | 18 | 19 | 20 | 21 | 22 |
| 23 | 24 | 25 | 26 | 27 | 28 | 29 |
| 30 | 31 | | | | | |

| September 2009 | | | | | | |
|---|---|---|---|---|---|---|
| S | M | T | W | T | F | S |
| | | 1 | 2 | 3 | 4 | 5 |
| 6 | 7 | 8 | 9 | 10 | 11 | 12 |
| 13 | 14 | 15 | 16 | 17 | 18 | 19 |
| 20 | 21 | 22 | 23 | 24 | 25 | 26 |
| 27 | 28 | 29 | 30 | | | |

| October 2009 | | | | | | |
|---|---|---|---|---|---|---|
| S | M | T | W | T | F | S |
| | | | | 1 | 2 | 3 |
| 4 | 5 | 6 | 7 | 8 | 9 | 10 |
| 11 | 12 | 13 | 14 | 15 | 16 | 17 |
| 18 | 19 | 20 | 21 | 22 | 23 | 24 |
| 25 | 26 | 27 | 28 | 29 | 30 | 31 |

| November 2009 | | | | | | |
|---|---|---|---|---|---|---|
| S | M | T | W | T | F | S |
| 1 | 2 | 3 | 4 | 5 | 6 | 7 |
| 8 | 9 | 10 | 11 | 12 | 13 | 14 |
| 15 | 16 | 17 | 18 | 19 | 20 | 21 |
| 22 | 23 | 24 | 25 | 26 | 27 | 28 |
| 29 | 30 | | | | | |

| December 2009 | | | | | | |
|---|---|---|---|---|---|---|
| S | M | T | W | T | F | S |
| | | 1 | 2 | 3 | 4 | 5 |
| 6 | 7 | 8 | 9 | 10 | 11 | 12 |
| 13 | 14 | 15 | 16 | 17 | 18 | 19 |
| 20 | 21 | 22 | 23 | 24 | 25 | 26 |
| 27 | 28 | 29 | 30 | 31 | | |

AAT SAMPLE SIMULATION

# MEMO

To: Payroll Assistant
From: Pam Palmer
Subject: Salary Reviews: September 2009
Date: 8 September 2009

Below is a schedule of the changes to be made to employees' pay in September following their annual reviews.

I have promised that these will be included in their September salary otherwise we will have to make back dated pay awards if they are paid later.

Please let me have a prompt response if you have any queries.

Pam Palmer

| Salary Amendment Details: Effective 1 September 2009 ||||
|---|---|---|---|
| **Employee number** | **Name** | **Old Salary (£)** | **New salary (£)** |
| JL - Director | James Last<br>*Director* | 45,000.00 | 48,000.00 |
| 00026 | Fred Dibnah<br>*Clerk* | 12,600.00 | 13,000.00 |
| 00166 | John Walker<br>*Clerk* | 31,485.00 | 31,995.00 |
| 00227 | Sally Oldfield<br>*Office Supervisor* | 21,764.00 | 22,486.00 |
| 00068 | Bruce Benyon<br>*Accounts Supervisor* | 18,465.00 | 19,000.00 |
| 00326 | Kathy Evans<br>*Stores Manager* | 25,670.00 | 26,216.00 |
| 00281 | Robin Williams<br>*Stores Supervisor* | 19,586.00 | 20,184.00 |
| 00019 | Kevin Klein<br>*Web Design Manager* | 25,000.00 | 26,500.00 |
| 00084 | John Steinbeck<br>*Web Designer* | 18,511.00 | 19,242.00 |
| 00099 | Evelyn Waugh<br>*Personnel Supervisor* | 23,734.00 | 24,319.00 |

# MEMO

To: Payroll Assistant
From: Pam Palmer
Subject: Miscellaneous issues: September 2009
Date: 8 September 2009

---

Can you please note the following changes for the Payroll for September 2009.

| Employee number | Name | Comments |
|---|---|---|
| 00274 | Jenny Wilson | Jenny has just got married and has advised me that she wants to be known as Mrs Jenny Agutter with immediate effect. |
| 00079 | John Nettles | John wants to contribute to the trade union with effect from 01-09-2009. He has given his verbal authority that we can deduct £5.00 per month from his pay. |
| 00384 | Alan Freeman | Has been promoted from Web Designer - code WD001 to Web Design Manager - code WD003. |
| 00359 | Andy Costello | Has moved and his new address is: 5 San Carlos House Midchester MD3 7AG |
| 00167 | Julie Andrews | Has been promoted from Office Supervisor - code AD002 to Office Manager - code AD003. |
| 00349 | Jim Broadbent | Has been moved from sales administration - code SA001 to Regional Sales - code SA101. |
| 00192 | Andy Peebles | Has just got divorced. |

I also enclose forms P6T from the Revenue in respect of David Soul (00472) and Sharon Stone (00481).

Please let me have a prompt response if you have any queries.

Pam Palmer

AAT SAMPLE SIMULATION

---

**HM Revenue & Customs**

Issued by
H.M. Inspector of Taxes

W MIDLANDS 4
WOLVERHAMPTON

**PAYE** – Notice to employer of employee's tax code (or amended code) and previous pay and tax

Advent Systems Ltd
Advent House
Central Avenue
Midchester MD4 6AF

Date: 1/09/09

Employer's PAYE reference: 054/ASL001

Employee's name: David Soul

National Insurance number
(To be entered on the Deductions Working Sheet and to be quoted in any communication): FF 48 61 49 B

Works/Payroll no., Branch etc.:

**Code:**
The code of this employee is amended to: K435

for the year to 5 April: 2010

*Please use this code from the next pay day after you receive this form and follow the instructions in Part A overleaf.*

**Previous Pay and Tax**
*Where there is an entry here please follow the instructions in both Parts A and B overleaf.*

Previous pay:

Previous tax:

**P6 (T)**

# AAT SAMPLE SIMULATION

**HM Revenue & Customs**

Issued by
H.M. Inspector of Taxes

W MIDLANDS 4
WOLVERHAMPTON

**PAYE** - Notice to employer of employee's tax code (or amended code) and previous pay and tax

Advent Systems Ltd
Advent House
Central Avenue
Midchester MD4 6AF

Date: 1/09/09

Employer's PAYE reference: 054/ASL001

Employee's name: Sharon Stone

National Insurance number (To be entered on the Deductions Working Sheet and to be quoted in any communication): KW 60 89 27 D

Works/Payroll no., Branch etc.:

**Code:**
The code of this employee is amended to: 6017

for the year to 5 April: 2010

Please use this code from the next pay day after you receive this form and follow the instructions in Part A overleaf.

**Previous Pay and Tax**

Where there is an entry here please follow the instructions in both Parts A and B overleaf.

Previous pay:

Previous tax:

**P6 (T)**

# MEMO

To: Payroll Assistant
From: Simon Callow
Subject: Data Protection
Date: 5 September 2009

We are conscious that the information held in the payroll department is very confidential and also personal. Can you please let me know what steps you take to ensure security is maintained.

In particular, can you please advise me:

- how you file paper payroll records;
- who has access to the paper and computerised records;
- how you ensure that no one else can gain access to paper records unless they have authority;
- how you secure your computer from unauthorised access;
- how you protect against loss of data through corruption, computer failure etc.

*Simon Callow*

Simon Callow

# MEMO

To: Payroll Assistant
From: Simon Callow
Subject: Court Orders
Date: 10 September 2009

Further to my memo of 5th September, I am looking to update our procedures, particularly in respect of court orders.

Can you please advise me:

- which organisations can authorise the issue of attachments of earnings and deductions from earnings orders?
- can you accept the written authority of the Human Resources Manager alone?
- how quickly do we have to start making deductions?

*Simon Callow*

Simon Callow

# AAT SAMPLE SIMULATION: ANSWER BOOKLET

# ANSWERS (Task 1)

| Employee Payroll Record Card ||||
|---|---|---|---|
| Name | | Employee number | |
| Address | | Bank Address | |
| Marital Status | | Cost Code | |
| Date of birth | | Start date | |
| Gender | | Grade | |
| Bank sort code | | Annual salary | £ |
| Bank A/c number | | Hourly rate | £ |
| Building society number | | Overtime rate @ 1½ times hourly rate | £ |
| Student Loan Deduction | Yes / No | Overtime rate @ one and one third times hourly rate | £ |
| | | Overtime rate @ double time | £ |
| Monthly Pension Contributions | | Tax code | |
| *COSR* | £ | Tax basis | |
| *COMP* | £ | *Cumulative* | Yes / No |
| *AVC* | £ | *Month1/Week 1* | Yes / No |
| | | N.I. category letter | |
| Trade union deduction | £ | N.I. Number | |
| Charitable giving deduction | £ | Occupational Sick Pay | Yes/No |
| Health club deduction | £ | Annual Holiday Entitlement (days – excluding public holidays) | |
| Permanent Contract | Yes/No | Temporary Contract End Date | |
| Leaving Date | | Commission Payable | Yes/No |
| P45 Joining Information ||||
| Pay to date | | Tax to date | |

# ANSWERS (Task 1, continued)

**Comments**

# ANSWERS (Task 1, continued)

| Employee Payroll Record Card |||||
|---|---|---|---|---|
| Name | | Employee number | | |
| Address | | Bank Address | | |
| Marital Status | | Cost Code | | |
| Date of birth | | Start date | | |
| Gender | | Grade | | |
| Bank sort code | | Annual salary | £ | |
| Bank A/c number | | Hourly rate | £ | |
| Building society number | | Overtime rate @ 1½ times hourly rate | £ | |
| Student Loan Deduction | Yes / No | Overtime rate @ one and one third times hourly rate | £ | |
| | | Overtime rate @ double time | £ | |
| Monthly Pension Contributions | | Tax code | | |
| *COSR* | £ | Tax basis | | |
| *COMP* | £ | *Cumulative* | Yes / No | |
| *AVC* | £ | *Month1/Week 1* | Yes / No | |
| | | N.I. category letter | | |
| Trade union deduction | £ | N.I. Number | | |
| Charitable giving deduction | £ | Occupational Sick Pay | Yes/No | |
| Health club deduction | £ | Annual Holiday Entitlement (days – excluding public holidays) | | |
| Permanent Contract | Yes/No | Temporary Contract End Date | | |
| Leaving Date | | Commission Payable | Yes/No | |
| P45 Joining Information |||||
| Pay to date | | Tax to date | | |

# ANSWERS (Task 1, continued)

**Comments**

# ANSWERS (Task 1, continued)

| Employee Payroll Record Card |||| 
|---|---|---|---|
| Name | | Employee number | |
| Address | | Bank Address | |
| Marital Status | | Cost Code | |
| Date of birth | | Start date | |
| Gender | | Grade | |
| Bank sort code | | Annual salary | £ |
| Bank A/c number | | Hourly rate | £ |
| Building society number | | Overtime rate @ 1½ times hourly rate | £ |
| Student Loan Deduction | Yes / No | Overtime rate @ one and one third times hourly rate | £ |
| | | Overtime rate @ double time | £ |
| Monthly Pension Contributions | | Tax code | |
| *COSR* | £ | Tax basis | |
| *COMP* | £ | *Cumulative* | Yes / No |
| *AVC* | £ | *Month1/Week 1* | Yes / No |
| | | N.I. category letter | |
| Trade union deduction | £ | N.I. Number | |
| Charitable giving deduction | £ | Occupational Sick Pay | Yes/No |
| Health club deduction | £ | Annual Holiday Entitlement (days – excluding public holidays) | |
| Permanent Contract | Yes/No | Temporary Contract End Date | |
| Leaving Date | | Commission Payable | Yes/No |
| P45 Joining Information ||||
| Pay to date | | Tax to date | |

# ANSWERS (Task 1, continued)

**Comments**

AAT SAMPLE SIMULATION: ANSWER BOOKLET

# ANSWERS (Task 1, continued)

| Employee Payroll Record Card |||||
|---|---|---|---|
| Name | | Employee number | |
| Address | | Bank Address | |
| Marital Status | | Cost Code | |
| Date of birth | | Start date | |
| Gender | | Grade | |
| Bank sort code | | Annual salary | £ |
| Bank A/c number | | Hourly rate | £ |
| Building society number | | Overtime rate @ 1½ times hourly rate | £ |
| Student Loan Deduction | Yes / No | Overtime rate @ one and one third times hourly rate | £ |
| | | Overtime rate @ double time | £ |
| Monthly Pension Contributions | | Tax code | |
| COSR | £ | Tax basis | |
| COMP | £ | *Cumulative* | Yes / No |
| AVC | £ | *Month 1/Week 1* | Yes / No |
| | | N.I. category letter | |
| Trade union deduction | £ | N.I. Number | |
| Charitable giving deduction | £ | Occupational Sick Pay | Yes/No |
| Health club deduction | £ | Annual Holiday Entitlement (days – excluding public holidays) | |
| Permanent Contract | Yes/No | Temporary Contract End Date | |
| Leaving Date | | Commission Payable | Yes/No |
| P45 Joining Information ||||
| Pay to date | | Tax to date | |

# ANSWERS (Task 1, continued)

**Comments**

AAT SAMPLE SIMULATION: ANSWER BOOKLET

# ANSWERS (Task 1, continued)

| Employee Payroll Record Card |||||
|---|---|---|---|---|
| Name | | Employee number | | |
| Address | | Bank Address | | |
| Marital Status | | Cost Code | | |
| Date of birth | | Start date | | |
| Gender | | Grade | | |
| Bank sort code | | Annual salary | £ | |
| Bank A/c number | | Hourly rate | £ | |
| Building society number | | Overtime rate @ 1½ times hourly rate | £ | |
| Student Loan Deduction | Yes / No | Overtime rate @ one and one third times hourly rate | £ | |
| | | Overtime rate @ double time | £ | |
| Monthly Pension Contributions | | Tax code | | |
| *COSR* | £ | Tax basis | | |
| *COMP* | £ | *Cumulative* | Yes / No | |
| *AVC* | £ | *Month1/Week 1* | Yes / No | |
| | | N.I. category letter | | |
| Trade union deduction | £ | N.I. Number | | |
| Charitable giving deduction | £ | Occupational Sick Pay | Yes/No | |
| Health club deduction | £ | Holiday Entitlement (days – excluding public holidays) | | |
| Permanent Contract | Yes/No | Temporary Contract End Date | | |
| Leaving Date | | Commission Payable | Yes/No | |
| P45 Joining Information |||||
| Pay to date | | Tax to date | | |

# ANSWERS (Task 1, continued)

**Comments**

AAT SAMPLE SIMULATION: ANSWER BOOKLET

**HM Revenue & Customs**

**P45 Part 3**
**New employee details**
For completion by new employer

File your employee's P45 online at www.hmrc.gov.uk

Use capital letters when completing this form

1. Employer PAYE reference
   Office number   Reference number
   0 4 4 / D G W 0 0 1 9 5

2. Employee's National Insurance number
   Y B 3 8 5 7 2 0 A

3. Title - enter MR, MRS, MISS, MS or other title
   MR

   Surname or family name
   MASON

   First or given name(s)
   JAMES

4. Leaving date DD MM YYYY
   2 7  0 8  2 0 0 9

5. Student Loan deductions
   Y   Student Loan deductions to continue

6. Tax Code at leaving date
   4 6 1 L
   If week 1 or month 1 applies, enter 'X' in the box below.
   Week 1/Month 1

7. Last entries on P11 *Deductions Working Sheet*.
   Complete only if Tax Code is cumulative. If there is an 'X' at box 6, there will be no entries here.
   Week number      Month number  0 5
   Total pay to date
   £          4 8 6 3 . 9 6
   Total tax to date
   £              5 8 7 . 8 0

*For information only*

**To the new employer** Complete boxes 8 to 18 and send P45 Part 3 only to your HMRC office immediately.

8. New employer PAYE reference
   Office number   Reference number
   □□□ / □□□□□□□

9. Date new employment started DD MM YYYY

10. Works number/Payroll number and Department or branch (if any)

11. Enter 'P' here if employee will not be paid by you between the date employment began and the next 5 April.

12. Enter Tax Code in use if different to the Tax Code at box 6
    If week 1 or month 1 applies, enter 'X' in the box below.
    Week 1/Month 1

13. If the tax figure you are entering on P11 *Deductions Working Sheet* differs from box 7 (see the E13 Employer Helpbook *Day-to-day payroll*) please enter the figure here.
    £

14. New employee's job title or job description

15. Employee's private address
    Postcode

16. Gender. Enter 'X' in the appropriate box
    Male □    Female □

17. Date of birth DD MM YYYY

**Declaration**

18. I have prepared a P11 *Deductions Working Sheet* in accordance with the details above.
    Employer name and address
    Postcode
    Date DD MM YYYY

P45(Manual) Part 3

HMRC 04/08

# P45 Part 3
## New employee details
### For completion by new employer

**HM Revenue & Customs**

File your employee's P45 online at www.hmrc.gov.uk

Use capital letters when completing this form

**1** Employer PAYE reference
Office number / Reference number
`025` / `AKE0019485`

**2** Employee's National Insurance number
`BA 68 20 49 C`

**3** Title - enter MR, MRS, MISS, MS or other title
`MS`

Surname or family name
`SMITH`

First or given name(s)
`JENNY`

**4** Leaving date DD MM YYYY
`27 08 2009`

**5** Student Loan deductions
☐ Student Loan deductions to continue

**6** Tax Code at leaving date
`586T`
If week 1 or month 1 applies, enter 'X' in the box below.
Week 1/Month 1 ☐

**7** Last entries on P11 Deductions Working Sheet.
Complete only if Tax Code is cumulative. If there is an 'X' at box 6, there will be no entries here.
Week number ☐  Month number `05`
Total pay to date
£ `11880.83`
Total tax to date
£ `1887.00`

*For information only*

---

To the new employer Complete boxes 8 to 18 and send P45 Part 3 only to your HMRC office immediately.

**8** New employer PAYE reference
Office number / Reference number

**9** Date new employment started DD MM YYYY

**10** Works number/Payroll number and Department or branch (if any)

**11** Enter 'P' here if employee will not be paid by you between the date employment began and the next 5 April.

**12** Enter Tax Code in use if different to the Tax Code at box 6
If week 1 or month 1 applies, enter 'X' in the box below.
Week 1/Month 1

**13** If the tax figure you are entering on P11 Deductions Working Sheet differs from box 7 (see the E13 Employer Helpbook Day-to-day payroll) please enter the figure here.
£

**14** New employee's job title or job description

**15** Employee's private address

Postcode

**16** Gender. Enter 'X' in the appropriate box
Male ☐  Female ☐

**17** Date of birth DD MM YYYY

### Declaration

**18** I have prepared a P11 Deductions Working Sheet in accordance with the details above.
Employer name and address

Postcode

Date DD MM YYYY

P45(Manual) Part 3

HMRC 04/08

# ANSWERS (Task 2, continued)

The P46 for Michael Jackson appears on the following page.

AAT SAMPLE SIMULATION: ANSWER BOOKLET

# HM Revenue & Customs
## P46: Employee without a Form P45

**Section one** To be completed by the employee

Please complete section one and then hand the form back to your present employer. If you later receive a form P45 from your previous employer, hand it to your present employer.
Use capital letters when completing this form.

### Your details

**National Insurance number**
This is very important in getting your tax and benefits right

**Title** - enter MR, MRS, MISS, MS or other title
MR

**Surname or family name**
JACKSON

**First or given name(s)**
MICHAEL

**Gender.** Enter 'X' in the appropriate box
Male [X]   Female [ ]

**Date of birth** DD MM YYYY
10 11 1963

**Address**
**House or flat number**

**Rest of address including house name or flat name**
GREY GABLES
SOUTHCHESTER

**Postcode**
M18 7EW

### Your present circumstances
Read all the following statements carefully and enter 'X' in **the one** box that applies to you.

**A** - This is my first job since last 6 April and **I have not** been receiving taxable Jobseeker's Allowance or taxable Incapacity Benefit or a state or occupational pension.

OR

**B** - This is now my only job, but since last 6 April **I have** had another job, or have received taxable Jobseeker's Allowance or Incapacity Benefit. I do not receive a state or occupational pension.

OR

**C** - I have another job or receive a state or occupational pension.  [C] ✓

### Student Loans
If you left a course of Higher Education before last 6 April and received your first Student Loan instalment on or after 1 September 1998 and you have not fully repaid your Student Loan, enter 'X' in box D. *(If you are required to repay your Student Loan through your bank or building society account do **not** enter an 'X' in box D.)*

### Signature and date
I can confirm that this information is correct

Signature
*Michael Jackson*

Date DD MM YYYY
08 09 2009

P46   Page 1   HMRC 02/08

AAT SAMPLE SIMULATION: ANSWER BOOKLET

**Section two** To be completed by the employer

File your employee's P46 online at **www.hmrc.gov.uk/employers/doitonline**
Use capital letters when completing this form. Guidance on how to fill it in, including what to do if your employee has not entered their National Insurance number on page 1, is at **www.hmrc.gov.uk/employers/working_out.htm** and in the E13 Employer Helpbook *Day-to-day payroll*.

### Employee's details

Date employment started  DD MM YYYY

Works/payroll number and department or branch (if any)

Job title

### Employer's details

Employer PAYE reference
Office number   Reference number

Address
Building number

Employer name

Rest of address

Postcode

### Tax code used

If you do not know the tax code to use or the current National Insurance contributions (NICs) lower earnings limit, go to **www.hmrc.gov.uk/employers/rates_and_limits.htm**

Enter 'X' in the appropriate box

**Box A**
Emergency code on a **cumulative** basis

**Box B**
Emergency code on a **non-cumulative**
Week 1/Month 1 basis

**Box C**
Code BR

Tax code used

If week 1 or month 1 applies, enter 'X' in this box

Send this form to your HM Revenue & Customs office on the first pay day.
If the employee has entered 'X' in box A or box B, on page 1, and their earnings are below the NICs lower earnings limit, **do not send the form until their earnings reach the NICs lower earnings limit.**

Page 2

AAT SAMPLE SIMULATION: ANSWER BOOKLET

# HM Revenue & Customs

**P45 Part 3**
**New employee details**
For completion by new employer

File your employee's P45 online at www.hmrc.gov.uk

Use capital letters when completing this form

**1** Employer PAYE reference
*Office number   Reference number*
`0 4 1` / `P D A 6 8 3 5`

**2** Employee's National Insurance number
`F W  2 6  6 8  9 2  A`

**3** Title - enter MR, MRS, MISS, MS or other title
`MR`

Surname or family name
`EASTWOOD`

First or given name(s)
`CLINT`

**4** Leaving date *DD MM YYYY*
`2 9  0 8  2 0 0 9`

**5** Student Loan deductions
☐ Student Loan deductions to continue

**6** Tax Code at leaving date
`K 4 2`

If week 1 or month 1 applies, enter 'X' in the box below.
Week 1/Month 1  `X`

**7** Last entries on P11 *Deductions Working Sheet*.
**Complete only if Tax Code is cumulative.** If there is an 'X' at box 6, there will be no entries here.

Week number ☐☐    Month number ☐☐

Total pay to date
£ ☐☐☐☐☐☐☐ . ☐☐

Total tax to date
£ ☐☐☐☐☐☐☐ . ☐☐

*For information only*

**To the new employer** complete boxes 8 to 18 and send P45 Part 3 only to your HMRC office immediately.

**8** New employer PAYE reference
*Office number   Reference number*
☐☐☐ / ☐☐☐☐☐☐☐

**9** Date new employment started *DD MM YYYY*
☐☐ ☐☐ ☐☐☐☐

**10** Works number/Payroll number and Department or branch (if any)

**11** Enter 'P' here if employee will not be paid by you between the date employment began and the next 5 April. ☐

**12** Enter Tax Code in use if different to the Tax Code at box 6
☐ ☐☐☐☐☐☐☐

If week 1 or month 1 applies, enter 'X' in the box below.
Week 1/Month 1 ☐

**13** If the tax figure you are entering on P11 *Deductions Working Sheet* differs from box 7 (see the E13 Employer Helpbook *Day-to-day payroll*) please enter the figure here.
£ ☐☐☐☐☐☐☐ . ☐☐

**14** New employee's job title or job description

**15** Employee's private address

Postcode ☐☐☐☐ ☐☐☐

**16** Gender. Enter 'X' in the appropriate box
Male ☐   Female ☐

**17** Date of birth *DD MM YYYY*
☐☐ ☐☐ ☐☐☐☐

**Declaration**

**18** I have prepared a P11 *Deductions Working Sheet* in accordance with the details above.
Employer name and address

Postcode ☐☐☐☐ ☐☐☐

Date *DD MM YYYY*
☐☐ ☐☐ ☐☐☐☐

P45(Manual) Part 3

HMRC 04/08

AAT SAMPLE SIMULATION: ANSWER BOOKLET

**HM Revenue & Customs**

**P45 Part 3**
**New employee details**
For completion by new employer

File your employee's P45 online at www.hmrc.gov.uk

Use capital letters when completing this form

**1** Employer PAYE reference
Office number   Reference number
0 3 3 / C D C 2 2 9 4 7 A

**2** Employee's National Insurance number
K S 3 7 6 8 5 4 D

**3** Title - enter MR, MRS, MISS, MS or other title
MRS

Surname or family name
LAMOUR

First or given name(s)
DOROTHY

**4** Leaving date DD MM YYYY
3 0 0 1 2 0 0 9

**5** Student Loan deductions
☐ Student Loan deductions to continue

**6** Tax Code at leaving date
3 4 5 L

If week 1 or month 1 applies, enter 'X' in the box below.
Week 1/Month 1  X

**7** Last entries on P11 Deductions Working Sheet.
Complete only if Tax Code is cumulative. If there is an 'X' at box 6, there will be no entries here.

Week number ☐☐   Month number ☐☐

Total pay to date
£

Total tax to date
£

*For information only*

To the new employer  Complete boxes 8 to 18 and send P45 Part 3 only to your HMRC office immediately.

**8** New employer PAYE reference
Office number   Reference number

**9** Date new employment started DD MM YYYY

**10** Works number/Payroll number and Department or branch (if any)

**11** Enter 'P' here if employee will not be paid by you between the date employment began and the next 5 April.

**12** Enter Tax Code in use if different to the Tax Code at box 6

If week 1 or month 1 applies, enter 'X' in the box below.
Week 1/Month 1

**13** If the tax figure you are entering on P11 Deductions Working Sheet differs from box 7 (see the E13 Employer Helpbook Day-to-day payroll) please enter the figure here.
£

**14** New employee's job title or job description

**15** Employee's private address

Postcode

**16** Gender. Enter 'X' in the appropriate box
Male ☐   Female ☐

**17** Date of birth DD MM YYYY

**Declaration**

**18** I have prepared a P11 Deductions Working Sheet in accordance with the details above.
Employer name and address

Postcode

Date DD MM YYYY

P45(Manual) Part 3

HMRC 04/08

# ANSWERS (Task 3)

| Leaver Input Form<br>September 2009 |||||
|---|---|---|---|
|  | Jane Seymour | Donald Sinden | Jerry Springer |
| Leaving Date |  |  |  |
| Salary to be paid in final month | £ | £ | £ |
| Holiday entitlement to be paid | £ | £ | £ |
| Commission | £ | £ | £ |
| Overtime | £ | £ | £ |
| Bonus | £ | £ | £ |

## ANSWERS (Task 4)

| | | | Payroll Input - Salary Adjustment Sheet | | | | |
|---|---|---|---|---|---|---|---|
| Name | Payroll Number | Old salary | New salary | Effective Date | Flat hourly rate | Hourly rate @ 1½ | Comments |
| | | | | | | | |
| | | | | | | | |
| | | | | | | | |
| | | | | | | | |
| | | | | | | | |
| | | | | | | | |
| | | | | | | | |
| | | | | | | | |
| | | | | | | | |
| | | | | | | | |
| | | | | | | | |

# ANSWERS (Task 5)

| Miscellaneous Payroll Amendment/Change Sheet ||||||||||
|---|---|---|---|---|---|---|---|---|---|
| Employee Number | Tax Code | Trade Union Deduction | Code | Surname | Title | Marital Status | Address | Post Code ||
|  |  |  |  |  |  |  |  |  ||
|  |  |  |  |  |  |  |  |  ||
|  |  |  |  |  |  |  |  |  ||
|  |  |  |  |  |  |  |  |  ||
|  |  |  |  |  |  |  |  |  ||
|  |  |  |  |  |  |  |  |  ||

# ANSWERS (Task 5, continued)

## MEMO

From:  Payroll Assistant                                    10 September 2009

To:      Pamela Palmer


**Payroll Changes – September 2009**

# ANSWERS (Task 5, continued)

**Memo Continued**

# ANSWERS (Task 6)

## MEMO

From: Payroll Assistant

10 September 2009

To: Simon Callow

**Data Protection**

# ANSWERS (Task 7)

**MEMO**

From: Payroll Assistant

10 September 2009

To: Simon Callow

**Court Orders**

# Unit 72

# AAT SAMPLE SIMULATION – 2003 STANDARDS

# LEVEL 2 CERTIFICATE IN PAYROLL ADMINISTRATION (QCF)

## UNIT 72

### ASCERTAINING GROSS PAY
### (REVISED FOR FINANCE ACT 2009)

## COVERAGE OF PERFORMANCE CRITERIA

All performance criteria are covered in this simulation.

| Element | PC Coverage |
|---|---|
| **72.1** | **Determine entitlements** |
| A | Evaluate all data relating to temporary variations for accuracy and reasonableness. |
| B | Ensure documentation relating to temporary variations is verified for authorisation. |
| C | Identify employees where input is required in order to ensure payment and ensure relevant details are correctly inserted. |
| D | Check rates for overtime payments against agreed scales for each type of employee affected. |
| E | Identify all payments in respect of their tax, National Insurance and pension liability. |
| F | Take appropriate action when employees are absent and apply the correct payment schemes with regard to adoption, maternity, paternity and sickness. |
| G | Identify and resolve all discrepancies directly or by reference to the appropriate person. |
| H | Process temporary payments and deductions accurately. |
| I | File source documentation in accordance with statutory and organisational requirements and in a logical and orderly manner. |
| J | Maintain security and confidentiality of sensitive information at all times. |
| **72.2** | **Determine statutory pay entitlements** |
| A | Determine entitlement to Statutory Sick Pay when entitlement to occupational sick pay expires or is not paid. |
| B | Process Statutory Sick Pay payments accurately on receipt of regulatory forms. |
| C | Determine entitlement to Statutory Maternity Pay, Statutory Adoption Pay, Statutory Paternity Pay, when entitlement to occupational payments are not made. |
| D | Process Statutory Maternity Pay, Statutory Adoption Pay, Statutory Paternity Pay payments accurately on receipt of regulatory forms. |
| E | Process Tax Credit payments on receipt of regulatory forms. |
| F | Contribute to the resolution of individual employees' queries by checking statutory pay entitlements manually, using the appropriate tables. |
| G | Identify and resolve all discrepancies directly or by reference to the appropriate person. |
| H | Issue the correct regulatory documentation where entitlement to statutory payments does not arise or ceases. |

All missing range statements should be assessed separately.

AAT SAMPLE SIMULATION

## ASSOCIATION OF ACCOUNTING TECHNICIANS
# DATA AND TASKS

## INSTRUCTIONS

This simulation is designed to let you show your ability to ascertain gross pay.

**You should read the whole simulation before you start work, so that you are fully aware of what you will have to do.**

You are allowed **four hours** to complete your work.

Write your answers in the answer booklet provided. Use a blue or black pen, not pencil. If you need more paper for your answers, ask the person in charge.

You may pull apart and rearrange your booklets if you wish to do so, but you must put them back in their original order before handing them in.

You may use correcting fluid, but in moderation. You should cross out your errors neatly and clearly.

Your work must be accurate, so check your work carefully before handing it in.

You are not allowed to refer to any unauthorised material, such as books or notes, while you are working on the simulation. If you have any such material with you, you must hand it to the person in charge before you start work.

Any instances of misconduct will be reported to the AAT, and disciplinary action may be taken.

*Coverage of performance criteria and range statements*

It is not always possible to cover all performance criteria and range statements in a single simulation. Any performance criteria and range statements not covered must be assessed by other means by the assessor before a candidate can be considered competent.

Performance criteria coverage for this simulation is shown on page 150.

# THE SITUATION

Watts and Stephenson is a paper merchants with a main office in Swansea and satellite offices in London, Glasgow, Liverpool and Belfast, each with its own payroll. You are the payroll supervisor, responsible for each of the payrolls in the UK.

The company operates weekly, monthly and directors' payrolls at each of the locations.
- The weekly payroll pays every Friday a week in arrears.
- The monthly payroll pays on the 20th of each month.

*Pension Scheme*

All employees in the UK are eligible to join the occupational pension scheme which is a contracted-out salary related scheme.
- Employee contributions are 5% of pensionable pay.
- Employer contributions are 7% of pensionable pay.
- Pensionable pay is basic pay, overtime, sales commission, statutory maternity pay, statutory adoption pay, statutory paternity pay.

Employees are entitled to pay additional voluntary contributions (AVCs).

The company will also make deductions from pay towards employees' own personal pension plans.

*Payment basis*

All employees are paid 1/12 of their annual salary each month. A days pay is calculated as 1/260 of the annual salary for each working day.

Employees starting or leaving part way through a month are paid 1/260 of their annual salary for each working day remaining in the month.

Overtime is only paid to supervisors and below on submission of an authority signed by Jerry Jackson the Operations Manager. Weekly paid staff overtime rates are as follows:
- Flat rate—for hours up to the full time equivalent of 40 hours per week;
- Time and third for weekday overtime;
- Time and half for weekend overtime;
- Double time for bank holiday working.

Hourly rates are always rounded according to the following rules:
- 0.5p or less rounded down;
- 0.51p or more rounded up.

All non-statutory payments for each branch must be agreed by the General Manager in the relevant branch. They are:

| Branch | Name | Signature |
| --- | --- | --- |
| London | George Shaw | *GB Shaw* |
| Glasgow | Dorothy Sayers | *Dorothy L Sayers* |
| Belfast | Henry Miller | *H Miller* |
| Liverpool | Albert Camus | *A Camus* |
| Swansea | Robert Stevenson | *RL Stevenson* |

Salary increases for all staff except directors can be authorised by Pamela Palmer, Human Resources Manager. Director's salaries can only be authorised by Sally Jenkins the Managing Director.

## Sickness Scheme

All employees are entitled to Statutory Sick Pay, but only directors are entitled to occupational sick pay.

For SSP purposes, all employees have 5 Qualifying days which are Monday to Friday.

SSP rates for 2009/2010 are as follows:

| Unrounded daily rates | Number of qualifying days in the week | 1 | 2 | 3 | 4 | 5 | 6 | 7 |
|---|---|---|---|---|---|---|---|---|
| £ | | £ | £ | £ | £ | £ | £ | £ |
| 11.3071 | 7 | 11.31 | 22.62 | 33.93 | 45.23 | 56.54 | 67.85 | 79.15 |
| 13.1916 | 6 | 13.20 | 26.39 | 39.58 | 52.77 | 65.96 | 79.15 | |
| 15.8300 | 5 | 15.83 | 31.66 | 47.49 | 63.32 | 79.15 | | |
| 19.7875 | 4 | 19.79 | 39.58 | 59.37 | 79.15 | | | |
| 26.3833 | 3 | 26.39 | 52.77 | 79.15 | | | | |
| 39.5750 | 2 | 39.58 | 79.15 | | | | | |
| 79.1500 | 1 | 79.15 | | | | | | |

## Maternity Pay

The company pays Statutory Maternity Pay only. There is no Occupational Maternity Pay.

SMP rates for 2009/2010 are as follows:

- 6 weeks at 90% of average earnings, plus up to
- 33 weeks at the lower of 90% of average earnings or £123.06 whichever is the lower.

## Bank Holidays

The Bank Holidays for 2009 are as follows:

| England and Wales | | 2009 |
|---|---|---|
| New Year's Day | | 1 Jan |
| Good Friday | | 10 Apr |
| Easter Monday | | 13 Apr |
| Early May Bank Holiday | | 4 May |
| Spring Bank Holiday | | 25 May |
| Summer Bank Holiday | | 31 Aug |
| Christmas Day | | 25 Dec |
| Boxing Day | | 28 Dec |

**Today's date is 23 June 2009.**

# TASKS TO BE COMPLETED

**All memos, letters and other communications have been received by you within 48 hours of the date of writing, unless stated otherwise.**

## Task 1

The input for the weekly payroll for Liverpool is to be processed. You have received the time sheet from the General Manager together with a covering memo on pages 156 and 157 of this booklet.

- Complete the payroll input sheet on page 169 of the answer booklet and reply to the General Manager's memo using the memo paper on page 168 of the answer booklet.

## Task 2

Jane Horrocks, who is employed at the London office, has advised her manager that she is expecting a baby. You have received the memo from Jane on page 158 of this booklet, requesting details of her SMP entitlement.

- Reply using the memo paper on page 170 of the answer booklet.

## Task 3

Refer to the memo on page 159 of this booklet.

- Reply using the memo paper on page 171 of the answer booklet.
- Complete the sickness report on page 172 of the answer booklet.

## Task 4

Refer to the memo regarding Statutory Sick Pay for Jenny Walker on page 160 of this booklet.

- Reply using the memo paper on page 173 of the answer booklet.

## Task 5

Refer to the memo you have received from the General Manager on page 161 of this booklet, asking you to process various bonus payments for the Swansea staff.

- Write a memo to the Financial Controller in response, with any comments you may have. Use the blank memo on page 174 of the answer booklet.
- Complete the additional bonus schedule on page 175 of the answer booklet.

## Task 6

You have received the memo on page 162 of this booklet, from the Chief Accountant concerning a forthcoming external audit.

- Reply using the memo paper on page 176 of the answer booklet.

## Task 7

You have received the memo on page 163 of this booklet, from Dorothy Sayers, the General Manager in Glasgow, asking for clarification of the tax and N.I. liability of certain benefits.

- Reply using the memo paper on page 177 of the answer booklet.

## Task 8

You have received the memo, on page 164 of this booklet, from Pamela Palmer, Human Resources Manager, concerning voluntary deductions.

- Complete the payroll deduction sheet on page 179 of the answer booklet.
- Reply to the memo from Pam Palmer using the memo paper on page 178 of the answer booklet.

## Task 9

You have received the memo on page 165 of this booklet, from Henry Miller, the General Manager in Belfast, with a query concerning a couple who both work for the company and are adopting a baby.

- Reply to the memo from Henry Miller on page 180 of the answer booklet.

# MEMO

**From:** General Manager—Liverpool   **Date:** 21 June 2009

**To:** Payroll Assistant

**Subject:** Time sheet and payroll changes for week ending 19 June 2009

---

Attached is the time sheet for the week ending 19 June. Can you please ensure it is processed for pay on Thursday 25 June.

Please confirm that this has been done and let me know if you have any queries.

N.B. If you have any queries please process what you can and omit those items with queries.


*A Camus*

Albert Camus

| Name | Employee Number | Hourly Rate £ | Flat Rate Hours | Weekday overtime @ time and a third | Weekend hours @ time and a half | Public holiday hours @ double time |
|---|---|---|---|---|---|---|
| Jenny Pitman | 00012 | 6.30 | 25 | 10 | 6 | |
| Frankie Detori | 00057 | 7.80 | 40 | 5 | 6 | |
| Jonnie Dankworth | 00082 | 5.40 | 40 | 8 | | 8 |
| Fred Mercury | 00142 | 9.32 | 40 | 6 | | |
| Roy Gibb | 00276 | 8.40 | 38 | | 7 | |
| Jimmie Saville | 00277 | 6.60 | 40 | 6 | 8 | |
| Paul Merton | 00306 | 7.30 | 35 | | 8 | |
| Daisy Springfield | 00311 | 5.80 | 40 | 8 | 4 | |
| Mary Hopkins | 00316 | 5.80 | 20 | | 8 | |
| Gary Rhodes | 00324 | 8.20 | 40 | 4 | | |
| Phil Collins | 00385 | 4.80 | 40 | | | |
| Eric Clapton | 00386 | 8.30 | 40 | 5 | 9 | |
| Eric Morcombe | 00414 | 7.90 | 40 | | 7 | |
| Erica Rowe | 00415 | 5.60 | 40 | 6 | 3 | |
| **Authorised Signature** | | *A Camus* | | | **20 June 2009** | |

# MEMO

**From:** Jane Horrocks—London  **Date:** 23 June 2009

**To:** Payroll Assistant

**Subject:** Pregnancy

---

I am expecting a baby on 15 October 2009.

I intend to start my maternity leave on Monday 21 September. As you are aware, I have been employed by Watts and Stephenson for some 8 years.

I believe my SMP will be based on my average earnings, but I am not sure which earnings are used. To help I have listed below my gross earnings over several months:

| | |
|---|---|
| April | £1,250.00 |
| May | £1,400.00 |
| June | £1,748.00 |
| July | £1,570.00 |

Can you please let me know:
- Am I entitled to SMP? Please give a reason for your response.
- How much leave am I entitled to? Please break it down into each type.
- How my SMP is calculated? Please give the formula.
- How much will I get per week? Please give a breakdown.
- What documentation do I need to give you?

Thank you.

# MEMO

**From:** Personnel Manager            **Date:** 19 June 2009

**To:** Payroll Assistant

**Subject:** Sickness Report

---

Peter Rason an employee in the Swansea branch was sick on the following days.
- 19, 20, 21, 22, 24, 25 and 26 May;
- 30 and 31 May;
- 1, 2 and 3 June;
- 8, 9, 10 and 11 June.

He works Monday to Friday and has not been off sick for over 6 months. You can assume that he is only actually sick on the days indicated above.

I am new to the personnel department and would be grateful if you could let me know how much SSP, if any, Peter is entitled to by completing a report. Indicate against each day of sickness:
- whether SSP is payable;
- if not, why not.

Also, could you please explain the following terms to me:
- Period of incapacity for work;
- Qualifying days;
- Waiting days;
- Linking of periods of incapacity for work.

Finally, please calculate the SSP and salary for June to ensure Peter receives the correct pay in June. His annual salary is £16,020.
- How much SSP will he receive for the month?
- What will be his salary for the month?


Personnel Manager

# MEMO

**From:** Personnel Manager  **Date:** 21 June 2009

**To:** Payroll Assistant

**Subject:** SSP and Jenny Walker

I forgot to raise the issue of Jenny Walker when I wrote to you. She is a part time clerk in Swansea who has average earnings of £50 per week.

She was sick for the whole week (7 days) beginning 7 June. She has not been sick before.

Can you please let me know:
- whether she is entitled to SSP;
- what action needs to be taken if she is not entitled.

Please give reasons for your answer.

Many thanks


Personnel Manager

# MEMO

**From:** General Manager      **Date:** 21 June 2009

**To:** Payroll Assistant

**Subject:** Bonus Payments—Swansea

---

I would like to pay a special, one off, bonus payment to the staff who gallantly helped out during the severe floods at the end of May. The bonus is to be based on a number of days pay for certain employees plus £50 as a one off payment for all employees.

Attached is a schedule listing the employees and setting out the days to be paid where appropriate.

Please confirm the total payments to be made by returning the completed schedule and let me know if you have any queries.


*RL Stevenson*

Robert Stevenson

# MEMO

**From:** Chief Accountant  **Date:** 21 June 2009

**To:** Payroll Assistant

**Subject:** Payroll Procedures

---

At the moment I am pulling together information with the prospect of revising our administration systems.

Can you please let me have the following information in respect of the payroll department:
- The statutory and recommended record retention period for payroll records.
- Your recommended method of filing that ensures it is easy to trace documents.
- The steps that can be taken to ensure security of:
    1. Documents;
    2. Computer information.

Please submit your response in bullet point format.


Chief Accountant

# MEMO

**From:** Dorothy Sayers  **Date:** 18 June 2009

**To:** Payroll Assistant

**Subject:** Expenses and Benefits

---

We make certain payments to employees in the Glasgow branch. My concern is that we may be making mistakes in the way the payments are made.

Can you please advise me of the tax, N.I. and Pension implications of the following payments:
- Annual bonus based on performance throughout the year;
- Attendance bonus of £10 for every month of attendance without sickness;
- Sales commission;
- Attendance allowance for working on bank holidays;
- Statutory Sick Pay;
- Statutory Maternity Pay;
- Statutory Adoption Pay;
- Statutory Paternity Pay.

I look forward to your response.


*Dorothy L Sayers*

Dorothy Sayers

# MEMO

**From:** Pamela Palmer  **Date:** 21 June 2009

**To:** Payroll Assistant

**Subject:** Collection of overpayments

---

The following workers were all overpaid last week due to an error within the time management system. Can you please deduct these from their pay next week. Their authority is below. However, I was not able to get the authority from Ben Kingsley.

Can you please confirm where we stand in respect of Ben Kingsley?

| Employee | Hourly Rate | Hours overpaid ||
|---|---|---|---|
|  |  | Flat hours | Hours @ time and half |
| H Johnson *Hugh Johnson* | 5.20 | 4.00 |  |
| W Wilkinson *WF Wilkinson* | 6.30 | 3.50 | 2.50 |
| F Watson *Fred Watson* | 5.40 | 6.50 | 2.00 |
| D Smith *Doug Smith* | 7.60 | 2.00 | 4.75 |
| A Thompson *Tony Thompson* | 6.50 |  | 7.50 |
| G Kerr *Graham Kerr* | 5.90 | 6.50 | 3.50 |
| B Kingsley | 6.40 | 7.25 | 2.75 |
| S Zander *Sara Zander* | 8.20 | 6.00 | 6.00 |

*Pam Palmer*

# MEMO

**From:** Henry Miller  **Date:** 18 June 2009

**To:** Payroll Assistant

**Subject:** Adoption

---

Can you please help me?

Angela and Barry McKay have both been employed by us for 6 years. They advised me two weeks ago that they have been accepted for adoption and the child is due to be placed with them on 6 September 2009.

Their earnings are £180.00 per week (Barry) and £250 per week (Angela).

They have advised me that Barry will take all the adoption leave and Angela will take the paternity leave.

Can you please advise me:
- what evidence is required from each of them?
- what will each of them be entitled to per week and for how long?
- what conditions specifically apply to how Angela can take her paternity leave?
- when will their adoption and paternity pay commence?

*Henry Miller*

**To be used for workings**

# AAT SAMPLE SIMULATION: ANSWER BOOKLET

## ANSWERS (Task 1)

# MEMO

**From:** Payroll Assistant                                **Date:**

**To:** General Manager—Liverpool

**Subject:** Time Sheet and payroll changes for week ending 20 June 2009

# ANSWERS (Task 1, continued)

## PAYROLL INPUT SHEET FOR LIVERPOOL

| Name | Employee Number | Hourly Rate £ | Flat Rate Hours |  | Weekday overtime @ time and a third |  | Weekend hours @ time and a half |  | Public holiday hours @ double time |  |
|---|---|---|---|---|---|---|---|---|---|---|
|  |  |  | Hours | Pay £ | Hours | Pay £ | Hours | Pay £ | Hours | Pay £ |
| Jenny Pitman | 00012 | 6.30 |  |  |  |  |  |  |  |  |
| Frankie Detori | 00057 | 7.80 |  |  |  |  |  |  |  |  |
| Jonnie Dankworth | 00082 | 5.40 |  |  |  |  |  |  |  |  |
| Fred Mercury | 00142 | 9.32 |  |  |  |  |  |  |  |  |
| Roy Gibb | 00276 | 8.40 |  |  |  |  |  |  |  |  |
| Jimmie Saville | 00277 | 6.60 |  |  |  |  |  |  |  |  |
| Paul Merton | 00306 | 7.30 |  |  |  |  |  |  |  |  |
| Daisy Springfield | 00311 | 5.80 |  |  |  |  |  |  |  |  |
| Mary Hopkins | 00316 | 5.80 |  |  |  |  |  |  |  |  |
| Gary Rhodes | 00324 | 8.20 |  |  |  |  |  |  |  |  |
| Phil Collins | 00385 | 4.80 |  |  |  |  |  |  |  |  |
| Eric Clapton | 00386 | 8.30 |  |  |  |  |  |  |  |  |
| Eric Morcombe | 00414 | 7.90 |  |  |  |  |  |  |  |  |
| Erica Rowe | 00415 | 5.60 |  |  |  |  |  |  |  |  |

## ANSWERS (Task 2)

# MEMO

**From:** Payroll Assistant  **Date:**

**To:** Jane Horrocks - London

**Subject:** **Pregnancy**

## ANSWERS (Task 3)

# MEMO

**From:** Payroll Assistant  **Date:**

**To:** Personnel Manager

**Subject:** Sickness Report

## ANSWERS (Task 3, continued)

### Sickness Report

**Peter Rason**

He works Monday to Friday and has not been off sick for over 6 months.

| Sun | Mon | Tues | Wed | Thurs | Fri | Sat | |
|-----|-----|------|-----|-------|-----|-----|------|
|     | 18  | 19   | 20  | 21    | 22  | 23  | May  |
|     |     | sick | sick| sick  | sick|     |      |
| 24  | 25  | 26   | 27  | 28    | 29  | 30  | May  |
| sick| sick| sick |     |       |     | sick|      |
| 31  | 1   | 2    | 3   | 4     | 5   | 6   | June |
| sick| sick| sick | sick|       |     |     |      |
| 7   | 8   | 9    | 10  | 11    | 12  | 13  | June |
|     | sick| sick | sick| sick  |     |     |      |

## ANSWERS (Task 4)

# MEMO

**From:** Payroll Assistant  **Date:**

**To:** Personnel Manager

**Subject:** SSP and Jenny Walker

## ANSWERS (Task 5)

# MEMO

**From:** Payroll Assistant  **Date:**

**To:** General Manager—Swansea

**Subject:** Bonus Payments—Swansea

# ANSWERS (Task 5, continued)

### Additional Bonus Schedule

| Name | Employee number | Salary £ | Days bonus to be paid | Bonus £ | Additional bonus £ |
|---|---|---|---|---|---|
| K Brockett | 00019 | 13,000.00 | 3 | | |
| S Field | 00023 | 24,500.00 | 6 | | |
| J Thompson | 00029 | 18,600.00 | 4 | | |
| P Delft | 00037 | 21,080.00 | | | |
| J Sainsbury | 00041 | 19,662.00 | | | |
| P Trewitt | 00042 | 20,050.00 | 3 | | |
| D Jones | 00055 | 18,600.00 | 3 | | |
| R Davies | 00064 | 19,520.00 | 3 | | |
| P Davies | 00064 | 18,618.00 | 3 | | |
| H Sanders | 00077 | 25,760.00 | 5 | | |
| F Saunders | 00078 | 17,648.00 | | | |
| P Davies | 00082 | 19,650.00 | 1 | | |
| | | | **Totals** | | |

## ANSWERS (Task 6)

# MEMO

**From:** Payroll Assistant      **Date:**

**To:** Chief Accountant

**Subject:** Payroll Procedures

## ANSWERS (Task 7)

# MEMO

**From:** Payroll Assistant  **Date:**

**To:** General Manager—Glasgow

**Subject:** Expenses and Benefits

# ANSWERS (Task 8)

# MEMO

**From:** Payroll Assistant  **Date:**

**To:** Pam Palmer

**Subject:** Collection of overpayments

## ANSWERS (Task 8, continued)

### Payroll Deduction Sheet

| Name | Flat Hourly £ | Time and half £ | Total £ |
|------|---------------|-----------------|---------|
|      |               |                 |         |
|      |               |                 |         |
|      |               |                 |         |
|      |               |                 |         |
|      |               |                 |         |
|      |               |                 |         |
|      |               |                 |         |
|      |               |                 |         |
|      |               |                 |         |
|      |               |                 |         |
|      |               |                 |         |
|      |               |                 |         |
|      |               |                 |         |
|      |               |                 |         |
|      |               |                 |         |

# ANSWERS (Task 9)

# MEMO

**From:** Payroll Assistant            **Date:**

**To:** Henry Miller

**Subject:** Adoption

# AAT Exams

# Unit 73

# AAT EXAM PAPER 1 – 2003 STANDARDS

# JUNE 2008

## LEVEL 2 CERTIFICATE IN PAYROLL ADMINISTRATION (QCF)

### UNIT 73

### DETERMINING NET PAY (DNP)
### (AMENDED FOR FINANCE ACT 2009)

# AAT EXAM PAPER 1 (JUNE 2008)

This exam paper is in TWO sections.

You must show competence in both sections. So, try to complete EVERY task in BOTH sections.

Section 1 contains 2 operational tasks and Section 2 contains 10 short answer questions.

You should spend about 130 minutes on Section 1 and about 50 minutes on Section 2.

There is blank space for your workings on pages 7, 18 and 23, but you should include all essential calculations in your answers.

You have been given a booklet containing all the tables you need to complete the exam, including the tax calculations tables, NIC earnings limits and rates and student loan deduction tables.

Please note that, for your calculations, only the NIC exact percentage method will be accepted.

Both sections relate to the scenario described below.

### Introduction

- You are the Payroll Clerk for Fictitious Ltd.

- The company main pension scheme is a COSR and contributions are paid by employees at 6% of basic pay only.

- There is an alternative group personal pension scheme with contributions set by employees at up to 100% of total gross pay.

- Charitable giving contributions are made to an agency approved by HMRC.

- Other 'one-off' donations are made directly to the charity.

### Assessment focus point

The AAT have advised that, from December 2009, there will no longer be a separate booklet of Tax tables. Instead the tables will form part of the exam paper. The table pages will be perforated and you will be able to tear them out for easy reference during the exam.

# Section 1

**You should spend about 130 minutes on this section.**

**Complete both tasks in full.**

## Data

**Employee 1**

| | |
|---|---|
| **Name:** | Paul Thomas |
| **Annual salary:** | £18,000.00 |
| **Monthly salary:** | £1,500.00 |
| **Deductions:** | |
| Charitable giving: | £57.00 a month |
| Staff loan: | £116.15 a month |
| Union subscriptions: | £8.75 a month |
| **Pension scheme member:** | No |

**April 2009:**

Paul's tax code of 350L is to be carried forward from 2008/09.

**May 2009:**

Paul was on unpaid sick leave in April 2009 and a deduction of £857.14 to cover 12 days of absence is to be taken this month.

You receive an instruction from HMRC to apply a code of 522L from this month.

You receive an instruction that Paul has decided to contribute £50.00 every month to the group personal pension scheme starting this month.

**Employee 2**

| Name: | Channo Cajero |
|---|---|
| **Annual salary:** | £96,300.00 |
| **Monthly salary:** | £8,025.00 |
| **Deductions:** | |
| AVC | £350.00 a month |
| Sharesave: | £200.00 a month |
| Health club: | £75.00 a month |
| **Pension scheme member:** | Yes – Main scheme |

**April 2009:**

You receive an instruction from HMRC to apply a tax code of K624 from this month.

Channo gives you a 'one-off' instruction to deduct £150.00 from his pay and send it to the local children's home.

**May 2009:**

Channo decides to go part time from 1 May 2009 working half the normal contractual hours each week with a consequent reduction in salary to £4,012.50 a month.

You receive a new instruction from HMRC to apply a tax allowance code of 522L from this month.

Channo signs a charitable giving instruction to make regular payments to the agency of £100.00 every month starting from this month.

## Task 1.1

(a) **Using all the information given, calculate Paul Thomas's and Channo Cajero's net pay for April and May 2009 showing all the gross to net calculations. Use the calculation sheets on pages 8, 10, 12 and 14.**

(b) **Using the results you calculated in (a) above, complete payslips for Paul and Channo for April and May 2009 on pages 9, 11, 13 and 15.**

## Notes:

Your calculations should be based on the values contained in the tables and rates supplied to you in the separate booklet and these will differ from the rates and values currently in use. You are being assessed on your ability to use the tables and rates supplied, not on your ability to remember a specific year's values.

You are reminded of the special rules which apply to the assessment of tax adjustments where the code to be used exceeds 500.

**Calculation for Task 1.1 – Paul Thomas – April 2009 gross to net pay**

Basic pay _____

Charitable giving for April 2009 _____

**Tax calculation**

Cumulative gross pay _____

Less cumulative allowable deductions (above) _____

Cumulative pay for tax purposes _____

Tax code used _____  Tax basis _____

Adjustment for tax code _____

Cumulative net taxable pay_____

Tax calculation                          Tables used _____

_____
_____
_____

Tax due for April 2009 _____

**NICs calculation**                     NI table letter used _____

Employee's contributions payable _____

_____
_____
_____

Employer's contributions payable _____

_____
_____
_____

**Payslip for April 2009**

| Employee: Paul Thomas | | Date: 30 April 2009 |
|---|---|---|
| **Payments** £ | **Deductions** £ | **Cumulatives** £ |
| Basic pay: | Income tax: | Gross pay: |
| | NIC: | Pay for tax purposes: |
| | Charitable giving: | Income tax: |
| | Staff loan: | Employee's NIC: |
| | Union: | Employer's NIC: |
| | | Charitable giving: |
| | | Staff loan: |
| | | Union: |
| | | |
| **Total gross pay:** | **Total deductions:** | **Net pay:** |

NI Number: BG490219D        Tax code: 350L

# AAT EXAM PAPER 1 (JUNE 2008)

**Calculation for Task 1.1 – Paul Thomas – May 2009 gross to net pay**

Basic pay _____

Less adjustment for leave _____

Total gross pay for May 2009 _____

Charitable giving for May 2009 _____

Cumulative charitable giving year to date _____

**Tax calculation**

Cumulative gross pay to May 2009 _____

Less cumulative allowable deductions (above) _____

Cumulative pay for tax purposes _____

Tax code used _____ Tax basis _____

Adjustment for tax code _____

Cumulative net taxable pay _____

Tax calculation                         Tables used _____

_____

_____

Tax due to May 2009 _____

Tax deducted in April 2009 _____

Tax due for May 2009 _____

**NICs calculation**                    NI table letter used _____

Employee's contribution payable _____

_____

_____

Employer's contribution payable _____

_____

_____

**Payslip for May 2009**

| Employee: Paul Thomas | | Date: 31 May 2009 |
|---|---|---|
| **Payments £** | **Deductions £** | **Cumulatives £** |
| Basic pay: | Income tax: | Gross pay: |
| Adjustment for leave: | NIC: | Pay for tax purposes: |
| | Charitable giving: | Income tax: |
| | Group personal pension: | Employee's NIC: |
| | Staff loan: | Employer's NIC: |
| | Union: | Charitable giving: |
| | | Group personal pension: |
| | | Staff loan: |
| | | Union: |
| **Total gross pay:** | **Total deductions:** | **Net pay:** |

NI Number: BG490219D         Tax Code: 522L

# AAT EXAM PAPER 1 (JUNE 2008)

### Calculation for Task 1.1 – Channo Cajero – April 2009 gross to net pay

Basic pay _____

Pension contribution for April 2009 _____

AVC payment for April 2009 _____

**Tax calculation**

Cumulative gross pay _____

Less cumulative allowable deductions (above) _____

Cumulative pay for tax purposes _____

Tax code used _____ Tax basis _____

Adjustment for tax code _____

Cumulative net taxable pay _____

Tax calculation                              Tables used _____

_____

_____

_____

Tax due for April 2009 _____

**NICs calculation**                         NI table letter used _____

Employee's contribution payable _____

_____

_____

_____

Employer's contribution payable _____

_____

_____

_____

**Payslip for April 2009**

| Employee: Channo Cajero | | Date: 30 April 2009 |
|---|---|---|

| Payments £ | Deductions £ | Cumulatives £ |
|---|---|---|
| Basic pay: | Income tax: | Gross pay: |
| | NIC: | Pay for tax purposes: |
| | Pension: | Tax: |
| | AVC: | Employee's NIC: |
| | Sharesave: | Employer's NIC: |
| | Health club: | Pension: |
| | Children's home: | AVC: |
| | | Sharesave: |
| | | Health club: |
| | | Children's home: |
| **Total gross pay:** | **Total deductions:** | **Net pay:** |

NI Number: AG623987B    Tax code: K624

**Calculation for Task 1.1 – Channo Cajero – May 2009 gross to net pay**

Basic pay _____

Pension contribution for May 2009 _____

AVC payment for May 2009 _____

Charitable giving for May 2009 _____

Cumulatives       Pension _____ AVC _____ Charitable Giving _____

**Tax calculation**

Cumulative gross pay to May 2009 _____

Less cumulative allowable deductions (above) _____

Cumulative pay for tax purposes _____

Tax code used _____ Tax basis _____

Adjustment for tax code _____

Cumulative net taxable pay _____

Tax calculation                               Tables used _____

_____

_____

_____

Tax due to May 2009 _____

Tax deducted in April 2009 _____

Tax due for May 2009 _____

**NICs calculation**                          NI table letter used _____

Employee's contribution payable _____

_____

_____

_____

Employer's contribution payable _____

_____

_____

_____

**Payslip for May 2009**

| Employee: Channo Cajero | | Date: 31 May 2009 |
|---|---|---|

| Payments £ | Deductions £ | Cumulatives £ |
|---|---|---|
| Basic pay: | Income tax: | Gross pay: |
| | NIC: | Pay for tax purposes: |
| | Pension: | Income tax: |
| | AVC: | Employee's NIC: |
| | Charitable giving: | Employer's NIC: |
| | Sharesave: | Pension: |
| | Health club: | AVC: |
| | | Charitable giving: |
| | | Sharesave: |
| | | Health club: |
| | | Children's home: |
| **Total gross pay:** | **Total deductions:** | **Net pay:** |

| NI Number: AG623987B | Tax code: 522L |
|---|---|

## Data

You have received the following e-mail from the company's Accounts Manager.

---

**From:** greg.salter@fictitious.co.uk
**To:** payroll@fictitious.co.uk
**Sent:** 17 June 2009
**Subject:** Payroll transfer to general ledger

Now that the new accounting system has been set up I wish to complete the code structures for the regular payroll transfers. Please supply me with information on the following two key control values and how the constituent parts work together to arrive at the total payment.

1. **The total gross cost of the payroll**
   How would you define this?
   Name four elements of pay and two employer costs.

2. **The total payment due to HM Revenue & Customs**
   Identify the two main constituents.
   List the components for each constituent payment.

Thank you for your help in this matter.

---

## Task 1.2

From the information given, reply to the above e-mail.

---

**From:** payroll@fictitious.co.uk
**To:** greg.salter@fictitious.co.uk
**Sent:** 19 June 2009
**Subject:** Re: Payroll transfer to general ledger

This page is for the continuation of your email. You may not need to use all of it.

## Section 2

You should spend about 50 minutes on this section.

Write in the space provided, tick the appropriate box OR circle the correct answer. Do not give your answer in any other way. In each case, tick or circle ONE box only.

Answer all the questions on pages 19 to 22.

### Task 2.1

A local loan company asks for financial details of Fictitious Ltd's employees in order to offer cut price loans to those who qualify. A travel voucher is being offered to each employee who takes out a loan and the company will get a payment for each enquiry. The directors think this is a good deal.

(a) Should you supply the information requested?

  Yes ☐   No ☐

(b) Give THREE reasons for your answer in (a) above.

1. _____

2. _____

3. _____

(c) Name ONE circumstance in which you would supply personal information without the express permission of the employee.

### Task 2.2

Explain how net taxable pay is calculated when an employee has the following allowance code.

(a) BR code

_____

_____

(b) K code

_____

_____

(c) Which ONE of the following codes is the Emergency Code for 2009/10?

  BR    647L    647LWk1    603L    603LWk1

## Task 2.3

**(a)** **There are three ways in which an employer is notified that an employee is to start paying student loan deductions. State TWO of the three ways.**

1. _____

2. _____

**(b)** One of the employees informs you that she has started to receive a pension from a former employer and this means you must stop taking student loan deductions from her.

**Will you agree to this?**

Yes ☐   No ☐

**(c)** **Which ONE of the following is the annual pay figure that is the starting point for student loan deductions?**

£10,000     £12,000     £15,000     £18,000

## Task 2.4

Holiday payments in advance attract special national insurance contribution calculation rules. Name ONE of them and explain how the calculation is carried out.

_____

_____

_____

_____

## Task 2.5

**(a)** **Which ONE of the following is the standard recovery amount for statutory adoption, maternity and paternity pay where the employer is not a small employer for recovery purposes?**

Nil     92%     95%     104.2%

**(b)** How does the employer recover this amount?

☐ The employer submits a special claim form to the Treasury.

☐ The recovery value is deducted from the regular payment to HMRC.

☐ The organisation sends a standard invoice to HMRC.

☐ An adjustment is made on the year end return.

**(c)** **Explain how you would determine if you can recover statutory sick pay when making the payment to HMRC.**

_____

_____

_____

## Task 2.5, continued

(d) Which ONE of the following is the amount of SSP which can be recovered if the circumstances in (c) above apply?

Excess over 13%    13%    92%    104.5%

## Task 2.6

(a) What is the earliest date in the month by which the regular PAYE payment must be made?

6$^{th}$    14$^{th}$    19$^{th}$    25$^{th}$

(b) Under what circumstances can the employer make payment later than the date you have identified in (a) above?

_____

_____

(c) What is the later date by which payment can be made if the circumstances in (b) above are met?

12$^{th}$    16$^{th}$    19$^{th}$    22$^{nd}$

## Task 2.7

Payments made to an ex-employee after they have left their employment can be subject to special income tax and national insurance rules.

(a) Which ONE of the following tax codes would apply to a payment made after the P45 has been issued?

The one on the P45    K647    647LWk1    BR

(b) At what point do the special NIC rules apply?

☐ One pay period after leaving

☐ One month after leaving

☐ 6 weeks after leaving

☐ After the end of the tax year

## Task 2.8

The main statutory deductions are income tax, student loans and national insurance contributions.

(a) State TWO other statutory deductions.

1. _____

2. _____

## Task 2.8, continued

**(b)** Which ONE of the following statements best describes the manner in which the employer should operate these other statutory deductions?

☐ Make a deduction in accordance with the instructions.

☐ Deduct whenever the employee says it is OK to do so.

☐ Make the deduction whenever a payment is made to the employee.

**(c)** What fees per deduction can the employer take from the employee towards the cost of operating these deductions?

Nil          50p          75p          £1.00

## Task 2.9

**(a)** Which ONE of the following types of pension scheme would be eligible for tax relief in the payroll?

☐ All pensions where the deductions are taken by the employer

☐ Only occupational pension schemes

☐ Occupational schemes and approved personal pensions

☐ Only approved occupational pension schemes

**b)** What basic NIC letter would apply to the following pension schemes if there are no other factors to consider?

COMP          _____

Stakeholder   _____

COSR          _____

## Task 2.10

One of your key functions is to check the validity of the payroll and ensure that only those entitled to be paid are to receive a payment.

**(a)** Describe how you would reconcile the number of payments made in a payroll run.

_____

_____

**(b)** What TWO checks would you use to ensure the payments calculated are to be made to genuine employees?

1. _____

2. _____

# AAT EXAM PAPER 2 – 2003 STANDARDS

# DECEMBER 2007

## LEVEL 2 CERTIFICATE IN PAYROLL ADMINISTRATION (QCF)

### UNIT 73

### DETERMINING NET PAY (DNP)
### (AMENDED FOR FINANCE ACT 2009)

**This exam paper is in TWO sections.**

**You must show competence in BOTH sections. So try to complete EVERY task in BOTH sections.**

**Section 1 contains 2 tasks and Section 2 contains 10 tasks.**

**You should spend about 130 minutes on Section 1, and 50 minutes on Section 2.**

**You should include all essential calculations in your answers.**

**Both Sections 1 and 2 are based on the business described below.**

### Introduction

- You work as a Payroll Clerk for Fictitious Ltd.
- The company has a pension scheme which is a COMP and contributions are paid by employees at 8% of pay.
- All pay is pensionable pay.
- All Charity Giving contributions are made to an agency approved by HMRC.

AAT EXAM PAPER 2 (DECEMBER 2007)

## Section 1 – operational tasks

You should spend about 130 minutes on this section.

Complete both tasks in full.

### Data

**Employee record card**

| Name: Trinidad Garcia | Start Date: 3 December 1992 |
|---|---|
| Department: Production<br>Position: Production Manager | Annual Salary: £58,165.00<br>Monthly Salary: £4,847.08 |
| NI Number: ST169528C | Deductions:<br>Staff loan £250.00 a month<br>Health club £25.00 a month |
|  | Pension Scheme Member: Yes |
|  | AVC: Yes – £287 a month |

**April 2009:**

Trinidad celebrates her 60th birthday at the beginning of April and gives you a Certificate of Age Exception, CA4140. National Insurance Contributions must be calculated at the appropriate rate.

You receive an instruction from HMRC to apply a code of 508L from this month.

**May 2009:**

Trinidad takes unpaid leave for most of May so only £1,118.56 is to be paid to her this month.

You receive a new instruction from HMRC to apply a tax allowance code of 508L Month 1 from this month.

Because of her low pay this month Trinidad asks you to suspend her loan, health club and AVC payments, and the company agrees to this.

## Data

**Employee record card**

| Name: Phillip Yoest | Start Date: 18 September 2005 |
|---|---|
| Department: ICT | Annual Salary: £31,800.00 |
| Position: Programmer | Monthly Salary: £2,650.00 |
| NI Number: TH638871D | Deductions:<br>Health club £25 a month |
| | Pension Scheme Member: Yes |
| | AVC: Yes – £175 a month |

**April 2009:**

You receive instructions to:

- apply a tax allowance code of K194 from this month
- deduct Charity Giving of £85 a month from Phillip's pay starting this month

**May 2009:**

The company decides to pay Phillip his annual bonus of £1,200 this month.

Philip instructs you to increase his AVC payments to £250 a month from this month.

## Task 1.1

(a) Using the information provided, calculate Trinidad Garcia's and Phillip Yoest's net pay for April and May 2009 showing all the gross to net calculations. Use the calculation sheets provided.

(b) Using the results calculated in (a) above, complete payslips for Trinidad and Phillip for April and May 2009.

**Note:**
All your calculations should be based on the values contained in the tables and rates supplied to you today and these may differ from actual current rates. You are being assessed on your ability to use the tables and rates supplied, not on your ability to remember a specific year's values.

You are reminded of the special rules which apply to the assessment of tax allowances where the code issued exceeds 500.

**Calculation for Task 1.1 – Trinidad Garcia – April 2009 gross to net pay**

Basic pay _____

Pension contribution for April 2009 _____

Pension contribution year to date _____

AVC for April 2009 _____

AVC year to date _____

**Tax calculation**

Cumulative gross pay _____

Less cumulative allowable deductions (above) _____

Cumulative pay for tax purposes _____

Tax code used _____  Tax basis _____

Adjustment for tax code _____

Cumulative net taxable pay _____

Tax calculation _____

continued _____

continued _____

Tax due for April 2009 _____

**NICs calculation**          **NI table letter used** _____

Employee's contributions payable _____

_____

_____

Employer's contributions payable _____

_____

Payslip – April 2009

Employee – Trinidad Garcia					Date – 30 April 2009

| Payments £ | Deductions £ | Cumulatives £ |
|---|---|---|
| Basic pay: | Income tax: | Gross pay: |
| | NIC: | Pay for tax purposes: |
| | Pension | Income tax: |
| | AVC: | Employee's NIC: |
| | Staff loan: | Employer's NIC: |
| | Health club: | Pension: |
| | | AVC: |
| | | Staff loan: |
| | | Health club: |
| Total gross pay: | Total deductions: | Net pay: |

NI number: ST169528C     Tax code: 508L

**Calculation for Task 1.1 – Trinidad Garcia – May 2009 gross to net pay**

Basic pay _____

Cumulative gross pay _____

Pension contribution for May 2009 _____

Pension contribution year to date _____

AVC contribution year to date _____

**Tax calculation**

Total gross pay _____

Less allowable deductions (above) _____

Pay for tax purposes _____

Tax code used _____ Tax basis _____

Adjustment for tax code _____

Net taxable pay for May 2009 only _____

Tax calculation _____

continued _____

continued _____

Tax due May 2009 _____

Plus tax paid in April 2009 _____

Cumulative tax due to May 2009 _____

**NICs calculation**          **NI table letter used** _____

Employee's contributions payable _____

_____

_____

Employer's contributions payable _____

_____

_____

**Payslip – May** 2009

**Employee – Trinidad Garcia**             **Date – 31 May** 2009

| Payments £ | Deductions £ | Cumulatives £ |
|---|---|---|
| Basic pay: | Income tax: | Gross pay: |
|  | NIC: | Pay for tax purposes: |
|  | Pension | Income tax: |
|  | AVC: | Employee's NIC: |
|  | Staff loan: | Employer's NIC: |
|  | Health club: | Pension: |
|  |  | AVC: |
|  |  | Staff loan: |
|  |  | Health club: |
| **Total gross pay:** | **Total deductions:** | **Net pay:** |

**NI number: ST169528C**     **Tax code: 508L Month 1**

**Calculation for Task 1.1 – Phillip Yoest – April 2009 gross to net pay**

Basic pay _____

Pension contribution for April 2009 _____

Pension contribution year to date _____

AVC for April 2009 _____

AVC year to date _____

Charity Giving for April 2009 _____

Charity Giving year to date _____

**Tax calculation**

Cumulative gross pay _____

Less cumulative allowable deductions (above) _____

Cumulative pay for tax purposes _____

Tax code used _____    Tax basis _____

Adjustment for tax code _____

Cumulative net taxable pay _____

Tax calculation _____

continued _____

continued _____

Cumulative tax due _____

**NICs calculation**          **NI table letter used** _____

Employee's contributions payable _____

_____

Employer's contributions payable _____

_____

| Payslip – April 2009 | | |
|---|---|---|
| Employee – Phillip Yoest | | Date – 30 April 2009 |

| Payments £ | Deductions £ | Cumulatives £ |
|---|---|---|
| Basic pay: | Income tax: | Gross pay: |
| | NIC: | Pay for tax purposes: |
| | Pension | Income tax: |
| | AVC: | Employee's NIC: |
| | Charity Giving: | Employer's NIC: |
| | Health club: | Pension: |
| | | AVC: |
| | | Charity Giving: |
| | | Health club: |
| **Total gross pay:** | **Total deductions:** | **Net pay:** |

NI number: TH638871D    Tax code: K194

## Calculation for Task 1.1 – Phillip Yoest – May 2009 gross to net pay

Basic pay _____

Bonus _____

Total gross pay for May 2009 _____

Cumulative gross pay, year to date _____

Pension contribution for May 2009 _____

Pension contribution year to date _____

AVC for May 2009 _____ year to date: _____

Charity Giving: for May 2009 _____ year to date: _____

**Tax calculation**

Cumulative gross pay _____

Less cumulative allowable deductions (above) _____

Cumulative pay for tax purposes _____

Tax code used _____ Tax basis _____

Adjustment for tax code _____

Cumulative net taxable pay _____

Tax calculation _____

continued _____

continued _____

Cumulative tax due _____

Less tax already paid _____

Tax due for May 2009 _____

**NICs calculation**           **NI table letter used** _____

Employee's contributions payable _____

_____

_____

Employer's contributions payable _____

_____

# AAT EXAM PAPER 2 (DECEMBER 2007)

Payslip – May 2009

Employee – Phillip Yoest                                    Date – 31 May 2009

| Payments £ | Deductions £ | Cumulatives £ |
|---|---|---|
| Basic pay: | Income tax: | Gross pay: |
| Bonus: | NIC: | Pay for tax purposes: |
|  | Pension | Income tax: |
|  | AVC: | Employee's NIC: |
|  | Charity Giving | Employer's NIC: |
|  | Health club: | Pension: |
|  |  | AVC: |
|  |  | Charity Giving: |
|  |  | Health club: |
| **Total gross pay:** | **Total deductions:** | **Net pay:** |

NI number: TH638871D         Tax code: K194

## Data

You have received the following e-mail from the company's Payments Manager:

| | |
|---|---|
| **From:** | chloe.nabarro@fictitious.ltd.uk |
| **Sent:** | 4 December 2009 |
| **To:** | payroll@fictitious.ltd.uk |
| **Subject:** | Payments to HMRC |

I am attempting to set up a formal schedule for the regular payments the company makes to various bodies. As this company has less than 250 employees will you please answer the following questions about the payments made to HMRC?

What two methods of payment can be used to make the regular remittance to HMRC?

What are the payment deadlines for each method?

## Task 1.2

**From the information given, reply to this e-mail.**

| | |
|---|---|
| **From:** | payroll@fictitious.ltd.uk |
| **Sent:** | 4 December 2009 |
| **To:** | chloe.nabarro@fictitious.ltd.uk |
| **Subject:** | Re: Payments to HMRC |

This page is for the continuation of your e-mail. You may not need all of it.

## Section 2 – short answer questions

You should spend about 50 minutes on this Section.

Write in the space provided, tick the appropriate box OR circle the correct answer. Do not give your answer in any other way.

Answer all the questions on pages 18 to 22.

### Task 2.1

(a) List the THREE statutory deductions which are included in the regular PAYE payments to HMRC

1. _____
2. _____
3. _____

(b) What is the standard amount of the following statutory payments which can be recovered from the sums paid to HMRC?

Statutory Adoption/Maternity/Paternity Pay          Amount _____ %

(c) Describe the circumstances under which the company can recover more than the standard amount and show the amount which can be recovered under these circumstances.

_____
_____
_____
_____
_____

## Task 2.2

Statutory Sick Pay (SSP) is a statutory payment employers must pay to employees. Employers are not permitted to recover any of the SSP they have paid out unless such recovery is covered by the Percentage Threshold Scheme.

(a) **Explain how the Percentage Threshold Scheme (PTS) works in respect of recovery of SSP payments made.**

_____

_____

_____

(b) **What amount of the SSP can be recovered if the PTS applies to the employer?**

        92%     100%     104.5%     Excess over 13%

## Task 2.3

The company management team decides that each employee is to receive a gift for the festive season and they contract with an outside organisation to provide a suitable item in each case. You have been instructed to provide the organisation with employees' home addresses so that it can deliver the gifts directly.

(a) **Should you comply with the instruction?**

        Yes     No

(b) **Give THREE reasons for your answer in (a) above.**

1. _____

2. _____

3. _____

## Task 2.4

(a) **List THREE items of pay you would expect to include in the gross pay figure for payroll.**

1. _____

2. _____

3. _____

(b) **List TWO items of additional employers' costs that would make up the gross cost of the payroll.**

1. _____

2. _____

## Task 2.5

(a) Which ONE of the following statements describes when an employee would begin to be liable for National Insurance Contributions?

☐ From the first payment made after attaining 16 years of age

☐ From the payment made in the month following the one in which they reach 16

☐ On all pay earned up to their 16th birthday

☐ From the payment made in the month prior to reaching age 16

(b) Hugo Chavez informs you that now he is 60 years of age he no longer has to pay National Insurance Contributions and instructs you to cease making such deductions from his pay.

**Should you agree to his instruction?**

Yes     No

## Task 2.6

(a) Hugo also informs you that since he is 60 he no longer has to repay his student loan and instructs you to stop deducting this.

**Will you agree to this instruction?**

Yes     No

(b) Explain your answer in (a) above.

_____

_____

_____

(c) List TWO circumstances in which student loan deductions must cease.

1. _____

2. _____

## Task 2.7

The training manager instructs you to deduct sums from employees' pay to cover fees for courses they were supposed to attend but failed to.

(a) **Should you make the deductions as instructed?**

                Yes     No

(b) Explain your answer in (a) above.

_____

_____

_____

## Task 2.8

(a) You are making a payment of outstanding bonus in December to an employee who left the company in September.

**Which one of the following tax codes will you use to calculate income tax?**

        OT     BR     647L     647L Wk1

(b) **The employee was a member of the company COMP pension scheme. Which ONE of the following National Insurance Contributions table letters would you use to calculate NICs on the delayed bonus payment?**

        A     C     F     X

## Task 2.9

**List FOUR checks you would carry out to ensure a payroll run is as accurate as possible.**

1. _____

2. _____

3. _____

4. _____

## Task 2.10

(a) Which ONE of the following is the current Emergency Allowance Code?

BR    647L    603L    647L Wk1

(b) Explain how a suffix code, for example 489L, is used when calculating income tax.

# AAT EXAM PAPER 3 – 2003 STANDARDS

# JUNE 2007

## LEVEL 2 CERTIFICATE IN PAYROLL ADMINISTRATION (QCF)

### UNIT 73

### DETERMINING NET PAY (DNP)
### (AMENDED FOR FINANCE ACT 2009)

# AAT EXAM PAPER 3 (JUNE 2007)

This exam paper is in TWO sections.

You must show competence in both sections. So, try to complete EVERY task in BOTH sections.

Section 1 contains 2 operational tasks and Section 2 contains 10 short answer questions.

You should spend about 130 minutes on Section 1 and about 50 minutes on Section 2.

You should include all essential calculations in your answers.

Please note that, for your calculations, only the NIC exact percentage method will be accepted.

Both sections relate to the scenario described below.

### Introduction

- You are the Payroll Clerk for Fictitious Ltd.

- There is a company pension scheme in operation. It is a COSR with contributions by employees set at 8% of pensionable pay if the employee is a member of the scheme.

- All gross pay is pensionable pay.

- Employees who are members of the pension scheme may also contribute to an AVC scheme.

- A Charitable Giving scheme is available to allow employees to make donations via an agency. The agency is registered with HMRC. The company matches all employee donations with a payment of its own, which is classified as an employer payment.

# Section 1

You should spend about 130 minutes on this section.

Complete both tasks in full.

## Data

**Employee record card**

| | | | |
|---|---|---|---|
| **Name:** | Frank Lee | **Start date:** | 18 July 2003 |
| **Department:** Accounting <br> **Position:** Finance Manager | | **Annual salary:** £45,780.00 <br> **Monthly salary:** £3,815.00 | |
| **NI number:** PN698247D | | **Deductions:** <br> Charitable Giving: £250.00 a month <br> Loan: £327.50 a month | |
| | | **Pension scheme member:** Yes | |
| | | **AVC:** £78.50 a month | |

**April 2009:**

You have an instruction from HMRC to apply immediately a tax allowance code of 15L.

Frank sends in an instruction to make an additional, one-off, Charitable Giving contribution of £150.00 through the agency.

**May 2009:**

You have received a new instruction from HMRC to change the tax allowance code to K82.

Frank is to be paid a one-off bonus of £2,800 this month.

**Employee record card**

| Name: | Kristina Strieff | Start date: | 23 April 2009 |
|---|---|---|---|
| Department: | Human Resources | Annual salary: | £28,698.00 |
| Position: | HR Adviser | Monthly salary: | £2,391.50 |
| NI number: | HZ638756A | Deductions:<br>**Personal pension**: £272.00 a month<br>**Charitable Giving**: £122.50 a month | |
| | | Pension scheme member: No | |
| | | AVC: No | |

**April 2009:**

Kristina started on 23 April so her payment for April is to be £956.60 only.

Kristina has not produced a P45 so she has completed a P46 stating that this is her only job. She has ticked Box A. Code 543L cumulative applies until HMRC advises otherwise.

Kristina has told you that she wants her pension and Charitable Giving deductions to be taken this month, even though this will significantly reduce her pay.

**May 2009:**

Kristina will receive a full month's pay of £2,391.50.

Kristina indicated on her P46 that she is liable to repay her student loan and that deductions based on her gross pay must commence this month.

## Task 1.1

(a) Using all the information given, calculate Frank Lee's and Kristina Strieff's net pay for April and May 2009 showing all the gross to net calculations.

(b) Using the results you calculated in (a) above, complete payslips for Frank and Kristina for April and May 2009.

**Notes:**
Your calculations should be based on the values contained in the tables and rates supplied to you in the separate booklet and these may differ from the rates and values currently in use. You are being assessed on your ability to use the tables and rates supplied, not on your ability to remember a specific year's values.

You are reminded of the special rules which apply to the assessment of tax adjustments where the code issued exceeds 500.

**Calculation for Task 1.1 – Frank Lee – April 2009 gross to net pay**

Basic pay _____

Total gross pay _____

Pension contribution for April 2009 _____

Pension contribution year to date _____

AVC contribution for April 2009 _____

AVC contribution year to date _____

Charitable Giving for April 2009 _____

Charitable Giving year to date _____

**Tax calculation**

Cumulative gross pay _____

Less cumulative allowable deductions (above) _____

Cumulative pay for tax purposes _____

Tax code used _____ Tax basis _____

Adjustment for tax code _____

Cumulative net taxable pay _____

Tax calculation _____

_____

_____

Tax due for April 2009 _____

**NICs calculation**                                NI table letter used _____

Employee's contributions payable _____

_____

_____

Employer's contributions payable _____

_____

_____

**Payslip for April 2009**

| Employee: Frank Lee | | Date: 30 April 2009 |
|---|---|---|

| Payments £ | Deductions £ | Cumulatives £ |
|---|---|---|
| Basic pay: | Income tax: | Gross pay: |
| | NIC: | Pay for tax purposes: |
| | Pension: | Tax: |
| | AVC: | Employee's NIC: |
| | Charitable Giving: | Employer's NIC: |
| | Loan: | Pension: |
| | | AVC: |
| | | Charitable Giving: |
| | | Loan: |
| **Total gross pay:** | **Total deductions:** | **Net pay:** |

**NI Number:** PN698247D  **Tax code:** 15L

## Calculation for Task 1.1 – Frank Lee – May 2009 gross to net pay

Basic pay _____

Bonus payment _____

Total gross for May 2009 _____

Cumulative gross pay _____

Pension contribution for May 2009 _____

Pension contribution year to date _____

AVC contribution for May 2009 _____

AVC contribution year to date _____

Charitable Giving for May 2009 _____

Charitable Giving year to date _____

**Tax calculation**

Cumulative gross pay _____

Less cumulative allowable deductions (above) _____

Cumulative pay for tax purposes _____

Tax code used _____ Tax basis _____

Adjustment for tax code _____

Cumulative net taxable pay _____

Tax calculation _____
_____
_____

Tax due year to date _____

Less tax already paid _____

Tax due for May 2009 _____

**NICs calculation**                NI table letter used _____

Employee's contributions payable _____
_____
_____

Employer's contributions payable _____
_____
_____

**Payslip for May 2009**

| Employee: Frank Lee | | Date: 31 May 2009 |
|---|---|---|

| Payments £ | Deductions £ | Cumulatives £ |
|---|---|---|
| Basic pay: | Income tax: | Gross pay: |
| Bonus: | NIC: | Pay for tax purposes: |
|  | Pension: | Income tax: |
|  | AVC: | Employee's NIC: |
|  | Charitable Giving: | Employer's NIC: |
|  | Loan: | Pension: |
|  |  | AVC: |
|  |  | Charitable Giving: |
|  |  | Loan: |
| **Total gross pay:** | **Total deductions:** | **Net pay:** |

| NI Number: PN698247D | Tax Code: K82 |
|---|---|

**Calculation for Task 1.1 – Kristina Strieff – April 2009 gross to net pay**

Basic pay _____

Gross pay year to date _____

Charitable Giving for April 2009 _____

Charitable Giving year to date _____

**Tax calculation**

Cumulative gross pay _____

Less cumulative allowable deductions (above) _____

Cumulative pay for tax purposes _____

Tax code used _____ Tax basis _____

Adjustment for tax code _____

Cumulative net taxable pay _____

Tax calculation _____

_____

_____

Tax due for April 2009 _____

**NICs calculation**                    NI table letter used _____

Employee's contributions payable _____

_____

_____

Employer's contributions payable _____

_____

_____

**Payslip for April 2009**

| Employee: Kristina Strieff | | Date: 30 April 2009 |
|---|---|---|

| Payments £ | Deductions £ | Cumulatives £ |
|---|---|---|
| Basic pay: | Income tax: | Gross pay: |
| | NIC: | Pay for tax purposes: |
| | Charitable Giving: | Income tax: |
| | Personal pension: | Employee's NIC: |
| | | Employer's NIC: |
| | | Charitable Giving: |
| | | Personal pension: |
| Total gross pay: | Total deductions: | **Net pay:** |

NI Number: HZ638756A    Tax code: 543L

# AAT EXAM PAPER 3 (JUNE 2007)

**Calculation for Task 1.1 – Kristina Strieff – May 2009 gross to net pay**

Basic pay _____

Gross pay year to date _____

Charitable Giving for May 2009 _____

Charitable Giving year to date _____

**Tax calculation**

Cumulative gross pay _____

Less cumulative allowable deductions (above) _____

Cumulative pay for tax purposes _____

Tax code used _____ Tax basis _____

Adjustment for tax code _____

Cumulative net taxable pay _____

Tax calculation _____

_____

_____

Cumulative tax due _____

Less tax already paid _____

Tax due for May 2009 _____

**NICs calculation**                    NI table letter used _____

Employee's contributions payable _____

_____

_____

Employer's contributions payable _____

_____

_____

AAT EXAM PAPER 3 (JUNE 2007)

**Payslip for May 2009**

| Employee: Kristina Strieff | | Date: 31 May 2009 |

| Payments £ | Deductions £ | Cumulatives £ |
|---|---|---|
| Basic pay: | Income tax: | Gross pay: |
| | NIC: | Pay for tax purposes: |
| | Charitable Giving: | Income tax: |
| | Personal pension: | Employee's NIC: |
| | Student loan: | Employer's NIC: |
| | | Charitable Giving: |
| | | Personal pension: |
| | | Student loan: |
| **Total gross pay:** | **Total deductions:** | **Net pay:** |

NI Number: HZ638756A    Tax code: 543L

237

## Data

You have the following information.

**Payroll summary – April 2009 pay run**

|  |  | £ | £ |
|---|---|---:|---:|
| **Pay items:** | Salaries | 482,685.78 | |
|  | Overtime payments | 63,132.95 | |
|  | Commissions | 5,750.00 | |
|  | SSP | 1,316.94 | |
|  | SMP | 17,862.23 | |
|  | SAP | 217.70 | |
|  |  |  | 570,965.60 |
| **Deductions:** | Income tax | 76,327.73 | |
|  | NIC | 58,083.85 | |
|  | Student loans | 18,862.00 | |
|  | Company pension contributions | 34,257.94 | |
|  | AVC | 1,750.00 | |
|  | Charitable Giving | 8,627.75 | |
|  | Staff loans | 5,863.50 | |
|  | Personal pension contributions | 272.00 | |
|  | Sports and social club | 2,786.00 | |
|  |  |  | 206,830.77 |
| **Employer payments:** | Employer's NI | 67,912.65 | |
|  | Company pension scheme | 68,515.88 | |
|  | Charitable Giving matched payment | 8,627.75 | |
|  |  |  | 145,056.28 |

**Note:**
The company cannot reclaim any of the SSP it has paid out. It reclaims 92% of all SAP and SMP it has paid to employees.

### Task 1.2

From the information given above, calculate the following:

(a) the total gross cost of April's payroll
(b) the total net payment due to the Collector of Taxes
(c) the total net pay to be paid to the company's employees

**Note:**
Use the space on pages 17 and 18 to list the component parts and the total of each of the above.

**Calculation of gross costs and distributions – April 2009**

(a)  Gross cost of April's payroll:

(b)  Payment due to the Collector of Taxes:

**(c)   Net pay to employees:**

## Section 2

You should spend about **50 minutes** on this section.

Write in the space provided, tick the appropriate box **OR** circle the correct answer. Do not give your answer in any other way. In each case, tick or circle **ONE** box only.

Answer all the questions on 20 to 26.

### Task 2.1

(a) **When, legally, must you supply an employee with an itemised payslip?**

☐ At the end of the pay period

☐ On or before pay day

☐ When they are ready for collection

(b) **Who is entitled to an itemised payslip?**

☐ Full time employees only

☐ Every employee who has been paid

☐ Employees who have paid income tax and NIC

☐ Anyone who asks for a payslip

### Task 2.2

Three types of personal allowance or tax code are issued by HMRC. There is the standard 'suffix' code, for example 647L, the special 'prefix' code, for example 'K' codes and finally there is 'BR'.

(a) **Explain the difference between the way suffix and the prefix K codes operate when calculating taxable pay.**

_____

_____

_____

_____

(b) **Which one of the following is the 2009/2010 emergency tax code?**

☐ 603L

☐ 647L

☐ BR

☐ 647L Wk1/Mn1

(c) What is the maximum amount of income tax that can be collected in a single pay period when a K code applies?

- ☐ 50% of the taxable pay
- ☐ 40% of the taxable pay
- ☐ 100% of the gross pay
- ☐ 50% of the gross pay

## Task 2.3

(a) Below what average monthly PAYE figure can an employer elect to pay its liability quarterly?

- ☐ £1,000
- ☐ £1,500
- ☐ £2,000
- ☐ £2,500

(b) Who are the PAYE payments made to each month or quarter?

- ☐ Treasury
- ☐ Status Inspector
- ☐ Collector of Taxes
- ☐ Inspector of Taxes

(c) What is the statutory deadline for making monthly electronic payments of PAYE?

- ☐ 6th of the month
- ☐ 14th of the month
- ☐ 19th of the month
- ☐ 22nd of the month

## Task 2.4

Operating student loan deductions is a statutory function of the employer.

(a) **There are three ways an employer can be notified that a student loan deduction is to commence for an employee. Name TWO of them.**

1. _____

2. _____

(b) **What is the minimum annual earnings level for an employee before a student loan deduction can be made?**

☐ £9,000

☐ £10,000

☐ £12,000

☐ £15,000

(c) **What sum per deduction can the employer take towards the administration costs of operating student loan deductions?**

☐ Nil

☐ 50p

☐ £1.00

☐ £2.00

## Task 2.5

A Council Tax Attachment of Earnings Order (CTAEO) is issued in order to collect outstanding council tax from an employee.

**(a)    To which one of the following would you send any sums collected from an employee?**

☐    Local Magistrates Court

☐    Local council

☐    Collector of Taxes

☐    Issuing council

**(b)    What sum per deduction can the employer take towards the administration costs of operating these deductions?**

☐    Nil

☐    50p

☐    £1.00

☐    £2.00

**(c)    Which one of the following would NOT stop the deduction of CTAEO?**

☐    Employee leaves employment

☐    Employee dies

☐    Employee withdraws authority to deduct

☐    Issuing council issues a cessation notice

## Task 2.6

Membership of a pension scheme can often affect the way income tax and NIC operate.

(a) **What NI table letter would you apply if an employee has a personal pension and there are no other factors to consider?**

☐ A

☐ C

☐ D

☐ F

(b) **What NI table letter would you apply if an employee is a member of an occupational Contracted Out Salary Related (COSR) pension scheme and there are no other factors to consider?**

☐ A

☐ C

☐ D

☐ F

(c) **Which one of the following types of pension scheme would NOT attract income tax relief when contributions are deducted from pay?**

☐ Occupational Contracted Out Defined Contributions scheme

☐ Appropriate Personal Pension Stakeholder pension scheme

☐ Contracted Out Salary Related pension scheme

☐ Contracted Out Money Purchase pension scheme

## Task 2.7

(a) **At what point does an employee cease to be liable for NICs?**

☐ When they retire

☐ When they reach State Pension Age

☐ When they declare they are no longer liable

(b) **Taking into consideration your answer to (a) above, exactly what salary payments will be exempt from NICs?**

☐ All payments in the tax year in which they cease to be liable

☐ All payments from the tax month in which they cease to be liable

☐ All payments which are made after the date when they cease to be liable

## Task 2.8

Payroll staff should operate basic controls to guard against administrative mistakes and fraud. Name THREE procedures you would follow to achieve this.

1. _____

2. _____

3. _____

## Task 2.9

(a) **Which one of the following would be permitted to receive employee information in respect of a mortgage application?**

☐ Mortgage company, if they make a written request

☐ Employee only

☐ Employee and spouse, where the spouse makes a written request

☐ Employee and anyone given written authority by the employee

(b) **A manager sends you an e-mail giving new bank account details for an employee. What would you do before you can process the bank account change for this employee?**

_____

_____

_____

_____

## Task 2.10

Employees can donate to charities of their choice using the statutory Charitable Giving or Give as You Earn (GAYE) process of deduction from pay.

(a) **Which one of the following is the maximum annual amount an employee can donate?**

☐ £120
☐ £360
☐ £720
☐ No limit

(b) **Which organisation are the deductions paid to?**

☐ Collector of Taxes
☐ The chosen charity
☐ Charities Aid Foundation
☐ An approved agency

(c) **By when must payments be made to the organisation in (b) above?**

☐ End of the pay period in which the deduction is taken
☐ End of the tax month in which the deduction is taken
☐ 19th of the month following the month of deduction
☐ 6 April following the deduction

# Answers to Practice Activities

ANSWERS TO PRACTICE ACTIVITIES

# Chapter 1 Starters and leavers

# 1 Retention

(a) Three years
(b) Six years

# 2 Paula Mell

(a) Having self-employed status means a person is more favourably treated for tax and NIC purposes. On the other hand, a self-employed person has far fewer rights under employment protection legislation (eg on dismissal), and other benefits such as holiday pay.

(b) HMRC will make up its own mind on the substance of the relationship, irrespective of its legal form. However, a number of possible criteria follows.

   (i) Does Paula work from home or have her own place of business?
   (ii) Does she use her own equipment?
   (iii) Is she entitled to holiday pay or sick pay?
   (iv) Does she, by and large, set her own work schedule?
   (v) Can she refuse to accept particular tasks of work?
   (vi) Does she work for more than one employer?

   None of these is conclusive. However, Paula's regular pattern of work for the two companies may well make her an employee of both of them.

# 3 Statutory data

- Name and title
- Address
- Date of birth
- Gender
- Pensions status
- NI number and category
- Tax code
- Starting date
- Leaving date

# 4 Change of name

As the employee is male, he can only change his name legally by deed poll. Therefore you will need a copy of the registered deed poll before changing the records. (A female can decide to change her name on marriage, in which case you would need a copy of the marriage certificate.)

ANSWERS TO PRACTICE ACTIVITIES

## 5 Filing

As there are only fifteen employees, the easiest way is to file their records in alphabetical order of surname. If two or more employees share the same surname, their record are filed in order of forenames. For example, John Smith and Joan Smith are filed in the order of Smith, Joan followed by Smith, John.

## 6 Freelance

Tell her that it is not in your power to determine if she is self-employed. Ultimately HMRC decides.

Tell her that the area is complex and there would have to be quite a significant change in her working relationship for self-employment to be accepted.

Tell her to talk to her Tax Office about the subject. You should supply the address and phone number, and give her her reference number.

# 7 Alan Wilson

**P45 Part 1**
**Details of employee leaving work**
Copy for HM Revenue & Customs

HM Revenue & Customs

File your employee's P45 online at www.hmrc.gov.uk — Use capital letters when completing this form

**1 Employer PAYE reference**
Office number / Reference number
123 / B1234

**2 Employee's National Insurance number**
AB 22 55 18 C

**3 Title** - enter MR, MRS, MISS, MS or other title
MR

Surname or family name
WILSON

First or given name(s)
ALAN

**4 Leaving date** DD MM YYYY
26 09 2009

**5 Student Loan deductions**
Enter 'Y' if Student Loan deduction is due to be made

**6 Tax Code at leaving date**
547L
If week 1 or month 1 applies, enter 'X' in the box below.
Week 1/Month 1

**7** Last entries on P11 *Deductions Working Sheet*. Complete only if Tax Code is cumulative. Make no entry if week 1 or month 1 applies, go straight to box 8.
Week number 2 5      Month number
Total pay to date
£ 3550.00
Total tax to date
£ 183.00

**8** This employment pay and tax. Leave blank if the Tax Code is cumulative and the amounts are the same as box 7.
Total pay in this employment
£
Total tax in this employment
£

**9** Works number/Payroll number and Department or branch (if any)

**10** Gender. Enter 'X' in the appropriate box
Male X    Female

**11** Date of birth DD MM YYYY
08 07 1973

**12** Employee's private address
5 RIVER STREET
DUTTON
WORCS
Postcode
DT13 9XX

**13** I certify that the details entered in items 1 to 11 on this form are correct.
Employer name and address
SHEPHERDS BRUSHES
3 LONG ROAD
DUTTON
WORCS
Postcode
DT2 3BP
Date DD MM YYYY
26 09 2009

**14 When an employee dies.** If the employee has died enter 'D' in the box and send all four parts of this form to your HMRC office immediately.

Instructions for the employer
- Complete this form following the 'What to do when an employee leaves' instructions in the Employer Helpbook E13 *Day-to-day payroll*. Make sure the details are clear on all four parts of this form and that your name and address is shown on Parts 1 and 1A.
- Send Part 1 to your HM Revenue & Customs office immediately.
- Hand Parts 1A, 2 and 3 to your employee when they leave.

P45(Manual) Part 1                                    HMRC 04/08

# ANSWERS TO PRACTICE ACTIVITIES

## 8 David Ricketts

A P45 should be prepared for all leavers. Assume that Mr Ricketts's dismissal occurred on 21 July and that he is not due any more pay from the company.

**P45 Part 1 — Details of employee leaving work (Copy for HM Revenue & Customs)**

1. Employer PAYE reference: Office number 011 / Reference number C2334
2. Employee's National Insurance number: DC 98 67 21 B
3. Title: MR; Surname: RICKETTS; First name: DAVID
4. Leaving date: 21 07 2009
5. Student Loan deductions: (blank)
6. Tax Code at leaving date: 350T; Week 1/Month 1: (blank)
7. Last entries on P11 Deductions Working Sheet:
   - Week number: 16
   - Total pay to date: £2,420.50
   - Total tax to date: £268.00
8. This employment pay and tax:
   - Total pay in this employment: £1,275.50
   - Total tax in this employment: £131.60
9. Works number/Payroll number: (blank)
10. Gender: Male X
11. Date of birth: 30 03 1970
12. Employee's private address:
    17 RIVER MANSIONS
    HADERTON
    LANCS
    Postcode: HA12 1YP
13. Employer name and address:
    GUMM BOOTS LTD
    7 WORPLE STREET
    HADERTON
    LANCS
    Postcode: HA1 2FT
    Date: 24 07 2009
14. When an employee dies: (blank)

ANSWERS TO PRACTICE ACTIVITIES

A **point to note** is that total pay to date and total tax to date (item 7 above) includes pay and tax in previous employment: these are included in the P11 running totals for Week 16. Therefore in item 8 the amounts from his joining P45 need to be deducted from the P11 totals to give the totals for **this employment**.

Part 1 of the form should be sent to the Tax Office immediately.

Parts 1A, 2 and 3 should be held until Mr Ricketts asks for them. Although the company has an address for him, it is possible that he no longer lives there, and it would be imprudent to send these parts of the P45 by post to that address.

ANSWERS TO PRACTICE ACTIVITIES

# 9 Deceased

(a)

**P45 Part 1 — Details of employee leaving work**
Copy for HM Revenue & Customs

|  |  |
|---|---|
| 1 Employer PAYE reference | 333 / C2468 |
| 2 Employee's National Insurance number | FG 23 32 45 A |
| 3 Title | MR |
| Surname or family name | WALLET |
| First or given name(s) | GERALD ANTHONY |
| 4 Leaving date | 11 11 2009 |
| 5 Student Loan deductions | (blank) |
| 6 Tax Code at leaving date | 640T |
| Week 1/Month 1 | (blank) |
| 7 Last entries on P11 — Month number | 07 |
| Total pay to date | £21000.00 |
| Total tax to date | £3452.20 |
| 8 This employment pay and tax | (blank — cumulative) |
| 9 Works number/Payroll number | 622 |
| 10 Gender | Male X |
| 11 Date of birth | 04 11 1946 |
| Further payments to be made | (noted) |
| 12 Employee's private address | MRS MARY WALLET (WIDOW), 17 CEDAR AVENUE, TOP VILLAGE, HERTS |
| Postcode | HE2 4TP |
| 13 Employer name and address | LARKS LTD, LARKS HOUSE, 5 HIGH STREET, BORTON, HERTS |
| Postcode | HE17 1JK |
| Date | 13 11 2009 |
| 14 When an employee dies | D |

P45(Manual) Part 1    HMRC 04/08

**Note:** Send all four parts to the Tax Office immediately you receive notification of the death. Since this is on 13 November, you do not wait until the end of Month 8 to complete the P45, and you should insert pay and tax details up to the latest known time, which is Month 7. You should write 'Further payments to be made' on the P45 (as shown).

(b) You do not issue a revised or further form P45. Instead you should provide Mrs Wallet with a detailed payslip showing the deductions made. You should also write to your tax office with the details of the further payment and deductions made. Remember that no NIC is due, but tax should be deducted at the basic rate (20%).

# 10 Joiners

(a) Before any further action is taken, the details in item 7 of the P45s must be checked.

|  | Ms Williams £ | Mr Smith £ |
|---|---|---|
| Tax due per tax tables | 69.40 | 86.60 |
| Per P45 | (69.40) | (89.90) |
| Discrepancy | Nil | 3.30 |

There is an incorrect entry for tax on Mr Smith's P45 and this should be noted on part 3 of his P45.

ANSWERS TO PRACTICE ACTIVITIES

**P45 Part 3**
**New employee details**
For completion by new employer

HM Revenue & Customs

File your employee's P45 online at www.hmrc.gov.uk — Use capital letters when completing this form

1. Employer PAYE reference
Office number / Reference number
152 / C3124

2. Employee's National Insurance number
AB 23 45 67 C

3. Title – enter MR, MRS, MISS, MS or other title
MS

Surname or family name
WILLIAMS

First or given name(s)
KAREN ALICE

4. Leaving date DD MM YYYY
30 04 2009

5. Student Loan deductions
☐ Student Loan deductions to continue

6. Tax Code at leaving date
379 L
If week 1 or month 1 applies, enter 'X' in the box below.
Week 1/Month 1 ☐

7. Last entries on P11 Deductions Working Sheet.
Complete only if Tax Code is cumulative. If there is an 'X' at box 6, there will be no entries here.
Week number 04    Month number ☐☐
Total pay to date
£ 640.00
Total tax to date
£ 69.40

To the new employer complete boxes 8 to 18 and send P45 Part 3 only to your HMRC office immediately.

8. New employer PAYE reference
Office number / Reference number
146 / B1323

9. Date new employment started DD MM YYYY
01 05 2009

10. Works number/Payroll number and Department or branch (if any)
351

11. Enter 'P' here if employee will not be paid by you between the date employment began and the next 5 April. ☐

12. Enter Tax Code in use if different to the Tax Code at box 6
☐☐☐☐☐☐☐☐
If week 1 or month 1 applies, enter 'X' in the box below.
Week 1/Month 1 ☐

13. If the tax figure you are entering on P11 Deductions Working Sheet differs from box 7 (see the E13 Employer Helpbook Day-to-day payroll) please enter the figure here.
£ ☐☐☐☐☐☐☐.☐☐

14. New employee's job title or job description
QUALITY CONTROLLER

15. Employee's private address
113A TOWN STREET
LITTLE SMELTING
GLOUCS
Postcode
G35 2HU

16. Gender. Enter 'X' in the appropriate box
Male ☐   Female X

17. Date of birth DD MM YYYY
12 12 1973

Declaration

18. I have prepared a P11 Deductions Working Sheet in accordance with the details above.
Employer name and address
FRY AND DICE LTD
HOME WORKS
RUDDERTON ESTATE
GLOUCESTER
Postcode
G99 1YY
Date DD MM YYYY
01 05 2009

P45(Manual) Part 3    HMRC 04/08

## ANSWERS TO PRACTICE ACTIVITIES

**HM Revenue & Customs**

**P45 Part 3**
**New employee details**
For completion by new employer

*File your employee's P45 online at www.hmrc.gov.uk*  *Use capital letters when completing this form*

**1** Employer PAYE reference
Office number  Reference number
`1 8 1 / B 2 6 9 7`

**2** Employee's National Insurance number
`L D 1 4 9 4 3 8 A`

**3** Title – enter MR, MRS, MISS, MS or other title
`MR`

Surname or family name
`SMITH`

First or given name(s)
`PETER BENJAMIN`

**4** Leaving date DD MM YYYY
`30 04 2009`

**5** Student Loan deductions
☐ Student Loan deductions to continue

**6** Tax Code at leaving date
`502 T`
If week 1 or month 1 applies, enter 'X' in the box below.
Week 1/Month 1 ☐

**7** Last entries on P11 Deductions Working Sheet.
Complete only if Tax Code is cumulative. If there is an 'X' at box 6, there will be no entries here.
Week number `04`   Month number ☐
Total pay to date
£ `820.00`
Total tax to date
£ `89.90`

*To the new employer Complete boxes 8 to 18 and send P45 Part 3 only to your HMRC office immediately.*

**8** New employer PAYE reference
Office number  Reference number
`1 4 6 / B 1 3 2 3`

**9** Date new employment started DD MM YYYY
`01 05 2009`

**10** Works number/Payroll number and Department or branch (if any)
`724`

**11** Enter 'P' here if employee will not be paid by you between the date employment began and the next 5 April. ☐

**12** Enter Tax Code in use if different to the Tax Code at box 6
☐☐☐☐☐
If week 1 or month 1 applies, enter 'X' in the box below.
Week 1/Month 1 ☐

**13** If the tax figure you are entering on P11 Deductions Working Sheet differs from box 7 (see the E13 Employer Helpbook Day-to-day payroll) please enter the figure here.
£ `86.60`

**14** New employee's job title or job description
`PERSONNEL ASSISTANT`

**15** Employee's private address
`4 CONSTABLE DRIVE`
`GLOUCESTER`

Postcode
`G22 4PQ`

**16** Gender. Enter 'X' in the appropriate box
Male `X`   Female ☐

**17** Date of birth DD MM YYYY
`29 05 1980`

**Declaration**

**18** I have prepared a P11 Deductions Working Sheet in accordance with the details above.
Employer name and address
`FRY AND DICE LTD`
`HOME WORKS`
`RUDDERTON ESTATE`
`GLOUCESTER`

Postcode
`G99 1YY`

Date DD MM YYYY
`01 05 2009`

P45(Manual) Part 3    HMRC 04/08

*For information only*

(b)

| | Tax code | Amended | | | | | | | | |
|---|---|---|---|---|---|---|---|---|---|---|
| | 502T | WK/mnth | | | | | | | | |
| | | | | K codes | | | | K codes | | K codes |
| W e e k | Pay in the week | Total pay to date | Total free pay to date | Total additional pay to date | Total taxable pay to date | Total tax due to date | Tax due at end of current period | Regulatory limit | Tax deducted in the week | Tax not deducted owing to the regulatory limit |
| | 2 | 3 | 4a | 4b | 5 | 6 | 6a | 6b | 7 | 8 |
| 1 | | | | | | | | | | |
| 2 | | | | | | | | | | |
| 3 | | | | | | | | | | |
| 4 | | 820.00 | 386.88 | | 433.12 | 86.60 | | | | |

# 11 Graduate

This activity is a straightforward test of your ability to fill in a P46. Three points to note are as follows.

(i) Ms Carlyle will be taxed on Emergency Code to begin with. This is 647L for 2009/10. By ticking Statement A, she will be taxed on a cumulative basis.

(ii) Note that she has put an 'X' in box D and so Student Loan Deductions will apply. You need to note this on the deduction card.

(iii) Use capital letters to complete the form.

ANSWERS TO PRACTICE ACTIVITIES

## HM Revenue & Customs
## P46: Employee without a Form P45

**Section one** To be completed by the employee

Please complete section one and then hand the form back to your present employer. If you later receive a form P45 from your previous employer, hand it to your present employer.
Use capital letters when completing this form.

### Your details

**National Insurance number**
This is very important in getting your tax and benefits right

Y C 6 5 7 8 9 9 B

**Title** - enter MR, MRS, MISS, MS or other title

MS

**Surname or family name**

CARLYLE

**First or given name(s)**

ROBERTA

**Gender.** Enter 'X' in the appropriate box

Male ☐   Female X

**Date of birth** DD MM YYYY

19 08 1986

**Address**
**House or flat number**

15

**Rest of address including house name or flat name**

CRESCENT LANE
WILLOWBY
BUCKS

**Postcode**

WL5 2TT

### Your present circumstances
Read all the following statements carefully and enter 'X' in **the one** box that applies to you.

**A** - This is my first job since last 6 April and **I have not** been receiving taxable Jobseeker's Allowance or taxable Incapacity Benefit or a state or occupational pension. **A** X

OR

**B** - This is now my only job, but since last 6 April **I have** had another job, or have received taxable Jobseeker's Allowance or Incapacity Benefit. I do not receive a state or occupational pension. **B** ☐

OR

**C** - I have another job or receive a state or occupational pension. **C** ☐

### Student Loans
If you left a course of Higher Education before last 6 April and received your first Student Loan instalment on or after 1 September 1998 and you have not fully repaid your Student Loan, enter 'X' in box D. *(If you are required to repay your Student Loan through your bank or building society account do **not** enter an 'X' in box D.)* **D** X

### Signature and date
I can confirm that this information is correct

**Signature**

*R. Carlyle*

**Date** DD MM YYYY

15 09 2009

P46　　　　　Page 1　　　　　HMRC 02/08

**261**

# ANSWERS TO PRACTICE ACTIVITIES

## Section two  To be completed by the employer

File your employee's P46 online at **www.hmrc.gov.uk/employers/doitonline**
Use capital letters when completing this form. Guidance on how to fill it in, including what to do if your employee has not entered their National Insurance number on page 1, is at **www.hmrc.gov.uk/employers/working_out.htm** and in the E13 Employer Helpbook *Day-to-day payroll*.

### Employee's details

**Date employment started** DD MM YYYY: 08 09 2009

**Works/payroll number and department or branch (if any):** 19

**Job title:** RESEARCH OFFICER

### Employer's details

**Employer PAYE reference**
Office number  Reference number
186 / D5432

**Employer name:** HEALTH AUDIT AGENCY

**Address**
Building number:
Rest of address: MUSSEL HOUSE
LYMM ROAD
LONDON

Postcode: EC5V 6ZP

### Tax code used

If you do not know the tax code to use or the current National Insurance contributions (NICs) lower earnings limit, go to **www.hmrc.gov.uk/employers/rates_and_limits.htm**

Enter 'X' in the appropriate box

**Box A** Emergency code on a **cumulative** basis — A: X

**Box B** Emergency code on a **non-cumulative** Week 1/Month 1 basis — B:

**Box C** Code BR — C:

**Tax code used:** 647L

If week 1 or month 1 applies, enter 'X' in this box:

**Send this form to your HM Revenue & Customs office on the first pay day.**
If the employee has entered 'X' in box A or box B, on page 1, and their earnings are below the NICs lower earnings limit, **do not send the form until their earnings reach the NICs lower earnings limit.**

Page 2

ANSWERS TO PRACTICE ACTIVITIES

## 12 Bonus after leaving

The bonus is assessed for NICs on the following basis.

(a) As a monthly payment (because Olly was a monthly paid employee and the bonus was a regular payment, otherwise the weekly table would have been used).

(b) Using Table D, as the payment was within 6 weeks of his leaving (otherwise Table A would have been used).

(c) Using the rates at the time of payment ie 15 July.

… ANSWERS TO PRACTICE ACTIVITIES

# Chapter 2: Instructions from external agencies

## 13 Verification

Before any deductions for pension contributions can be made, the employee must be a member of the scheme. On joining the scheme, the employee should complete an instruction form enabling payroll to deduct the contribution from his or her pay. The form should be placed on the employee's personal file and details noted on the employee record. Therefore you should check the employee's record card and personal file.

## 14 CSA 1

You need to note the details on Joe Johnson's personal record card and keep the order in his personal file.

**Record card extract**

*Joe Johnson*

Attachment of earnings order dated X/X/0X from CSA. Deduction £130 pm. Protected rate £350 pm.

## 15 CSA 2

You should have told Joe Johnson that the CSA can force employers to give details of an employee's pay, even when the employee has refused to co-operate with the CSA. When you receive the letter from the CSA, you must reply giving details of Joe's pay rise.

## 16 Trade union subs

Where deductions for trade union subscriptions are made under the 'check'off' system, the employer can automatically deduct subscriptions from all employees who are members of the trade union at the new rate. This is an exception to the normal rule, under which the employee would have to give specific written authority for you to vary the amount of any deductions.

In order to avoid these types of queries, the employer is supposed to advise employees of the increase **prior to deduction**. You need to explain the system to Marlene and make sure that all employees are aware of the increase.

# Chapter 3: Recording permanent payroll variations

## 17 Promotion

(a) The amount that you are authorised to pay ie £19,500 pa as stated in the personnel department's memorandum.

(b) In order to avoid future problems you should immediately send Joe a copy of personnel's memorandum. You should tell Joe that you are only authorised to pay him £19,500 pa not £20,000 pa. If he thinks that this is wrong, could he please speak to his supervisor to confirm his new rate. If it should be £20,000 pa, then perhaps both of them should go to see personnel to sort out the problem.

## 18 Overtime

Marlene is a Grade D employee. Her conditions have changed and you need to update her record file with the new rate of double time. Keep a copy of the memo with her contract of employment in her personal file.

## 19 Change of conditions

(a) 40 × £4.75 = £190 per week
(b) 35 × £5.50 = £192.50 per week

ANSWERS TO PRACTICE ACTIVITIES

# Chapter 4: Calculation of gross pay

## 20 Agreed rate

Personnel should send you details of an employee's pay and this should be in the employee's records. You can also check the details to the contract of employment (eg overtime entitlement and rates, shift allowances, etc).

## 21 Contract of employment

(a) The names of the employer and employee.
(b) The employee's job title (eg Payroll Assistant), or a description of duties.
(c) When the employee is to commence employment.
(d) How much the employee is to be paid (hourly rate, annual salary, overtime etc).
(e) When the employee is to be paid (eg weekly, two weekly, four weekly or monthly).
(f) Normal working hours (including requirement for overtime).
(g) Holiday entitlement, including any entitlement to accrued holiday pay.
(h) Notice period for leaving.
(i) Pension scheme details, if any.
(j) Disciplinary and grievance procedures.
(k) Injury and sickness terms.
(l) Place of work.

## 22 Coding

Accounts is usually part of the financial department and so the code is F01.

## 23 Commission

Joe's original contract of employment, when he was employed in sales, will have altered on moving to accounts. Personnel should have told him of the revised terms (eg higher basic salary, but no commission) before he moved departments. Explain this to Joe and, if he is still not happy, refer him to the Personnel Department.

## 24 Payment changes

First check your in-tray and filing tray to ensure that the notification of change of bank account is not there. If you can find no evidence of a change in Joe Johnson's bank account details, you should notify your supervisor, as it is possible that someone has committed a fraud. You will also need to speak to Joe to ensure that he has received his salary. If he has changed his bank account, ask him to complete the appropriate form.

ANSWERS TO PRACTICE ACTIVITIES

## 25 Payroll processing

Accuracy, timeliness, security, confidentiality.

## 26 Hourly pay

|     |                                |      £   |
|-----|--------------------------------|----------|
| (a) | 40 hours × £6.50 =             | 260      |
| (b) | 32 hours × £6.50 =             | 208      |
|     | 8 hours × £10 =                | 80       |
|     |                                | 288      |
| (c) | 40 hours × £7.50 =             | 300      |
|     | 4 hours × £7.50 =              | 30       |
|     |                                | 330      |

**Tutorial note:** All the rates paid exceed the National Minimum Wage.

## 27 Piecework

|     |                                |      £   |
|-----|--------------------------------|----------|
| (a) | 50 widgets × £5 =              | 250      |
|     | Overtime 4 hours × £4 =        | 16       |
|     |                                | 266      |
|     | (NMW: 44 × £5.80 = £255.20)    |          |
| (b) | Guaranteed minimum             | 235      |
| (c) | 34 widgets × £5 =              | 170      |
|     | So pay guaranteed minimum      | 235      |
| (d) | 1st 60 widgets × £5 =          | 300      |
|     | Next 10 widgets × £6 =         | 60       |
|     | 6 hours overtime × £4 =        | 24       |
|     |                                | 384      |
|     | (NMW: 46 × £5.80 = £266.80)    |          |

**Tutorial note:** The guaranteed minimum wage exceeds the National Minimum Wage (40 × £5.80 = £232.00).

## 28 Bonus and commission

| End of | | £ |
|---|---|---|
| January | £900 + (5% × £5,000) (December) | 1,150 |
| February | £900 + (5% × £5,000) (January) | 1,150 |
| March | £900 + (5% × £4,000) (February) | 1,100 |
| April | £900 + (5% × £3,000) (March) + £1,000 bonus (Total sales Jan-March of £12,000 exceed £10,000) | 2,050 |
| May | £900 + (5% × £2,000) (April) | 1,000 |
| June | £900 + (5% × £3,000) (May) | 1,050 |

**Tutorial note.** Total sales April to June of £9,000 do not exceed £10,000, so no one-off bonus is payable in July.

## 29 Annual

Dana's last full payday is the month ended 31 August 20X1. For the period from 1 to 15 September 20X1, you will have to calculate a part month. This will depend on your firm's policy for calculating the number of days in a working year. This could be:

(a) 365 days

(b) 261 days (if weekends are ignored) or

(c) 253 days (if weekends and Bank Holidays are ignored)

(a) $\dfrac{30,000}{365} \times 15 = £1,232.88$

(b) $\dfrac{30,000}{261} \times 10 = £1,149.43$

(c) $\dfrac{30,000}{253} \times 10 = £1,185.77$

**Tutorial note.** Under (a) all 365 days count and so 15 days are used in the calculations. For (b) and (c) only working days count and so the calculation uses 10 days.

## 30 Back pay

| | £ |
|---|---|
| Basic salary £15,000/12 | 1,250.00 |
| Overtime (175 – 156) × £10 | 190.00 |
| Productivity bonus 5% × £1,250 | 62.50 |
| | 1,502.50 |
| Back pay Jan – April (£15,000 – £12,000) × 4/12 | 1,000.00 |
| | 2,502.50 |

ANSWERS TO PRACTICE ACTIVITIES

# 31 Mary Down

(a) and (b)

|  | £ |
|---|---|
| Basic pay | 150 |
| Bonus | 30 |
| Staff suggestion award | 20 |
| Back pay | 15 |
| Overtime | 20 |
| = Gross pay | 235 |
| Income tax | (25) |
| National Insurance contribution | (10) |
| Pay advance reclaimed | (20) |
| Net pay (as on pay cheque) | 180 |

# 32 Gosplan plc 1

| PAYROLL – 20X1 WEEK 13<br>Employee | Staff number | Basic<br>£   p | Saturday & overtime<br>£   p | Total<br>£   p |
|---|---|---|---|---|
| Ashdown P | 071 | 208.00 | 104.00 | 312.00 |
| Baker K | 659 | 198.90 | 0.00 | 198.90 |
| Blair T | 660 | 184.00 | 92.00 | 276.00 |
| Callaghan J | 661 | 280.00 | 0.00 | 280.00 |
| Clarke K | 624 | 182.00 | 0.00 | 182.00 |
| Delors J | 010 | 300.00 | 90.00 | 390.00 |
| Heath E | 970 | 170.00 | 0.00 | 170.00 |
| Heseltine M | 664 | 208.00 | 7.80 | 215.80 |
| Hurd D | 663 | 230.00 | 43.13 | 273.13 |
| King T | 662 | 153.00 | 102.00 | 255.00 |
| Kinnock N | 992 | 260.00 | 61.75 | 321.75 |
| Lamont N | 666 | 166.40 | 0.00 | 166.40 |
| Lilley P | 665 | 208.00 | 0.00 | 208.00 |
| Major J | 990 | 175.00 | 80.00 | 255.00 |
| Patten C | 696 | 168.30 | 0.00 | 168.30 |
| Rifkind M | 621 | 163.20 | 81.60 | 244.80 |
| Scargill A | 917 | 230.00 | 17.25 | 247.25 |
| Thatcher M | 999 | 200.00 | 80.00 | 280.00 |
| Waldegrave W | 721 | 204.00 | 0.00 | 204.00 |
| Wilson H | 964 | 196.00 | 168.00 | 364.00 |
| TOTAL |  | £4,084.80 | £927.53 | £5,012.33 |

ANSWERS TO PRACTICE ACTIVITIES

**Workings**

1.  Ashdown, P is an Underforeman, so is paid £6.50 per hour basic.

    |  | £ |
    |---|---|
    | 32 hours at £6.50 | 208 |
    | 8 hours at (£6.50 × 2) Saturday | 104 |
    |  | 312 |

2.  Baker, K is a Templateer, and so is paid £5.10 per hour basic. Baker has worked 39 hours this week. He has not worked on Saturday.

    Baker's pay is thus £5.10 × 39 = £198.90

3.  Blair, T is in Boiler maintenance, and so earns £5.75 an hour basic.

    |  | £ |
    |---|---|
    | 32 × £5.75 | 184 |
    | 8 × (£5.75 × 2) Saturday | 92 |
    |  | 276 |

4.  Callaghan, J is an Optical Fibre Twister, and so earns £7.00 an hour. For 40 hours (weekday) he earns £280.

5.  Clarke, K is a Hopper Steerer, earning £5.20 per hour, which for 35 hours gives £182.00.

6.  Delors, J the Foreman works for 48 hours. The basic rate is £7.50. Delors did not work on Saturday.

    |  | £ |
    |---|---|
    | 40 × £7.50 basic | 300 |
    | 8 × (£7.50 × 1.5) overtime | 90 |
    |  | 390 |

7.  Heath, E is a Chargehand, at £5.00 per hour, which for 34 hours gives £170.

8.  Heseltine, M is a Hopper Steerer, and so earns basic of £5.20 per hour.

    |  | £ |
    |---|---|
    | 40 × £5.20 basic | 208.00 |
    | 1 × (£5.20 × 1.5) overtime | 7.80 |
    |  | 215.80 |

9.  Hurd, D is in Boiler maintenance who worked 45 hours at £5.75 basic.

    |  | £ |
    |---|---|
    | 40 × £5.75 basic | 230.00 |
    | 5 × (£5.75 × 1.5) overtime | 43.13 |
    |  | 273.13 |

10. King, T is a Templateer (£5.10 basic) who worked 40 hours, 10 on Saturday.

    |  | £ |
    |---|---|
    | 30 × £5.10 basic | 153 |
    | 10 × (£5.10 × 2) Saturday | 102 |
    |  | 255 |

ANSWERS TO PRACTICE ACTIVITIES

11. Kinnock, N is an Underforeman, at £6.50 per hour basic.

|  | £ |
|---|---|
| 40 × £6.50 basic | 260.00 |
| 1 × (£6.50 × 1.5) overtime | 9.75 |
| 4 × (£6.50 × 2) Saturday | 52.00 |
|  | 321.75 |

12. Lamont, N is a Hopper Steerer at £5.20 per hour basic

    32 × £5.20 basic = £166.40

13. Lilley, P is a Hopper Steerer at £5.20 an hour.

    40 × £5.20 basic = £208

14. Major, J is a Chargehand at £5.00 an hour basic.

|  | £ |
|---|---|
| 35 × £5 basic | 175 |
| 8 × (£5 × 2) Saturday | 80 |
|  | 255 |

15. Patten, C is a Templateer at £5.10 an hour basic.

    33 × £5.10 = £168.30

16. Rifkind, M is a Templateer at £5.10 an hour basic.

|  | £ |
|---|---|
| 32 × £5.10 | 163.20 |
| 8 × (£5.10 × 2) Saturday | 81.60 |
|  | 244.80 |

17. Scargill, A is in Boiler maintenance at £5.75 an hour basic.

|  | £ |
|---|---|
| 40 × £5.75 | 230.00 |
| 2 × (£5.75 × 1.5) overtime | 17.25 |
|  | 247.25 |

18. Thatcher, M is a Chargehand at £5.00 an hour basic.

|  | £ |
|---|---|
| 40 × £5 basic | 200.00 |
| 8 × (£5 × 2) Saturday | 80.00 |
|  | 280.00 |

19. Waldegrave, W is a Templateer at £5.10 an hour basic.

    40 × £5.10 basic = £204

20. Wilson, H is an Optical Fibre Twister at £7.00 an hour basic.

|  | £ |
|---|---|
| 28 × £7 | 196 |
| 12 × (£7 × 2) Saturday | 168 |
|  | 364 |

ANSWERS TO PRACTICE ACTIVITIES

# 33 Gosplan plc 2

| PAYROLL – 20X2 WEEK 20<br>Employee | Staff number | Basic<br>£ p | Overtime<br>£ p | Bonus<br>£ p | Other<br>£ p | Total<br>£ p |
|---|---|---|---|---|---|---|
| Ashdown P | 071 | 230.00 | 15.50 | 30.00 | – | 275.50 |
| Baker K | 659 | 180.00 | 25.20 | 30.00 | – | 235.20 |
| Blair T | 660 | 230.00 | 38.75 | 30.00 | – | 298.75 |
| Callaghan J | 661 | 285.00 | 46.50 | 30.00 | – | 361.50 |
| Clarke K | 624 | 180.00 | 6.30 | 30.00 | – | 216.30 |
| Delors J | 010 | 285.00 | 127.88 | 30.00 | 30.00 | 472.88 |
| Heath E | 970 | 180.00 | 6.30 | 30.00 | – | 216.30 |
| Heseltine M | 664 | 180.00 | 44.10 | 30.00 | – | 254.10 |
| Hurd D | 663 | 230.00 | 77.50 | 30.00 | – | 337.50 |
| King T | 662 | 180.00 | 44.10 | 30.00 | – | 254.10 |
| Kinnock N | 992 | 230.00 | 96.88 | 30.00 | – | 356.88 |
| Lamont N | 666 | 180.00 | 18.90 | 30.00 | – | 228.90 |
| Lilley P | 665 | 180.00 | 31.50 | 30.00 | – | 241.50 |
| Major J | 990 | 180.00 | 31.50 | 30.00 | – | 241.50 |
| Patten C | 696 | 180.00 | 12.60 | 30.00 | – | 222.60 |
| Rifkind M | 621 | 180.00 | – | 30.00 | – | 210.00 |
| Scargill A | 917 | 230.00 | 62.00 | 30.00 | 50.00 | 372.00 |
| Thatcher M | 999 | 180.00 | 37.80 | 30.00 | – | 247.80 |
| Waldegrave W | 721 | 180.00 | 37.80 | 30.00 | – | 247.80 |
| Wilson H | 964 | 285.00 | 9.30 | 30.00 | – | 324.30 |
| TOTAL | | 4,165.00 | 770.41 | 600.00 | 80.00 | 5,615.41 |

**Workings**

1. For the basic pay, just check the grades and write down the weekly standard for the grade.

2. Overtime (hours × rate)

|  |  | £ |
|---|---|---|
| 1. | Ashdown, Grade B (37 – 35) × £7.75 | 15.50 |
| 2. | Baker, Grade C (39 – 35) × £6.30 | 25.20 |
| 3. | Blair, Grade B (40 – 35) × £7.75 | 38.75 |
| 4. | Callaghan, Grade A (40 – 35) × £9.30 | 46.50 |
| 5. | Clarke (C) (36 – 35) × £6.30 | 6.30 |
| 6. | Delors (A) ((48 – 45) × £9.30 × 1.25) + ((45 - 35) × £9.30) | 127.88 |
| 7. | Heath (C) (36 – 35) × £6.30 | 6.30 |
| 8. | Heseltine (C) (42 – 35) × £6.30 | 44.10 |
| 9. | Hurd (B) (45 – 35) × £7.75 | 77.50 |
| 10. | King (C) (42 – 35) × £6.30 | 44.10 |
| 11. | Kinnock (B) ((47 – 45) × £7.75 × 1.25) + ((45 – 35) × £7.75) | 96.88 |
| 12. | Lamont (C) (38 – 35) × £6.30 | 18.90 |
| 13. | Lilley (C) (40 – 35) × £6.30 | 31.50 |

|     |     |                              | £     |
| --- | --- | ---------------------------- | ----- |
| 14. |     | Major (C) (40 – 35) × £6.30  | 31.50 |
| 15. |     | Patten (C) (37 – 35) × £6.30 | 12.60 |
| 16. |     | Rifkind (C) (35 – 35) × £6.30 | NIL  |
| 17. |     | Scargill (B) (43 – 35) × £7.75 | 62.00 |
| 18. |     | Thatcher (C) (41 – 35) × £6.30 | 37.80 |
| 19. |     | Waldegrave (C) (41 – 35) × £6.30 | 37.80 |
| 20. |     | Wilson (A) (36 – 35) × £9.30 | 9.30  |

3. Group bonus scheme

The bonus per employee is ((1,120 – 1,000) × £5)/20 = £30 each

# 34 Design

The **payroll proforma** needs to be redesigned. It needs a column showing the grade of each employee, a column for the number of basic hours, and a column for the number of hours at each overtime rate. The **timesheet summary** should also show the total number of hours at each rate for each employee as well as an overall total. In fact this company has enough employees for it to be cost effective to **computerise** the system, given the amount of calculation required and the potential for error.

ANSWERS TO PRACTICE ACTIVITIES

# Chapter 5: Statutory pay entitlements

## 35 Sick pay

Assuming that Joe normally works five days a week, then the self certification is sufficient for the first week. However, under the firm's rules, Joe needs to supply a doctor's certificate for the second week. You need to contact Joe to tell him that you can pay him occupational sick pay for the first week, but you will need a doctor's certificate for the second week. If he does not provide a doctor's certificate for the second week, then he will not be paid for that week.

## 36 SSP

The weekly rate of SSP is £79.15. The total period of illness exceeds 4 days and so a PIW is formed. K Baker had his three waiting days in week 19. Therefore the whole of his sickness in week 20 qualifies for SSP. He is due the following SSP.

$$\frac{79.15}{5} \times 3 = \underline{£47.49}$$

## 37 SMP

As this is the first week of SMP, the higher rate is paid. The question states that pay in week 20 is the same as the average over the last 8 weeks. Therefore average pay exceeds £95 per week.

SMP = 90% × £324.30 = £291.87

After the first six weeks SMP drops to the lower of 90% of average weekly earnings or £123.06. So H Maranthawalla will receive £123.06 per week for the final 33 weeks SMP.

## 38 SPP

Weekly earnings = $\frac{20,000}{52}$ = £384.62

SPP = 90% × £384.62 = £346.15, or £123.06 whichever is **lower**.

Therefore SPP = 2 × £123.06 = £246.12

## 39 SAP

Nothing. SAP is available to foster carers in certain circumstances but **not** if they apply directly to the courts for an adoption order.

**Tutorial note.** Remember to check that an employee satisfies the conditions for a statutory payment.

# Chapter 6: Income tax: simple cases

## 40 Ghost

George Ghost's taxable pay in Month 4 is as follows.

|     |     | £ |
| --- | --- | --- |
| (a) | Months 1 - 3 gross pay 3 × £1,000 | 3,000 |
|     | Gross pay in Month 4 | 1,500 |
|     | Total pay to date | 4,500 |
|     | Less free pay Months 1 - 4 | 603 |
|     | Taxable pay to date | 3,897 |
| (b) | Total tax due (table B) (760.00 + 19.40) | 779.40 |
|     | Less tax paid to date | 509.40 |
|     | Tax to be paid | 270.00 |

## 41 Tax code

A tax code tells you how much tax-free pay a person is entitled to. HMRC will send a Form P6(T) to advise an employer of an individual's tax code. They will also instruct employers to change employees' codes at the beginning of a new tax year. The code is also shown on the P45 which a new employee should give you.

## 42 Emergency code

The emergency code is a code giving only the personal allowance. It should be used in some cases where you do not know an employee's tax code. For the tax year 2009/10, the emergency code is 647L. The emergency code can be used on a cumulative or week 1/month 1 basis, depending on the employee's circumstances (ie which boxes have been ticked on form P46).

## 43 Tax calculations

You look up the total for the Week or Month in Table C, and add it to the amount calculated from Table D.

ANSWERS TO PRACTICE ACTIVITIES

## 44 Ralph Thomas

|  |  | 8th April<br>Week 1<br>472T | 15th April<br>Week 2<br>472T | 22nd April<br>Week 3<br>472T |
|---|---|---|---|---|
| (a) | Tax code |  |  |  |
|  |  | £ | £ | £ |
|  | Pay in the week | 240.60 | 290.30 | 260.00 |
|  | Total pay to date | 240.60 | 530.90 | 790.90 |
|  | Free pay (Tables A) to date | 90.95 | 181.90 | 272.85 |
|  | Taxable pay to date | 149.65 | 349.00 | 518.05 |
|  | Use Table B if pay does not exceed | £720.00 | £1,439.00 | £2,158.00 |
|  | Taxable Pay Table to use | B | B | B |
|  |  | £ | £ | £ |
|  | Tax due to date per Table B |  |  |  |
|  | On £100/£300/£500 | 20.00 | 60.00 | 100.00 |
|  | On £49/£49/£18 | 9.80 | 9.80 | 3.60 |
|  |  | 29.80 | 69.80 | 103.60 |
|  | Total tax deducted in the week | 29.80 | 40.00 | 33.80 |

(b)

| | Tax code | | Amended | | | | | | | |
|---|---|---|---|---|---|---|---|---|---|---|---|
| | 472T | | WK/mnth | | | | | | | |
| | | | | K codes | | | | K codes | | | K codes |
| Week | Pay in the week | Total pay to date | Total free pay to date | Total additional pay to date | Total taxable pay to date | Total tax due to date | Tax due at end of current period | Regulatory limit | Tax deducted in the week | Tax not deducted owing to the regulatory limit |
| | 2 | 3 | 4a | 4b | 5 | 6 | 6a | 6b | 7 | 8 |
| 1 | 240.60 | 240.60 | 90.95 | | 149.65 | 29.80 | | | 29.80 | |
| 2 | 290.30 | 530.90 | 181.90 | | 349.00 | 69.80 | | | 40.00 | |
| 3 | 260.00 | 790.90 | 272.85 | | 518.05 | 103.60 | | | 33.80 | |

ANSWERS TO PRACTICE ACTIVITIES

# 45 Barbara Walton

(a)

|  | End of April Month 1 £ | End of May Month 2 £ |
|---|---|---|
| Pay in the month | 3,600.00 | 3,600.00 |
| Total pay to date | 3,600.00 | 7,200.00 |
| Tax free pay, Tables A Codes 5 + boxed 500 | 421.59 (4.92 + 416.67) | 843.18 (9.84 + 833.34) |
| Taxable pay to date | 3,178.41 | 6,356.82 |
| Limitation on use of Table B | £3,117.00 | £6,234.00 |
| Taxable Pay Tables to use | C and D | C and D |
|  | £ | £ |
| Taxable pay (ignoring pence) | 3,178 | 6,356 |
| Taxable at basic rate (Table C) | 3,117 | 6,234 |
| Taxable at higher rate (Table D) | 61 | 122 |

|  |  | £ | £ |
|---|---|---|---|
| At basic rate, Table C | On £3,117/£6,234 | 623.46 | 1,246.93 |
| Table D | On £61/£122 | 24.40 | 48.80 |
| Total tax to date |  | 647.86 | 1,295.73 |
| Tax due in month |  | £647.86 | £647.87 |

(b)

| | Tax code | | Amended | | | | | K codes | | | K codes | | K codes |
|---|---|---|---|---|---|---|---|---|---|---|---|---|---|
| | 505T | | WK/mnth | | | | | | | | | | |
| | | | | K codes | | | | | | | | | |
| Month | Pay in the month | Total pay to date | Total free pay to date | Total additional pay to date | Total taxable pay to date | Total tax due to date | Tax due at end of current period | Regulatory limit | Tax deducted in the month | Tax not deducted owing to the regulatory limit |
| | 2 | 3 | 4a | 4b | 5 | 6 | 6a | 6b | 7 | 8 |
| 1 | 3,600.00 | 3,600.00 | 421.59 | | 3,178.41 | 647.86 | | | 647.86 | |
| 2 | 3,600.00 | 7,200.00 | 843.18 | | 6,356.82 | 1,295.73 | | | 647.87 | |

# 46 Burnham Peters Ltd

The most important point to remember is that enquiries about pay must be treated with the utmost courtesy. People do a job to earn money, and if they are worried about their pay, they will be unhappy at their work. When you have answered their query, they should feel comfortable with the idea of speaking to you again, if problems arise in the future.

Our answers are quite full ones: you need only have given the gist of what we say.

ANSWERS TO PRACTICE ACTIVITIES

(a) *Ellen Priestley.* You need to tell her that, unfortunately, she is subject to PAYE income tax on her earnings, even though she is a pensioner. If she is 65 or over her tax code will be higher because of her age, so she pays less tax than a young person. It is the law that an employer should tax employees who are pensioners according to the appropriate tax code. (A pensioner is not required to pay National Insurance contributions, but that is not the subject of this activity.)

You should suggest to Ellen that she should get the Tax Office to check her tax coding. Give her the address and telephone number of the Tax Office, and suggest that she contacts them.

(b) *Tina Gonzalez.* You will obviously be sympathetic because the agency is not paying Tina on time. Unfortunately, you have to tell her that, because she is an agency worker, the agency is her 'official employer'. You can speak to your supervisor, who might be able to put some pressure on the agency to start paying Tina more promptly than in the past. Alternatively, the company may talk to Tina's agency about taking Tina on permanently. In this case, the agency may well charge the company a fee.

(c) *Bob Harkins.* A tax code BR means that all of Bob's pay will be taxable at the basic rate of 20%, and he will be entitled to no allowances at all on his pay (so there is no free pay) nor will he be taxable at the higher rate (40%). This is an unusual situation, as every individual is entitled to at least a personal allowance. It might be the case that Bob has another job, where the employer is giving him his allowances in his tax code, or is receiving a pension from a former employer. There could be other reasons why he should not be entitled to any allowances. He should be advised to telephone or write to his Tax Office. (You should give him the address and telephone number.)

(d) *Simone Michel.* Every employee should be subject to tax on income in one country or another (but not two!). When someone goes to work abroad, they might become subject to different treatment for tax purposes, but until you are told this officially by the Tax Office, Simone will still be subject to UK PAYE and National Insurance rules. Before she goes abroad, you should do the following.

 (i) Speak to your supervisor about writing to the Tax Office on Simone's behalf.
 (ii) Write to the Tax Office notifying HMRC of her change of job location.

(e) *Ali Shah.* You must tell Ali, as politely as possible, that you cannot treat him as a self-employed person if he is working for you regularly, even if only on a part-time basis, unless he can provide official confirmation of his new status from the Tax Office. He should be kept on the payroll, and PAYE income tax (and NI) deducted. You should advise him to write to the Tax Office if he is dissatisfied, and give him the address to write to (or number to telephone).

(f) *Goran Ivanov.* Goran presumably doesn't understand about PAYE, and you might need to explain the system to him very carefully. Emergency code (647L for tax year 2009/10) is a code that gives the individual the allowances of a single person (no more and no less). If he believes he is due more allowances, he should write to the Tax Office and ask for a 'revised' coding. Emergency coding is temporary, and it is probable anyway that the Tax Office is in the process of re-coding him. If he gets a higher code eventually, he will benefit from a lower tax payment on the first pay day afterwards, or might even be entitled to a refund of tax previously paid.

'Emergency' is not really a very good word to use because it sounds so alarming. You might be able to reassure people by telling them that all it means is that a 'revised' code will emerge from the Tax Office in due course. Remember that the emergency code is for a full single personal allowance. The 'proper' code may well be the same as the 'emergency' code; except that where the emergency code has been applied on a week 1/month 1 basis, the 'proper' code may be on a cumulative basis.

# Chapter 7: Income tax: more complex cases

## 47 Code and pay changes

| | Tax code | | Amended | | 130L | | | | | |
|---|---|---|---|---|---|---|---|---|---|---|
| | ~~433L~~ | | WK/mnth | | 4 | | | | | |
| | | | | K codes | | | K codes | | | K codes |
| Month | Pay in the month | Total pay to date | Total free pay to date | Total additional pay to date | Total taxable pay to date | Total tax due to date | Tax due at end of current period | Regulatory limit | Tax deducted in the month | Tax not deducted owing to the regulatory limit |
| | 2 | 3 | 4a | 4b | 5 | 6 | 6a | 6b | 7 | 8 |
| 1 | 1,250.00 | 1,250.00 | 361.59 | | 888.41 | 177.60 | | | 177.60 | |
| 2 | 1,250.00 | 2,500.00 | 723.18 | | 1,776.82 | 355.20 | | | 177.60 | |
| 3 | 1,250.00 | 3,750.00 | 1,084.77 | | 2,665.23 | 533.00 | | | 177.80 | |
| 4 | 1,250.00 | 5,000.00 | 436.36 | | 4,563.64 | 912.60 | | | 379.60 | |
| 5 | 1,250.00 | 6,250.00 | 545.45 | | 5,704.55 | 1,140.80 | | | 228.20 | |
| 6 | 1,250.00 | 7,500.00 | 654.54 | | 6,845.46 | 1,369.00 | | | 228.20 | |
| 7 | 1,250.00 | 8,750.00 | 763.63 | | 7,986.37 | 1,597.20 | | | 228.20 | |
| 8 | 1,250.00 | 10,000.00 | 872.72 | | 9,127.28 | 1,825.40 | | | 228.20 | |
| 9 | 1,250.00 | 11,250.00 | 981.81 | | 10,268.19 | 2,053.60 | | | 228.20 | |
| 10 | 1,312.50 | 12,562.50 | 1,090.90 | | 11,471.60 | 2,294.20 | | | 240.60 | |
| 11 | 1,312.50 | 13,875.00 | 1,199.99 | | 12,675.01 | 2,535.00 | | | 240.80 | |
| 12 | 1,312.50 | 15,187.50 | 1,309.08 | | 13,878.42 | 2,775.60 | | | 240.60 | |

The most likely assumptions are that Maria is paid at the end of the month (which would be normal) and that the new tax code would be used in Month 4. Also the first payment at the increased salary level would be on 31 January (in Month 10).

**Lecturer's note.** Notice how much tax is deduced in month 4. This is due to the code being applied on a cumulative basis and so back tax for months 1, 2 and 3 is collected in month 4. It is likely, in practice, that the new code would be issued on a Wk1/Mth1 basis.

## 48 Philip Phantom

(a) (i) *Week 1/Month 1 basis*

| | Month 1 £ | Month 2 £ |
|---|---|---|
| Gross pay | 1,500.00 | 2,000.00 |
| Free pay | (415.75) | (415.75) |
| Taxable pay | 1,084.25 | 1,584.25 |

ANSWERS TO PRACTICE ACTIVITIES

(ii) *Cumulative basis*

|  | Month 1 £ | Month 2 £ |
|---|---|---|
| Gross pay | 1,500.00 | 3,500.00 |
| Free pay | (415.75) | (831.50) |
| Taxable pay | 1,084.25 | 2,668.50 |

(b) (i) *Week 1/Month 1 basis*

Tax for Month 1: (£1,084 × 20%) = £216.80
Tax for Month 2: (£1,584 × 20%) = £316.80

(ii) *Cumulative basis*

Tax for month 1: (£1,084 × 20%) = £216.80
Tax for month 2: (£2,668 × 20%) – £216.80 = £316.80

These figures can also be found using Table B.

(c) (i) A code D0 indicates that no allowances are due and all pay is taxed at 40%. Remember a D code operates on a week 1/month 1 basis.

Month 1: £1,500 @ 40% = £600.00
Month 2: £2,000 @ 40% = £800.00

These amounts can also be taken direct from Table D

(ii) Code BR means that no allowances are available and no tax is payable at 40%. All pay is taxed at 20%. Remember a BR code can operate on a cumulative basis or a week 1/month 1 basis. As no week 1/month 1 indicator is shown in the question, calculate tax on a cumulative basis.

Month 1: £1,500 @ 20% = £300.00
Month 2: (£3,500 @ 20%) – £300.00 = £400.00

These amounts can be taken direct from Table B.

(iii) A code NT means that no tax is due.

Month 1: Tax is nil
Month 2: Tax is nil

(iv) A code 0T means no allowances are due, but pay is taxed normally ie at 20% and 40% as appropriate. The code operates on a cumulative basis.

Month 1: (£1,500 × 20%) = £300.00
Month 2: (£3,500 × 20%) – £300.00 = £400.00

These amounts can be taken from Table B.

(d) (i) Code BR means tax at 20%.

Month 1: £3,500 × 20% = £700.00
Month 2: £7,000 × 20% – £700.00 = £700.00

These amounts can be taken from Table B.

(ii) Code OT means tax as usual at 20% and 40% rate bands.

Month 1: (£3,117 × 20%) + (£383 × 40%) = £776.60
Month 2: (£6,234 × 20%) + (£766 × 40%) − £776.60 = £776.60

These amounts can be taken from Tables C and D.

# 49 John David Rose

Since John Rose is being taxed on a Week 1/Month 1 basis and earns a constant monthly salary, the tax computations for his pay will be the same every month (until his tax code changes in June).

(a) *For April and May*

|  | £ |
|---|---|
| Total pay for the month | 3,000.00 |
| Tax free pay (code 608 = 108 + boxed 500) − Table A Month 1 £(90.75 + 416.67) | 507.42 |
| Taxable pay | 2,492.58 |

|  | £ |
|---|---|
| On £2,492 | 498.40 |

(b) *For June*

|  | £ |
|---|---|
| Total pay to date (3 months) | 9,000.00 |
| Tax free pay (code 620 = 120 + boxed 500) − Table A Month 3 £(302.25 + 1,250.01) | 1,552.26 |
| Taxable pay | 7,447.74 |

Table B should be used.

*Tax payable in June*

|  | £ |
|---|---|
| On £7,447 | 1,489.40 |

The tax payable in June is as follows.

|  | £ |
|---|---|
| To date in June | 1,489.40 |
| To date in May (2 × £498.40) | 996.80 |
|  | 492.60 |

ANSWERS TO PRACTICE ACTIVITIES

| | Tax code | | Amended | | 620T | | K codes | | | K codes |
|---|---|---|---|---|---|---|---|---|---|---|
| | ~~608T M1~~ | | WK/mnth | | 3 | | | | | |
| | | | | K codes | | | | | | Tax not deducted owing to the regulatory limit |
| M o n t h | Pay in the month | Total pay to date | Total free pay to date | Total additional pay to date | Total taxable pay to date | Total tax due to date | Tax due at end of current period | Regulatory limit | Tax deducted in the month | |
| | 2 | 3 | 4a | 4b | 5 | 6 | 6a | 6b | 7 | 8 |
| 1 | 3,000.00 | | 507.42 | | 2,492.58 | | | | 498.40 | |
| 2 | 3,000.00 | 6,000.00 | 507.42 | | 2,492.58 | 996.80 | | | 498.40 | |
| 3 | 3,000.00 | 9,000.00 | 1,552.26 | | 7,447.74 | 1,489.40 | | | 492.60 | |

Note that the total pay to date and total tax to date (columns 3 and 6) are entered in the Month 2 row in Month 3, when John Rose changes to the cumulative basis.

# 50 Week 53

In Week 53, compute free pay on a Week 1 basis, using the same tax code for the employee as before.

|  | Week 53 £ |
|---|---|
| Pay for Week 53 | 300.00 |
| Less free pay for Week 1 | (63.45) |
| Taxable pay | 236.55 |

|  | £ |
|---|---|
| Table B applies | |
| On £200 | 40.00 |
| On £36 | 7.20 |
| Tax for Week 53 | 47.20 |

… ANSWERS TO PRACTICE ACTIVITIES

For Week 53, fill in column 7 of the P11 **before** you fill in column 6. Then column 6 is £2,460.00 + £47.20.

| Week | Pay in the week 2 | Total pay to date 3 | Total free pay to date 4a | K codes Total additional pay to date 4b | Total taxable pay to date 5 | Total tax due to date 6 | K codes Tax due at end of current period 6a | Regulatory limit 6b | Tax deducted in the week 7 | K codes Tax not deducted owing to the regulatory limit 8 |
|---|---|---|---|---|---|---|---|---|---|---|
| 47 | 300.00 | 14,100.00 | 2,982.15 |  | 11,117.85 | 2,223.40 |  |  | 47.20 |  |
| 48 | 300.00 | 14,400.00 | 3,045.60 |  | 11,354.40 | 2,270.80 |  |  | 47.40 |  |
| 49 | 300.00 | 14,700.00 | 3,109.05 |  | 11,590.95 | 2,318.00 |  |  | 47.20 |  |
| 50 | 300.00 | 15,000.00 | 3,172.50 |  | 11,827.50 | 2,365.40 |  |  | 47.40 |  |
| 51 | 300.00 | 15,300.00 | 3,235.95 |  | 12,064.05 | 2,412.80 |  |  | 47.40 |  |
| 52 | 300.00 | 15,600.00 | 3,299.40 |  | 12,300.60 | 2,460.00 |  |  | 47.20 |  |
| 53 | 300.00 | 15,900.00 | 3,362.85 |  | 12,537.15 | 2,507.20 |  |  | 47.20 |  |

# 51 Trade dispute

(a) **Paul Rodgers**

He is on strike and is not paid in Week 2. You should not fill in the P11 for him for Week 2 or compute any refund.

| | Tax code 300T | | | Amended WK/mnth | | | | | | | |
|---|---|---|---|---|---|---|---|---|---|---|---|
| Week | Pay in the week 2 | Total pay to date 3 | Total free pay to date 4a | K codes Total additional pay to date 4b | Total taxable pay to date 5 | Total tax due to date 6 | K codes Tax due at end of current period 6a | Regulatory limit 6b | Tax deducted in the month 7 | K codes Tax not deducted owing to the regulatory limit 8 |
| 1 | 250.00 | 250.00 | 57.87 |  | 192.13 | 38.40 |  |  | 38.40 |  |
| 2 |  |  |  |  |  |  |  |  |  |  |

ANSWERS TO PRACTICE ACTIVITIES

**Richard Stout**

| | Tax code | | Amended | | | | | | | |
|---|---|---|---|---|---|---|---|---|---|---|
| | 300T | | WK/mnth | | | | | | | |
| | | | | K codes | | | | K codes | | K codes |
| W e e k | Pay in the week | Total pay to date | Total free pay to date | Total additional pay to date | Total taxable pay to date | Total tax due to date | Tax due at end of current period | Regulatory limit | Tax deducted in the month | Tax not deducted owing to the regulatory limit |
| | 2 | 3 | 4a | 4b | 5 | 6 | 6a | 6b | 7 | 8 |
| 1 | 200.00 | 200.00 | 57.87 | | 142.13 | 28.40 | | | 28.40 | |
| 2 | 50.00 | 250.00 | 115.74 | | 134.26 | 26.80 | | | (1.60) R | |

(b) The refund should not be paid during the lay-off, but Richard Stout's P11 should be filled in.

The refund should be paid on the pay day following Richard Stout's eventual return to work. By that time, more refunds might be due.

Paul Rodgers' tax refund will not be calculated until the first pay day after he returns to work. The refund will be given on that pay day.

# 52 K Codes

(a) The Tax Office assigns K codes to people when their taxable benefits are greater than the allowances that they are entitled to.

(b) 
**MEMO**

To: Carol Lewis
From: P Administrator
Subject: PAYE income tax
Date: 10 July 20X0

Following our telephone conversation today I have looked into the sudden change in the amount of PAYE income tax deducted from your salary.

The calculations have been done correctly. The increase in tax is due to a change in your tax code which was notified to us last month. As these matters depend on personal circumstances, we are simply told what figures to use. The Tax Office should have notified you separately of this change and provided an explanation.

The tax code number determines the amount of adjustment to basic pay before calculating the tax due, both to give credit for personal tax allowances and to ensure that tax is collected on taxable benefits such as company cars. You have been given a code K321. This means that, according to HMRC's records, the amount of your taxable benefits exceeds the amount of your allowances by about £3,215.

ANSWERS TO PRACTICE ACTIVITIES

Unless we are notified of a further change, this means that in future income tax will be payable on an amount in addition to your basic salary each month. However, the maximum amount of income tax that can be deducted each month is 50% of your gross pay (ie your pay excluding benefits).

Please contact me again if I can be of further assistance. If you need to contact the Tax Office about this, their address (and your reference, which you should quote in any correspondence) is as follows:

Address of Tax Office

Employee's reference number

(c) You should certainly not leave the memo anywhere where it can be read by other people because this is a confidential matter. You should institute whatever procedure is used to deliver confidential messages in your organisation - perhaps use a sealed envelope and mark it 'Private and Confidential'.

(d) It is bad practice to leave any task unfinished, because you might forget to come back to it. In any case, since the information is to hand and fresh in your mind, now is the best time to deal with it.

# 53 Mushtaq Ahmed

**Note**: Did you check the monthly limits? You should have used Tables C and D.

| | Tax code | | Amended | | | | | | | |
| --- | --- | --- | --- | --- | --- | --- | --- | --- | --- | --- |
| | K149 | | WK/mnth | | | | | | | |
| | | | | K codes | | | K codes | | | K codes |
| Month | Pay in the month | Total pay to date | Total free pay to date | Total additional pay to date | Total taxable pay to date | Total tax due to date | Tax due at end of current period | Regulatory limit | Tax deducted in the month | Tax not deducted owing to the regulatory limit |
| | 2 | 3 | 4a | 4b | 5 | 6 | 6a | 6b | 7 | 8 |
| 1 | 3,200.00 | 3,200.00 | | 124.92 | 3,324.92 | 706.26 | 706.26 | 1,600.00 | 706.26 | |
| 2 | 3,200.00 | 6,400.00 | | 249.84 | 6,649.84 | 1,412.93 | 706.67 | 1,600.00 | 706.67 | |
| 3 | 3,200.00 | 9,600.00 | | 374.76 | 9,974.76 | 2,119.60 | 706.67 | 1,600.00 | 706.67 | |

ANSWERS TO PRACTICE ACTIVITIES

## 54 Martin Carr

(a)

| Tax code | Amended | | |
|---|---|---|---|
| K491 | WK/mnth | | |

| Month | Pay in the month 2 | Total pay to date 3 | Total free pay to date 4a | Total additional pay to date (K codes) 4b | Total taxable pay to date 5 | Total tax due to date 6 | Tax due at end of current period (K codes) 6a | Regulatory limit (K codes) 6b | Tax deducted in the month 7 | Tax not deducted owing to the regulatory limit (K codes) 8 |
|---|---|---|---|---|---|---|---|---|---|---|
| 1 | 125.00 | 125.00 | | 409.92 | 534.92 | 106.80 | 106.80 | 62.50 | 62.50 | 44.30 |
| 2 | 125.00 | 250.00 | | 819.84 | 1,069.84 | 213.80 | 151.30 | 62.50 | 62.50 | 88.80 |

(b)

| Tax code | Amended | | |
|---|---|---|---|
| K491 Mth 1 | WK/mnth | | |

| Month | Pay in the month 2 | Total pay to date 3 | Total free pay to date 4a | Total additional pay to date (K codes) 4b | Total taxable pay to date 5 | Total tax due to date 6 | Tax due at end of current period (K codes) 6a | Regulatory limit (K codes) 6b | Tax deducted in the month 7 | Tax not deducted owing to the regulatory limit (K codes) 8 |
|---|---|---|---|---|---|---|---|---|---|---|
| 1 | 125.00 | | | 409.92 | 534.92 | | 106.80 | 62.50 | 62.50 | |
| 2 | 125.00 | | | 409.92 | 534.92 | | 106.80 | 62.50 | 62.50 | |

**No entry is made in Column 8.**

# Chapter 8: National Insurance: basic NICs

## 55 NI Tables

(a) None. People aged under 16 do not pay NICs, nor do their employers.
(b) Table C.
(c) Table D. Although she is married, she does not have a reduced rate certificate.
(d) Table A.

## 56 NICs

(a) The upper earnings limit less the earnings threshold: £844 – £110 = £734 at 11%, plus 1% on (£850 – £844).
(b) All earnings over the earnings threshold: £850 – £110 = £740 at 12.8%.

## 57 Earnings

False. There may be occasions when items are assessable for NICs but are not taxable, and vice versa. Remember that pension contributions and GAYE are deducted for PAYE but not NICs.

## 58 Knowledge

Employees normally pay NICs when earnings are paid. Form P45 doesn't include details of NICs as these are not usually cumulative. All that is needed is the NINO, which is shown on form P45. Each employer then has to decide which table letter to use, based on the employee's circumstances.

## 59 Water babies

NICs are not payable by persons under 16. His sixteenth birthday has no significance for tax purposes as he can be taxed at any age.

## 60 Harold Childe 1

To:     Harold Childe
From:   Payroll Administrator

From the age of 16 you must pay National Insurance Contributions (NICs) on your pay, if your pay is at least as high as the earnings threshold (£110 a week for the tax year 2009/10).

Your employer is required by law to deduct NICs. These are worked out using Tables supplied to us by HMRC.

ANSWERS TO PRACTICE ACTIVITIES

For pay of £120 a week, we are required to deduct £1.10 a week from your pay.

Your National Insurance Contributions are used to fund a number of social benefits. If you are ill, for example, then you can be paid Statutory Sick Pay.

# 61 Harold Childe 2

To:     Harold Childe
From:   Payroll Administrator

**Contracting out**

It is true that some people are entitled to contract out of paying full National Insurance Contributions.

Contracting out means that you pay NICs at a lower rate because you are not participating in the State Second Pension (S2P). You are only allowed to contract out if the employer runs a contracted-out occupational pension scheme of which you are a member. This usually means, of course, that you have to pay pension contributions as well as NICs.

I hope this clarifies the matter for you.

# 62 Churne Orvill

**Notes to the solution**

1.  Did you remember to fill in the NI contribution table letter at the bottom?

2.  Did you remember the procedure? Look up the employee's gross earnings in the appropriate table. If there is no exact match, take the nearest lower amount.

(a) *Diane Geness*

   We use Table A. To work out the NICs on £1,577.33, go to the next lower figure of £1,576.

(b) *Horace Inkley*

   Horace's Table changes during the year.

   For his payments up to, but not including, Week 7 he pays contributions under Table A. Once he has reached pension age he goes to Table C. He pays nothing, but Churne Orvill Ltd still contributes.

   You can fill in the totals for letter A at the bottom of the P11.

(c) *Maggie Knox*

   For Maggie Knox go to Table A and read off the figures for £380.

(d) *Silas Izewell*

   Silas Izewell, being over pension age, pays no employee's contribution. The employer, however, is still liable on all Silas Izewell's salary.

ANSWERS TO PRACTICE ACTIVITIES

Go to Table C. The fact that he gives his bonuses to charity has no effect on his NIC liability. The Month 3 bonus relates to Month 2 but is subject to NICs in the month it is paid ie Month 3.

So: Month 1: £2,300
    Month 2: £2,000
    Month 3: £2,700

## Diane Geness

### National Insurance contributions

|  |  |  | Earnings details ||||  Contribution details || Statutory payments ||||  |
|---|---|---|---|---|---|---|---|---|---|---|---|---|---|
| MONTH NO | WEEK NO | For employer's use only | Earnings at the LEL (where earnings are equal to or exceed the LEL) 1a £ p | Earnings above the LEL, up to and including the ET 1b £ p | Earnings above the ET, up to and including the UAP 1c £ p | Earnings above the UAP, up to and including the UEL 1d £ p | Total of employee's and employer's contributions 1e £ p | Employee's contribution due on all earnings above the ET 1f £ p | SSP 1g £ p | SMP 1h £ p | SPP 1i £ p | SAP 1j £ p | Student Loan Deductions 1k £ |
| 1 | 1 |  |  |  |  |  |  |  |  |  |  |  |  |
|   | 2 |  |  |  |  |  |  |  |  |  |  |  |  |
|   | 3 |  |  |  |  |  |  |  |  |  |  |  |  |
|   | 4 |  | 412 | 64 | 1,100 | 0 | 262.28 | 121.22 |  |  |  |  |  |
| 2 | 5 |  |  |  |  |  |  |  |  |  |  |  |  |
|   | 6 |  |  |  |  |  |  |  |  |  |  |  |  |
|   | 7 |  |  |  |  |  |  |  |  |  |  |  |  |
|   | 8 |  | 412 | 64 | 1,724 | 0 | 410.79 | 189.86 |  |  |  |  |  |
| 3 | 9 |  |  |  |  |  |  |  |  |  |  |  |  |
|   | 10 |  |  |  |  |  |  |  |  |  |  |  |  |
|   | 11 |  |  |  |  |  |  |  |  |  |  |  |  |
|   | 12 |  |  |  |  |  |  |  |  |  |  |  |  |
|   | 13 |  | 412 | 64 | 1,724 | 0 | 410.79 | 189.86 |  |  |  |  |  |

*Enter NIC Contribution Table letter here*

**End of Year Summary**

|   | 1a £ p | 1b £ p | 1c £ p | 1d £ p | 1e £ p | 1f £ p |
|---|---|---|---|---|---|---|
| A |  |  |  |  |  |  |
|   |  |  |  |  |  |  |

P11(1999)                                BMSD 11/98

# ANSWERS TO PRACTICE ACTIVITIES

## Horace Inkley

**National Insurance contributions**

| MONTH NO | WEEK NO | For employer's use only | Earnings at the LEL (where earnings are equal to or exceed the LEL) 1a £ p | Earnings above the LEL, up to and including the ET 1b £ p | Earnings above the ET, up to and including the UAP 1c £ p | Earnings above the UAP, up to and including the UEL 1d £ p | Total of employee's and employer's contributions 1e £ p | Employee's contribution due on all earnings above the ET 1f £ p | SSP 1g £ p | SMP 1h £ p | SPP 1i £ p | SAP 1j £ p | Student Loan Deductions 1k £ |
|---|---|---|---|---|---|---|---|---|---|---|---|---|---|
| 1 | 1 | | 95 | 15 | 70 | 0 | 16.77 | 7.75 | | | | | |
| | 2 | | 95 | 15 | 70 | 0 | 16.77 | 7.75 | | | | | |
| | 3 | | 95 | 15 | 70 | 0 | 16.77 | 7.75 | | | | | |
| | 4 | | 95 | 15 | 70 | 0 | 16.77 | 7.75 | | | | | |
| 2 | 5 | | 95 | 15 | 70 | 0 | 16.77 | 7.75 | | | | | |
| | 6 | | 95 | 15 | 70 | 0 | 16.77 | 7.75 | | | | | |
| | 7 | | 95 | 15 | 70 | 0 | 9.02 | - | | | | | |
| | 8 | | 95 | 15 | 70 | 0 | 9.02 | - | | | | | |
| 3 | 9 | | 95 | 15 | 70 | 0 | 9.02 | - | | | | | |
| | 10 | | 95 | 15 | 70 | 0 | 9.02 | - | | | | | |
| | 11 | | 95 | 15 | 70 | 0 | 9.02 | - | | | | | |
| | 12 | | 95 | 15 | 70 | 0 | 9.02 | - | | | | | |
| | 13 | | 95 | 15 | 70 | 0 | 9.02 | - | | | | | |

*Enter NIC Contribution Table letter here*     **End of Year Summary**

| | 1a £ p | 1b £ p | 1c £ p | 1d £ p | 1e £ p | 1f £ p |
|---|---|---|---|---|---|---|
| A | 570.00 | 90.00 | 420.00 | 0 | 100.62 | 46.50 |
| C | | | | | | |

P11(1999)                  BMSD 11/98

ANSWERS TO PRACTICE ACTIVITIES

## Maggie Knox

### National Insurance contributions

| MONTH NO | WEEK NO | For employer's use only | Earnings details ||||| Contribution details || Statutory payments |||| Student Loan Deductions 1k £ |
|---|---|---|---|---|---|---|---|---|---|---|---|---|---|
| | | | Earnings at the LEL (where earnings are equal to or exceed the LEL) 1a £ p | Earnings above the LEL, up to and including the ET 1b £ p | Earnings above the ET, up to and including the UAP 1c £ p | Earnings above the UAP, up to and including the UEL 1d £ p | Total of employee's and employer's contributions 1e £ p | Employee's contribution due on all earnings above the ET 1f £ p | SSP 1g £ p | SMP 1h £ p | SPP 1i £ p | SAP 1j £ p | |
| 1 | 1 | | | | | | | | | | | | |
| | 2 | | | | | | | | | | | | |
| | 3 | | | | | | | | | | | | |
| | 4 | | 380 | – | – | – | – | – | | | | | |
| 2 | 5 | | | | | | | | | | | | |
| | 6 | | | | | | | | | | | | |
| | 7 | | | | | | | | | | | | |
| | 8 | | 380 | – | – | – | – | – | | | | | |
| 3 | 9 | | | | | | | | | | | | |
| | 10 | | | | | | | | | | | | |
| | 11 | | | | | | | | | | | | |
| | 12 | | | | | | | | | | | | |
| | 13 | | 380 | – | – | – | – | – | | | | | |

Enter NIC Contribution Table letter here

**End of Year Summary**

| | 1a £ p | 1b £ p | 1c £ p | 1d £ p | 1e £ p | 1f £ p |
|---|---|---|---|---|---|---|
| A | | | | | | |
| | | | | | | |

P11(1999)　　　　　　　　　　　　　　　　　　　BMSD 11/98

**Note**: As Maggie's earnings are below the LEL of £412, we don't have to fill in a P11 for her. However, this is a useful record of her earnings for the year end reports (see Level 3).

# ANSWERS TO PRACTICE ACTIVITIES

## Silas Izewell

### National Insurance contributions

| MONTH NO | WEEK NO | For employer's use only | Earnings at the LEL (where earnings are equal to or exceed the LEL) 1a £ p | Earnings above the LEL, up to and including the ET 1b £ p | Earnings above the ET, up to and including the UAP 1c £ p | Earnings above the UAP, up to and including the UEL 1d £ p | Total of employee's and employer's contributions 1e £ p | Employee's contribution due on all earnings above the ET 1f £ p | SSP 1g £ p | SMP 1h £ p | SPP 1i £ p | SAP 1j £ p | Student Loan Deductions 1k £ |
|---|---|---|---|---|---|---|---|---|---|---|---|---|---|
| 1 | 1 | | | | | | | | | | | | |
|   | 2 | | | | | | | | | | | | |
|   | 3 | | | | | | | | | | | | |
|   | 4 | | 412 | 64 | 1,824 | 0 | 233.73 | - | | | | | |
| 2 | 5 | | | | | | | | | | | | |
|   | 6 | | | | | | | | | | | | |
|   | 7 | | | | | | | | | | | | |
|   | 8 | | 412 | 64 | 1,524 | 0 | 195.33 | - | | | | | |
| 3 | 9 | | | | | | | | | | | | |
|   | 10 | | | | | | | | | | | | |
|   | 11 | | | | | | | | | | | | |
|   | 12 | | | | | | | | | | | | |
|   | 13 | | 412 | 64 | 2,224 | 0 | 284.93 | - | | | | | |

*Enter NIC Contribution Table letter here*     **End of Year Summary**

|   | 1a £ p | 1b £ p | 1c £ p | 1d £ p | 1e £ p | 1f £ p |
|---|---|---|---|---|---|---|
| C | | | | | | |
|   | | | | | | |

P11(1999)                                            BMSD 11/98

ANSWERS TO PRACTICE ACTIVITIES

# Chapter 9: National Insurance: advanced NICs

# 63 Exact percentage

(a) (i) *P Morris* - Table A (£2,000 a month)

| | £ |
|---|---|
| Employee's contribution (£2,000 − £476) × 11% | 167.64 |
| Employer's contribution: (£2,000 − £476) × 12.8% | 195.07 |

(ii) *B Jones* – Table A (£150 a week)

| | £ |
|---|---|
| Employee's contribution (£150 − £110) × 11% | 4.40 |
| Employer's contribution (£150 − £110) × 12.8% | 5.12 |

(iii) *F Sanders* – Table A (£98 a week)

| | £ |
|---|---|
| Employee's contribution not required; earnings below threshold | Nil |
| Employer's contribution not required; earnings below threshold | Nil |

However, a deduction card is needed as earnings exceed the LEL of £95 per week

(iv) *J Jellicoe* – Table A (£880 a week)

| | £ |
|---|---|
| Employee's contribution: (£844 − £110) × 11%; (£880 − £844) × 1% | 81.10 |
| Employer's contribution (£880 − £110) × 12.8% | 98.56 |

(v) *F Majid* - Table B (£115 a week)

| | £ |
|---|---|
| Employee's contribution (£115 − £110) × 4.85% | 0.24 |
| Employer's contribution (£115 − £110) × 12.8% | 0.64 |

(b)

| Name | Column 1a £ | Column 1b £ | Column 1c £ | Column 1d £ | Column 1e £ | Column 1f £ |
|---|---|---|---|---|---|---|
| P Morris | 412 | 64 | 1,524 | - | 362.71 | 167.64 |
| B Jones | 95 | 15 | 40 | - | 9.52 | 4.40 |
| F Sanders | 95 | 3 | - | - | - | - |
| J Jellicoe | 95 | 15 | 660 | 74 | 179.66 | 81.10 |
| F Majid | 95 | 15 | 15 | - | 0.88 | 0.24 |

**Note**: For J Jellicoe, did you remember that the column 1d figure is for earnings up to the UEL? So on this line the total of 1a + 1b + 1c + 1d = £844, not £880.

ANSWERS TO PRACTICE ACTIVITIES

## 64 COSRS

Although Penny does not have to pay tax on her pension contribution, the amount she contributes is still included in **gross pay for NIC purposes.** Therefore her pay is £3,700 for NIC.

Contracting out means that earnings between the earnings threshold (ET) and upper accrual point (UAP) are assessed for reduced employee's contributions.

The employer reverts to the normal rate beyond the UAP but pays a reduced rate on earnings between the earnings threshold and the UAP. Both employee and employer get a rebate on earnings between the LEL and the earnings threshold.

**Workings**

|  | £ |
|---|---:|
| *Employer's contributions* | |
| On earnings above UAP: (£3,700 − £3,337) × 12.8% | 46.46 |
| On earnings between ET and UAP: (£3,337 − £476) × 9.1% | 260.35 |
| Employer's rebate: (£476 − £412) × 3.7% | (2.37) |
| | 304.44 |
| *Employee's contributions* | |
| (£3,700 − £3,656) × 1% | 0.44 |
| (£3,656 − £3,337) × 11% | 35.09 |
| (£3,337 − £476) × 9.4% | 268.93 |
| Employee's rebate: (£476 − £412) × 1.6% | (1.02) |
| | 303.44 |
| Total of employee's and employer's contributions | 607.88 |

*Summary*

Per exact percentage calculations

| 1a | 1b | 1c | 1d | 1e | 1f |
|---|---|---|---|---|---|
| 412 | 64 | 2,861 | 319 | 607.88 | 303.44 |

## ANSWERS TO PRACTICE ACTIVITIES

**National Insurance contributions**

| MONTH NO | WEEK NO | For employer's use only | Earnings at the LEL (where earnings are equal to or exceed the LEL) 1a £ p | Earnings above the LEL, up to and including the ET 1b £ p | Earnings above the ET, up to and including the UAP 1c £ p | Earnings above the UAP, up to and including the UEL 1d £ p | Total of employee's and employer's contributions 1e £ p | Employee's contribution due on all earnings above the ET 1f £ p | SSP 1g £ p | SMP 1h £ p | SPP 1i £ p | SAP 1j £ p | Student Loan Deductions 1k £ |
|---|---|---|---|---|---|---|---|---|---|---|---|---|---|
| 1 | 1 | | | | | | | | | | | | |
|   | 2 | | | | | | | | | | | | |
|   | 3 | | | | | | | | | | | | |
|   | 4 | | 412 | 64 | 2,861 | 319 | 607.88 | 303.44 | | | | | |
| 2 | 5 | | | | | | | | | | | | |
|   | 6 | | | | | | | | | | | | |
|   | 7 | | | | | | | | | | | | |
|   | 8 | | | | | | | | | | | | |
| 3 | 9 | | | | | | | | | | | | |
|   | 10 | | | | | | | | | | | | |
|   | 11 | | | | | | | | | | | | |
|   | 12 | | | | | | | | | | | | |
|   | 13 | | | | | | | | | | | | |

ANSWERS TO PRACTICE ACTIVITIES

# Chapter 10: Other deductions

# 65 Gilberta Sullivan

**MEMO**

To: Gilberta Sullivan
From: A Payroll Clerk
Subject: Gross and net pay

Gross pay is all the income you have earned for the work you have done. Gross pay comprises basic pay, overtime, bonuses, commission, holiday pay, statutory sick pay and statutory maternity pay. Net pay is gross pay minus deductions, like income tax, NICs, pension contributions, season ticket loan repayments and advances of pay.

Tax and NICs are calculated on gross pay following rules laid down by HMRC. Some deductions from gross pay (like Give As You Earn and pension contributions) reduce the amount of tax due.

A deduction from pay after tax reduces the amount of your pay cheque, but does not affect the tax computation. Loan repayments fall into this category.

# 66 Groddy Ltd

(a) Charles Kingsley does not need a P11 for the following reasons.

   (i) He is too young (under 16) for NICs.

   (ii) He earns less than the basic level at which NICs and income tax are payable. The earnings threshold for tax and NICs is £110 per week (2009/10).

   Note down his name, NI number and earnings, and send in the details at the end of the year. Keep his P46 and ensure that he signs it as a school leaver. He will need a P11 after the age of 16, as his earnings exceed the LEL of £95 per week and the P46 must then be sent to HMRC.

(b) Freddie Scullion should be given form P38(S) to sign to state that he is a student in full time education and that his income for the year to the following 5 April will be less than the personal allowance. Then no tax needs to be deducted.

   However, NICs are still relevant for Freddie. As his weekly earnings (£98) are above the lower earnings limit (£95), a P11 will have to be prepared, but no contributions are due until his salary exceeds the earnings threshold of £110.

(c) Oliver Spend works for one evening a week during term time. In this case, his status as a student is irrelevant. Tax and NICs must be deducted if he earns enough. He does not at the moment (provided that he has signed a P46 stating that he doesn't have another job), so just note down his name, NI number and earnings.

ANSWERS TO PRACTICE ACTIVITIES

# 67 Gill Tee Ltd

(a) See the form below.

(b) (i) Elizabeth Windsor is obviously a higher rate tax payer so each month she is saving:

£15 × 40% = £6

(ii) Elizabeth Windsor saves nothing in NICs, as GAYE is only deducted from earnings for tax purposes, *not* for NIC purposes.

```
                    INSTRUCTIONS FOR SUBMITTING DONATIONS
1. Quote your CONTRACT NUMBER and PAYROLL NAME on all documentation.
2. Check that the Employee identification number on each Charity Choice Form is correct.
3. Check that the Employee identification number which you quote on your monthly deduction
   list is also the same on the Charity Choice form.
4. Send us the completed TOP SECTION of the Charity Choice form AND keep a copy or the yellow
   carbonated copy on your file for future reference.
5. Please arrange for your monthly lists to be in this format or PHOTOCOPY FREELY and write or
   type the information required.
6. Please arrange for your monthly lists to show the MONTH OF DEDUCTION where possible.
7. Please submit donations by cheque. Other means of payment should be agreed with Give As
   You Earn prior to any change.
8. Please arrange for all Give As You Earn documentation to come to us in one monthly packet.
9. Use this as an example of the format needed for computer printouts.
10. It will help us if we could have both these numbers. If this poses a problem, please submit
    one or the other (see * overleaf).
```

GIVE AS YOU EARN EMPLOYEE DONATIONS     PAYLISTING/DEDUCTION STATEMENT

CONTRACT NUMBER: 9752
MONTH OF DEDUCTION: March 2010
PAYROLL NAME/ID/CODE: N/A

EMPLOYER NAME: GILL TEE LTD
EMPLOYER ADDRESS: Workhouse Buildings
Almshouse Lane
Workington

| NI NUMBER AND PAYROLL NUMBER | DONATION | NAME | STARTER/LEAVER |
|---|---|---|---|
| QE201649C  02 | 15 | Windsor, E. | — |
| AJ999999D  07 | 15 | Ayre, M. | — |
| KE777777B  03 | 20 | Croesus, R.S.I. | — |
| ON222222A  33 | 20 | Pope, B. | — |

PAGE TOTAL: 70
OPTIONAL 5% ADMIN: —
REMITTANCE ENCLOSED: 70    MUST AGREE WITH ENCLOSED CHEQUE

## ANSWERS TO PRACTICE ACTIVITIES

# 68 Sandy Shore

(a) **National Insurance contributions**

| MONTH NO | WEEK NO | For employer's use only | Earnings at the LEL (where earnings are equal to or exceed the LEL) 1a £ p | Earnings above the LEL, up to and including the ET 1b £ p | Earnings above the ET, up to and including the UAP 1c £ p | Earnings above the UAP, up to and including the UEL 1d £ p | Total of employee's and employer's contributions 1e £ p | Employee's contribution due on all earnings above the ET 1f £ p | SSP 1g £ p | SMP 1h £ p | SPP 1i £ p | SAP 1j £ p | Student Loan Deductions 1k £ |
|---|---|---|---|---|---|---|---|---|---|---|---|---|---|
| 1 | 1 | | 95 | 15 | 57 | 0 | 13.57 | 6.27 | | | | | |
|   | 2 | | 95 | 15 | 15 | 0 | 3.57 | 1.65 | | | | | |
|   | 3 | | 95 | 15 | 15 | 0 | 3.57 | 1.65 | | | | | |
|   | 4 | | | | | | | | | | | | |
| 2 | 5 | | | | | | | | | | | | |
|   | 6 | | | | | | | | | | | | |
|   | 7 | | | | | | | | | | | | |
|   | 8 | | | | | | | | | | | | |
| 3 | 9 | | | | | | | | | | | | |
|   | 10 | | | | | | | | | | | | |
|   | 11 | | | | | | | | | | | | |
|   | 12 | | | | | | | | | | | | |
|   | 13 | | | | | | | | | | | | |

Enter NIC Contribution Table letter here

**End of Year Summary**

| | 1a £ p | 1b £ p | 1c £ p | 1d £ p | 1e £ p | 1f £ p |
|---|---|---|---|---|---|---|
| A | | | | | | |
| | | | | | | |

# ANSWERS TO PRACTICE ACTIVITIES

P11(1999)  BMSD 11/98

| | Tax code | | Amended | | | | | | | | |
|---|---|---|---|---|---|---|---|---|---|---|---|
| | 419T | | WK/mnth | | | | | | | | |
| | | | | K codes | | | | K codes | | K codes | |
| W e e k | Pay in the week | Total pay to date | Total free pay to date | Total additional pay to date | Total taxable pay to date | Total tax due to date | Tax due at end of current period | Regulatory limit | Tax deducted in the week | Tax not deducted owing to the regulatory limit | Tax Credits |
| | 2 | 3 | 4a | 4b | 5 | 6 | 6a | 6b | 7 | 8 | 9 |
| 1 | 167.00 | 167.00 | 80.75 | | 86.25 | 17.20 | | | 17.20 | | |
| 2 | | | | | | | | | | | |
| 3 | 250.00 | 417.00 | 242.25 | | 174.75 | 34.80 | | | 17.60 | | |

**Notes**

*NICs*

NICs are recorded on a payment by payment basis; that is, even though the holiday pay is for the future it is being paid *now*. Pretend that the holiday pay is being paid at the right time, and so calculate each week separately.

*Income tax*

Here the situation is a little different. Income tax is cumulative.

Work out the tax on the holiday pay as if it had been received at the end of Week 3, and note down the amounts at the end of Week 3 on the P11. Table B should be used throughout.

|   |   | £ |
|---|---|---|
| (b) | Gross pay (ie £167 + £125 + £125) | 417.00 |
| | Less employee's NICs | (9.57) |
| | Less tax due to date (week 3!) | (34.80) |
| | Amount actually paid | 372.63 |

Note that this covers Week 1 to Week 3.

ANSWERS TO PRACTICE ACTIVITIES

## 69 Pension scheme

All are eligible *except the following*.

*A Foot* has not been in permanent full-time employment for long enough. This employee was a temporary worker (perhaps sent by an agency) for three months.

*B Quiet* has only been working for the company for 5 months so is not yet eligible.

**Note.** Although R Dworkin has left the company scheme, there is no harm in suggesting rejoining. The company scheme might offer greater security or benefits than the personal pension plan.

## 70 Panther Ltd

(a) Employee name
Date employment commenced with employer
Date joined scheme
Date left employer
Expected date of retirement
Date of reaching state retirement age
Employee NI number
Date of birth
Marital status
Sex
Amounts transferred into scheme from another scheme
Next of kin
Salary, and all increases
Contracted percentage contribution for employer and employee
Actual employee's and employer's pension contributions
AVCs
Whether or not employee is contracted out of S2P

# ANSWERS TO PRACTICE ACTIVITIES

(b)

| NAME: | A. HOPEFUL | NI NO: | WC963123X | A/C: | H0943 |
|---|---|---|---|---|---|

| SEX: M/F | M | BIRTHDATE: | 3/6/1965 |
|---|---|---|---|

| DATE JOINED COMPANY: | 15/6/2008 | DATE JOINED SCHEME: | 1/1/2009 |
|---|---|---|---|

| ESTIMATED DATE OF RETIREMENT: | 3/6/2030 | DATE LEFT SCHEME: | |
|---|---|---|---|

YEARS (cross off): ~~1~~,~~2~~,3,4,5,6,7,8,9,10,11,12,13,14,15,16,17,18,19,20,21,22,23,24,25,26,27,28,29,30,31,32,33,34,35,36,37,38,39,40

| YEAR | PENSIONABLE EARNINGS (from 1/1) | YEAR | PENSIONABLE EARNINGS (from 1/1) | YEAR | PENSIONABLE EARNINGS (from 1/1) | YEAR | PENSIONABLE EARNINGS (from 1/1) |
|---|---|---|---|---|---|---|---|
| 1 | £22,000 | 11 | | 21 | | 31 | |
| 2 | £27,500 | 12 | | 22 | | 32 | |
| 3 | | 13 | | 23 | | 33 | |
| 4 | | 14 | | 24 | | 34 | |
| 5 | | 15 | | 25 | | 35 | |
| 6 | | 16 | | 26 | | 36 | |
| 7 | | 17 | | 27 | | 37 | |
| 8 | | 18 | | 28 | | 38 | |
| 9 | | 19 | | 29 | | 39 | |
| 10 | | 20 | | 30 | | 40 | |

Pensionable earnings are earnings at 1 January of each year

**Notes**

Pensionable earnings are those at 1 January.

Year 1 (2009) Earnings at 1 January 2009 are £22,000, so these are pensionable earnings.

|  |  | £ |
|---|---|---|
| Year 2 (2010) | Basic pay at 1 January 2010 is | 14,500 |
| | Commission earned in 2009 | 13,000 |
| | Pensionable earnings 2010 | 27,500 |

(c) £22,000 × 6% = £1,320 pa or £110 per month

(d) £27,500 × 10% = £2,750 pa or £229.17 per month

(e)

| | Pensionable earnings £ | Employee (6%) £ | Employer (10%) £ | Total (16%) £ |
|---|---|---|---|---|
| 2009 | 22,000 | 1,320 | 2,200 | 3,520 |
| 2010 | 27,500 | 1,650 | 2,750 | 4,400 |
| | | 2,970 | 4,950 | 7,920 |

# 71 Harris Ltd

(a)

NAME: Jill Kernot   ACCOUNT:

| YEAR | B/F | JAN | FEB | MAR | APR | MAY | JUNE | JULY | AUG | SEP | OCT | NOV | DEC | C/F |
|---|---|---|---|---|---|---|---|---|---|---|---|---|---|---|
| 1 EMP'EE |  | 62.50 | 62.50 | 68.68 | 62.50 | 62.50 | 62.50 | 62.50 | 62.50 | 74.33 | 79.24 | 70.83 | 70.83 | 801.41 |
| 1 EMP'ER | — | 125.00 | 125.00 | 137.36 | 125.00 | 125.00 | 125.00 | 125.00 | 125.00 | 148.67 | 158.48 | 141.67 | 141.67 | 1,602.85 |
| 2 EMP'EE | 801.41 | 70.83 | 70.83 | 70.83 | 70.83 | 70.83 | 70.83 | 70.83 | 70.83 | 87.50 | 99.68 | 87.50 | 87.50 | 1,730.23 |
| 2 EMP'ER | 1,602.85 | 141.67 | 141.67 | 141.67 | 141.67 | 141.67 | 141.67 | 141.67 | 141.67 | 175.00 | 199.22 | 175.00 | 175.00 | 3,460.43 |
| EMP'EE |  |  |  |  |  |  |  |  |  |  |  |  |  |  |

**Workings**

1. Contributions in months when no overtime is worked January to August 2009

    £15,000/12 × 5% = £62.50
    £15,000/12 × 10% = £125.00

2. March 2009 10 hours overtime is paid at time and a half

    $$\frac{£15,000}{(35 \times 52)} \times 1.5 = £12.36 \text{ per hour}$$

    10 × £12.36 = £123.60

    5% × £123.60 = £6.18
    10% × £123.60 = £12.36

    These amounts are added to the basic contributions (W1).

3. September and October 2009

    £17,000/12 × 5% = £70.83
    £17,000/12 × 10% = £141.67

    Overtime hours affect the contributions in September (5 hours) and October (12 hours).

    $$\frac{£17,000}{(35 \times 52)} \times 1.5 = £14.01 \text{ per hour}$$

    *September 2009*
    5 × £14.01 = £70.05
    5% × £70.05 = £3.50
    10% × £70.05 = £7.00

    *October 2009*
    12 × £14.01 = £168.12
    5% × £168.12 = £8.41
    10% × £168.12 = £16.81

    These amounts are added to the basic calculation above (£70.83 and £141.67).

4. September 2010: £21,000/12 × 5% = £87.50 (£175 for employer)

5   October 2010 $\dfrac{£21{,}000}{(35 \times 52)} \times 1.5 \times 5\%$ = £0.87 per hour (£1.73 for employer) to be added to contributions per W4 (so £12.18 employee's and £24.22 employer's)

(b) Jill would receive back the contributions she had paid, less 20% tax. She would receive nothing in respect of the employer's contributions.

|  | £ |
|---|---|
| Contributions | 801.41 |
| Tax deducted | (160.28) |
|  | 641.13 |

(c) The contributions would be frozen. They would be used to give Jill some small pension when she retired.

Alternatively, they could be transferred to another scheme.

(d) 

**MEMO**

To:        Jill Kernot
From:    A Clerk
Subject: Additional pension contributions

If you want to increase your pension above what is already provided in your company scheme you have a number of choices.

**Additional Voluntary Contributions (AVCs)**

These can be paid to the company pension fund. You will receive tax relief on them at source. They form part of your contribution record to the company scheme, so should you leave they would make up part of the frozen pension, or transfer value to another scheme.

**Free Standing AVCs (FSAVCs) or personal pension scheme contributions**

In this case an arrangement, outside the company pension scheme, is made by you with another pension provider. The provider receives the tax relief on your behalf.

These contributions do not form part of your contribution record to the company scheme, and so will not go to make up a transfer value or frozen pension should you leave.

You can claim the relief on **total** pension contributions of up to the limit of your net earnings, subject to the annual limit (£245,000 for 2009/10).

## 72 Holmes plc

|  | £ |
|---|---|
| Per payroll   employees | 18,000 |
| employer | 30,000 |
| Total deductions | 48,000 |
| Reimburse Dr Watson | (100) |
| Registration fee 500 × 10p | (50) |
| AVC - from employee | 80 |
| Tax relief on AVC | 20 |
| Per contribution record | 47,950 |

ANSWERS TO PRACTICE ACTIVITIES

# Chapter 11: Net pay and aggregate payroll

## 73 Cash wages

(a) Put the packet in the safe.

(b) Call her over the PA system.

(c) Phone her home.

(d) 'Do you have a letter from Miss Humbert and some means of identification?'

(e) Lolita's letter has not been signed by her, and so it should be returned to her for her signature. Moreover the procedures manual requires that the representative's address on the identification is correct as well as the name, so you should ask Mr Nabokov for some other means of identification to verify the address given in Lolita's letter (which is different from that on his driving licence).

You might phone Lolita at home again, just to check the situation. If in doubt consult your supervisor.

## 74 Cash reconciliation

(a) Cash payments

| Denomination | Mr Barnet (no) | Mrs Bromley (no) | Mr Ealing (no) | Mr Kensington (no) | Mrs Wandsworth (no) | Mr Westminster (no) | Total (no) | Total (£) |
|---|---|---|---|---|---|---|---|---|
| £50 | 3 | 4 | 2 | 4 | 2 | 3 | 18 | 900.00 |
| £20 | 1 | – | 1 | 1 | 2 | – | 5 | 100.00 |
| £10 | – | 1 | 1 | 1 | – | – | 3 | 30.00 |
| £5 | 1 | – | – | – | 1 | 1 | 3 | 15.00 |
| £2 | – | 1 | 1 | 1 | 1 | 2 | 6 | 12.00 |
| £1 | – | 1 | – | – | 1 | – | 2 | 2.00 |
| 50p | 1 | – | – | 1 | – | 1 | 3 | 1.50 |
| 20p | 2 | 2 | – | 2 | – | 2 | 8 | 1.60 |
| 10p | – | – | 1 | – | – | – | 1 | 0.10 |
| 5p | – | – | – | – | – | – | – | – |
| 2p | – | 1 | – | – | 2 | – | 3 | 0.06 |
| 1p | 1 | 1 | – | 1 | – | 1 | 4 | 0.04 |
| Total (£) | 175.91 | 213.43 | 132.10 | 232.91 | 148.04 | 159.91 | | 1,062.30 |

ANSWERS TO PRACTICE ACTIVITIES

(b)

|  |  |  |  | £ |
|---|---|---|---|---|
| Cash |  |  |  | 1,062.30 |
| Cheque | 10855 | Mr Camden |  | 141.32 |
|  | 10856 | Mrs Enfield |  | 241.53 |
|  | 10857 | Mr Hackney |  | 113.95 |
|  | 10858 | Mrs Hammersmith |  | 204.11 |
|  | 10859 | Mr Haringey |  | 123.45 |
|  | 10860 | Mrs Islington |  | 67.89 |
|  | 10861 | Mrs Lambeth |  | 184.32 |
|  | 10862 | Mr Redditch |  | 166.66 |
|  | 10863 | Mr Southwark |  | 297.43 |
| Per payroll |  |  |  | 2,602.96 |

# 75 Direct credit

**MEMO**

To: A N Employee
From: A Clerk
Date: X/X/XX
Subject: Payment of wages by Direct Credit

Thank you for getting in touch with the payroll department about Direct Credit. I hope the following sets your mind at rest.

Direct Credit is a system which enables us to make wages payments by electronic transfer from our bank account directly into our employees' bank or building society accounts. It is operated by BACS, the UK's authorised payments clearing service which is owned by the major banks and building societies.

There is a minimum of paperwork. The information detailing net pay for each employee is sent to BACS via a telephone line so it can be input directly to the BACS system.

The advantages of direct credit over cash or cheques are as follows.

(a) It is much cheaper, as all the payroll department has to do is press a button, and the banks charge less for direct credit than they do for processing cheques.

(b) It is much safer, as there is no chance of cash or cheques being stolen.

(c) It is quicker, as the money does not have to be counted, nor does each cheque have to be signed, if you are paid by cheque.

(d) The money is available in your account immediately on pay day.

If you wish, you can open a building society account instead of a bank account.

The company is paying £50 (before tax and national insurance) to every employee who switches over to the BACS system. The company is also happy to help you in your arrangements for opening a bank or building society account.

# Unit 71 Sample Simulation answers

# AAT SAMPLE SIMULATION: ANSWERS

**DO NOT TURN THIS PAGE UNTIL YOU HAVE COMPLETED THE SIMULATION**

# ANSWERS (Task 1)

## Employee Payroll Record Card

| | | | |
|---|---|---|---|
| Name | James W Mason | Employee number | 00583 |
| Address | 3 Ulverston Road Midchester MI6 7SF | Bank Address | Lloyds TSB Middle Path Midchester |
| Marital Status | Single | Cost Code | S0056 |
| Date of birth | 27-08-1980 | Start date | 01-09-2009 |
| Gender | Male | Grade | SA001 |
| Bank sort code | 45-07-96 | Annual salary | £18,000.00 |
| Bank A/c number | 1856920 | Hourly rate | £9.89 |
| Building society number | | Overtime rate @ 1½ times hourly rate | £14.83 |
| Student Loan Deduction | Yes / **No** | Overtime rate @ one and one third times hourly rate | £13.19 |
| | | Overtime rate @ double time | £19.78 |
| Monthly Pension Contributions | | Tax code | 461L |
| COSR | £ | Tax basis | |
| COMP | £45.00 | *Cumulative* | **Yes** / No |
| AVC | £ | *Month1/Week 1* | Yes / **No** |
| | | N.I. category letter | F |
| Trade union deduction | £5.00 | N.I. Number | YB385720A |
| Charitable giving deduction | £ | Occupational Sick Pay | Yes/**No** |
| Health club deduction | £ | Annual Holiday Entitlement (days – excluding public holidays) | |
| Permanent Contract | **Yes**/No | Temporary Contract End Date | |
| Leaving Date | | Commission Payable | Yes/**No** |
| **P45 Joining Information** | | | |
| Pay to date | 4,863-96 | Tax to date | 587.80 |

# ANSWERS (Task 1, continued)

**Comments**
- James Mason signed to say he wanted to pay AVCs into his pension fund. This option is not open to him in the COMP scheme.
- James Mason has been told he is entitled to 20 days holiday per annum when the company rules state 25 days.

I would query these with Pam Palmer, the Personnel Manager.

## ANSWERS (Task 1, continued)

| Employee Payroll Record Card |||||
|---|---|---|---|
| Name | Jenny P Smith | Employee number | 00584 |
| Address | Bluebell Cottage<br>Midchester<br>MI5 8RE | Bank Address | Nat West<br>West Bank<br>Midchester |
| Marital Status | Divorced | Cost Code | W0114 |
| Date of birth | 02-01-1949 | Start date | 08-09-2009 |
| Gender | Female | Grade | WD003 |
| Bank sort code | 60-08-18 | Annual salary | £29,600.00 |
| Bank A/c number | 16378942 | Hourly rate | £ |
| Building society number | | Overtime rate @ 1½ times hourly rate | £ |
| Student Loan Deduction | Yes / **No** | Overtime rate @ one and one third times hourly rate | £ |
| | | Overtime rate @ double time | £ |
| Monthly Pension Contributions | | Tax code | 586T |
| *COSR* | £ | Tax basis | |
| *COMP* | £ | *Cumulative* | **Yes** / No |
| *AVC* | £ | *Month1/Week 1* | Yes / **No** |
| | | N.I. category letter | A |
| Trade union deduction | £ | N.I. Number | BA682049C |
| Charitable giving deduction | £25.00 | Occupational Sick Pay | **Yes**/No |
| Health club deduction | £25.00 | Annual Holiday Entitlement (days – excluding public holidays) | 25 |
| Permanent Contract | **Yes**/No | Temporary Contract End Date | |
| Leaving Date | | Commission Payable | Yes /**No** |
| P45 Information |||||
| Pay to date | 11,880.83 | Tax to date | 1,887.00 |

# ANSWERS (Task 1, continued)

**Comments**
- Jenny Smith – has been entered for the COSR pension scheme when she is only eligible for the COMP pension.

I would query this with Pam Palmer, the Personnel Manager.

# ANSWERS (Task 1, continued)

| Employee Payroll Record Card ||||
|---|---|---|---|
| Name | Michael B Jackson | Employee number | MBJ |
| Address | Grey Gables<br>Southchester<br>MI8 7EW | Bank Address | NatWest<br>North Street<br>Midchester |
| Marital status | Single | Cost Code | D0010 |
| Date of birth | 17-11-1963 | Start date | 08-09-2009 |
| Gender | Male | Grade | DIR002 |
| Bank sort code | 61-45-32 | Annual salary | £36,000.00 |
| Bank A/c number | | Hourly rate | £ |
| Building society number | | Overtime rate @ 1½ times hourly rate | £ |
| Student Loan Deduction | Yes / **No** | Overtime rate @ one and one third times hourly rate | £ |
| | | Overtime rate @ double time | £ |
| Monthly Pension Contributions | | Tax code | BR |
| *COSR* | £150.00 | Tax basis | |
| *COMP* | £ | *Cumulative* | **Yes** / No |
| *AVC* | £200.00 | *Month1/Week 1* | Yes /**No** |
| | | N.I. category letter | D |
| Trade union deduction | £ | N.I. Number | |
| Charitable giving deduction | £100.00 | Occupational Sick Pay | **Yes**/No |
| Health club deduction | £25.00 | Annual Holiday Entitlement (days – excluding public holidays) | 30 |
| Permanent Contract | Yes/**No** | Temporary Contract End Date | 31-12-2011 |
| Leaving Date | | Commission Payable | Yes/ **No** |
| P45 Information ||||
| Pay to date | | Tax to date | |

# ANSWERS (Task 1, continued)

**Comments**

Expect candidate to identify that:
- Michael Jackson – has no NI number; and
- He has no bank account number.

I would query both of these directly with the individual.

# ANSWERS (Task 1, continued)

| Employee Payroll Record Card |||||
|---|---|---|---|
| Name | Clint Eastwood | Employee number | 00585 |
| Address | Cuddlers Cottage<br>Southchester<br>SO21 5RT | Bank Address | Lloyds TSB<br>Middle Path<br>Midchester |
| Marital status | Single | Cost Code | WO114 |
| Date of birth | 20-02-1981 | Start date | 15-09-2009 |
| Gender | Male | Grade | SA001 |
| Bank sort code | 45-07-96 | Annual salary | £25,700.00 |
| Bank A/c number | 1469482 | Hourly rate | £ |
| Building society number | | Overtime rate @ 1½ times hourly rate | £ |
| Student Loan Deduction | Yes / **No** | Overtime rate @ one and one third times hourly rate | £ |
| | | Overtime rate @ double time | £ |
| Monthly Pension Contributions | | Tax code | K42 |
| COSR | £ | Tax basis | |
| COMP | £64.25 | *Cumulative* | Yes / **No** |
| AVC | £ | *Month1/Week 1* | **Yes** / No |
| | | N.I. category letter | F |
| Trade union deduction | £ | N.I. Number | FW266892A |
| Charitable giving deduction | £ | Occupational Sick Pay | **Yes**/No |
| Health club deduction | £25.00 | Annual Holiday Entitlement (days – excluding public holidays) | 25 |
| Permanent Contract | **Yes**/No | Temporary Contract End Date | |
| Leaving Date | | Commission Payable | **Yes**/No |
| P45 Information ||||
| Pay to date | | Tax to date | |

# ANSWERS (Task 1, continued)

**Comments**

# ANSWERS (Task 1, continued)

| Employee Payroll Record Card |||| 
|---|---|---|---|
| Name | Dorothy Lamour | Employee number | 00586 |
| Address | 15A Court House<br>Midchester<br>MI4 7WD | Bank Address | NatWest<br>West Bank<br>Midchester |
| Marital status | Married | Cost Code | A0004 |
| Date of birth | 02-08-1957 | Start date | 22-09-2009 |
| Gender | Female | Grade | AD001 |
| Bank sort code | 60-08-18 | Annual salary | £14,000.00 |
| Bank A/c number | 16938285 | Hourly rate | £7.69 |
| Building society number | | Overtime rate @ 1½ times hourly rate | £11.53 |
| Student Loan Deduction | Yes / **No** | Overtime rate @ one and one third times hourly rate | £10.25 |
| | | Overtime rate @ double time | £15.38 |
| Monthly Pension Contributions | | Tax code | 647L |
| *COSR* | £ | Tax basis | |
| *COMP* | £ | *Cumulative* | Yes / **No** |
| *AVC* | £ | *Month1/Week 1* | **Yes** / No |
| | | N.I. category letter | A |
| Trade union deduction | £ | N.I. Number | KS376854D |
| Charitable giving deduction | £ | Occupational Sick Pay | Yes/**No** |
| Health club deduction | £ | Annual Holiday Entitlement (days – excluding public holidays) | 25 |
| Permanent Contract | **Yes**/No | Temporary Contract End Date | |
| Leaving Date | | Commission Payable | Yes/No |
| P45 Information ||||
| Pay to date | | Tax to date | |

# ANSWERS (Task 1, continued)

**Comments**

Expect candidate to identify:
- The P45 is out of date and tax code to be used should be emergency code on a week 1 / month 1 basis.

The memo from Pam Palmer asking for health club deductions cannot be processed because there is no employee signature.

Contact employee direct to explain emergency code and get her to sign authorisation form for health club deductance. Advise Pam Palmer about health club deductions

# ANSWERS TO AAT SAMPLE SIMULATION

**HM Revenue & Customs**

**P45 Part 3**
**New employee details**
For completion by new employer

File your employee's P45 online at www.hmrc.gov.uk — Use capital letters when completing this form

**1** Employer PAYE reference
Office number / Reference number
`0 4 4 / D G W 0 0 1 9 5`

**2** Employee's National Insurance number
`Y B 3 8 5 7 2 0 A`

**3** Title - enter MR, MRS, MISS, MS or other title
`MR`

Surname or family name
`MASON`

First or given name(s)
`JAMES`

**4** Leaving date DD MM YYYY
`2 7 0 8 2 0 0 9`

**5** Student Loan deductions
`Y` Student Loan deductions to continue

**6** Tax Code at leaving date
`4 6 1 L`
If week 1 or month 1 applies, enter 'X' in the box below.
Week 1/Month 1

**7** Last entries on P11 *Deductions Working Sheet*.
Complete only if Tax Code is cumulative. If there is an 'X' at box 6, there will be no entries here.
Week number          Month number `0 5`

Total pay to date
£ `4 8 6 3 . 9 6`

Total tax to date
£ `5 8 7 . 8 0`

*To the new employer* Complete boxes 8 to 18 and send P45 Part 3 only to your HMRC office immediately.

**8** New employer PAYE reference
Office number / Reference number
`0 5 4 / A S L 0 0 1`

**9** Date new employment started DD MM YYYY
`0 1 0 9 2 0 0 9`

**10** Works number/Payroll number and Department or branch (if any)
`00583`

**11** Enter 'P' here if employee will not be paid by you between the date employment began and the next 5 April.

**12** Enter Tax Code in use if different to the Tax Code at box 6

If week 1 or month 1 applies, enter 'X' in the box below.
Week 1/Month 1

**13** If the tax figure you are entering on P11 *Deductions Working Sheet* differs from box 7 (see the E13 Employer Helpbook *Day-to-day payroll*) please enter the figure here.
£

**14** New employee's job title or job description
`SALES ASSISTANT`

**15** Employee's private address
`3 ULVERSTON ROAD`
`MIDCHESTER`

Postcode
`M 1 6   7 S F`

**16** Gender. Enter 'X' in the appropriate box
Male `X`    Female

**17** Date of birth DD MM YYYY
`2 7 0 8 1 9 8 0`

**Declaration**

**18** I have prepared a P11 *Deductions Working Sheet* in accordance with the details above.
Employer name and address
`ADVENT SYSTEMS LTD`
`ADVENT HOUSE`
`CENTRAL AVENUE`
`MIDCHESTER`

Postcode
`M D 4   6 A F`

Date DD MM YYYY
`1 0 0 9 2 0 0 9`

P45(Manual) Part 3                                              HMRC 04/08

# ANSWERS TO AAT SAMPLE SIMULATION

**HM Revenue & Customs**

**P45 Part 3**
**New employee details**
For completion by new employer

File your employee's P45 online at www.hmrc.gov.uk — Use capital letters when completing this form

**1 Employer PAYE reference**
Office number / Reference number
0 2 5 / A K E 0 0 1 9 4 8 5

**2 Employee's National Insurance number**
B A 6 8 2 0 4 9 C

**3 Title** – enter MR, MRS, MISS, MS or other title
MS

Surname or family name
SMITH

First or given name(s)
JENNY

**4 Leaving date** DD MM YYYY
2 7 0 8 2 0 0 9

**5 Student Loan deductions**
☐ Student Loan deductions to continue

**6 Tax Code at leaving date**
5 8 6 T

If week 1 or month 1 applies, enter 'X' in the box below.
Week 1/Month 1 ☐

**7** Last entries on P11 Deductions Working Sheet.
Complete only if Tax Code is cumulative. If there is an 'X' at box 6, there will be no entries here.

Week number ☐☐   Month number 0 5

Total pay to date
£ 1 1 8 8 0 . 8 3

Total tax to date
£ 1 8 8 7 . 0 0

*For information only*

**To the new employer** Complete boxes 8 to 18 and send P45 Part 3 only to your HMRC office immediately.

**8 New employer PAYE reference**
Office number / Reference number
0 5 4 / A S L 0 0 1

**9 Date new employment started** DD MM YYYY
0 8 0 9 2 0 0 9

**10 Works number/Payroll number and Department or branch (if any)**
00584

**11** Enter 'P' here if employee will not be paid by you between the date employment began and the next 5 April. ☐

**12** Enter Tax Code in use if different to the Tax Code at box 6
☐ ☐☐☐☐☐☐☐

If week 1 or month 1 applies, enter 'X' in the box below.
Week 1/Month 1 ☐

**13** If the tax figure you are entering on P11 Deductions Working Sheet differs from box 7 (see the E13 Employer Helpbook Day-to-day payroll) please enter the figure here.
£ ☐☐☐☐☐☐ . ☐☐

**14 New employee's job title or job description**
WEB DESIGN MANAGER

**15 Employee's private address**
BLUEBELL COTTAGE
MIDCHESTER

Postcode
M 1 5   8 R E

**16 Gender.** Enter 'X' in the appropriate box
Male ☐   Female X

**17 Date of birth** DD MM YYYY
0 2 0 1 1 9 4 9

**Declaration**

**18** I have prepared a P11 Deductions Working Sheet in accordance with the details above.
Employer name and address
ADVENT SYSTEMS LTD
ADVENT HOUSE
CENTRAL AVENUE
MIDCHESTER

Postcode
M D 4   6 A F

Date DD MM YYYY
1 0 0 9 2 0 0 9

P45(Manual) Part 3                                HMRC 04/08

## ANSWERS (Task 2, continued)

The P46 for Michael Jackson appears on the following page.

## HM Revenue & Customs

## P46: Employee without a Form P45

**Section one** To be completed by the employee

Please complete section one and then hand the form back to your present employer. If you later receive a form P45 from your previous employer, hand it to your present employer.
Use capital letters when completing this form.

### Your details

**National Insurance number**
This is very important in getting your tax and benefits right

**Title** - enter MR, MRS, MISS, MS or other title
MR

**Surname or family name**
JACKSON

**First or given name(s)**
MICHAEL

**Gender.** Enter 'X' in the appropriate box
Male [X]   Female [ ]

**Date of birth** DD MM YYYY
17 11 1963

**Address**
**House or flat number**

**Rest of address including house name or flat name**
GREY GABLES
SOUTHCHESTER

**Postcode**
M18 7EW

### Your present circumstances
Read all the following statements carefully and enter 'X' in **the one** box that applies to you.

**A** - This is my first job since last 6 April and **I have not** been receiving taxable Jobseeker's Allowance or taxable Incapacity Benefit or a state or occupational pension. [A]

OR

**B** - This is now my only job, but since last 6 April **I have** had another job, or have received taxable Jobseeker's Allowance or Incapacity Benefit. I do not receive a state or occupational pension. [B]

OR

**C** - I have another job or receive a state or occupational pension. [C] X

### Student Loans
If you left a course of Higher Education before last 6 April and received your first Student Loan instalment on or after 1 September 1998 and you have not fully repaid your Student Loan, enter 'X' in box D. *(If you are required to repay your Student Loan through your bank or building society account do **not** enter an 'X' in box D.)* [D]

### Signature and date
I can confirm that this information is correct

**Signature**
*Michael Jackson*

**Date** DD MM YYYY
08 09 2009

P46                     Page 1                     HMRC 02/08

## ANSWERS TO AAT SAMPLE SIMULATION

### Section two  To be completed by the employer

File your employee's P46 online at www.hmrc.gov.uk/employers/doitonline
Use capital letters when completing this form. Guidance on how to fill it in, including what to do if your employee has not entered their National Insurance number on page 1, is at www.hmrc.gov.uk/employers/working_out.htm and in the E13 Employer Helpbook *Day-to-day payroll.*

#### Employee's details

Date employment started DD MM YYYY: 08 09 2009

Works/payroll number and department or branch (if any): MBJ

Job title: NON EXECUTIVE DIRECTOR

#### Employer's details

Employer PAYE reference
Office number  Reference number
054 / ASL001

Employer name: ADVENT SYSTEMS LTD

Address
Building number:

Rest of address:
ADVENT HOUSE
CENTRAL AVENUE
MIDCHESTER

Postcode: MD4 6AF

#### Tax code used

If you do not know the tax code to use or the current National Insurance contributions (NICs) lower earnings limit, go to www.hmrc.gov.uk/employers/rates_and_limits.htm

Enter 'X' in the appropriate box

**Box A** Emergency code on a **cumulative** basis — A ☐

**Box B** Emergency code on a **non-cumulative** Week 1/Month 1 basis — B ☐

**Box C** Code BR — C [X]

Tax code used: BR

If week 1 or month 1 applies, enter 'X' in this box ☐

**Send this form to your HM Revenue & Customs office on the first pay day.**
If the employee has entered 'X' in box A or box B, on page 1, and their earnings are below the NICs lower earnings limit, **do not send the form until their earnings reach the NICs lower earnings limit.**

Page 2

## ANSWERS TO AAT SAMPLE SIMULATION

**HM Revenue & Customs**

**P45 Part 3**
**New employee details**
For completion by new employer

File your employee's P45 online at www.hmrc.gov.uk — Use capital letters when completing this form

**1 Employer PAYE reference**
Office number / Reference number
041 / PDA6835

**2 Employee's National Insurance number**
FW 26 68 92 A

**3 Title** - enter MR, MRS, MISS, MS or other title
MR

Surname or family name
EASTWOOD

First or given name(s)
CLINT

**4 Leaving date** DD MM YYYY
29 08 2009

**5 Student Loan deductions**
☐ Student Loan deductions to continue

**6 Tax Code at leaving date**
K 42
If week 1 or month 1 applies, enter 'X' in the box below.
Week 1/Month 1  X

**7 Last entries on P11 Deductions Working Sheet.**
Complete only if Tax Code is cumulative. If there is an 'X' at box 6, there will be no entries here.
Week number ☐   Month number ☐
Total pay to date £
Total tax to date £

*For information only*

**To the new employer** Complete boxes 8 to 18 and send P45 Part 3 only to your HMRC office immediately.

**8 New employer PAYE reference**
Office number / Reference number
054 / ASL001

**9 Date new employment started** DD MM YYYY
15 09 2009

**10 Works number/Payroll number and Department or branch (if any)**
00585

**11** Enter 'P' here if employee will not be paid by you between the date employment began and the next 5 April. ☐

**12** Enter Tax Code in use if different to the Tax Code at box 6
☐☐☐☐☐☐☐
If week 1 or month 1 applies, enter 'X' in the box below.
Week 1/Month 1 ☐

**13** If the tax figure you are entering on P11 Deductions Working Sheet differs from box 7 (see the E13 Employer Helpbook Day-to-day payroll) please enter the figure here.
£

**14** New employee's job title or job description
ACCOUNT MANAGER

**15 Employee's private address**
CUDDLERS COTTAGE
SOUTHCHESTER

Postcode
SO21 5RT

**16 Gender.** Enter 'X' in the appropriate box
Male X   Female ☐

**17 Date of birth** DD MM YYYY
20 02 1981

**Declaration**

**18** I have prepared a P11 Deductions Working Sheet in accordance with the details above.
Employer name and address
ADVENT SYSTEMS LTD
ADVENT HOUSE
CENTRAL AVENUE
MIDCHESTER

Postcode
MD4 6AF

Date DD MM YYYY
10 09 2009

P45(Manual) Part 3                                HMRC 04/08

# P45 Part 3
## New employee details
### For completion by new employer

**HM Revenue & Customs**

File your employee's P45 online at www.hmrc.gov.uk

Use capital letters when completing this form

**1** Employer PAYE reference
Office number  Reference number
`033` / `CDC22947A`

**2** Employee's National Insurance number
`KS 37 68 54 D`

**3** Title – enter MR, MRS, MISS, MS or other title
`MRS`

Surname or family name
`LAMOUR`

First or given name(s)
`DOROTHY`

**4** Leaving date DD MM YYYY
`30 01 2009`

**5** Student Loan deductions
☐ Student Loan deductions to continue

**6** Tax Code at leaving date
`345 L`
If week 1 or month 1 applies, enter 'X' in the box below.
Week 1/Month 1  `X`

**7** Last entries on P11 Deductions Working Sheet.
Complete only if Tax Code is cumulative. If there is an 'X' at box 6, there will be no entries here.

Week number ☐☐    Month number ☐☐

Total pay to date
£ ☐☐☐☐☐☐☐.☐☐

Total tax to date
£ ☐☐☐☐☐☐☐.☐☐

---

**To the new employer** Complete boxes 8 to 18 and send P45 Part 3 only to your HMRC office immediately.

**8** New employer PAYE reference
Office number  Reference number
`054` / `ASL001`

**9** Date new employment started DD MM YYYY
`22 09 2009`

**10** Works number/Payroll number and Department or branch (if any)
`00586`

**11** Enter 'P' here if employee will not be paid by you between the date employment began and the next 5 April. ☐

**12** Enter Tax Code in use if different to the Tax Code at box 6
`647 L`
If week 1 or month 1 applies, enter 'X' in the box below.
Week 1/Month 1  `X`

**13** If the tax figure you are entering on P11 Deductions Working Sheet differs from box 7 (see the E13 Employer Helpbook Day-to-day payroll) please enter the figure here.
£ ☐☐☐☐☐☐.☐☐

**14** New employee's job title or job description
`ADMINISTRATION CLERK`

**15** Employee's private address
`15A COURT HOUSE`
`MIDCHESTER`

Postcode
`M14 7WD`

**16** Gender. Enter 'X' in the appropriate box
Male ☐    Female `X`

**17** Date of birth DD MM YYYY
`02 08 1957`

### Declaration

**18** I have prepared a P11 Deductions Working Sheet in accordance with the details above.
Employer name and address
`ADVENT SYSTEMS LTD`
`ADVENT HOUSE`
`CENTRAL AVENUE`
`MIDCHESTER`

Postcode
`MD4 6AF`

Date DD MM YYYY
`10 09 2009`

P45(Manual) Part 3    HMRC 04/08

# ANSWERS (Task 3)

| | Leaver Input Form September 2009 | | |
|---|---|---|---|
| | Jane Seymour | Donald Sinden | Jerry Springer |
| Leaving Date | 10-09-2009 | 17-09-2009 | 30-09-2009 |
| Salary to be paid in final month | £568.62 | £829.10 | £1,812.33 |
| Holiday entitlement to be paid | £213.23 | £ | £ |
| Commission | £ | £865.00 | £ |
| Overtime | £ | £ | £ |
| Bonus | £ | £ | £ |

**Workings**

1. *Jane Seymour*

    Salary: £18,480/260 × 8 = £568.62
    Holiday pay: £18,480/260 × 3 = £213.23

2. *Donald Sinden*

    Salary: £16,582/260 × 13 = £829.10

3. *Jerry Springer*

    Full month's salary: £21,748/12 = £1,812.33

# ANSWERS (Task 4)

| \multicolumn{8}{c|}{Payroll Input - Salary Adjustment Sheet} |
|---|---|---|---|---|---|---|---|
| Name | Payroll Number | Old salary | New salary | Effective Date | Flat hourly rate | Hourly rate @ 1½ | Comments |
| James Last *Director* | JL - Director | 45,000-00 | 48,000-00 | 01-09-2009 | | | Cannot be actioned as no approval from the MD. |
| Fred Dibnah *Clerk* | 00026 | 12,600-00 | 13,000-00 | 01-09-2009 | 7.14 | 10.71 | |
| John Walker *Clerk* | 00166 | 31,485-00 | 31,995-00 | 01-09-2009 | 17.58 | 26.37 | |
| Sally Oldfield *Office Supervisor* | 00227 | 21,764-00 | 22,486-00 | 01-09-2009 | 12.35 | 18.52 | |
| Bruce Benyon *Accounts Supervisor* | 00068 | 18,465-00 | 19,000-00 | 01-09-2009 | 10.44 | 15.66 | |
| Kathy Evans *Stores Manager* | 00326 | 25,670-00 | 26,216-00 | 01-09-2009 | 14.40 | | Manager – no overtime payable |
| Robin Williams *Stores Supervisor* | 00281 | 19,586-00 | 20,184-00 | 01-09-2009 | 11.09 | 16.63 | |
| Kevin Klein *Web Design Manager* | 00019 | 25,000-00 | 26,500-00 | 01-09-2009 | 14.56 | | Manager – no overtime payable |
| John Steinbeck *Web Designer* | 00084 | 18,511-00 | 19,242-00 | 01-09-2009 | 10.57 | 15.85 | |
| Evelyn Waugh *Personnel Supervisor* | 00099 | 23,734-00 | 24,319-00 | 01-09-2009 | 13.36 | 20.04 | |

ANSWERS TO AAT SAMPLE SIMULATION

## ANSWERS (Task 5)

| \multicolumn{10}{|c|}{Miscellaneous Payroll Amendment/Change Sheet} |
|---|---|---|---|---|---|---|---|---|
| Employee Number | Tax Code | Trade Union Deduction | Code | Surname | Title | Marital Status | Address | Post Code |
| 00274 | | | | Agutter | Mrs | Married | | |
| 00079 | | | | | | | | |
| 00384 | | | WD003 | | | | | |
| 00359 | | | | | | | 5 San Carlos House Midchester | MD3 7AG |
| 00167 | | | AD003 | | | | | |
| 00349 | | | SA101 | | | | | |
| 00192 | | | | | | Divorced | | |
| 00472 | K435 | | | | | | | |
| 00481 | 601T | | | | | | | |

# ANSWERS (Task 5, continued)

## MEMO

From: Payroll Assistant                                                                            10 September 2009

To:      Pamela Palmer

**Payroll Changes – September 2009**

I would like to raise the following issues concerning the September payroll:

- James Mason – He has signed for AVCs of £50 pm but this is not available in the COMP scheme. Also his contract states that he is entitled to 20 days holiday per annum when company rules state 25 days. Please can you clarify these points for me?
- Jenny Smith – has been shown on the new starter memo from you as being in the COSR pension scheme when she is not a director of the company. Can you please advise me what action I should take?
- Dorothy Lamour – your memo about the health club deductions is not sufficient. I need Dorothy's written permission before I can make the deductions. I have sent her a new deduction authority sheet.
- James Last – I cannot process the pay increase for him as I do not have the authority of the Managing Director – Sally Jenkins
- John Nettles – I cannot action his request for a trade union deduction without his prior written approval and at the moment he has only given his verbal authority

Payroll Assistant

# ANSWERS (Task 6)

## MEMO

10 September 2009

From: Payroll Assistant

To: Simon Callow

**Data Protection**

In response to your memo:
*How I file paper payroll records*
- All documents are filed in individual files for each employee
- In alpha or numeric (employee number) order
- In locked filing cabinets
- With the office locked when no authorised personnel present
- Care is taken to ensure no documents are left in the open when non authorised employees are present

*Who has access to the paper and computer records*
- Only me and Pam Palmer, my immediate manager
- Also, employees may see their own files on giving notice to us.

*How I ensure that no one else can gain access to paper records unless they have authority*
- The office is locked when Pam Palmer and I are not in the office
- All records are kept in locked filing cabinets
- Employees are allowed to see their own file only

*How I secure the computer from unauthorised access*
- Computers are password protected and passwords changed regularly
- Computers are switched off when not being used
- Visitors are not allowed to see confidential information on the screen

*How I protect the data*
- Data is backed up regularly
- Back ups are tested on a regular basis to ensure they can be read

Payroll Assistant

# ANSWERS (Task 7)

## MEMO

10 September 2009

From: Payroll Assistant

To: Simon Callow

**Court Orders**

In response to your memo:

*Which organisations can authorise the issue of attachments of earnings and deductions from earnings orders?*
Orders can be issued by:
- Local authorities for council tax arrears
- Child Support Agency
- Courts

*Can you accept the written authority of the Human Resources Manager?*
- No, all orders must be on original documentation, though the employee authority is not required as the orders are statutory

*How quickly do we have to start making deduction?*
- By the next payday unless the next payday is within 7 days of receipt of the order

Payroll Assistant

ANSWERS TO AAT SAMPLE SIMULATION

## ASSESSMENT CRITERIA

Assessors must refer to the Standards of Competence for Payroll Administration and be guided by the performance criteria when evaluating candidates' work.

In all cases where memos form part of the answer, alternative, but appropriate wording is acceptable.

| Task | Commentary | Mapping to PCs |
|---|---|---|
| **1. Completing payroll record cards** | Candidates should make no errors in entering information on the record card.<br>Expect candidates to pick up that new employee<ul><li>James Mason – has only been told he is entitled to 20 days annual leave when company policy is for 25 days</li><li>Jenny Smith – has been entered for the COSR pension scheme when she is only eligible for the COMP pension</li><li>Michael Jackson – has no NI number or bank account number.</li><li>Dorothy Lamour – has a P45 from an earlier tax year and so cannot be used. She should be put on emergency tax code using a week 1 / month 1 basis. Also, the deduction request submitted by Pam Palmer cannot be processed as it is necessary to have the employee's own written authority.</li></ul> | 71.1 a, b, e, f<br>71.2 a |
| **2. Completing statutory documentation** | Candidates should make no errors in completing the P45s and P46 | 71.1 d |
| **3. Dealing with leavers** | Candidates should make no mistakes | 71.1 c |
| **4. Dealing with salary reviews** | Allow one error.<br>Expect candidates to pick up that<ul><li>James Last is a director and that Pam Palmer does not have authority to adjust his pay.</li><li>The following employees are not entitled to overtime and so no premium hourly rates needed – Kathy Evans and Kevin Klein</li></ul> | 71.2 a<br>71.3 a, b, c, d |

| 5. Dealing with changes to the payroll | Allow one error.<br>Expect candidates to pick up that<br>• John Nettles has not given written permission for the deduction from pay. | 71.2 a, b, c, d<br>71.3 a, b, c, d |
|---|---|---|
| 6. Dealing with enquiry regarding data protection and confidentiality | Expect candidate to pick up on major points as highlighted in the model answers. | 71.1 g, h |
| 7. Dealing with the principles of court orders | Expect candidate to pick up on major points as highlighted in the model answers. | 71.2 b |

# Unit 72 Sample Simulation answers

# AAT SAMPLE SIMULATION: ANSWERS

**DO NOT TURN THIS PAGE UNTIL YOU HAVE COMPLETED THE SIMULATION**

# ANSWERS (Task 1)

# MEMO

**From:** Payroll Assistant  **Date:** 23 June 2009

**To:** General Manager—Liverpool

**Subject:** Time Sheet and payroll changes for week ending 19 June 2009

I can confirm that, subject to the points listed below, I have taken action on the time sheet as requested and that employees will be paid on time.

I do have the following queries:
- The time sheet shows Jenny Pitman as having 10 hours weekday overtime at time and a third when she has only worked 25 hours. Company rules state that weekday overtime is only paid at time and a third once the employee has worked 40 hours.
- Roy Gibb, Paul Merton and Mary Hopkins have not worked 40 hours in the week and yet are receiving overtime at time and a half for the weekend.
- Jonnie Dankworth is shown as having 8 hours overtime at double time. This is only paid on bank holidays and we do not have one in June.

Can you please clarify what you would like me to do in respect of these three queries.

# ANSWERS (Task 1, continued)

## PAYROLL INPUT SHEET FOR LIVERPOOL

| Name | Employee Number | Hourly Rate £ | Flat Rate Hours | Flat Rate Pay £ | Weekday overtime @ time and a third Hours | Weekday overtime @ time and a third Pay £ | Weekend hours @ time and a half Hours | Weekend hours @ time and a half Pay £ | Public holiday hours @ double time Hours | Public holiday hours @ double time Pay £ |
|---|---|---|---|---|---|---|---|---|---|---|
| Jenny Pitman | 00012 | 6.30 | 25 | 157.50 | 10 | Not processed | 6 | Not processed | | |
| Frankie Detori | 00057 | 7.80 | 40 | 312.00 | 5 | 52.00 | 6 | 70.20 | | |
| Jonnie Dankworth | 00082 | 5.40 | 40 | 216.00 | 8 | 57.60 | | | 8 | Not processed |
| Fred Mercury | 00142 | 9.32 | 40 | 372.80 | 6 | 74.58 | | | | |
| Roy Gibb | 00276 | 8.40 | 38 | 319.20 | | | 7 | Not processed | | |
| Jimmie Saville | 00277 | 6.60 | 40 | 264.00 | 6 | 52.80 | 8 | 79.20 | | |
| Paul Merton | 00306 | 7.30 | 35 | 255.50 | | | 8 | Not processed | | |
| Daisy Springfield | 00311 | 5.80 | 40 | 232.00 | 8 | 61.84 | 4 | 34.80 | | |
| Mary Hopkins | 00316 | 5.80 | 20 | 116.00 | | | 8 | Not processed | | |
| Gary Rhodes | 00324 | 8.20 | 40 | 328.00 | 4 | 43.72 | | | | |
| Phil Collins | 00385 | 4.80 | 40 | 192.00 | | | | | | |
| Eric Clapton | 00386 | 8.30 | 40 | 332.00 | 5 | 55.35 | 9 | 112.05 | | |
| Eric Morcombe | 00414 | 7.90 | 40 | 316.00 | | | 7 | 82.95 | | |
| Erica Rowe | 00415 | 5.60 | 40 | 224.00 | 6 | 44.82 | 3 | 25.20 | | |

# ANSWERS (Task 2)

# MEMO

**From:** Payroll Assistant  **Date:** 23 June 2009

**To:** Jane Horrocks—London

**Subject:** Pregnancy

---

Congratulations on your good news.

I can respond to your questions as follows:

- *Am I entitled to SMP?* Yes you are entitled to SMP. You have the requisite 26 weeks employment at the Qualifying Week (15th week before the expected week of childbirth) and your average earnings are greater than the lower earnings limit for N.I. purposes.
- *How much leave am I entitled to?* You are entitled to 26 weeks ordinary maternity leave and a further 26 weeks additional maternity leave.
- *How is my SMP calculated?* The first 6 weeks SMP is based on 90% of your average earnings over the eight weeks prior to the end of the Qualifying Week which is the 15th week before the Expected Week of Childbirth.
- *How much will I get per week?* For the first 6 weeks you will get £326.91 per week. (This is calculated as follows: £1,400 (May) plus £1,748 (June) × 6/52 = £363.23 × 90%.) The other 33 weeks are paid at the lower of 90% of average earnings or £123.06. In this case, you are entitled to £123.06 per week.
- *What documentation do I need to give you?* I must have the original of form MAT B1 for my files.

# ANSWERS (Task 3)

# MEMO

**From:** Payroll Assistant  **Date:** 23 June 2009

**To:** Personnel Manager

**Subject:** Sickness Report

---

I have completed the sickness report for Peter Rason that you requested and am attaching it.

Please see below explanations for the terms listed in your memo:

- *Period of incapacity for work* is a period of sickness of at least four consecutive days where all days count regardless of whether they are Qualifying Days or not.
- *Qualifying days* are the only days for which SSP is paid. They are normally the days the employee works.
- *Waiting days* are the first three Qualifying Days of sickness in any PIW or linked PIW. No SSP is paid for Waiting Days.
- *Linking of periods of incapacity for work*—PIWs separated by 56 calendar days or less are said to link. If they do, Waiting Days do not need to be served again.

Finally, Peter Rason will receive the following for June:

- Salary = £16,020/12 = £1,335.00 less 13 working days of sickness (£16,020/260 = £61.62 × 13 = £801.06) = £533.94.
- SSP of 8 days (8 × £15.83) = £126.64
- His total pay will be £660.58

Please let me know if you have any queries.

# ANSWERS (Task 3, continued)

## Sickness Report

**Peter Rason**

He works Monday to Friday and has not been off sick for over 6 months.

| Sun | Mon | Tues | Wed | Thurs | Fri | Sat | |
|---|---|---|---|---|---|---|---|
| | 18 | 19 | 20 | 21 | 22 | 23 | May |
| | | sick | sick | sick | sick | | |
| | | There is a PIW. No SSP paid for the first three days as they are Waiting Days. SSP is paid for one day. | | | | | |
| 24 | 25 | 26 | 27 | 28 | 29 | 30 | May |
| sick | sick | sick | | | | sick | |
| There is not a PIW. Therefore, no entitlement to SSP. | | | | | | No SSP– not a Qualifying Day. | |
| 31 | 1 | 2 | 3 | 4 | 5 | 6 | June |
| sick | sick | sick | sick | | | | |
| No SSP– not a Qualifying Day. | The 5 days sickness represents a PIW, however no SSP for the first two days as they are not Qualifying Days. SSP is paid for three days. Waiting days do not need to be served again as this PIW links to the previous one. | | | | | | |
| 7 | 8 | 9 | 10 | 11 | 12 | 13 | June |
| | sick | sick | sick | sick | | | |
| | There is a PIW. It links to the previous one. All four days are Qualifying Days. SSP is paid for all four days. | | | | | | |

# ANSWERS (Task 4)

# MEMO

**From:** Payroll Assistant      **Date:** 23 June 2009

**To:** Personnel Manager

**Subject:** SSP and Jenny Walker

---

To respond to your questions:

- *Whether she is entitled to SSP*—no she is not entitled to SSP because her earnings are too low. One of the qualifying criteria for SSP is that the employee must have average earnings that are equal to or greater than the lower earnings limit for N.I. purposes. The current lower earnings limit is £95 per week and Jenny Walker's average earnings are £50 per week.
- *What action needs to be taken if she is not entitled*—we need to issue a form SSP1 to Jenny and she may be able to claim benefits from the government.

Please let me know if you have any further questions.

## ANSWERS (Task 5)

# MEMO

**From:** Payroll Assistant **Date:** 23 June 2009

**To:** General Manager—Swansea

**Subject:** Bonus Payments—Swansea

---

Attached is the completed schedule as requested.

However, I cannot process the payments for P Davies and R Davies as both have been shown under the same employee number. Can you please confirm as soon as possible what you would like me to do in respect of these staff?

# ANSWERS (Task 5, continued)

### Additional Bonus Schedule

| Name | Employee number | Salary £ | Days bonus to be paid | Bonus £ | Additional bonus £ |
|---|---|---|---|---|---|
| K Brockett | 00019 | 13,000.00 | 3 | 150.00 | 50.00 |
| S Field | 00023 | 24,500.00 | 6 | 565.38 | 50.00 |
| J Thompson | 00029 | 18,600.00 | 4 | 286.16 | 50.00 |
| P Delft | 00037 | 21,080.00 | | | 50.00 |
| J Sainsbury | 00041 | 19,662.00 | | | 50.00 |
| P Trewitt | 00042 | 20,050.00 | 3 | 231.36 | 50.00 |
| D Jones | 00055 | 18,600.00 | 3 | 214.62 | 50.00 |
| R Davies | 00064 | 19,520.00 | 3 | | |
| P Davies | 00064 | 18,618.00 | 3 | | |
| H Sanders | 00077 | 25,760.00 | 5 | 495.40 | 50.00 |
| F Saunders | 00078 | 17,648.00 | | | 50.00 |
| P Davies | 00082 | 19,650.00 | 1 | 75.58 | 50.00 |
| | | | **Totals** | **2,018.50** | **500.00** |

# ANSWERS (Task 6)

# MEMO

**From:** Payroll Assistant             **Date:** 23 June 2009

**To:** Chief Accountant

**Subject:** Payroll Procedures

---

In response to your memo of 21 June:

- *The statutory and recommended record retention period for payroll records*
  — Statutory record retention period is 3 years.
  — Recommended record retention period is at least 6 years because the Revenue can go back 6 years.
- *Your recommended method of filing that ensures it is easy to trace documents*
  — All documents to be filed in individual files for each employee.
  — In alpha or numeric (employee number) order.
  — In locked filing cabinets.
  — With the office locked when no authorised personnel present.
- *The steps that can be taken to ensure security of:*
  1. Documents
     — All files to be put into locked filing units.
     — Office to be locked when no authorised employees present.
     — Care must be taken to ensure no documents are left in the open when non-authorised employees are present.
     — Filing should be done regularly to ensure as few papers as possible are out

  2. Computer information
     — Computers should be password protected and passwords changed regularly.
     — Computers should be switched off when not being used.
     — Visitors should not be allowed to see confidential information on the screen.
     — Data should be backed up regularly.
     — Back ups should be tested.

# ANSWERS (Task 7)

# MEMO

**From:** Payroll Assistant    **Date:** 23 June 2009

**To:** General Manager—Glasgow

**Subject:** Expenses and Benefits

---

Thank you for your memo of 18 June.

I can advise you as follows:

| Payments | Taxable | Pensionable | NICable |
|---|---|---|---|
| Annual Bonus | Yes | No | Yes |
| Attendance Bonus | Yes | No | Yes |
| Sales Commission | Yes | Yes | Yes |
| Attendance Allowance | Yes | No | Yes |
| Statutory Sick Pay | Yes | No | Yes |
| Statutory Maternity Pay | Yes | Yes | Yes |
| Statutory Adoption Pay | Yes | Yes | Yes |
| Statutory Paternity Pay | Yes | Yes | Yes |

Please let me know if I can be of any further assistance.

## ANSWERS (Task 8)

# MEMO

**From:** Payroll Assistant  **Date:** 23 June 2009

**To:** Pam Palmer

**Subject:** Collection of overpayments

---

Thank you for your memo of 21 June 2009.

I can confirm that we are able to collect Ben Kingsley's overpayment even if he has not agreed in writing.

Under the Employment Rights Act 1996, we do not need his authority. I therefore, intend collecting his overpayment along with everyone else's next week.

I hope this clarifies the matter for you.

## ANSWERS (Task 8, continued)

### Payroll Deduction Sheet

| Name | Flat Hourly £ | Time and half £ | Total £ |
|---|---|---|---|
| H Johnson | 20.80 |  | 20.80 |
| W Wilkinson | 22.05 | 23.62 | 45.67 |
| F Watson | 35.10 | 16.20 | 51.30 |
| D Smith | 15.20 | 54.15 | 69.35 |
| A Thompson |  | 73.12 | 73.12 |
| G Kerr | 38.35 | 30.97 | 69.32 |
| B Kingsley | 46.40 | 26.40 | 72.80 |
| S Zander | 49.20 | 73.80 | 123.00 |
|  |  |  |  |
|  |  |  |  |
|  |  |  |  |
|  |  |  |  |
|  |  |  |  |
|  |  |  |  |
|  |  |  |  |

## ANSWERS (Task 9)

# MEMO

**From:** Payroll Assistant  **Date:** 23 June 2009

**To:** Henry Miller

**Subject:** Adoption

---

Thank you for your memo of 18 June.

I can advise you as follows.

Angela, who will be taking the paternity leave:
- will have to provide a self certificate form for becoming a parent–adoption (SC4);
- will be entitled to two weeks leave which must be completed within 56 days of the date on which the baby is adopted;
- has the option of taking one week or two consecutive weeks for Statutory Paternity Pay purposes, no other options;
- will be entitled to pay of £123.06 for each week of her leave.

Barry, who will be taking the adoption leave:
- will have to provide the original of a Matching Certificate from the registered UK agency;
- will be entitled to 26 weeks ordinary adoption leave and a further 26 weeks additional adoption leave which follows on from the ordinary leave;
- will be entitled to Statutory Adoption Pay for 39 weeks;
- will be entitled to pay of £123.06 for each week of the 39 weeks.

For both of them their paternity and adoption pay will commence on the day the baby is adopted unless either of them is at work that day in which case it will commence the following day.

## ASSESSMENT CRITERIA

Assessors must refer to the Standards of Competence for Payroll Administration and be guided by the performance criteria when evaluating candidates' work.

| Task | Comments | Mapping to PCs |
|---|---|---|
| **1. Completing payroll input and changes from sheets** | Allow two calculation errors in entering information on the record card. Candidates should spot that Jenny Pitman cannot get overtime at a premium rate when she has not worked the full equivalent, and that Jonnie Dankworth cannot get overtime at double time when there is not a bank holiday in the month. Candidates should also spot that Roy Gibb, Paul Merton and Mary Hopkins have not worked 40 hours, and so question the weekend overtime. | **72.1 A, B, C, D, G, H** |
| **2. Understanding of the SMP rules** | Candidate should provide all points listed in main answer, but allow a shortfall of one. | **72.2 C, D** |
| **3. Dealing with entitlement to SSP** | Candidates should provide all points listed in main answer, but allow a shortfall of one. | **72.1 F** <br> **72.2 A, B** |
| **4. Dealing with entitlement to SSP** | Allow no errors. | **72.2 H** |
| **5. Dealing with additional payments** | Allow no errors to the calculations. Candidates should identify that two employees have the same employee number and hence payments cannot be made. | **72.1 G, H** |
| **6. Dealing with enquiry regarding data protection and confidentiality** | Candidates should pick up on major points as highlighted in the suggested answers. | **72.1 I, J** |
| **7. Dealing with the principles of tax and N.I. liability on benefits** | Candidates should pick up on major points as highlighted in the suggested answers. | **72.1 F** |
| **8. Dealing with deductions from pay** | Allow one mistake in calculations. However, candidates should identify that correcting errors do not require employee authority. | **72.1 G** <br> **72.1 H** |
| **9. Dealing with paternity and adoption leave and pay** | Candidates should get 7 of the 8 bulleted points as outlined in the suggested answers. | **72.2 C, D** |
|  |  |  |

## OVERALL ASSESSMENT

Candidates may be allowed to make further minor errors, provided such errors do not suggest a fundamental lack of understanding.

*General*
- Work should be neatly and competently presented.
- Pencil is not acceptable.
- Correcting fluid may be used but in moderation.

*Discretion*

In having regard to the above criteria, the assessor is entitled in marginal cases to exercise discretion in the candidate's favour. Such discretion shall only be exercised where other criteria are met to above the required standard and, in the opinion of the assessor, the assessment overall demonstrates competence and would be of an acceptable standard in the workplace.

# Unit 73
# Answers to Exams

# AAT EXAM PAPER 1: ANSWERS

**DO NOT TURN THIS PAGE UNTIL YOU HAVE COMPLETED THE EXAM**

**June 2008**

# SECTION 1

**Calculation for Task 1.1 – Paul Thomas – April 2009 gross to net pay**

| | |
|---|---|
| Basic pay | 1,500.00 |
| Charitable giving for April 2009 | 57.00 |

**Tax calculation**

| | |
|---|---|
| Cumulative gross pay | 1,500.00 |
| Less cumulative allowable deductions (above) | (57.00) |
| Cumulative pay for tax purposes | 1,443.00 |

Tax code used __350L__    Tax basis __Cumulative__

| | |
|---|---|
| Adjustment for tax code | 292.42 |
| Cumulative net taxable pay | 1,150.58 |

Tax calculation    Tables used __B__

| | |
|---|---|
| £1,150 @ 20% | 230.00 |
| Tax due for April 2009 | 230.00 |

**NICs calculation**    NI table letter used __A__

Employee's contributions payable

| | |
|---|---|
| (1,500 – 476) x 11% | 112.64 |

Employer's contributions payable

| | |
|---|---|
| (1,500 – 476) x 12.8% | 131.07 |

**Payslip for April 2009**

| Employee: Paul Thomas | | Date: 30 April 2009 |
|---|---|---|

| Payments £ | | Deductions £ | | Cumulatives £ | |
|---|---|---|---|---|---|
| Basic pay: | 1,500.00 | Income tax: | 230.00 | Gross pay: | 1,500.00 |
| | | NIC: | 112.64 | Pay for tax purposes: | 1,443.00 |
| | | Charitable giving: | 57.00 | Income tax: | 230.00 |
| | | Staff loan: | 116.15 | Employee's NIC: | 112.64 |
| | | Union: | 8.75 | Employer's NIC: | 131.07 |
| | | | | Charitable giving: | 57.00 |
| | | | | Staff loan: | 116.15 |
| | | | | Union: | 8.75 |
| | | | | | |
| **Total gross pay:** | 1,500.00 | **Total deductions:** | 524.54 | **Net pay:** | 975.46 |

| NI Number: BG490219D | Tax code: 350L |
|---|---|

## Calculation for Task 1.1 – Paul Thomas – May 2009 gross to net pay

| | |
|---|---:|
| Basic pay | 1,500.00 |
| Less adjustment for leave | (857.14) |
| Total gross pay for May 2009 | 642.86 |
| Charitable giving for May 2009 | 57.00 |
| Cumulative charitable giving year to date | 114.00 |

**Tax calculation**

| | | |
|---|---|---:|
| Cumulative gross pay to May 2009 | (1,500.00 + 642.86) | 2,142.86 |
| Less cumulative allowable deductions (above) | | (114.00) |
| Cumulative pay for tax purposes | | 2,028.86 |
| Tax code used __522L__ | Tax basis __Cumulative__ | |
| Adjustment for tax code | | 871.52 |
| Cumulative net taxable pay | | 1,157.34 |
| Tax calculation | Tables used __B__ | |

| | |
|---|---:|
| £1,157 @ 20% | 231.40 |
| Tax due to May 2009 | 231.40 |
| Tax deducted in April 2009 | 230.00 |
| Tax due for May 2009 | 1.40 |

**NICs calculation**    NI table letter used __A__

| | |
|---|---:|
| Employee's contribution payable | |
| (642.86 – 476) x 11% | 18.36 |
| | |
| Employer's contribution payable | |
| (642.86 – 476) x 12.8% | 21.36 |

**Payslip for May** 2009

| Employee: Paul Thomas | | Date: 31 May 2009 |

| Payments £ | | Deductions £ | | Cumulatives £ | |
|---|---|---|---|---|---|
| Basic pay: | 1,500.00 | Income tax: | 1.40 | Gross pay: | 2,142.86 |
| Adjustment for leave: | (857.14) | NIC: | 18.36 | Pay for tax purposes: | 2,028.86 |
| | | Charitable giving: | 57.00 | Income tax: | 231.40 |
| | | Group personal pension: | 50.00 | Employee's NIC: | 131.00 |
| | | Staff loan: | 116.15 | Employer's NIC: | 152.43 |
| | | Union: | 8.75 | Charitable giving: | 114.00 |
| | | | | Group personal pension: | 50.00 |
| | | | | Staff loan: | 232.30 |
| | | | | Union: | 17.50 |
| **Total gross pay:** | 642.86 | **Total deductions:** | 251.66 | **Net pay:** | 391.20 |

NI Number: BG490219D          Tax Code: 522L

### Calculation for Task 1.1 – Channo Cajero – April 2009 gross to net pay

| | | |
|---|---|---|
| Basic pay | | 8,025.00 |
| Pension contribution for April 2009 | (6% x 8,025.00) | 481.50 |
| AVC payment for April 2009 | | 350.00 |

**Tax calculation**

| | | |
|---|---|---|
| Cumulative gross pay | | 8,025.00 |
| Less cumulative allowable deductions (above) | (481.50 + 350.00) | (831.50) |
| Cumulative pay for tax purposes | | 7,193.50 |
| Tax code used K624 | Tax basis Cumulative | |
| Adjustment for tax code | | 520.76 |
| Cumulative net taxable pay | | 7,714.26 |
| Tax calculation | Tables used C + D | |
| 3,117 | | 623.46 |
| 4,597 | | 1,838.80 |
| 7,714 | | |
| Tax due for April 2009 | | 2,462.26 |

**NICs calculation**  NI table letter used **D**

| | | |
|---|---|---|
| Employee's contribution payable | (8,025 – 3,656) x 1% | 43.69 |
| | (3,656 – 3,337) x 11% | 35.09 |
| | (3,337 – 476) x 9.4% | 268.93 |
| | (476 – 412) x 1.6% | (1.02) |
| | | 346.69 |
| Employer's contribution payable | | |
| | (8,025 – 3,337) x 12.8% | 600.06 |
| | (3,337 – 476) x 9.1% | 260.35 |
| | (476 – 412) x 3.7% | (2.37) |
| | | 858.04 |

**Payslip for April 2009**

| Employee: Channo Cajero | | Date: 30 April 2009 |

| Payments £ | Deductions £ | Cumulatives £ |
|---|---|---|
| Basic pay: 8,025.00 | Income tax: 2,462.26 | Gross pay: 8,025.00 |
| | NIC: 346.69 | Pay for tax purposes: 7,193.50 |
| | Pension: 481.50 | Tax: 2,462.26 |
| | AVC: 350.00 | Employee's NIC: 346.69 |
| | Sharesave: 200.00 | Employer's NIC: 858.04 |
| | Health club: 75.00 | Pension: 481.50 |
| | Children's home: 150.00 | AVC: 350.00 |
| | | Sharesave: 200.00 |
| | | Health club: 75.00 |
| | | Children's home: 150.00 |
| **Total gross pay:** 8,025.00 | **Total deductions:** 4,065.45 | **Net pay:** 3,959.55 |

NI Number: AG623987B          Tax code: K624

## Calculation for Task 1.1 – Channo Cajero – May 2009 gross to net pay

| | | |
|---|---|---|
| Basic pay | | 4,012.50 |
| Pension contribution for May 2009 | (6% x £4,012.50) | 240.75 |
| AVC payment for May 2009 | | 350.00 |
| Charitable giving for May 2009 | | 100.00 |
| Cumulatives    Pension  722.25    AVC  700.00    Charitable Giving | | 100.00 |

**Tax calculation**

| | | |
|---|---|---|
| Cumulative gross pay to May 2009 | (8,025.00 + 4,012.50) | 12,037.50 |
| Less cumulative allowable deductions (above) | | (1,522.25) |
| Cumulative pay for tax purposes | | 10,515.25 |
| Tax code used  522L    Tax basis  Cumulative | | |
| Adjustment for tax code | | (871.52) |
| Cumulative net taxable pay | | 9,643.75 |
| Tax calculation | Tables used  C+D | |
| 6,234 | | 1,246.93 |
| 3,409 | | 1,363.60 |
| 9,643 | | |
| Tax due to May 2009 | | 2,610.53 |
| Tax deducted in April 2009 | | (2,462.26) |
| Tax due for May 2009 | | 148.27 |

**NICs calculation**    NI table letter used  D

| | | |
|---|---|---|
| Employee's contribution payable | (4,012.50 – 3,656) x 1% | 3.57 |
| | (3,656 – 3,337) x 11% | 35.09 |
| | (3,337 – 476) x 9.4% | 268.93 |
| | (476 – 412) x 1.6% | (1.02) |
| Employer's contribution payable | | 306.57 |
| | (4,012.50 – 3,337) x 12.8% | 86.46 |
| | (3,337.00 – 476) x 9.1% | 260.35 |
| | (476.00 – 412) x 1.6% | (2.37) |
| | | 344.44 |

**Payslip for May 2009**

| Employee: Channo Cajero | | Date: 31 May 2009 |
|---|---|---|

| Payments £ | Deductions £ | Cumulatives £ |
|---|---|---|
| Basic pay: 4,012.50 | Income tax: 148.27 | Gross pay: 12,037.50 |
| | NIC: 306.57 | Pay for tax purposes: 10,515.25 |
| | Pension: 240.75 | Income tax: 2,610.53 |
| | AVC: 350.00 | Employee's NIC: 653.26 |
| | Charitable giving: 100.00 | Employer's NIC: 1,202.48 |
| | Sharesave: 200.00 | Pension: 722.25 |
| | Health club: 75.00 | AVC: 700.00 |
| | | Charitable giving: 100.00 |
| | | Sharesave: 400.00 |
| | | Health club: 150.00 |
| | | Children's home: 150.00 |
| **Total gross pay:** 4,012.50 | **Total deductions:** 1,420.59 | **Net pay:** 2,591.91 |

| NI Number: AG623987B | Tax code: 522L |
|---|---|

## Task 1.2

| |
|---|
| **From:** payroll@fictitious.co.uk<br>**To:** greg.salter@fictitious.co.uk<br>**Sent:** 19 June<br>**Subject:** Re: Payroll transfer to general ledger |
| Thank you for your e-mail. The answers to your questions follow. |
| **1  The total gross cost of the payroll** |
| The total gross cost is the total of all payments made to the employee. For example: |
| Basic salary and wages, overtime, bonuses, statutory payments (such as SSP, SMP SAP, SPP). |
| [Tutor note: You were asked for four elements. Others could be comissions, holiday pay, backdated payrises etc.] |
| It also includes employer's costs, such as employers NIC and employer's pension contributions. |

This page is for the continuation of your email. You may not need to use all of it.

**2 The total payment due to HMRC:**

The two main constituents are tax and NIC.

The tax element includes tax deducted and student loan deductions.

The NIC element consists of:

Employee's NIC + employer's NIC – the appropriate percentage recoverable of statutory payments (SSP, SMP, SAP, SPP).

Regards,

Payroll Clerk

# SECTION 2

## Task 2.1

A local loan company asks for financial details of Fictitious Ltd's employees in order to offer cut price loans to those who qualify. A travel voucher is being offered to each employee who takes out a loan and the company will get a payment for each enquiry. The directors think this is a good deal.

(a) Should you supply the information requested?

Yes ☐   No ☑

(b) Give THREE reasons for your answer in (a) above.

1. Data Protection Acts forbid disclosure to unauthorised third parties
2. Data must be used for legitimate payroll purposes only
3. Employees have not been told

(c) Name ONE circumstance in which you would supply personal information without the express permission of the employee.

Required by law (eg. Child Support Agency)

## Task 2.2

Explain how net taxable pay is calculated when an employee has the following allowance code.

(a) BR code

No allowances to deduct. All taxable pay taxed at basic rate.

(b) K code

The adjusting figure is added to taxable pay, so net taxable pay is higher than gross taxable pay.

(c) Which ONE of the following codes is the Emergency Code 2009/2010?

BR   **(647L)**   647LWk1   603L   603LWk1

## Task 2.3

(a) **There are three ways in which an employer is notified that an employee is to start paying student loan deductions. State TWO of the three ways.**

1. 'Y' in box 5 of form P45
2. 'X' in box D of from P46

(Tutor note: the 3rd way is a start notice from HMRC)

(b) One of the employees informs you that she has started to receive a pension from a former employer and this means you must stop taking student loan deductions from her.

**Will you agree to this?**

Yes ☐   No ☑

(c) **Which ONE of the following is the annual pay figure that is the starting point for student loan deductions?**

£10,000   £12,000   (£15,000)   £18,00

## Task 2.4

**Holiday payments in advance attract special national insurance contribution calculation rules. Name ONE of them and explain how the calculation is carried out.**

One of the following:

Method A – Total pay divided by number of pay periods. NIC then calculated on average amount and multiplied by number of pay periods.

Method B – Total pay allocated to actual amounts due for each pay period. NIC is calculated for each pay period and the results are added together.

## Task 2.5

(a) **Which ONE of the following is the standard recovery amount for statutory adoption, maternity and paternity pay where the employer is not a small employer for recovery purposes?**

Nil   (92%)   95%   104.2%

(b) **How does the employer recover this amount?**

☐ The employer submits a special claim form to the Treasury.
☑ The recovery value is deducted from the regular payment to HMRC.
☐ The organisation sends a standard invoice to HMRC.
☐ An adjustment is made on the year end return.

(c) **Explain how you would determine if you can recover statutory sick pay when making the payment to HMRC.**

Calculate 13% of gross NIC for month. If SSP paid is higher, then some of the SSP can be reclaimed.

# ANSWERS TO AAT EXAM PAPER 1 (JUNE 2008)

## Task 2.5, continued

(d) Which ONE of the following is the amount of SSP which can be recovered if the circumstances in (c) above apply?

**Excess over 13%** | 13% | 92% | 104.5%

## Task 2.6

(a) What is the earliest date in the month by which the regular PAYE payment must be made?

6th | 14th | **19th** | 25th

(b) Under what circumstances can the employer make payment later than the date you have identified in (a) above?

If paying electronically

(c) What is the later date by which payment can be made if the circumstances in (b) above are met?

12th | 16th | 19th | **22nd**

## Task 2.7

Payments made to an ex-employee after they have left their employment can be subject to special income tax and national insurance rules.

(a) Which ONE of the following tax codes would apply to a payment made after the P45 has been issued?

The one on the P45 | K647 | 647L Wk1 | **BR**

(b) At what point do the special NIC rules apply?

- [ ] One pay period after leaving
- [ ] One month after leaving
- [x] 6 weeks after leaving
- [ ] After the end of the tax year

## Task 2.8

The main statutory deductions are income tax, student loans and national insurance contributions.

(a) State TWO other statutory deductions.

1. Attachment of earnings orders
2. Child Support Agency DEO

## Task 2.8, continued

(b) **Which ONE of the following statements best describes the manner in which the employer should operate these other statutory deductions?**

- [✓] Make a deduction in accordance with the instructions.
- [ ] Deduct whenever the employee says it is OK to do so.
- [ ] Make the deduction whenever a payment is made to the employee.

(c) **What fees per deduction can the employer take from the employee towards the cost of operating these deductions?**

Nil    50p    75p    (£1.00)

## Task 2.9

(a) **Which ONE of the following types of pension scheme would be eligible for tax relief in the payroll?**

- [ ] All pensions where the deductions are taken by the employer
- [ ] Only occupational pension schemes
- [ ] Occupational schemes and approved personal pensions
- [✓] Only approved occupational pension schemes

b) **What basic NIC letter would apply to the following pension schemes if there are no other factors to consider?**

| | |
|---|---|
| COMP | F |
| Stakeholder | A |
| COSR | D |

## Task 2.10

One of your key functions is to check the validity of the payroll and ensure that only those entitled to be paid are to receive a payment.

(a) **Describe how you would reconcile the number of payments made in a payroll run.**

Number paid in previous period + starters − leavers + those not paid last time but due to be paid this time − those not being paid this time.

(b) **What TWO checks would you use to ensure the payments calculated are to be made to genuine employees?**

1. Properly authorised new starter forms
2. Correct use of P45/P46 procedures

# ANSWERS TO AAT EXAM PAPER 1 (JUNE 2008)

# AAT EXAM PAPER 2: ANSWERS

**DO NOT TURN THIS PAGE UNTIL YOU HAVE COMPLETED THE EXAM**

# December 2007

# SECTION 1

**Calculation for Task 1.1 – Trinidad Garcia – April 2009 gross to net pay**

| | | |
|---|---|---|
| Basic pay | | 4,847.08 |
| Pension contribution for April 2009 | (8% × £4,847.08) | 387.77 |
| Pension contribution year to date | | 387.77 |
| AVC for April 2009 | | 287.00 |
| AVC year to date | | 287.00 |

**Tax calculation**

| | | |
|---|---|---|
| Cumulative gross pay | | 4,847.08 |
| Less cumulative allowable deductions (above) | (387.77 + 287.00) | 674.77 |
| Cumulative pay for tax purposes | | 4,172.31 |
| Tax code used | 508L    Tax basis    Cumulative | |
| Adjustment for tax code | | 424.09 |
| Cumulative net taxable pay | | 3,748.22 |
| Tax calculation | Table C: £3,177 | 623.46 |
| continued | Table D: £600 | 240.00 |
| continued | £31 | 12.40 |
| Tax due for April 2009 | | 875.86 |

**NICs calculation**    NI table letter used    C

| | | |
|---|---|---|
| Employee's contributions payable | | NIL |
| | | |
| Employer's contributions payable | (4,847.08 – 476) × 12.8% | 559.50 |

| Payslip – April 2009 | | |
|---|---|---|
| Employee – Trinidad Garcia | | Date – 30 April 2009 |

| Payments £ | Deductions £ | Cumulatives £ |
|---|---|---|
| Basic pay: 4,847.08 | Income tax: 875.86 | Gross pay: 4,847.08 |
| | NIC: NIL | Pay for tax purposes: 4,172.31 |
| | Pension: 387.77 | Income tax: 875.86 |
| | AVC: 287.00 | Employee's NIC: NIL |
| | Staff loan: 250.00 | Employer's NIC: 559.50 |
| | Health club: 25.00 | Pension: 387.77 |
| | | AVC: 287.00 |
| | | Staff loan: 250.00 |
| | | Health club: 25.00 |
| Total gross pay: 4,847.08 | Total deductions: 1,825.63 | Net pay: 3,021.45 |

NI number: ST169528C    Tax code: 508L

## ANSWERS TO AAT EXAM PAPER 2 (DECEMBER 2007)

**Calculation for Task 1.1 – Trinidad Garcia – May 2009 gross to net pay**

| | | |
|---|---|---:|
| Basic pay | | 1,118.56 |
| Cumulative gross pay | (4,847.08 + 1,118.56) | 5,965.64 |
| Pension contribution for May 2009 | (8% × 1,118.56) | 89.48 |
| Pension contribution year to date | (387.77 + 89.48) | 477.25 |
| AVC contribution year to date | | 287.00 |

**Tax calculation**

| | | |
|---|---|---:|
| Total gross pay | | 5,965.44 |
| Less allowable deductions (above) | (477.25 + 287.00) | 764.25 |
| Pay for tax purposes | | 5,201.39 |
| Tax code used | 508L     Tax basis     Wk1/Mth1 | |
| Adjustment for tax code | | 424.09 |
| Net taxable pay for May 2009 only | (1,118.56 – 89.48 – 424.09) | 604.99 |
| Tax calculation | Table B | |
| continued | 600 | 120.00 |
| continued | 4 | 0.80 |
| Tax due May 2009 | | 120.80 |
| Plus tax paid in April 2009 | | 875.86 |
| Cumulative tax due to May 2009 | | 996.66 |

**NICs calculation**    NI table letter used    C

| | | |
|---|---|---:|
| Employee's contributions payable | | NIL |
| Employer's contributions payable | (1,118.56 – 476) × 12.8% | 82.25 |

### Payslip – May 2009

**Employee – Trinidad Garcia**

Date – 31 May 2009

| Payments £ | Deductions £ | Cumulatives £ |
|---|---|---|
| Basic pay: 1,118.56 | Income tax: 120.80 | Gross pay: 5,965.64 |
|  | NIC: NIL | Pay for tax purposes: 5,201.39 |
|  | Pension: 89.48 | Income tax: 996.66 |
|  | AVC: - | Employee's NIC: NIL |
|  | Staff loan: - | Employer's NIC: 641.75 |
|  | Health club: - | Pension: 477.25 |
|  |  | AVC: 287.00 |
|  |  | Staff loan: 250.00 |
|  |  | Health club: 25.00 |
| **Total gross pay:** 1,118.56 | **Total deductions:** 210.28 | **Net pay:** 908.28 |

**NI number:** ST169528C  **Tax code:** 508L Month 1

## Calculation for Task 1.1 – Phillip Yoest – April 2009 gross to net pay

| | | |
|---|---|---:|
| Basic pay | | 2,650.00 |
| Pension contribution for April 2009 | (8% × £2,650) | 212.00 |
| Pension contribution year to date | | 212.00 |
| AVC for April 2009 | | 175.00 |
| AVC year to date | | 175.00 |
| Charity Giving for April 2009 | | 85.00 |
| Charity Giving year to date | | 85.00 |

**Tax calculation**

| | | |
|---|---|---:|
| Cumulative gross pay | | 2,650.00 |
| Less cumulative allowable deductions (above) | (212.00 + 175.00 + 85.00) | 472.00 |
| Cumulative pay for tax purposes | | 2,178.00 |
| Tax code used | K194    Tax basis   Cumulative | |
| Adjustment for tax code | | 162.42 |
| Cumulative net taxable pay | | 2,340.42 |
| Tax calculation | Table B | |
| continued | 2,300 | 460.00 |
| continued | 40 | 8.00 |
| Cumulative tax due | | 468.00 |

| **NICs calculation** | NI table letter used   F | |
|---|---|---:|
| Employee's contributions payable | (2,650.00 – 476) × 9.4% | 204.36 |
| | (476 – 412) × 1.6% | (1.02) |
| | | 203.34 |
| Employer's contributions payable | (2,650.00 – 476) × 11.4% | 247.84 |
| | (476 – 412) × 1.4% | (0.90) |
| | | 246.94 |

## Payslip – April 2009

**Employee – Phillip Yoest**  
**Date – 30 April 2009**

| Payments £ | Deductions £ | Cumulatives £ |
|---|---|---|
| Basic pay: 2,650.00 | Income tax: 468.00 | Gross pay: 2,650.00 |
| | NIC: 203.34 | Pay for tax purposes: 2,178.00 |
| | Pension: 212.00 | Income tax: 468.00 |
| | AVC: 175.00 | Employee's NIC: 203.34 |
| | Charity Giving: 85.00 | Employer's NIC: 246.94 |
| | Health club: 25.00 | Pension: 212.00 |
| | | AVC: 175.00 |
| | | Charity Giving: 85.00 |
| | | Health club: 25.00 |
| **Total gross pay:** 2,650.00 | **Total deductions:** 1,168.34 | **Net pay:** 1,481.66 |

**NI number: TH638871D**     **Tax code: K194**

## Calculation for Task 1.1 – Phillip Yoest – May 2009 gross to net pay

| | | |
|---|---|---|
| Basic pay | | 2,650.00 |
| Bonus | | 1,200.00 |
| Total gross pay for May 2009 | | 3,850.00 |
| Cumulative gross pay, year to date | | 6,500.00 |
| Pension contribution for May 2009 | (8% × £3,850.00) | 308.00 |
| Pension contribution year to date | | 520.00 |
| AVC for May | 250.00   year to date: | 425.00 |
| Charity Giving: for May 2009 | 85.00   year to date: | 170.00 |

**Tax calculation**

| | | |
|---|---|---|
| Cumulative gross pay | | 6,500.00 |
| Less cumulative allowable deductions (above) | (520.00 + 425.00 + 170.00) | 1,115.00 |
| Cumulative pay for tax purposes | | 5,385.00 |
| Tax code used | K194   Tax basis   Cumulative | |
| Adjustment for tax code | | 324.84 |
| Cumulative net taxable pay | | 5,709.84 |
| Tax calculation | Table B | |
| continued | 5,700 | 1,140.00 |
| continued | 9 | 1.80 |
| Cumulative tax due | | 1,141.80 |
| Less tax already paid | | 468.00 |
| Tax due for May 2009 | | 673.80 |

**NICs calculation**   NI table letter used   F

| | | | |
|---|---|---|---|
| Employee's contributions payable | (3,850 – 3,656) × 1% | | 1.94 |
| | (3,656 – 3,337) × 11% | | 35.09 |
| | ~~(3,337 – 476) × 9.4%~~ | | ~~268.93~~ |
| | (476 – 412) × 1.6% | | (1.02) |
| | | | 304.94 |
| Employer's contributions payable | (3,850 – 3,337) × 12.8% | 65.66 | |
| | (3,337 – 476) × 11.4% | 326.15 | |
| | (476 – 412) × 1.4% | (0.90) | |
| | | 390.91 | |

**Payslip – May 2009**

Employee – Phillip Yoest

Date – 31 May 2009

| Payments £ | Deductions £ | Cumulatives £ |
|---|---|---|
| Basic pay: 2,650.00 | Income tax: 673.80 | Gross pay: 6,500.00 |
| Bonus: 1,200.00 | NIC: 304.94 | Pay for tax purposes: 5,385.00 |
|  | Pension 308.00 | Income tax: 1,141.80 |
|  | AVC: 250.00 | Employee's NIC: 508.28 |
|  | Charity Giving 85.00 | Employer's NIC: 637.85 |
|  | Health club: 25.00 | Pension: 520.00 |
|  |  | AVC: 425.00 |
|  |  | Charity Giving: 170.00 |
|  |  | Health club: 50.00 |
| **Total gross pay:** 3,850.00 | **Total deductions:** 1,646.74 | **Net pay:** 2,203.26 |

NI number: TH638871D    Tax code: K194

## Task 1.2

| | |
|---|---|
| From: | payroll@fictitious.ltd.uk |
| Sent: | 6 December 2009 |
| To: | chloe.nabarro@fictitious.ltd.uk |
| Subject: | Re: Payments to HMRC |

Dear Chloe

Thank you for your e-mail.

As we have less than 250 employees, we can pay HMRC by cheque, using the Giro system or electronically.

We are not obliged to pay electronically, but we could use BACS, Internet or CHAPS if we wish.

Payment must reach HMRC accounts office by 19th of the month. However, if we decide to pay electronically, then the payment must reach the HMRC account by 22nd of the month. Note that if the 19th or 22nd fall on a weekend or bank holiday, then payment must reach HMRC by the last working day prior to those dates.

# SECTION 2

## Task 2.1

(a) Income tax
NIC (employees' and employer's)
SLDs

(b) 92%

(c) If the employer is classified as a small employer (annual Class 1 NIC liability is £45,000 or less), then 100% of SMP/SPP/SAP can be recovered together with 4.5% compensation (a total of 104.5%).

## Task 2.2

(a) SSP can only be recovered if the amount of SSP paid in the month exceeds 13% of the total Class 1 NIC liability for that month.

(b) Excess over 13%.

## Task 2.3

(a) No.

(b) Breach of confidentiality
Data Protection Act
Employers may not have permission to use data in this way

## Task 2.4

(a) Any three from:

Basic wage
Salary
Overtime
Bonus
Commission
Shift pay
SSP/SMP/SPP/SAP

(b) Employer's NIC
Employer's pension contributions

## Task 2.5

(a) From the first payment made after attaining 16 years of age
(b) No (state retirement age for men is 65 and Hugo needs an age exemption certificate)

## Task 2.6

(a) No

(b) SLDs can only be stopped if HMRC sends a stop notice

(c) Any two of the following:

Employee reaches 65
HMRC issue a stop notice
Employee dies

## Task 2.7

(a) No
(b) Cannot deduct such sums without employee's written consent.

## Task 2.8

(a) BR
(b) A

## Task 2.9

Any of the following:

Control account balances
Reasonability check to previous month
Check parameters are current, eg tax and NIC rates
Correct numbers of payslips
Reconciliation of gross pay to net pay and deductions

## Task 2.10

(a) 647L
(b) The suffix code represents the amount of pay that can be earned in a year without paying tax.

# AAT EXAM PAPER 3: ANSWERS

## DO NOT TURN THIS PAGE UNTIL YOU HAVE COMPLETED THE EXAM

## June 2007

# SECTION 1

**Calculation for Task 1.1 – Frank Lee – April 2009 gross to net pay**

| | | |
|---|---|---:|
| Basic pay | | 3,815.00 |
| Total gross pay | | 3,815.00 |
| Pension contribution for April | (8% × £3,815) | 305.20 |
| Pension contribution year to date | | 305.20 |
| AVC contribution for April 2009 | | 78.50 |
| AVC contribution year to date | | 78.50 |
| Charitable Giving for April 2009 | (250 + 150) | 400.00 |
| Charitable Giving year to date | | 400.00 |

**Tax calculation**

| | | |
|---|---|---:|
| Cumulative gross pay | | 3,815.00 |
| Less cumulative allowable deductions (above) | (305.20 + 78.50 + 400.00) | 783.70 |
| Cumulative pay for tax purposes | | 3,031.30 |
| Tax code used __15L__ | Tax basis __Cumulative__ | |
| Adjustment for tax code | | 13.25 |
| Cumulative net taxable pay | | 3,018.05 |
| Tax calculation | Table B: 3,000 | 600.00 |
| | : 18 | 3.60 |
| Tax due for April 2009 | | 603.60 |

**NICs calculation**     NI table letter used __D__

| | | | |
|---|---|---:|---:|
| Employee's contributions payable | (3,815 – 3,656) × 1% | | 1.59 |
| | (3,656 – 3,337) × 11% | | 35.09 |
| | (3,337 – 476) × 9.4% | | 268.93 |
| | (476 – 412) × 1.6% | | (1.02) |
| Employer's contributions payable | (3,815 – 3,337) × 12.8% | 61.18 | 304.59 |
| | (3,337 – 476) × 9.1% | 260.35 | |
| | (476 – 412) × 3.7% | (2.37) | |
| | | 319.16 | |

**Payslip – April 2009**

| Employee: Frank Lee | | Date – 30 April 2009 |
|---|---|---|

| Payments £ | | Deductions £ | | Cumulatives £ | |
|---|---|---|---|---|---|
| Basic pay: | 3,815.00 | Income tax: | 603.60 | Gross pay: | 3,815.00 |
| | | NIC: | 304.59 | Pay for tax purposes: | 3,031.30 |
| | | Pension: | 305.20 | Tax: | 603.60 |
| | | AVC: | 78.50 | Employee's NIC: | 304.59 |
| | | Charitable Giving: | 400.00 | Employer's NIC: | 319.16 |
| | | Loan: | 327.50 | Pension: | 305.20 |
| | | | | AVC: | 78.50 |
| | | | | Charitable Giving: | 400.00 |
| | | | | Loan: | 327.50 |
| **Total gross pay:** | 3,815.00 | **Total deductions:** | 2,019.39 | **Net pay:** | 1,795.61 |

| NI Number: PN698247D | Tax code: 15L |
|---|---|

## Calculation for Task 1.1 – Frank Lee – May 2009 gross to net pay

| | | |
|---|---|---:|
| Basic pay | | 3,815.00 |
| Bonus payment | | 2,800.00 |
| Total gross for May 2009 | | 6,615.00 |
| Cumulative gross pay | | 10,430.00 |
| Pension contribution for May 2009 | (8% × £6,615) | 529.20 |
| Pension contribution year to date | | 834.40 |
| AVC contribution for May 2009 | | 78.50 |
| AVC contribution year to date | | 157.00 |
| Charitable Giving for May 2009 | | 250.00 |
| Charitable Giving year to date | | 650.00 |

### Tax calculation

| | | |
|---|---|---:|
| Cumulative gross pay | | 10,430.00 |
| Less cumulative allowable deductions (above) | (834.40 + 157.00 + 650.00) | 1,641.40 |
| Cumulative pay for tax purposes | | 8,788.60 |
| Tax code used  K82 | Tax basis  Cumulative | |
| Adjustment for tax code | | 138.18 |
| Cumulative net taxable pay | | 8,926.78 |
| Tax calculation | Table C: 6,234 | 1,246.93 |
| | Table D: 2,600 | 1,040.00 |
| | 92 | 36.80 |
| Tax due year to date | | 2,323.73 |
| Less tax already paid | | 603.60 |
| Tax due for May 2009 | | 1,720.13 |

### NICs calculation  NI table letter used  D

| | | |
|---|---|---:|
| Employee's contributions payable | (6,615 – 3,656) × 1% | 29.59 |
| | (3,656 – 3,337) × 11% | 35.09 |
| | (3,337 – 476) × 9.4% – £1.02 | 267.91 |
| | | 332.59 |
| Employer's contributions payable | (6,615 – 3,337) × 12.8% | 419.58 |
| | (3,337 – 476) × 9.1% – £2.37 | 257.98 |
| | | 677.56 |

**Payslip – May 2009**

| Employee: Frank Lee | | Date – 31 May 2009 |
|---|---|---|

| Payments £ | | Deductions £ | | Cumulatives £ | |
|---|---|---|---|---|---|
| Basic pay: | 3,815.00 | Income tax: | 1,720.13 | Gross pay: | 10,430.00 |
| Bonus: | 2,800.00 | NIC: | 332.59 | Pay for tax purposes: | 8,788.60 |
| | | Pension: | 529.20 | Income tax: | 2,323.73 |
| | | AVC: | 78.50 | Employee's NIC: | 637.18 |
| | | Charitable Giving: | 250.00 | Employer's NIC: | 996.72 |
| | | Loan: | 327.50 | Pension: | 834.40 |
| | | | | AVC: | 157.00 |
| | | | | Charitable Giving: | 650.00 |
| | | | | Loan: | 655.00 |
| **Total gross pay:** | 6,615.00 | **Total deductions:** | 3,237.92 | **Net pay:** | 3,377.08 |

NI Number: PN698247D    Tax Code: K82

**Calculation for Task 1.1 – Kristina Strieff – April 2009 gross to net pay**

| | |
|---|---:|
| Basic pay | 956.60 |
| Gross pay year to date | 956.60 |
| Charitable Giving for April 2009 | 122.50 |
| Charitable Giving year to date | 122.50 |

**Tax calculation**

| | |
|---|---:|
| Cumulative gross pay | 956.60 |
| Less cumulative allowable deductions (above) | 122.50 |
| Cumulative pay for tax purposes | 834.10 |
| Tax code used ___647L___  Tax basis ___Cumulative___ | |
| Adjustment for tax code | 539.92 |
| Cumulative net taxable pay | 294.18 |
| Tax calculation     Table B | |
| 200 | 40.00 |
| 94 | 18.80 |
| Tax due for April | 58.80 |

**NICs calculation**         NI table letter used ___A___

| | | |
|---|---|---:|
| Employee's contributions payable | (956.60 – 476) × 11% | 52.87 |
| Employer's contributions payable | (956.60 – 476) × 12.8% | 61.52 |

**Payslip – April 2009**

| Employee: Kristina Strieff | | Date – 30 April 2009 |

| Payments £ | Deductions £ | Cumulatives £ |
|---|---|---|
| Basic pay: 956.60 | Income tax: 58.80 | Gross pay: 956.60 |
| | NIC: 52.87 | Pay for tax purposes: 834.10 |
| | Charitable Giving: 122.50 | Income tax: 58.80 |
| | Personal pension: 272.00 | Employee's NIC: 52.87 |
| | | Employer's NIC: 61.52 |
| | | Charitable Giving: 122.50 |
| | | Personal pension: 272.00 |
| **Total gross pay:** 956.60 | **Total deductions:** 506.17 | **Net pay:** 450.43 |

NI Number: HZ638756A        Tax code: 647L

## Calculation for Task 1.1 – Kristina Strieff – May 2009 gross to net pay

| | |
|---|---:|
| Basic pay | 2,391.50 |
| Gross pay year to date | 3,348.10 |
| Charitable Giving for May 2009 | 122.50 |
| Charitable Giving year to date | 245.00 |

### Tax calculation

| | |
|---|---:|
| Cumulative gross pay | 3,348.10 |
| Less cumulative allowable deductions (above) | 245.00 |
| Cumulative pay for tax purposes | 3,103.10 |

Tax code used  647L         Tax basis  Cumulative

| | |
|---|---:|
| Adjustment for tax code | 1,079.84 |
| Cumulative net taxable pay | 2,023.26 |

Tax calculation    Table B

| | |
|---:|---:|
| 2,000 | 400.00 |
| 23 | 4.60 |

| | |
|---|---:|
| Cumulative tax due | 404.60 |
| Less tax already paid | 58.80 |
| Tax due for May | 345.80 |

### NICs calculation

NI table letter used   A

| | | |
|---|---|---:|
| Employee's contributions payable | (2,391.50 – 476) × 11% | 210.70 |
| Employer's contributions payable | (2,391.50 – 476) × 12.8% | 245.18 |

**Payslip – May 2009**

| Employee: Kristina Strieff | Date – 31 May 2009 |
|---|---|

| Payments £ | Deductions £ | Cumulatives £ |
|---|---|---|
| Basic pay: 2,391.50 | Income tax: 345.80 | Gross pay: 3,348.10 |
| | NIC: 210.70 | Pay for tax purposes 3,103.10 |
| | Charitable Giving: 122.50 | Income tax: 404.60 |
| | Personal pension: 272.00 | Employee's NIC: 263.57 |
| | Student loan: 102.00 | Employer's NIC: 306.70 |
| | | Charitable Giving: 245.00 |
| | | Personal pension: 544.00 |
| | | Student loan: 102.00 |
| **Total gross pay:** 2,391.50 | **Total deductions:** 1,053.00 | **Net pay:** 1,338.50 |

| NI Number: HZ638756A | Tax code: 647L |
|---|---|

**Note.** SLDs based on pay for NIC purposes: £2,391.50.

## Task 1.2

**Calculation of gross costs and distributions – April 2009**

(a) Gross cost of April's payroll:

| | |
|---|---:|
| Pay items | 570,965.60 |
| SMP/SAP recovery (92% × £18,079.93) | (16,633.53) |
| Employer payments | 145,056.28 |
| | 699,388.35 |

(b) Payment due to the Collector of Taxes:

| | |
|---|---:|
| Income tax | 76,327.73 |
| NIC  – employees' | 58,083.85 |
|  – employer's | 67,912.65 |
| SMP/SAP recovery (as above) | (16,633.53) |
| Student loan | 18,862.00 |
| | 204,552.70 |

**(c) Net pay to employees:**

| | |
|---|---|
| Pay items | 570,965.60 |
| Deductions | (206,830.77) |
| Net pay | 364,134.83 |

# SECTION 2

## Task 2.1

(a) On or before pay day
(b) Every employee who has been paid

## Task 2.2

(a) A suffix code shows the amount of 'free pay' to be deducted from gross pay to arrive at taxable pay. The prefix K code shows the amount to be added to gross pay to arrive at taxable pay.

(b) 647L

(c) 50% of the taxable pay

## Task 2.3

(a) £1,500
(b) Collector of taxes
(c) 22nd of the month

## Task 2.4

(a) Any two of the following:

Start notice (SL 1)
P45 with 'Y' in box 5
P46 with 'X' in appropriate box

(b) £15,000

(c) Nil

## Task 2.5

(a) Issuing council
(b) £1.00
(c) Employee withdraws authority to deduct (it is a statutory deduction and so must be made)

## Task 2.6

(a) A
(b) D
(c) Appropriate Personal Pension Stakeholder pension scheme

## Task 2.7

(a) When they reach State Pension Age
(b) All payments which are made after the date when they cease to be liable

## Task 2.8

Any three of the following

Checking payslip totals against input
Checking a sample of payments
Proper authorisation
Effective procedures
Work rotation

## Task 2.9

(a) Employee and anyone given written authority by the employee
(b) Ask the employee to complete and sign a change of bank account form

## Task 2.10

(a) No limit
(b) An approved agency
(c) 19th of the month following the month of deduction

# Tax Tables

# TAX TABLES

**HM Revenue & Customs**

**Pay Adjustment Tables**

# Tables A

**Week 1** Apr 6 to Apr 12                      **Tables A** - Pay Adjustment Tables

| Code | Total pay adjustment to date £ | Code | Total pay adjustment to date £ | Code | Total pay adjustment to date £ | Code | Total pay adjustment to date £ | Code | Total pay adjustment to date £ | Code | Total pay adjustment to date £ | Code | Total pay adjustment to date £ | Code | Total pay adjustment to date £ | Code | Total pay adjustment to date £ |
|---|---|---|---|---|---|---|---|---|---|---|---|---|---|---|---|---|---|
| 0 | NIL | | | | | | | | | | | | | | | | |
| 1 | 0.37 | 61 | 11.91 | 121 | 23.45 | 181 | 34.99 | 241 | 46.52 | 301 | 58.06 | 351 | 67.68 | 401 | 77.29 | 451 | 86.91 |
| 2 | 0.56 | 62 | 12.10 | 122 | 23.64 | 182 | 35.18 | 242 | 46.72 | 302 | 58.25 | 352 | 67.87 | 402 | 77.49 | 452 | 87.10 |
| 3 | 0.75 | 63 | 12.29 | 123 | 23.83 | 183 | 35.37 | 243 | 46.91 | 303 | 58.45 | 353 | 68.06 | 403 | 77.68 | 453 | 87.29 |
| 4 | 0.95 | 64 | 12.49 | 124 | 24.02 | 184 | 35.56 | 244 | 47.10 | 304 | 58.64 | 354 | 68.25 | 404 | 77.87 | 454 | 87.49 |
| 5 | 1.14 | 65 | 12.68 | 125 | 24.22 | 185 | 35.75 | 245 | 47.29 | 305 | 58.83 | 355 | 68.45 | 405 | 78.06 | 455 | 87.68 |
| 6 | 1.33 | 66 | 12.87 | 126 | 24.41 | 186 | 35.95 | 246 | 47.49 | 306 | 59.02 | 356 | 68.64 | 406 | 78.25 | 456 | 87.87 |
| 7 | 1.52 | 67 | 13.06 | 127 | 24.60 | 187 | 36.14 | 247 | 47.68 | 307 | 59.22 | 357 | 68.83 | 407 | 78.45 | 457 | 88.06 |
| 8 | 1.72 | 68 | 13.25 | 128 | 24.79 | 188 | 36.33 | 248 | 47.87 | 308 | 59.41 | 358 | 69.02 | 408 | 78.64 | 458 | 88.25 |
| 9 | 1.91 | 69 | 13.45 | 129 | 24.99 | 189 | 36.52 | 249 | 48.06 | 309 | 59.60 | 359 | 69.22 | 409 | 78.83 | 459 | 88.45 |
| 10 | 2.10 | 70 | 13.64 | 130 | 25.18 | 190 | 36.72 | 250 | 48.25 | 310 | 59.79 | 360 | 69.41 | 410 | 79.02 | 460 | 88.64 |
| 11 | 2.29 | 71 | 13.83 | 131 | 25.37 | 191 | 36.91 | 251 | 48.45 | 311 | 59.99 | 361 | 69.60 | 411 | 79.22 | 461 | 88.83 |
| 12 | 2.49 | 72 | 14.02 | 132 | 25.56 | 192 | 37.10 | 252 | 48.64 | 312 | 60.18 | 362 | 69.79 | 412 | 79.41 | 462 | 89.02 |
| 13 | 2.68 | 73 | 14.22 | 133 | 25.75 | 193 | 37.29 | 253 | 48.83 | 313 | 60.37 | 363 | 69.99 | 413 | 79.60 | 463 | 89.22 |
| 14 | 2.87 | 74 | 14.41 | 134 | 25.95 | 194 | 37.49 | 254 | 49.02 | 314 | 60.56 | 364 | 70.18 | 414 | 79.79 | 464 | 89.41 |
| 15 | 3.06 | 75 | 14.60 | 135 | 26.14 | 195 | 37.68 | 255 | 49.22 | 315 | 60.75 | 365 | 70.37 | 415 | 79.99 | 465 | 89.60 |
| 16 | 3.25 | 76 | 14.79 | 136 | 26.33 | 196 | 37.87 | 256 | 49.41 | 316 | 60.95 | 366 | 70.56 | 416 | 80.18 | 466 | 89.79 |
| 17 | 3.45 | 77 | 14.99 | 137 | 26.52 | 197 | 38.06 | 257 | 49.60 | 317 | 61.14 | 367 | 70.75 | 417 | 80.37 | 467 | 89.99 |
| 18 | 3.64 | 78 | 15.18 | 138 | 26.72 | 198 | 38.25 | 258 | 49.79 | 318 | 61.33 | 368 | 70.95 | 418 | 80.56 | 468 | 90.18 |
| 19 | 3.83 | 79 | 15.37 | 139 | 26.91 | 199 | 38.45 | 259 | 49.99 | 319 | 61.52 | 369 | 71.14 | 419 | 80.75 | 469 | 90.37 |
| 20 | 4.02 | 80 | 15.56 | 140 | 27.10 | 200 | 38.64 | 260 | 50.18 | 320 | 61.72 | 370 | 71.33 | 420 | 80.95 | 470 | 90.56 |
| 21 | 4.22 | 81 | 15.75 | 141 | 27.29 | 201 | 38.83 | 261 | 50.37 | 321 | 61.91 | 371 | 71.52 | 421 | 81.14 | 471 | 90.75 |
| 22 | 4.41 | 82 | 15.95 | 142 | 27.49 | 202 | 39.02 | 262 | 50.56 | 322 | 62.10 | 372 | 71.72 | 422 | 81.33 | 472 | 90.95 |
| 23 | 4.60 | 83 | 16.14 | 143 | 27.68 | 203 | 39.22 | 263 | 50.75 | 323 | 62.29 | 373 | 71.91 | 423 | 81.52 | 473 | 91.14 |
| 24 | 4.79 | 84 | 16.33 | 144 | 27.87 | 204 | 39.41 | 264 | 62.49 | 324 | 62.49 | 374 | 72.10 | 424 | 81.72 | 474 | 91.33 |
| 25 | 4.99 | 85 | 16.52 | 145 | 28.06 | 205 | 39.60 | 265 | 51.14 | 325 | 62.68 | 375 | 72.29 | 425 | 81.91 | 475 | 91.52 |
| 26 | 5.18 | 86 | 16.72 | 146 | 28.25 | 206 | 39.79 | 266 | 51.33 | 326 | 62.87 | 376 | 72.49 | 426 | 82.10 | 476 | 91.72 |
| 27 | 5.37 | 87 | 16.91 | 147 | 28.45 | 207 | 39.99 | 267 | 51.52 | 327 | 63.06 | 377 | 72.68 | 427 | 82.29 | 477 | 91.91 |
| 28 | 5.56 | 88 | 17.10 | 148 | 28.64 | 208 | 40.18 | 268 | 51.72 | 328 | 63.25 | 378 | 72.87 | 428 | 82.49 | 478 | 92.10 |
| 29 | 5.75 | 89 | 17.29 | 149 | 28.83 | 209 | 40.37 | 269 | 51.91 | 329 | 63.45 | 379 | 73.06 | 429 | 82.68 | 479 | 92.29 |
| 30 | 5.95 | 90 | 17.49 | 150 | 29.02 | 210 | 40.56 | 270 | 52.10 | 330 | 63.64 | 380 | 73.25 | 430 | 82.87 | 480 | 92.49 |
| 31 | 6.14 | 91 | 17.68 | 151 | 29.22 | 211 | 40.75 | 271 | 52.29 | 331 | 63.83 | 381 | 73.45 | 431 | 83.06 | 481 | 92.68 |
| 32 | 6.33 | 92 | 17.87 | 152 | 29.41 | 212 | 40.95 | 272 | 52.49 | 332 | 64.02 | 382 | 73.64 | 432 | 83.25 | 482 | 92.87 |
| 33 | 6.52 | 93 | 18.06 | 153 | 29.60 | 213 | 41.14 | 273 | 52.68 | 333 | 64.22 | 383 | 73.83 | 433 | 83.45 | 483 | 93.06 |
| 34 | 6.72 | 94 | 18.25 | 154 | 29.79 | 214 | 41.33 | 274 | 52.87 | 334 | 64.41 | 384 | 74.02 | 434 | 83.64 | 484 | 93.25 |
| 35 | 6.91 | 95 | 18.45 | 155 | 29.99 | 215 | 41.52 | 275 | 53.06 | 335 | 64.60 | 385 | 74.22 | 435 | 83.83 | 485 | 93.45 |
| 36 | 7.10 | 96 | 18.64 | 156 | 30.18 | 216 | 41.72 | 276 | 53.25 | 336 | 64.79 | 386 | 74.41 | 436 | 84.02 | 486 | 93.64 |
| 37 | 7.29 | 97 | 18.83 | 157 | 30.37 | 217 | 41.91 | 277 | 53.45 | 337 | 64.99 | 387 | 74.60 | 437 | 84.22 | 487 | 93.83 |
| 38 | 7.49 | 98 | 19.02 | 158 | 30.56 | 218 | 42.10 | 278 | 53.64 | 338 | 65.18 | 388 | 74.79 | 438 | 84.41 | 488 | 94.02 |
| 39 | 7.68 | 99 | 19.22 | 159 | 30.75 | 219 | 42.29 | 279 | 53.83 | 339 | 65.37 | 389 | 74.99 | 439 | 84.60 | 489 | 94.22 |
| 40 | 7.87 | 100 | 19.41 | 160 | 30.95 | 220 | 42.49 | 280 | 54.02 | 340 | 65.56 | 390 | 75.18 | 440 | 84.79 | 490 | 94.41 |
| 41 | 8.06 | 101 | 19.60 | 161 | 31.14 | 221 | 42.68 | 281 | 54.22 | 341 | 65.75 | 391 | 75.37 | 441 | 84.99 | 491 | 94.60 |
| 42 | 8.25 | 102 | 19.79 | 162 | 31.33 | 222 | 42.87 | 282 | 54.41 | 342 | 65.95 | 392 | 75.56 | 442 | 85.18 | 492 | 94.79 |
| 43 | 8.45 | 103 | 19.99 | 163 | 31.52 | 223 | 43.06 | 283 | 54.60 | 343 | 66.14 | 393 | 75.75 | 443 | 85.37 | 493 | 94.99 |
| 44 | 8.64 | 104 | 20.18 | 164 | 31.72 | 224 | 43.25 | 284 | 54.79 | 344 | 66.33 | 394 | 75.95 | 444 | 85.56 | 494 | 95.18 |
| 45 | 8.83 | 105 | 20.37 | 165 | 31.91 | 225 | 43.45 | 285 | 54.99 | 345 | 66.52 | 395 | 76.14 | 445 | 85.75 | 495 | 95.37 |
| 46 | 9.02 | 106 | 20.56 | 166 | 32.10 | 226 | 43.64 | 286 | 55.18 | 346 | 66.72 | 396 | 76.33 | 446 | 85.95 | 496 | 95.56 |
| 47 | 9.22 | 107 | 20.75 | 167 | 32.29 | 227 | 43.83 | 287 | 55.37 | 347 | 66.91 | 397 | 76.52 | 447 | 86.14 | 497 | 95.75 |
| 48 | 9.41 | 108 | 20.95 | 168 | 32.49 | 228 | 44.02 | 288 | 55.56 | 348 | 67.10 | 398 | 76.72 | 448 | 86.33 | 498 | 95.95 |
| 49 | 9.60 | 109 | 21.14 | 169 | 32.68 | 229 | 44.22 | 289 | 55.75 | 349 | 67.29 | 399 | 76.91 | 449 | 86.52 | 499 | 96.14 |
| 50 | 9.79 | 110 | 21.33 | 170 | 32.87 | 230 | 44.41 | 290 | 55.95 | 350 | 67.49 | 400 | 77.10 | 450 | 86.72 | 500 | 96.33 |
| 51 | 9.99 | 111 | 21.52 | 171 | 33.06 | 231 | 44.60 | 291 | 56.14 | | | | | | | | |
| 52 | 10.18 | 112 | 21.72 | 172 | 33.25 | 232 | 44.79 | 292 | 56.33 | | | | | | | | |
| 53 | 10.37 | 113 | 21.91 | 173 | 33.45 | 233 | 44.99 | 293 | 56.52 | | | | | | | | |
| 54 | 10.56 | 114 | 22.10 | 174 | 33.64 | 234 | 45.18 | 294 | 56.72 | | | | | | | | |
| 55 | 10.75 | 115 | 22.29 | 175 | 33.83 | 235 | 45.37 | 295 | 56.91 | | | | | | | | |
| 56 | 10.95 | 116 | 22.49 | 176 | 34.02 | 236 | 45.56 | 296 | 57.10 | | | | | | | | |
| 57 | 11.14 | 117 | 22.68 | 177 | 34.22 | 237 | 45.75 | 297 | 57.29 | | | | | | | | |
| 58 | 11.33 | 118 | 22.87 | 178 | 34.41 | 238 | 45.95 | 298 | 57.49 | | | | | | | | |
| 59 | 11.52 | 119 | 23.06 | 179 | 34.60 | 239 | 46.14 | 299 | 57.68 | | | | | | | | |
| 60 | 11.72 | 120 | 23.25 | 180 | 34.79 | 240 | 46.33 | 300 | 57.87 | | | | | | | | |

**Code more than 500**

1 Where the code is in the range **501** to **1000** inclusive:
   a. Subtract **500** from the code and use the balance of the code to obtain a pay adjustment figure from the table above.
   b. Add this pay adjustment figure to the figure given in the box alongside to obtain the figure of total pay adjustment to date *    **96.16**

2 Where the code **exceeds 1000** follow the instructions on **page 3**.

400

# TAX TABLES

**Tables A** - Pay Adjustment Tables    Apr 13 to Apr 19  **Week 2**

| Code | Total pay adjustment to date £ | Code | Total pay adjustment to date £ | Code | Total pay adjustment to date £ | Code | Total pay adjustment to date £ | Code | Total pay adjustment to date £ | Code | Total pay adjustment to date £ | Code | Total pay adjustment to date £ | Code | Total pay adjustment to date £ | Code | Total pay adjustment to date £ |
|---|---|---|---|---|---|---|---|---|---|---|---|---|---|---|---|---|---|---|
| 0 | NIL | | | | | | | | | | | | | | | | | | |
| 1 | 0.74 | 61 | 23.82 | 121 | 46.90 | 181 | 69.98 | 241 | 93.04 | 301 | 116.12 | 351 | 135.36 | 401 | 154.58 | 451 | 173.82 |
| 2 | 1.12 | 62 | 24.20 | 122 | 47.28 | 182 | 70.36 | 242 | 93.44 | 302 | 116.50 | 352 | 135.74 | 402 | 154.98 | 452 | 174.20 |
| 3 | 1.50 | 63 | 24.58 | 123 | 47.66 | 183 | 70.74 | 243 | 93.82 | 303 | 116.90 | 353 | 136.12 | 403 | 155.36 | 453 | 174.58 |
| 4 | 1.90 | 64 | 24.98 | 124 | 48.04 | 184 | 71.12 | 244 | 94.20 | 304 | 117.28 | 354 | 136.50 | 404 | 155.74 | 454 | 174.98 |
| 5 | 2.28 | 65 | 25.36 | 125 | 48.44 | 185 | 71.50 | 245 | 94.58 | 305 | 117.66 | 355 | 136.90 | 405 | 156.12 | 455 | 175.36 |
| 6 | 2.66 | 66 | 25.74 | 126 | 48.82 | 186 | 71.90 | 246 | 94.98 | 306 | 118.04 | 356 | 137.28 | 406 | 156.50 | 456 | 175.74 |
| 7 | 3.04 | 67 | 26.12 | 127 | 49.20 | 187 | 72.28 | 247 | 95.36 | 307 | 118.44 | 357 | 137.66 | 407 | 156.90 | 457 | 176.12 |
| 8 | 3.44 | 68 | 26.50 | 128 | 49.58 | 188 | 72.66 | 248 | 95.74 | 308 | 118.82 | 358 | 138.04 | 408 | 157.28 | 458 | 176.50 |
| 9 | 3.82 | 69 | 26.90 | 129 | 49.98 | 189 | 73.04 | 249 | 96.12 | 309 | 119.20 | 359 | 138.44 | 409 | 157.66 | 459 | 176.90 |
| 10 | 4.20 | 70 | 27.28 | 130 | 50.36 | 190 | 73.44 | 250 | 96.50 | 310 | 119.58 | 360 | 138.82 | 410 | 158.04 | 460 | 177.28 |
| 11 | 4.58 | 71 | 27.66 | 131 | 50.74 | 191 | 73.82 | 251 | 96.90 | 311 | 119.98 | 361 | 139.20 | 411 | 158.44 | 461 | 177.66 |
| 12 | 4.98 | 72 | 28.04 | 132 | 51.12 | 192 | 74.20 | 252 | 97.28 | 312 | 120.36 | 362 | 139.58 | 412 | 158.82 | 462 | 178.04 |
| 13 | 5.36 | 73 | 28.44 | 133 | 51.50 | 193 | 74.58 | 253 | 97.66 | 313 | 120.74 | 363 | 139.98 | 413 | 159.20 | 463 | 178.44 |
| 14 | 5.74 | 74 | 28.82 | 134 | 51.90 | 194 | 74.98 | 254 | 98.04 | 314 | 121.12 | 364 | 140.36 | 414 | 159.58 | 464 | 178.82 |
| 15 | 6.12 | 75 | 29.20 | 135 | 52.28 | 195 | 75.36 | 255 | 98.44 | 315 | 121.50 | 365 | 140.74 | 415 | 159.98 | 465 | 179.20 |
| 16 | 6.50 | 76 | 29.58 | 136 | 52.66 | 196 | 75.74 | 256 | 98.82 | 316 | 121.90 | 366 | 141.12 | 416 | 160.36 | 466 | 179.58 |
| 17 | 6.90 | 77 | 29.98 | 137 | 53.04 | 197 | 76.12 | 257 | 99.20 | 317 | 122.28 | 367 | 141.50 | 417 | 160.74 | 467 | 179.98 |
| 18 | 7.28 | 78 | 30.36 | 138 | 53.44 | 198 | 76.50 | 258 | 99.58 | 318 | 122.66 | 368 | 141.90 | 418 | 161.12 | 468 | 180.36 |
| 19 | 7.66 | 79 | 30.74 | 139 | 53.82 | 199 | 76.90 | 259 | 99.98 | 319 | 123.04 | 369 | 142.28 | 419 | 161.50 | 469 | 180.74 |
| 20 | 8.04 | 80 | 31.12 | 140 | 54.20 | 200 | 77.28 | 260 | 100.36 | 320 | 123.44 | 370 | 142.66 | 420 | 161.90 | 470 | 181.12 |
| 21 | 8.44 | 81 | 31.50 | 141 | 54.58 | 201 | 77.66 | 261 | 100.74 | 321 | 123.82 | 371 | 143.04 | 421 | 162.28 | 471 | 181.50 |
| 22 | 8.82 | 82 | 31.90 | 142 | 54.98 | 202 | 78.04 | 262 | 101.12 | 322 | 124.20 | 372 | 143.44 | 422 | 162.66 | 472 | 181.90 |
| 23 | 9.20 | 83 | 32.28 | 143 | 55.36 | 203 | 78.44 | 263 | 101.50 | 323 | 124.58 | 373 | 143.82 | 423 | 163.04 | 473 | 182.28 |
| 24 | 9.58 | 84 | 32.66 | 144 | 55.74 | 204 | 78.82 | 264 | 101.90 | 324 | 124.98 | 374 | 144.20 | 424 | 163.44 | 474 | 182.66 |
| 25 | 9.98 | 85 | 33.04 | 145 | 56.12 | 205 | 79.20 | 265 | 102.28 | 325 | 125.36 | 375 | 144.58 | 425 | 163.82 | 475 | 183.04 |
| 26 | 10.36 | 86 | 33.44 | 146 | 56.50 | 206 | 79.58 | 266 | 102.66 | 326 | 125.74 | 376 | 144.98 | 426 | 164.20 | 476 | 183.44 |
| 27 | 10.74 | 87 | 33.82 | 147 | 56.90 | 207 | 79.98 | 267 | 103.04 | 327 | 126.12 | 377 | 145.36 | 427 | 164.58 | 477 | 183.82 |
| 28 | 11.12 | 88 | 34.20 | 148 | 57.28 | 208 | 80.36 | 268 | 103.44 | 328 | 126.50 | 378 | 145.74 | 428 | 164.98 | 478 | 184.20 |
| 29 | 11.50 | 89 | 34.58 | 149 | 57.66 | 209 | 80.74 | 269 | 103.82 | 329 | 126.90 | 379 | 146.12 | 429 | 165.36 | 479 | 184.58 |
| 30 | 11.90 | 90 | 34.98 | 150 | 58.04 | 210 | 81.12 | 270 | 104.20 | 330 | 127.28 | 380 | 146.50 | 430 | 165.74 | 480 | 184.98 |
| 31 | 12.28 | 91 | 35.36 | 151 | 58.44 | 211 | 81.50 | 271 | 104.58 | 331 | 127.66 | 381 | 146.90 | 431 | 166.12 | 481 | 185.36 |
| 32 | 12.66 | 92 | 35.74 | 152 | 58.82 | 212 | 81.90 | 272 | 104.98 | 332 | 128.04 | 382 | 147.28 | 432 | 166.50 | 482 | 185.74 |
| 33 | 13.04 | 93 | 36.12 | 153 | 59.20 | 213 | 82.28 | 273 | 105.36 | 333 | 128.44 | 383 | 147.66 | 433 | 166.90 | 483 | 186.12 |
| 34 | 13.44 | 94 | 36.50 | 154 | 59.58 | 214 | 82.66 | 274 | 105.74 | 334 | 128.82 | 384 | 148.04 | 434 | 167.28 | 484 | 186.50 |
| 35 | 13.82 | 95 | 36.90 | 155 | 59.98 | 215 | 83.04 | 275 | 106.12 | 335 | 129.20 | 385 | 148.44 | 435 | 167.66 | 485 | 186.90 |
| 36 | 14.20 | 96 | 37.28 | 156 | 60.36 | 216 | 83.44 | 276 | 106.50 | 336 | 129.58 | 386 | 148.82 | 436 | 168.04 | 486 | 187.28 |
| 37 | 14.58 | 97 | 37.66 | 157 | 60.74 | 217 | 83.82 | 277 | 106.90 | 337 | 129.98 | 387 | 149.20 | 437 | 168.44 | 487 | 187.66 |
| 38 | 14.98 | 98 | 38.04 | 158 | 61.12 | 218 | 84.20 | 278 | 107.28 | 338 | 130.36 | 388 | 149.58 | 438 | 168.82 | 488 | 188.04 |
| 39 | 15.36 | 99 | 38.44 | 159 | 61.50 | 219 | 84.58 | 279 | 107.66 | 339 | 130.74 | 389 | 149.98 | 439 | 169.20 | 489 | 188.44 |
| 40 | 15.74 | 100 | 38.82 | 160 | 61.90 | 220 | 84.98 | 280 | 108.04 | 340 | 131.12 | 390 | 150.36 | 440 | 169.58 | 490 | 188.82 |
| 41 | 16.12 | 101 | 39.20 | 161 | 62.28 | 221 | 85.36 | 281 | 108.44 | 341 | 131.50 | 391 | 150.74 | 441 | 169.98 | 491 | 189.20 |
| 42 | 16.50 | 102 | 39.58 | 162 | 62.66 | 222 | 85.74 | 282 | 108.82 | 342 | 131.90 | 392 | 151.12 | 442 | 170.36 | 492 | 189.58 |
| 43 | 16.90 | 103 | 39.98 | 163 | 63.04 | 223 | 86.12 | 283 | 109.20 | 343 | 132.28 | 393 | 151.50 | 443 | 170.74 | 493 | 189.98 |
| 44 | 17.28 | 104 | 40.36 | 164 | 63.44 | 224 | 86.50 | 284 | 109.58 | 344 | 132.66 | 394 | 151.90 | 444 | 171.12 | 494 | 190.36 |
| 45 | 17.66 | 105 | 40.74 | 165 | 63.82 | 225 | 86.90 | 285 | 109.98 | 345 | 133.04 | 395 | 152.28 | 445 | 171.50 | 495 | 190.74 |
| 46 | 18.04 | 106 | 41.12 | 166 | 64.20 | 226 | 87.28 | 286 | 110.36 | 346 | 133.44 | 396 | 152.66 | 446 | 171.90 | 496 | 191.12 |
| 47 | 18.44 | 107 | 41.50 | 167 | 64.58 | 227 | 87.66 | 287 | 110.74 | 347 | 133.82 | 397 | 153.04 | 447 | 172.28 | 497 | 191.50 |
| 48 | 18.82 | 108 | 41.90 | 168 | 64.98 | 228 | 88.04 | 288 | 111.12 | 348 | 134.20 | 398 | 153.44 | 448 | 172.66 | 498 | 191.90 |
| 49 | 19.20 | 109 | 42.28 | 169 | 65.36 | 229 | 88.44 | 289 | 111.50 | 349 | 134.58 | 399 | 153.82 | 449 | 173.04 | 499 | 192.28 |
| 50 | 19.58 | 110 | 42.66 | 170 | 65.74 | 230 | 88.82 | 290 | 111.90 | 350 | 134.98 | 400 | 154.20 | 450 | 173.44 | 500 | 192.66 |
| 51 | 19.98 | 111 | 43.04 | 171 | 66.12 | 231 | 89.20 | 291 | 112.28 | | | | | | | | |
| 52 | 20.36 | 112 | 43.44 | 172 | 66.50 | 232 | 89.58 | 292 | 112.66 | | | | | | | | |
| 53 | 20.74 | 113 | 43.82 | 173 | 66.90 | 233 | 89.98 | 293 | 113.04 | | | | | | | | |
| 54 | 21.12 | 114 | 44.20 | 174 | 67.28 | 234 | 90.36 | 294 | 113.44 | | | | | | | | |
| 55 | 21.50 | 115 | 44.58 | 175 | 67.66 | 235 | 90.74 | 295 | 113.82 | | | | | | | | |
| 56 | 21.90 | 116 | 44.98 | 176 | 68.04 | 236 | 91.12 | 296 | 114.20 | | | | | | | | |
| 57 | 22.28 | 117 | 45.36 | 177 | 68.44 | 237 | 91.50 | 297 | 114.58 | | | | | | | | |
| 58 | 22.66 | 118 | 45.74 | 178 | 68.82 | 238 | 91.90 | 298 | 114.98 | | | | | | | | |
| 59 | 23.04 | 119 | 46.12 | 179 | 69.20 | 239 | 92.28 | 299 | 115.36 | | | | | | | | |
| 60 | 23.44 | 120 | 46.50 | 180 | 69.58 | 240 | 92.66 | 300 | 115.74 | | | | | | | | |

**Code more than 500**

1 Where the code is in the range **501** to **1000** inclusive:
   a. Subtract **500** from the code and use the balance of the code to obtain a pay adjustment figure from the table above.
   b. Add this pay adjustment figure to the figure given in the box alongside to obtain the figure of total pay adjustment to date * **192.32**

2 Where the code **exceeds 1000** follow the instructions on **page 3**.

# TAX TABLES

**Week 3** Apr 20 to Apr 26      **Tables A** - Pay Adjustment Tables

| Code | Total pay adjustment to date £ | Code | Total pay adjustment to date £ | Code | Total pay adjustment to date £ | Code | Total pay adjustment to date £ | Code | Total pay adjustment to date £ | Code | Total pay adjustment to date £ | Code | Total pay adjustment to date £ | Code | Total pay adjustment to date £ | Code | Total pay adjustment to date £ |
|---|---|---|---|---|---|---|---|---|---|---|---|---|---|---|---|---|---|
| 0 | NIL | | | | | | | | | | | | | | | | |
| 1 | 1.11 | 61 | 35.73 | 121 | 70.35 | 181 | 104.97 | 241 | 139.56 | 301 | 174.18 | 351 | 203.04 | 401 | 231.87 | 451 | 260.73 |
| 2 | 1.68 | 62 | 36.30 | 122 | 70.92 | 182 | 105.54 | 242 | 140.16 | 302 | 174.75 | 352 | 203.61 | 402 | 232.47 | 452 | 261.30 |
| 3 | 2.25 | 63 | 36.87 | 123 | 71.49 | 183 | 106.11 | 243 | 140.73 | 303 | 175.35 | 353 | 204.18 | 403 | 233.04 | 453 | 261.87 |
| 4 | 2.85 | 64 | 37.47 | 124 | 72.06 | 184 | 106.68 | 244 | 141.30 | 304 | 175.92 | 354 | 204.75 | 404 | 233.61 | 454 | 262.47 |
| 5 | 3.42 | 65 | 38.04 | 125 | 72.66 | 185 | 107.25 | 245 | 141.87 | 305 | 176.49 | 355 | 205.35 | 405 | 234.18 | 455 | 263.04 |
| 6 | 3.99 | 66 | 38.61 | 126 | 73.23 | 186 | 107.85 | 246 | 142.47 | 306 | 177.06 | 356 | 205.92 | 406 | 234.75 | 456 | 263.61 |
| 7 | 4.56 | 67 | 39.18 | 127 | 73.80 | 187 | 108.42 | 247 | 143.04 | 307 | 177.66 | 357 | 206.49 | 407 | 235.35 | 457 | 264.18 |
| 8 | 5.16 | 68 | 39.75 | 128 | 74.37 | 188 | 108.99 | 248 | 143.61 | 308 | 178.23 | 358 | 207.06 | 408 | 235.92 | 458 | 264.75 |
| 9 | 5.73 | 69 | 40.35 | 129 | 74.97 | 189 | 109.56 | 249 | 144.18 | 309 | 178.80 | 359 | 207.66 | 409 | 236.49 | 459 | 265.35 |
| 10 | 6.30 | 70 | 40.92 | 130 | 75.54 | 190 | 110.16 | 250 | 144.75 | 310 | 179.37 | 360 | 208.23 | 410 | 237.06 | 460 | 265.92 |
| 11 | 6.87 | 71 | 41.49 | 131 | 76.11 | 191 | 110.73 | 251 | 145.35 | 311 | 179.97 | 361 | 208.80 | 411 | 237.66 | 461 | 266.49 |
| 12 | 7.47 | 72 | 42.06 | 132 | 76.68 | 192 | 111.30 | 252 | 145.92 | 312 | 180.54 | 362 | 209.37 | 412 | 238.23 | 462 | 267.06 |
| 13 | 8.04 | 73 | 42.66 | 133 | 77.25 | 193 | 111.87 | 253 | 146.49 | 313 | 181.11 | 363 | 209.97 | 413 | 238.80 | 463 | 267.66 |
| 14 | 8.61 | 74 | 43.23 | 134 | 77.85 | 194 | 112.47 | 254 | 147.06 | 314 | 181.68 | 364 | 210.54 | 414 | 239.37 | 464 | 268.23 |
| 15 | 9.18 | 75 | 43.80 | 135 | 78.42 | 195 | 113.04 | 255 | 147.66 | 315 | 182.25 | 365 | 211.11 | 415 | 239.97 | 465 | 268.80 |
| 16 | 9.75 | 76 | 44.37 | 136 | 78.99 | 196 | 113.61 | 256 | 148.23 | 316 | 182.85 | 366 | 211.68 | 416 | 240.54 | 466 | 269.37 |
| 17 | 10.35 | 77 | 44.97 | 137 | 79.56 | 197 | 114.18 | 257 | 148.80 | 317 | 183.42 | 367 | 212.25 | 417 | 241.11 | 467 | 269.97 |
| 18 | 10.92 | 78 | 45.54 | 138 | 80.16 | 198 | 114.75 | 258 | 149.37 | 318 | 183.99 | 368 | 212.85 | 418 | 241.68 | 468 | 270.54 |
| 19 | 11.49 | 79 | 46.11 | 139 | 80.73 | 199 | 115.35 | 259 | 149.97 | 319 | 184.56 | 369 | 213.42 | 419 | 242.25 | 469 | 271.11 |
| 20 | 12.06 | 80 | 46.68 | 140 | 81.30 | 200 | 115.92 | 260 | 150.54 | 320 | 185.16 | 370 | 213.99 | 420 | 242.85 | 470 | 271.68 |
| 21 | 12.66 | 81 | 47.25 | 141 | 81.87 | 201 | 116.49 | 261 | 151.11 | 321 | 185.73 | 371 | 214.56 | 421 | 243.42 | 471 | 272.25 |
| 22 | 13.23 | 82 | 47.85 | 142 | 82.47 | 202 | 117.06 | 262 | 151.68 | 322 | 186.30 | 372 | 215.16 | 422 | 243.99 | 472 | 272.85 |
| 23 | 13.80 | 83 | 48.42 | 143 | 83.04 | 203 | 117.66 | 263 | 152.25 | 323 | 186.87 | 373 | 215.73 | 423 | 244.56 | 473 | 273.42 |
| 24 | 14.37 | 84 | 48.99 | 144 | 83.61 | 204 | 118.23 | 264 | 152.85 | 324 | 187.47 | 374 | 216.30 | 424 | 245.16 | 474 | 273.99 |
| 25 | 14.97 | 85 | 49.56 | 145 | 84.18 | 205 | 118.80 | 265 | 153.42 | 325 | 188.04 | 375 | 216.87 | 425 | 245.73 | 475 | 274.56 |
| 26 | 15.54 | 86 | 50.16 | 146 | 84.75 | 206 | 119.37 | 266 | 153.99 | 326 | 188.61 | 376 | 217.47 | 426 | 246.30 | 476 | 275.16 |
| 27 | 16.11 | 87 | 50.73 | 147 | 85.35 | 207 | 119.97 | 267 | 154.56 | 327 | 189.18 | 377 | 218.04 | 427 | 246.87 | 477 | 275.73 |
| 28 | 16.68 | 88 | 51.30 | 148 | 85.92 | 208 | 120.54 | 268 | 155.16 | 328 | 189.75 | 378 | 218.61 | 428 | 247.47 | 478 | 276.30 |
| 29 | 17.25 | 89 | 51.87 | 149 | 86.49 | 209 | 121.11 | 269 | 155.73 | 329 | 190.35 | 379 | 219.18 | 429 | 248.04 | 479 | 276.87 |
| 30 | 17.85 | 90 | 52.47 | 150 | 87.06 | 210 | 121.68 | 270 | 156.30 | 330 | 190.92 | 380 | 219.75 | 430 | 248.61 | 480 | 277.47 |
| 31 | 18.42 | 91 | 53.04 | 151 | 87.66 | 211 | 122.25 | 271 | 156.87 | 331 | 191.49 | 381 | 220.35 | 431 | 249.18 | 481 | 278.04 |
| 32 | 18.99 | 92 | 53.61 | 152 | 88.23 | 212 | 122.85 | 272 | 157.47 | 332 | 192.06 | 382 | 220.92 | 432 | 249.75 | 482 | 278.61 |
| 33 | 19.56 | 93 | 54.18 | 153 | 88.80 | 213 | 123.42 | 273 | 158.04 | 333 | 192.66 | 383 | 221.49 | 433 | 250.35 | 483 | 279.18 |
| 34 | 20.16 | 94 | 54.75 | 154 | 89.37 | 214 | 123.99 | 274 | 158.61 | 334 | 193.23 | 384 | 222.06 | 434 | 250.92 | 484 | 279.75 |
| 35 | 20.73 | 95 | 55.35 | 155 | 89.97 | 215 | 124.56 | 275 | 159.18 | 335 | 193.80 | 385 | 222.66 | 435 | 251.49 | 485 | 280.35 |
| 36 | 21.30 | 96 | 55.92 | 156 | 90.54 | 216 | 125.16 | 276 | 159.75 | 336 | 194.37 | 386 | 223.23 | 436 | 252.06 | 486 | 280.92 |
| 37 | 21.87 | 97 | 56.49 | 157 | 91.11 | 217 | 125.73 | 277 | 160.35 | 337 | 194.97 | 387 | 223.80 | 437 | 252.66 | 487 | 281.49 |
| 38 | 22.47 | 98 | 57.06 | 158 | 91.68 | 218 | 126.30 | 278 | 160.92 | 338 | 195.54 | 388 | 224.37 | 438 | 253.23 | 488 | 282.06 |
| 39 | 23.04 | 99 | 57.66 | 159 | 92.25 | 219 | 126.87 | 279 | 161.49 | 339 | 196.11 | 389 | 224.97 | 439 | 253.80 | 489 | 282.66 |
| 40 | 23.61 | 100 | 58.23 | 160 | 92.85 | 220 | 127.47 | 280 | 162.06 | 340 | 196.68 | 390 | 225.54 | 440 | 254.37 | 490 | 283.23 |
| 41 | 24.18 | 101 | 58.80 | 161 | 93.42 | 221 | 128.04 | 281 | 162.66 | 341 | 197.25 | 391 | 226.11 | 441 | 254.97 | 491 | 283.80 |
| 42 | 24.75 | 102 | 59.37 | 162 | 93.99 | 222 | 128.61 | 282 | 163.23 | 342 | 197.85 | 392 | 226.68 | 442 | 255.54 | 492 | 284.37 |
| 43 | 25.35 | 103 | 59.97 | 163 | 94.56 | 223 | 129.18 | 283 | 163.80 | 343 | 198.42 | 393 | 227.25 | 443 | 256.11 | 493 | 284.97 |
| 44 | 25.92 | 104 | 60.54 | 164 | 95.16 | 224 | 129.75 | 284 | 164.37 | 344 | 198.99 | 394 | 227.85 | 444 | 256.68 | 494 | 285.54 |
| 45 | 26.49 | 105 | 61.11 | 165 | 95.73 | 225 | 130.35 | 285 | 164.97 | 345 | 199.56 | 395 | 228.42 | 445 | 257.25 | 495 | 286.11 |
| 46 | 27.06 | 106 | 61.68 | 166 | 96.30 | 226 | 130.92 | 286 | 165.54 | 346 | 200.16 | 396 | 228.99 | 446 | 257.85 | 496 | 286.68 |
| 47 | 27.66 | 107 | 62.25 | 167 | 96.87 | 227 | 131.49 | 287 | 166.11 | 347 | 200.73 | 397 | 229.56 | 447 | 258.42 | 497 | 287.25 |
| 48 | 28.23 | 108 | 62.85 | 168 | 97.47 | 228 | 132.06 | 288 | 166.68 | 348 | 201.30 | 398 | 230.16 | 448 | 258.99 | 498 | 287.85 |
| 49 | 28.80 | 109 | 63.42 | 169 | 98.04 | 229 | 132.66 | 289 | 167.25 | 349 | 201.87 | 399 | 230.73 | 449 | 259.56 | 499 | 288.42 |
| 50 | 29.37 | 110 | 63.99 | 170 | 98.61 | 230 | 133.23 | 290 | 167.85 | 350 | 202.47 | 400 | 231.30 | 450 | 260.16 | 500 | 288.99 |
| 51 | 29.97 | 111 | 64.56 | 171 | 99.18 | 231 | 133.80 | 291 | 168.42 | | | | | | | | |
| 52 | 30.54 | 112 | 65.16 | 172 | 99.75 | 232 | 134.37 | 292 | 168.99 | | | | | | | | |
| 53 | 31.11 | 113 | 65.73 | 173 | 100.35 | 233 | 134.97 | 293 | 169.56 | | | | | | | | |
| 54 | 31.68 | 114 | 66.30 | 174 | 100.92 | 234 | 135.54 | 294 | 170.16 | | | | | | | | |
| 55 | 32.25 | 115 | 66.87 | 175 | 101.49 | 235 | 136.11 | 295 | 170.73 | | | | | | | | |
| 56 | 32.85 | 116 | 67.47 | 176 | 102.06 | 236 | 136.68 | 296 | 171.30 | | | | | | | | |
| 57 | 33.42 | 117 | 68.04 | 177 | 102.66 | 237 | 137.25 | 297 | 171.87 | | | | | | | | |
| 58 | 33.99 | 118 | 68.61 | 178 | 103.23 | 238 | 137.85 | 298 | 172.47 | | | | | | | | |
| 59 | 34.56 | 119 | 69.18 | 179 | 103.80 | 239 | 138.42 | 299 | 173.04 | | | | | | | | |
| 60 | 35.16 | 120 | 69.75 | 180 | 104.37 | 240 | 138.99 | 300 | 173.61 | | | | | | | | |

**Code more than 500**

1. Where the code is in the range **501** to **1000** inclusive:
   a. Subtract **500** from the code and use the balance of the code to obtain a pay adjustment figure from the table above.
   b. Add this pay adjustment figure to the figure given in the box alongside to obtain the figure of total pay adjustment to date * **288.48**

2. Where the code **exceeds 1000** follow the instructions on **page 3**.

**Tables A** - Pay Adjustment Tables  Apr 27 to May 3  **Week 4**

| Code | Total pay adjustment to date £ | Code | Total pay adjustment to date £ | Code | Total pay adjustment to date £ | Code | Total pay adjustment to date £ | Code | Total pay adjustment to date £ | Code | Total pay adjustment to date £ | Code | Total pay adjustment to date £ | Code | Total pay adjustment to date £ | Code | Total pay adjustment to date £ |
|---|---|---|---|---|---|---|---|---|---|---|---|---|---|---|---|---|---|
| 0 | NIL | | | | | | | | | | | | | | | | | |
| 1 | 1.48 | 61 | 47.64 | 121 | 93.80 | 181 | 139.96 | 241 | 186.08 | 301 | 232.24 | 351 | 270.72 | 401 | 309.16 | 451 | 347.64 |
| 2 | 2.24 | 62 | 48.40 | 122 | 94.56 | 182 | 140.72 | 242 | 186.88 | 302 | 233.00 | 352 | 271.48 | 402 | 309.96 | 452 | 348.40 |
| 3 | 3.00 | 63 | 49.16 | 123 | 95.32 | 183 | 141.48 | 243 | 187.64 | 303 | 233.80 | 353 | 272.24 | 403 | 310.72 | 453 | 349.16 |
| 4 | 3.80 | 64 | 49.96 | 124 | 96.08 | 184 | 142.24 | 244 | 188.40 | 304 | 234.56 | 354 | 273.00 | 404 | 311.48 | 454 | 349.96 |
| 5 | 4.56 | 65 | 50.72 | 125 | 96.88 | 185 | 143.00 | 245 | 189.16 | 305 | 235.32 | 355 | 273.80 | 405 | 312.24 | 455 | 350.72 |
| 6 | 5.32 | 66 | 51.48 | 126 | 97.64 | 186 | 143.80 | 246 | 189.96 | 306 | 236.08 | 356 | 274.56 | 406 | 313.00 | 456 | 351.48 |
| 7 | 6.08 | 67 | 52.24 | 127 | 98.40 | 187 | 144.56 | 247 | 190.72 | 307 | 236.88 | 357 | 275.32 | 407 | 313.80 | 457 | 352.24 |
| 8 | 6.88 | 68 | 53.00 | 128 | 99.16 | 188 | 145.32 | 248 | 191.48 | 308 | 237.64 | 358 | 276.08 | 408 | 314.56 | 458 | 353.00 |
| 9 | 7.64 | 69 | 53.80 | 129 | 99.96 | 189 | 146.08 | 249 | 192.24 | 309 | 238.40 | 359 | 276.88 | 409 | 315.32 | 459 | 353.80 |
| 10 | 8.40 | 70 | 54.56 | 130 | 100.72 | 190 | 146.88 | 250 | 193.00 | 310 | 239.16 | 360 | 277.64 | 410 | 316.08 | 460 | 354.56 |
| 11 | 9.16 | 71 | 55.32 | 131 | 101.48 | 191 | 147.64 | 251 | 193.80 | 311 | 239.96 | 361 | 278.40 | 411 | 316.88 | 461 | 355.32 |
| 12 | 9.96 | 72 | 56.08 | 132 | 102.24 | 192 | 148.40 | 252 | 194.56 | 312 | 240.72 | 362 | 279.16 | 412 | 317.64 | 462 | 356.08 |
| 13 | 10.72 | 73 | 56.88 | 133 | 103.00 | 193 | 149.16 | 253 | 195.32 | 313 | 241.48 | 363 | 279.96 | 413 | 318.40 | 463 | 356.88 |
| 14 | 11.48 | 74 | 57.64 | 134 | 103.80 | 194 | 149.96 | 254 | 196.08 | 314 | 242.24 | 364 | 280.72 | 414 | 319.16 | 464 | 357.64 |
| 15 | 12.24 | 75 | 58.40 | 135 | 104.56 | 195 | 150.72 | 255 | 196.88 | 315 | 243.00 | 365 | 281.48 | 415 | 319.96 | 465 | 358.40 |
| 16 | 13.00 | 76 | 59.16 | 136 | 105.32 | 196 | 151.48 | 256 | 197.64 | 316 | 243.80 | 366 | 282.24 | 416 | 320.72 | 466 | 359.16 |
| 17 | 13.80 | 77 | 59.96 | 137 | 106.08 | 197 | 152.24 | 257 | 198.40 | 317 | 244.56 | 367 | 283.00 | 417 | 321.48 | 467 | 359.96 |
| 18 | 14.56 | 78 | 60.72 | 138 | 106.88 | 198 | 153.00 | 258 | 199.16 | 318 | 245.32 | 368 | 283.80 | 418 | 322.24 | 468 | 360.72 |
| 19 | 15.32 | 79 | 61.48 | 139 | 107.64 | 199 | 153.80 | 259 | 199.96 | 319 | 246.08 | 369 | 284.56 | 419 | 323.00 | 469 | 361.48 |
| 20 | 16.08 | 80 | 62.24 | 140 | 108.40 | 200 | 154.56 | 260 | 200.72 | 320 | 246.88 | 370 | 285.32 | 420 | 323.80 | 470 | 362.24 |
| 21 | 16.88 | 81 | 63.00 | 141 | 109.16 | 201 | 155.32 | 261 | 201.48 | 321 | 247.64 | 371 | 286.08 | 421 | 324.56 | 471 | 363.00 |
| 22 | 17.64 | 82 | 63.80 | 142 | 109.96 | 202 | 156.08 | 262 | 202.24 | 322 | 248.40 | 372 | 286.88 | 422 | 325.32 | 472 | 363.80 |
| 23 | 18.40 | 83 | 64.56 | 143 | 110.72 | 203 | 156.88 | 263 | 203.00 | 323 | 249.16 | 373 | 287.64 | 423 | 326.08 | 473 | 364.56 |
| 24 | 19.16 | 84 | 65.32 | 144 | 111.48 | 204 | 157.64 | 264 | 203.80 | 324 | 249.96 | 374 | 288.40 | 424 | 326.88 | 474 | 365.32 |
| 25 | 19.96 | 85 | 66.08 | 145 | 112.24 | 205 | 158.40 | 265 | 204.56 | 325 | 250.72 | 375 | 289.16 | 425 | 327.64 | 475 | 366.08 |
| 26 | 20.72 | 86 | 66.88 | 146 | 113.00 | 206 | 159.16 | 266 | 205.32 | 326 | 251.48 | 376 | 289.96 | 426 | 328.40 | 476 | 366.88 |
| 27 | 21.48 | 87 | 67.64 | 147 | 113.80 | 207 | 159.96 | 267 | 206.08 | 327 | 252.24 | 377 | 290.72 | 427 | 329.16 | 477 | 367.64 |
| 28 | 22.24 | 88 | 68.40 | 148 | 114.56 | 208 | 160.72 | 268 | 206.88 | 328 | 253.00 | 378 | 291.48 | 428 | 329.96 | 478 | 368.40 |
| 29 | 23.00 | 89 | 69.16 | 149 | 115.32 | 209 | 161.48 | 269 | 207.64 | 329 | 253.80 | 379 | 292.24 | 429 | 330.72 | 479 | 369.16 |
| 30 | 23.80 | 90 | 69.96 | 150 | 116.08 | 210 | 162.24 | 270 | 208.40 | 330 | 254.56 | 380 | 293.00 | 430 | 331.48 | 480 | 369.96 |
| 31 | 24.56 | 91 | 70.72 | 151 | 116.88 | 211 | 163.00 | 271 | 209.16 | 331 | 255.32 | 381 | 293.80 | 431 | 332.24 | 481 | 370.72 |
| 32 | 25.32 | 92 | 71.48 | 152 | 117.64 | 212 | 163.80 | 272 | 209.96 | 332 | 256.08 | 382 | 294.56 | 432 | 333.00 | 482 | 371.48 |
| 33 | 26.08 | 93 | 72.24 | 153 | 118.40 | 213 | 164.56 | 273 | 210.72 | 333 | 256.88 | 383 | 295.32 | 433 | 333.80 | 483 | 372.24 |
| 34 | 26.88 | 94 | 73.00 | 154 | 119.16 | 214 | 165.32 | 274 | 211.48 | 334 | 257.64 | 384 | 296.08 | 434 | 334.56 | 484 | 373.00 |
| 35 | 27.64 | 95 | 73.80 | 155 | 119.96 | 215 | 166.08 | 275 | 212.24 | 335 | 258.40 | 385 | 296.88 | 435 | 335.32 | 485 | 373.80 |
| 36 | 28.40 | 96 | 74.56 | 156 | 120.72 | 216 | 166.88 | 276 | 213.00 | 336 | 259.16 | 386 | 297.64 | 436 | 336.08 | 486 | 374.56 |
| 37 | 29.16 | 97 | 75.32 | 157 | 121.48 | 217 | 167.64 | 277 | 213.80 | 337 | 259.96 | 387 | 298.40 | 437 | 336.88 | 487 | 375.32 |
| 38 | 29.96 | 98 | 76.08 | 158 | 122.24 | 218 | 168.40 | 278 | 214.56 | 338 | 260.72 | 388 | 299.16 | 438 | 337.64 | 488 | 376.08 |
| 39 | 30.72 | 99 | 76.88 | 159 | 123.00 | 219 | 169.16 | 279 | 215.32 | 339 | 261.48 | 389 | 299.96 | 439 | 338.40 | 489 | 376.88 |
| 40 | 31.48 | 100 | 77.64 | 160 | 123.80 | 220 | 169.96 | 280 | 216.08 | 340 | 262.24 | 390 | 300.72 | 440 | 339.16 | 490 | 377.64 |
| 41 | 32.24 | 101 | 78.40 | 161 | 124.56 | 221 | 170.72 | 281 | 216.88 | 341 | 263.00 | 391 | 301.48 | 441 | 339.96 | 491 | 378.40 |
| 42 | 33.00 | 102 | 79.16 | 162 | 125.32 | 222 | 171.48 | 282 | 217.64 | 342 | 263.80 | 392 | 302.24 | 442 | 340.72 | 492 | 379.16 |
| 43 | 33.80 | 103 | 79.96 | 163 | 126.08 | 223 | 172.24 | 283 | 218.40 | 343 | 264.56 | 393 | 303.00 | 443 | 341.48 | 493 | 379.96 |
| 44 | 34.56 | 104 | 80.72 | 164 | 126.88 | 224 | 173.00 | 284 | 219.16 | 344 | 265.32 | 394 | 303.80 | 444 | 342.24 | 494 | 380.72 |
| 45 | 35.32 | 105 | 81.48 | 165 | 127.64 | 225 | 173.80 | 285 | 219.96 | 345 | 266.08 | 395 | 304.56 | 445 | 343.00 | 495 | 381.48 |
| 46 | 36.08 | 106 | 82.24 | 166 | 128.40 | 226 | 174.56 | 286 | 220.72 | 346 | 266.88 | 396 | 305.32 | 446 | 343.80 | 496 | 382.24 |
| 47 | 36.88 | 107 | 83.00 | 167 | 129.16 | 227 | 175.32 | 287 | 221.48 | 347 | 267.64 | 397 | 306.08 | 447 | 344.56 | 497 | 383.00 |
| 48 | 37.64 | 108 | 83.80 | 168 | 129.96 | 228 | 176.08 | 288 | 222.24 | 348 | 268.40 | 398 | 306.88 | 448 | 345.32 | 498 | 383.80 |
| 49 | 38.40 | 109 | 84.56 | 169 | 130.72 | 229 | 176.88 | 289 | 223.00 | 349 | 269.16 | 399 | 307.64 | 449 | 346.08 | 499 | 384.56 |
| 50 | 39.16 | 110 | 85.32 | 170 | 131.48 | 230 | 177.64 | 290 | 223.80 | 350 | 269.96 | 400 | 308.40 | 450 | 346.88 | 500 | 385.32 |
| 51 | 39.96 | 111 | 86.08 | 171 | 132.24 | 231 | 178.40 | 291 | 224.56 | | | | | | | | |
| 52 | 40.72 | 112 | 86.88 | 172 | 133.00 | 232 | 179.16 | 292 | 225.32 | | | | | | | | |
| 53 | 41.48 | 113 | 87.64 | 173 | 133.80 | 233 | 179.96 | 293 | 226.08 | | | | | | | | |
| 54 | 42.24 | 114 | 88.40 | 174 | 134.56 | 234 | 180.72 | 294 | 226.88 | | | | | | | | |
| 55 | 43.00 | 115 | 89.16 | 175 | 135.32 | 235 | 181.48 | 295 | 227.64 | | | | | | | | |
| 56 | 43.80 | 116 | 89.96 | 176 | 136.08 | 236 | 182.24 | 296 | 228.40 | | | | | | | | |
| 57 | 44.56 | 117 | 90.72 | 177 | 136.88 | 237 | 183.00 | 297 | 229.16 | | | | | | | | |
| 58 | 45.32 | 118 | 91.48 | 178 | 137.64 | 238 | 183.80 | 298 | 229.96 | | | | | | | | |
| 59 | 46.08 | 119 | 92.24 | 179 | 138.40 | 239 | 184.56 | 299 | 230.72 | | | | | | | | |
| 60 | 46.88 | 120 | 93.00 | 180 | 139.16 | 240 | 185.32 | 300 | 231.48 | | | | | | | | |

**Code more than 500**

1 Where the code is in the range **501 to 1000** inclusive:
   a. Subtract **500** from the code and use the balance of the code to obtain a pay adjustment figure from the table above.
   b. Add this pay adjustment figure to the figure given in the box alongside to obtain the figure of total pay adjustment to date * **384.64**

2 Where the code **exceeds 1000** follow the instructions on **page 3**.

# TAX TABLES

**Week 5** May 4 to May 10      **Tables A** - Pay Adjustment Tables

| Code | Total pay adjustment to date £ | Code | Total pay adjustment to date £ | Code | Total pay adjustment to date £ | Code | Total pay adjustment to date £ | Code | Total pay adjustment to date £ | Code | Total pay adjustment to date £ | Code | Total pay adjustment to date £ | Code | Total pay adjustment to date £ | Code | Total pay adjustment to date £ |
|---|---|---|---|---|---|---|---|---|---|---|---|---|---|---|---|---|---|
| 0 | NIL | | | | | | | | | | | | | | | | |
| 1 | 1.85 | 61 | 59.55 | 121 | 117.25 | 181 | 174.95 | 241 | 232.60 | 301 | 290.30 | 351 | 338.40 | 401 | 386.45 | 451 | 434.55 |
| 2 | 2.80 | 62 | 60.50 | 122 | 118.20 | 182 | 175.90 | 242 | 233.60 | 302 | 291.25 | 352 | 339.35 | 402 | 387.45 | 452 | 435.50 |
| 3 | 3.75 | 63 | 61.45 | 123 | 119.15 | 183 | 176.85 | 243 | 234.55 | 303 | 292.25 | 353 | 340.30 | 403 | 388.40 | 453 | 436.45 |
| 4 | 4.75 | 64 | 62.45 | 124 | 120.10 | 184 | 177.80 | 244 | 235.50 | 304 | 293.20 | 354 | 341.25 | 404 | 389.35 | 454 | 437.45 |
| 5 | 5.70 | 65 | 63.40 | 125 | 121.10 | 185 | 178.75 | 245 | 236.45 | 305 | 294.15 | 355 | 342.25 | 405 | 390.30 | 455 | 438.40 |
| 6 | 6.65 | 66 | 64.35 | 126 | 122.05 | 186 | 179.75 | 246 | 237.45 | 306 | 295.10 | 356 | 343.20 | 406 | 391.25 | 456 | 439.35 |
| 7 | 7.60 | 67 | 65.30 | 127 | 123.00 | 187 | 180.70 | 247 | 238.40 | 307 | 296.10 | 357 | 344.15 | 407 | 392.25 | 457 | 440.30 |
| 8 | 8.60 | 68 | 66.25 | 128 | 123.95 | 188 | 181.65 | 248 | 239.35 | 308 | 297.05 | 358 | 345.10 | 408 | 393.20 | 458 | 441.25 |
| 9 | 9.55 | 69 | 67.25 | 129 | 124.95 | 189 | 182.60 | 249 | 240.30 | 309 | 298.00 | 359 | 346.10 | 409 | 394.15 | 459 | 442.25 |
| 10 | 10.50 | 70 | 68.20 | 130 | 125.90 | 190 | 183.60 | 250 | 241.25 | 310 | 298.95 | 360 | 347.05 | 410 | 395.10 | 460 | 443.20 |
| 11 | 11.45 | 71 | 69.15 | 131 | 126.85 | 191 | 184.55 | 251 | 242.25 | 311 | 299.95 | 361 | 348.00 | 411 | 396.10 | 461 | 444.15 |
| 12 | 12.45 | 72 | 70.10 | 132 | 127.80 | 192 | 185.50 | 252 | 243.20 | 312 | 300.90 | 362 | 348.95 | 412 | 397.05 | 462 | 445.10 |
| 13 | 13.40 | 73 | 71.10 | 133 | 128.75 | 193 | 186.45 | 253 | 244.15 | 313 | 301.85 | 363 | 349.95 | 413 | 398.00 | 463 | 446.10 |
| 14 | 14.35 | 74 | 72.05 | 134 | 129.75 | 194 | 187.45 | 254 | 245.10 | 314 | 302.80 | 364 | 350.90 | 414 | 398.95 | 464 | 447.05 |
| 15 | 15.30 | 75 | 73.00 | 135 | 130.70 | 195 | 188.40 | 255 | 246.10 | 315 | 303.75 | 365 | 351.85 | 415 | 399.95 | 465 | 448.00 |
| 16 | 16.25 | 76 | 73.95 | 136 | 131.65 | 196 | 189.35 | 256 | 247.05 | 316 | 304.75 | 366 | 352.80 | 416 | 400.90 | 466 | 448.95 |
| 17 | 17.25 | 77 | 74.95 | 137 | 132.60 | 197 | 190.30 | 257 | 248.00 | 317 | 305.70 | 367 | 353.75 | 417 | 401.85 | 467 | 449.95 |
| 18 | 18.20 | 78 | 75.90 | 138 | 133.60 | 198 | 191.25 | 258 | 248.95 | 318 | 306.65 | 368 | 354.75 | 418 | 402.80 | 468 | 450.90 |
| 19 | 19.15 | 79 | 76.85 | 139 | 134.55 | 199 | 192.25 | 259 | 249.95 | 319 | 307.60 | 369 | 355.70 | 419 | 403.75 | 469 | 451.85 |
| 20 | 20.10 | 80 | 77.80 | 140 | 135.50 | 200 | 193.20 | 260 | 250.90 | 320 | 308.60 | 370 | 356.65 | 420 | 404.75 | 470 | 452.80 |
| 21 | 21.10 | 81 | 78.75 | 141 | 136.45 | 201 | 194.15 | 261 | 251.85 | 321 | 309.55 | 371 | 357.60 | 421 | 405.70 | 471 | 453.75 |
| 22 | 22.05 | 82 | 79.75 | 142 | 137.45 | 202 | 195.10 | 262 | 252.80 | 322 | 310.50 | 372 | 358.60 | 422 | 406.65 | 472 | 454.75 |
| 23 | 23.00 | 83 | 80.70 | 143 | 138.40 | 203 | 196.10 | 263 | 253.75 | 323 | 311.45 | 373 | 359.55 | 423 | 407.60 | 473 | 455.70 |
| 24 | 23.95 | 84 | 81.65 | 144 | 139.35 | 204 | 197.05 | 264 | 254.75 | 324 | 312.45 | 374 | 360.50 | 424 | 408.60 | 474 | 456.65 |
| 25 | 24.95 | 85 | 82.60 | 145 | 140.30 | 205 | 198.00 | 265 | 255.70 | 325 | 313.40 | 375 | 361.45 | 425 | 409.55 | 475 | 457.60 |
| 26 | 25.90 | 86 | 83.60 | 146 | 141.25 | 206 | 198.95 | 266 | 256.65 | 326 | 314.35 | 376 | 362.45 | 426 | 410.50 | 476 | 458.60 |
| 27 | 26.85 | 87 | 84.55 | 147 | 142.25 | 207 | 199.95 | 267 | 257.60 | 327 | 315.30 | 377 | 363.40 | 427 | 411.45 | 477 | 459.55 |
| 28 | 27.80 | 88 | 85.50 | 148 | 143.20 | 208 | 200.90 | 268 | 258.60 | 328 | 316.25 | 378 | 364.35 | 428 | 412.45 | 478 | 460.50 |
| 29 | 28.75 | 89 | 86.45 | 149 | 144.15 | 209 | 201.85 | 269 | 259.55 | 329 | 317.25 | 379 | 365.30 | 429 | 413.40 | 479 | 461.45 |
| 30 | 29.75 | 90 | 87.45 | 150 | 145.10 | 210 | 202.80 | 270 | 260.50 | 330 | 318.20 | 380 | 366.25 | 430 | 414.35 | 480 | 462.45 |
| 31 | 30.70 | 91 | 88.40 | 151 | 146.10 | 211 | 203.75 | 271 | 261.45 | 331 | 319.15 | 381 | 367.25 | 431 | 415.30 | 481 | 463.40 |
| 32 | 31.65 | 92 | 89.35 | 152 | 147.05 | 212 | 204.75 | 272 | 262.45 | 332 | 320.10 | 382 | 368.20 | 432 | 416.25 | 482 | 464.35 |
| 33 | 32.60 | 93 | 90.30 | 153 | 148.00 | 213 | 205.70 | 273 | 263.40 | 333 | 321.10 | 383 | 369.15 | 433 | 417.25 | 483 | 465.30 |
| 34 | 33.60 | 94 | 91.25 | 154 | 148.95 | 214 | 206.65 | 274 | 264.35 | 334 | 322.05 | 384 | 370.10 | 434 | 418.20 | 484 | 466.25 |
| 35 | 34.55 | 95 | 92.25 | 155 | 149.95 | 215 | 207.60 | 275 | 265.30 | 335 | 323.00 | 385 | 371.10 | 435 | 419.15 | 485 | 467.25 |
| 36 | 35.50 | 96 | 93.20 | 156 | 150.90 | 216 | 208.60 | 276 | 266.25 | 336 | 323.95 | 386 | 372.05 | 436 | 420.10 | 486 | 468.20 |
| 37 | 36.45 | 97 | 94.15 | 157 | 151.85 | 217 | 209.55 | 277 | 267.25 | 337 | 324.95 | 387 | 373.00 | 437 | 421.10 | 487 | 469.15 |
| 38 | 37.45 | 98 | 95.10 | 158 | 152.80 | 218 | 210.50 | 278 | 268.20 | 338 | 325.90 | 388 | 373.95 | 438 | 422.05 | 488 | 470.10 |
| 39 | 38.40 | 99 | 96.10 | 159 | 153.75 | 219 | 211.45 | 279 | 269.15 | 339 | 326.85 | 389 | 374.95 | 439 | 423.00 | 489 | 471.10 |
| 40 | 39.35 | 100 | 97.05 | 160 | 154.75 | 220 | 212.45 | 280 | 270.10 | 340 | 327.80 | 390 | 375.90 | 440 | 423.95 | 490 | 472.05 |
| 41 | 40.30 | 101 | 98.00 | 161 | 155.70 | 221 | 213.40 | 281 | 271.10 | 341 | 328.75 | 391 | 376.85 | 441 | 424.95 | 491 | 473.00 |
| 42 | 41.25 | 102 | 98.95 | 162 | 156.65 | 222 | 214.35 | 282 | 272.05 | 342 | 329.75 | 392 | 377.80 | 442 | 425.90 | 492 | 473.95 |
| 43 | 42.25 | 103 | 99.95 | 163 | 157.60 | 223 | 215.30 | 283 | 273.00 | 343 | 330.70 | 393 | 378.75 | 443 | 426.85 | 493 | 474.95 |
| 44 | 43.20 | 104 | 100.90 | 164 | 158.60 | 224 | 216.25 | 284 | 273.95 | 344 | 331.65 | 394 | 379.75 | 444 | 427.80 | 494 | 475.90 |
| 45 | 44.15 | 105 | 101.85 | 165 | 159.55 | 225 | 217.25 | 285 | 274.95 | 345 | 332.60 | 395 | 380.70 | 445 | 428.75 | 495 | 476.85 |
| 46 | 45.10 | 106 | 102.80 | 166 | 160.50 | 226 | 218.20 | 286 | 275.90 | 346 | 333.60 | 396 | 381.65 | 446 | 429.75 | 496 | 477.80 |
| 47 | 46.10 | 107 | 103.75 | 167 | 161.45 | 227 | 219.15 | 287 | 276.85 | 347 | 334.55 | 397 | 382.60 | 447 | 430.70 | 497 | 478.75 |
| 48 | 47.05 | 108 | 104.75 | 168 | 162.45 | 228 | 220.10 | 288 | 277.80 | 348 | 335.50 | 398 | 383.60 | 448 | 431.65 | 498 | 479.75 |
| 49 | 48.00 | 109 | 105.70 | 169 | 163.40 | 229 | 221.10 | 289 | 278.75 | 349 | 336.45 | 399 | 384.55 | 449 | 432.60 | 499 | 480.70 |
| 50 | 48.95 | 110 | 106.65 | 170 | 164.35 | 230 | 222.05 | 290 | 279.75 | 350 | 337.45 | 400 | 385.50 | 450 | 433.60 | 500 | 481.65 |
| 51 | 49.95 | 111 | 107.60 | 171 | 165.30 | 231 | 223.00 | 291 | 280.70 | | | | | | | | |
| 52 | 50.90 | 112 | 108.60 | 172 | 166.25 | 232 | 223.95 | 292 | 281.65 | | | | | | | | |
| 53 | 51.85 | 113 | 109.55 | 173 | 167.25 | 233 | 224.95 | 293 | 282.60 | | | | | | | | |
| 54 | 52.80 | 114 | 110.50 | 174 | 168.20 | 234 | 225.90 | 294 | 283.60 | | | | | | | | |
| 55 | 53.75 | 115 | 111.45 | 175 | 169.15 | 235 | 226.85 | 295 | 284.55 | | | | | | | | |
| 56 | 54.75 | 116 | 112.45 | 176 | 170.10 | 236 | 227.80 | 296 | 285.50 | | | | | | | | |
| 57 | 55.70 | 117 | 113.40 | 177 | 171.10 | 237 | 228.75 | 297 | 286.45 | | | | | | | | |
| 58 | 56.65 | 118 | 114.35 | 178 | 172.05 | 238 | 229.75 | 298 | 287.45 | | | | | | | | |
| 59 | 57.60 | 119 | 115.30 | 179 | 173.00 | 239 | 230.70 | 299 | 288.40 | | | | | | | | |
| 60 | 58.60 | 120 | 116.25 | 180 | 173.95 | 240 | 231.65 | 300 | 289.35 | | | | | | | | |

**Code more than 500**

1 Where the code is in the range **501** to **1000** inclusive:
   a. Subtract **500** from the code and use the balance of the code to obtain a pay adjustment figure from the table above.
   b. Add this pay adjustment figure to the figure given in the box alongside to obtain the figure of total pay adjustment to date *   **480.80**

2 Where the code **exceeds 1000** follow the instructions on **page 3**.

## Tables A - Pay Adjustment Tables

May 11 to May 17 **Week 6**

| Code | Total pay adjustment to date £ | Code | Total pay adjustment to date £ | Code | Total pay adjustment to date £ | Code | Total pay adjustment to date £ | Code | Total pay adjustment to date £ | Code | Total pay adjustment to date £ | Code | Total pay adjustment to date £ | Code | Total pay adjustment to date £ | Code | Total pay adjustment to date £ | Code | Total pay adjustment to date £ |
|---|---|---|---|---|---|---|---|---|---|---|---|---|---|---|---|---|---|---|---|
| 0 | NIL | | | | | | | | | | | | | | | | | | |
| 1 | 2.22 | 61 | 71.46 | 121 | 140.70 | 181 | 209.94 | 241 | 279.12 | 301 | 348.36 | 351 | 406.08 | 401 | 463.74 | 451 | 521.46 | | |
| 2 | 3.36 | 62 | 72.60 | 122 | 141.84 | 182 | 211.08 | 242 | 280.32 | 302 | 349.50 | 352 | 407.22 | 402 | 464.94 | 452 | 522.60 | | |
| 3 | 4.50 | 63 | 73.74 | 123 | 142.98 | 183 | 212.22 | 243 | 281.46 | 303 | 350.70 | 353 | 408.36 | 403 | 466.08 | 453 | 523.74 | | |
| 4 | 5.70 | 64 | 74.94 | 124 | 144.12 | 184 | 213.36 | 244 | 282.60 | 304 | 351.84 | 354 | 409.50 | 404 | 467.22 | 454 | 524.94 | | |
| 5 | 6.84 | 65 | 76.08 | 125 | 145.32 | 185 | 214.50 | 245 | 283.74 | 305 | 352.98 | 355 | 410.70 | 405 | 468.36 | 455 | 526.08 | | |
| 6 | 7.98 | 66 | 77.22 | 126 | 146.46 | 186 | 215.70 | 246 | 284.94 | 306 | 354.12 | 356 | 411.84 | 406 | 469.50 | 456 | 527.22 | | |
| 7 | 9.12 | 67 | 78.36 | 127 | 147.60 | 187 | 216.84 | 247 | 286.08 | 307 | 355.32 | 357 | 412.98 | 407 | 470.70 | 457 | 528.36 | | |
| 8 | 10.32 | 68 | 79.50 | 128 | 148.74 | 188 | 217.98 | 248 | 287.22 | 308 | 356.46 | 358 | 414.12 | 408 | 471.84 | 458 | 529.50 | | |
| 9 | 11.46 | 69 | 80.70 | 129 | 149.94 | 189 | 219.12 | 249 | 288.36 | 309 | 357.60 | 359 | 415.32 | 409 | 472.98 | 459 | 530.70 | | |
| 10 | 12.60 | 70 | 81.84 | 130 | 151.08 | 190 | 220.32 | 250 | 289.50 | 310 | 358.74 | 360 | 416.46 | 410 | 474.12 | 460 | 531.84 | | |
| 11 | 13.74 | 71 | 82.98 | 131 | 152.22 | 191 | 221.46 | 251 | 290.70 | 311 | 359.94 | 361 | 417.60 | 411 | 475.32 | 461 | 532.98 | | |
| 12 | 14.94 | 72 | 84.12 | 132 | 153.36 | 192 | 222.60 | 252 | 291.84 | 312 | 361.08 | 362 | 418.74 | 412 | 476.46 | 462 | 534.12 | | |
| 13 | 16.08 | 73 | 85.32 | 133 | 154.50 | 193 | 223.74 | 253 | 292.98 | 313 | 362.22 | 363 | 419.94 | 413 | 477.60 | 463 | 535.32 | | |
| 14 | 17.22 | 74 | 86.46 | 134 | 155.70 | 194 | 224.94 | 254 | 294.12 | 314 | 363.36 | 364 | 421.08 | 414 | 478.74 | 464 | 536.46 | | |
| 15 | 18.36 | 75 | 87.60 | 135 | 156.84 | 195 | 226.08 | 255 | 295.32 | 315 | 364.50 | 365 | 422.22 | 415 | 479.94 | 465 | 537.60 | | |
| 16 | 19.50 | 76 | 88.74 | 136 | 157.98 | 196 | 227.22 | 256 | 296.46 | 316 | 365.70 | 366 | 423.36 | 416 | 481.08 | 466 | 538.74 | | |
| 17 | 20.70 | 77 | 89.94 | 137 | 159.12 | 197 | 228.36 | 257 | 297.60 | 317 | 366.84 | 367 | 424.50 | 417 | 482.22 | 467 | 539.94 | | |
| 18 | 21.84 | 78 | 91.08 | 138 | 160.32 | 198 | 229.50 | 258 | 298.74 | 318 | 367.98 | 368 | 425.70 | 418 | 483.36 | 468 | 541.08 | | |
| 19 | 22.98 | 79 | 92.22 | 139 | 161.46 | 199 | 230.70 | 259 | 299.94 | 319 | 369.12 | 369 | 426.84 | 419 | 484.50 | 469 | 542.22 | | |
| 20 | 24.12 | 80 | 93.36 | 140 | 162.60 | 200 | 231.84 | 260 | 301.08 | 320 | 370.32 | 370 | 427.98 | 420 | 485.70 | 470 | 543.36 | | |
| 21 | 25.32 | 81 | 94.50 | 141 | 163.74 | 201 | 232.98 | 261 | 302.22 | 321 | 371.46 | 371 | 429.12 | 421 | 486.84 | 471 | 544.50 | | |
| 22 | 26.46 | 82 | 95.70 | 142 | 164.94 | 202 | 234.12 | 262 | 303.36 | 322 | 372.60 | 372 | 430.32 | 422 | 487.98 | 472 | 545.70 | | |
| 23 | 27.60 | 83 | 96.84 | 143 | 166.08 | 203 | 235.32 | 263 | 304.50 | 323 | 373.74 | 373 | 431.46 | 423 | 489.12 | 473 | 546.84 | | |
| 24 | 28.74 | 84 | 97.98 | 144 | 167.22 | 204 | 236.46 | 264 | 305.70 | 324 | 374.94 | 374 | 432.60 | 424 | 490.32 | 474 | 547.98 | | |
| 25 | 29.94 | 85 | 99.12 | 145 | 168.36 | 205 | 237.60 | 265 | 306.84 | 325 | 376.08 | 375 | 433.74 | 425 | 491.46 | 475 | 549.12 | | |
| 26 | 31.08 | 86 | 100.32 | 146 | 169.50 | 206 | 238.74 | 266 | 307.98 | 326 | 377.22 | 376 | 434.94 | 426 | 492.60 | 476 | 550.32 | | |
| 27 | 32.22 | 87 | 101.46 | 147 | 170.70 | 207 | 239.94 | 267 | 309.12 | 327 | 378.36 | 377 | 436.08 | 427 | 493.74 | 477 | 551.46 | | |
| 28 | 33.36 | 88 | 102.60 | 148 | 171.84 | 208 | 241.08 | 268 | 310.32 | 328 | 379.50 | 378 | 437.22 | 428 | 494.94 | 478 | 552.60 | | |
| 29 | 34.50 | 89 | 103.74 | 149 | 172.98 | 209 | 242.22 | 269 | 311.46 | 329 | 380.70 | 379 | 438.36 | 429 | 496.08 | 479 | 553.74 | | |
| 30 | 35.70 | 90 | 104.94 | 150 | 174.12 | 210 | 243.36 | 270 | 312.60 | 330 | 381.84 | 380 | 439.50 | 430 | 497.22 | 480 | 554.94 | | |
| 31 | 36.84 | 91 | 106.08 | 151 | 175.32 | 211 | 244.50 | 271 | 313.74 | 331 | 382.98 | 381 | 440.70 | 431 | 498.36 | 481 | 556.08 | | |
| 32 | 37.98 | 92 | 107.22 | 152 | 176.46 | 212 | 245.70 | 272 | 314.94 | 332 | 384.12 | 382 | 441.84 | 432 | 499.50 | 482 | 557.22 | | |
| 33 | 39.12 | 93 | 108.36 | 153 | 177.60 | 213 | 246.84 | 273 | 316.08 | 333 | 385.32 | 383 | 442.98 | 433 | 500.70 | 483 | 558.36 | | |
| 34 | 40.32 | 94 | 109.50 | 154 | 178.74 | 214 | 247.98 | 274 | 317.22 | 334 | 386.46 | 384 | 444.12 | 434 | 501.84 | 484 | 559.50 | | |
| 35 | 41.46 | 95 | 110.70 | 155 | 179.94 | 215 | 249.12 | 275 | 318.36 | 335 | 387.60 | 385 | 445.32 | 435 | 502.98 | 485 | 560.70 | | |
| 36 | 42.60 | 96 | 111.84 | 156 | 181.08 | 216 | 250.32 | 276 | 319.50 | 336 | 388.74 | 386 | 446.46 | 436 | 504.12 | 486 | 561.84 | | |
| 37 | 43.74 | 97 | 112.98 | 157 | 182.22 | 217 | 251.46 | 277 | 320.70 | 337 | 389.94 | 387 | 447.60 | 437 | 505.32 | 487 | 562.98 | | |
| 38 | 44.94 | 98 | 114.12 | 158 | 183.36 | 218 | 252.60 | 278 | 321.84 | 338 | 391.08 | 388 | 448.74 | 438 | 506.46 | 488 | 564.12 | | |
| 39 | 46.08 | 99 | 115.32 | 159 | 184.50 | 219 | 253.74 | 279 | 322.98 | 339 | 392.22 | 389 | 449.94 | 439 | 507.60 | 489 | 565.32 | | |
| 40 | 47.22 | 100 | 116.46 | 160 | 185.70 | 220 | 254.94 | 280 | 324.12 | 340 | 393.36 | 390 | 451.08 | 440 | 508.74 | 490 | 566.46 | | |
| 41 | 48.36 | 101 | 117.60 | 161 | 186.84 | 221 | 256.08 | 281 | 325.32 | 341 | 394.50 | 391 | 452.22 | 441 | 509.94 | 491 | 567.60 | | |
| 42 | 49.50 | 102 | 118.74 | 162 | 187.98 | 222 | 257.22 | 282 | 326.46 | 342 | 395.70 | 392 | 453.36 | 442 | 511.08 | 492 | 568.74 | | |
| 43 | 50.70 | 103 | 119.94 | 163 | 189.12 | 223 | 258.36 | 283 | 327.60 | 343 | 396.84 | 393 | 454.50 | 443 | 512.22 | 493 | 569.94 | | |
| 44 | 51.84 | 104 | 121.08 | 164 | 190.32 | 224 | 259.50 | 284 | 328.74 | 344 | 397.98 | 394 | 455.70 | 444 | 513.36 | 494 | 571.08 | | |
| 45 | 52.98 | 105 | 122.22 | 165 | 191.46 | 225 | 260.70 | 285 | 329.94 | 345 | 399.12 | 395 | 456.84 | 445 | 514.50 | 495 | 572.22 | | |
| 46 | 54.12 | 106 | 123.36 | 166 | 192.60 | 226 | 261.84 | 286 | 331.08 | 346 | 400.32 | 396 | 457.98 | 446 | 515.70 | 496 | 573.36 | | |
| 47 | 55.32 | 107 | 124.50 | 167 | 193.74 | 227 | 262.98 | 287 | 332.22 | 347 | 401.46 | 397 | 459.12 | 447 | 516.84 | 497 | 574.50 | | |
| 48 | 56.46 | 108 | 125.70 | 168 | 194.94 | 228 | 264.12 | 288 | 333.36 | 348 | 402.60 | 398 | 460.32 | 448 | 517.98 | 498 | 575.70 | | |
| 49 | 57.60 | 109 | 126.84 | 169 | 196.08 | 229 | 265.32 | 289 | 334.50 | 349 | 403.74 | 399 | 461.46 | 449 | 519.12 | 499 | 576.84 | | |
| 50 | 58.74 | 110 | 127.98 | 170 | 197.22 | 230 | 266.46 | 290 | 335.70 | 350 | 404.94 | 400 | 462.60 | 450 | 520.32 | 500 | 577.98 | | |
| 51 | 59.94 | 111 | 129.12 | 171 | 198.36 | 231 | 267.60 | 291 | 336.84 | | | | | | | | | | |
| 52 | 61.08 | 112 | 130.32 | 172 | 199.50 | 232 | 268.74 | 292 | 337.98 | | | | | | | | | | |
| 53 | 62.22 | 113 | 131.46 | 173 | 200.70 | 233 | 269.94 | 293 | 339.12 | | | | | | | | | | |
| 54 | 63.36 | 114 | 132.60 | 174 | 201.84 | 234 | 271.08 | 294 | 340.32 | | | | | | | | | | |
| 55 | 64.50 | 115 | 133.74 | 175 | 202.98 | 235 | 272.22 | 295 | 341.46 | | | | | | | | | | |
| 56 | 65.70 | 116 | 134.94 | 176 | 204.12 | 236 | 273.36 | 296 | 342.60 | | | | | | | | | | |
| 57 | 66.84 | 117 | 136.08 | 177 | 205.32 | 237 | 274.50 | 297 | 343.74 | | | | | | | | | | |
| 58 | 67.98 | 118 | 137.22 | 178 | 206.46 | 238 | 275.70 | 298 | 344.94 | | | | | | | | | | |
| 59 | 69.12 | 119 | 138.36 | 179 | 207.60 | 239 | 276.84 | 299 | 346.08 | | | | | | | | | | |
| 60 | 70.32 | 120 | 139.50 | 180 | 208.74 | 240 | 277.98 | 300 | 347.22 | | | | | | | | | | |

**Code more than 500**

1 Where the code is in the range 501 to 1000 inclusive:
   a. Subtract 500 from the code and use the balance of the code to obtain a pay adjustment figure from the table above.
   b. Add this pay adjustment figure to the figure given in the box alongside to obtain the figure of total pay adjustment to date * **576.96**

2 Where the code **exceeds 1000** follow the instructions on **page 3**.

# TAX TABLES

**Tables A** - Pay Adjustment Tables  Apr 6 to May 5 **Month 1**

| Code | Total pay adjustment to date £ | Code | Total pay adjustment to date £ | Code | Total pay adjustment to date £ | Code | Total pay adjustment to date £ | Code | Total pay adjustment to date £ | Code | Total pay adjustment to date £ | Code | Total pay adjustment to date £ | Code | Total pay adjustment to date £ | Code | Total pay adjustment to date £ |
|---|---|---|---|---|---|---|---|---|---|---|---|---|---|---|---|---|---|
| 0 | NIL | | | | | | | | | | | | | | | | |
| 1 | 1.59 | 61 | 51.59 | 121 | 101.59 | 181 | 151.59 | 241 | 201.59 | 301 | 251.59 | 351 | 293.25 | 401 | 334.92 | 451 | 376.59 |
| 2 | 2.42 | 62 | 52.42 | 122 | 102.42 | 182 | 152.42 | 242 | 202.42 | 302 | 252.42 | 352 | 294.09 | 402 | 335.75 | 452 | 377.42 |
| 3 | 3.25 | 63 | 53.25 | 123 | 103.25 | 183 | 153.25 | 243 | 203.25 | 303 | 253.25 | 353 | 294.92 | 403 | 336.59 | 453 | 378.25 |
| 4 | 4.09 | 64 | 54.09 | 124 | 104.09 | 184 | 154.09 | 244 | 204.09 | 304 | 254.09 | 354 | 295.75 | 404 | 337.42 | 454 | 379.09 |
| 5 | 4.92 | 65 | 54.92 | 125 | 104.92 | 185 | 154.92 | 245 | 204.92 | 305 | 254.92 | 355 | 296.59 | 405 | 338.25 | 455 | 379.92 |
| 6 | 5.75 | 66 | 55.75 | 126 | 105.75 | 186 | 155.75 | 246 | 205.75 | 306 | 255.75 | 356 | 297.42 | 406 | 339.09 | 456 | 380.75 |
| 7 | 6.59 | 67 | 56.59 | 127 | 106.59 | 187 | 156.59 | 247 | 206.59 | 307 | 256.59 | 357 | 298.25 | 407 | 339.92 | 457 | 381.59 |
| 8 | 7.42 | 68 | 57.42 | 128 | 107.42 | 188 | 157.42 | 248 | 207.42 | 308 | 257.42 | 358 | 299.09 | 408 | 340.75 | 458 | 382.42 |
| 9 | 8.25 | 69 | 58.25 | 129 | 108.25 | 189 | 158.25 | 249 | 208.25 | 309 | 258.25 | 359 | 299.92 | 409 | 341.59 | 459 | 383.25 |
| 10 | 9.09 | 70 | 59.09 | 130 | 109.09 | 190 | 159.09 | 250 | 209.09 | 310 | 259.09 | 360 | 300.75 | 410 | 342.42 | 460 | 384.09 |
| 11 | 9.92 | 71 | 59.92 | 131 | 109.92 | 191 | 159.92 | 251 | 209.92 | 311 | 259.92 | 361 | 301.59 | 411 | 343.25 | 461 | 384.92 |
| 12 | 10.75 | 72 | 60.75 | 132 | 110.75 | 192 | 160.75 | 252 | 210.75 | 312 | 260.75 | 362 | 302.42 | 412 | 344.09 | 462 | 385.75 |
| 13 | 11.59 | 73 | 61.59 | 133 | 111.59 | 193 | 161.59 | 253 | 211.59 | 313 | 261.59 | 363 | 303.25 | 413 | 344.92 | 463 | 386.59 |
| 14 | 12.42 | 74 | 62.42 | 134 | 112.42 | 194 | 162.42 | 254 | 212.42 | 314 | 262.42 | 364 | 304.09 | 414 | 345.75 | 464 | 387.42 |
| 15 | 13.25 | 75 | 63.25 | 135 | 113.25 | 195 | 163.25 | 255 | 213.25 | 315 | 263.25 | 365 | 304.92 | 415 | 346.59 | 465 | 388.25 |
| 16 | 14.09 | 76 | 64.09 | 136 | 114.09 | 196 | 164.09 | 256 | 214.09 | 316 | 264.09 | 366 | 305.75 | 416 | 347.42 | 466 | 389.09 |
| 17 | 14.92 | 77 | 64.92 | 137 | 114.92 | 197 | 164.92 | 257 | 214.92 | 317 | 264.92 | 367 | 306.59 | 417 | 348.25 | 467 | 389.92 |
| 18 | 15.75 | 78 | 65.75 | 138 | 115.75 | 198 | 165.75 | 258 | 215.75 | 318 | 265.75 | 368 | 307.42 | 418 | 349.09 | 468 | 390.75 |
| 19 | 16.59 | 79 | 66.59 | 139 | 116.59 | 199 | 166.59 | 259 | 216.59 | 319 | 266.59 | 369 | 308.25 | 419 | 349.92 | 469 | 391.59 |
| 20 | 17.42 | 80 | 67.42 | 140 | 117.42 | 200 | 167.42 | 260 | 217.42 | 320 | 267.42 | 370 | 309.09 | 420 | 350.75 | 470 | 392.42 |
| 21 | 18.25 | 81 | 68.25 | 141 | 118.25 | 201 | 168.25 | 261 | 218.25 | 321 | 268.25 | 371 | 309.92 | 421 | 351.59 | 471 | 393.25 |
| 22 | 19.09 | 82 | 69.09 | 142 | 119.09 | 202 | 169.09 | 262 | 219.09 | 322 | 269.09 | 372 | 310.75 | 422 | 352.42 | 472 | 394.09 |
| 23 | 19.92 | 83 | 69.92 | 143 | 119.92 | 203 | 169.92 | 263 | 219.92 | 323 | 269.92 | 373 | 311.59 | 423 | 353.25 | 473 | 394.92 |
| 24 | 20.75 | 84 | 70.75 | 144 | 120.75 | 204 | 170.75 | 264 | 220.75 | 324 | 270.75 | 374 | 312.42 | 424 | 354.09 | 474 | 395.75 |
| 25 | 21.59 | 85 | 71.59 | 145 | 121.59 | 205 | 171.59 | 265 | 221.59 | 325 | 271.59 | 375 | 313.25 | 425 | 354.92 | 475 | 396.59 |
| 26 | 22.42 | 86 | 72.42 | 146 | 122.42 | 206 | 172.42 | 266 | 222.42 | 326 | 272.42 | 376 | 314.09 | 426 | 355.75 | 476 | 397.42 |
| 27 | 23.25 | 87 | 73.25 | 147 | 123.25 | 207 | 173.25 | 267 | 223.25 | 327 | 273.25 | 377 | 314.92 | 427 | 356.59 | 477 | 398.25 |
| 28 | 24.09 | 88 | 74.09 | 148 | 124.09 | 208 | 174.09 | 268 | 224.09 | 328 | 274.09 | 378 | 315.75 | 428 | 357.42 | 478 | 399.09 |
| 29 | 24.92 | 89 | 74.92 | 149 | 124.92 | 209 | 174.92 | 269 | 224.92 | 329 | 274.92 | 379 | 316.59 | 429 | 358.25 | 479 | 399.92 |
| 30 | 25.75 | 90 | 75.75 | 150 | 125.75 | 210 | 175.75 | 270 | 225.75 | 330 | 275.75 | 380 | 317.42 | 430 | 359.09 | 480 | 400.75 |
| 31 | 26.59 | 91 | 76.59 | 151 | 126.59 | 211 | 176.59 | 271 | 226.59 | 331 | 276.59 | 381 | 318.25 | 431 | 359.92 | 481 | 401.59 |
| 32 | 27.42 | 92 | 77.42 | 152 | 127.42 | 212 | 177.42 | 272 | 227.42 | 332 | 277.42 | 382 | 319.09 | 432 | 360.75 | 482 | 402.42 |
| 33 | 28.25 | 93 | 78.25 | 153 | 128.25 | 213 | 178.25 | 273 | 228.25 | 333 | 278.25 | 383 | 319.92 | 433 | 361.59 | 483 | 403.25 |
| 34 | 29.09 | 94 | 79.09 | 154 | 129.09 | 214 | 179.09 | 274 | 229.09 | 334 | 279.09 | 384 | 320.75 | 434 | 362.42 | 484 | 404.09 |
| 35 | 29.92 | 95 | 79.92 | 155 | 129.92 | 215 | 179.92 | 275 | 229.92 | 335 | 279.92 | 385 | 321.59 | 435 | 363.25 | 485 | 404.92 |
| 36 | 30.75 | 96 | 80.75 | 156 | 130.75 | 216 | 180.75 | 276 | 230.75 | 336 | 280.75 | 386 | 322.42 | 436 | 364.09 | 486 | 405.75 |
| 37 | 31.59 | 97 | 81.59 | 157 | 131.59 | 217 | 181.59 | 277 | 231.59 | 337 | 281.59 | 387 | 323.25 | 437 | 364.92 | 487 | 406.59 |
| 38 | 32.42 | 98 | 82.42 | 158 | 132.42 | 218 | 182.42 | 278 | 232.42 | 338 | 282.42 | 388 | 324.09 | 438 | 365.75 | 488 | 407.42 |
| 39 | 33.25 | 99 | 83.25 | 159 | 133.25 | 219 | 183.25 | 279 | 233.25 | 339 | 283.25 | 389 | 324.92 | 439 | 366.59 | 489 | 408.25 |
| 40 | 34.09 | 100 | 84.09 | 160 | 134.09 | 220 | 184.09 | 280 | 234.09 | 340 | 284.09 | 390 | 325.75 | 440 | 367.42 | 490 | 409.09 |
| 41 | 34.92 | 101 | 84.92 | 161 | 134.92 | 221 | 184.92 | 281 | 234.92 | 341 | 284.92 | 391 | 326.59 | 441 | 368.25 | 491 | 409.92 |
| 42 | 35.75 | 102 | 85.75 | 162 | 135.75 | 222 | 185.75 | 282 | 235.75 | 342 | 285.75 | 392 | 327.42 | 442 | 369.09 | 492 | 410.75 |
| 43 | 36.59 | 103 | 86.59 | 163 | 136.59 | 223 | 186.59 | 283 | 236.59 | 343 | 286.59 | 393 | 328.25 | 443 | 369.92 | 493 | 411.59 |
| 44 | 37.42 | 104 | 87.42 | 164 | 137.42 | 224 | 187.42 | 284 | 237.42 | 344 | 287.42 | 394 | 329.09 | 444 | 370.75 | 494 | 412.42 |
| 45 | 38.25 | 105 | 88.25 | 165 | 138.25 | 225 | 188.25 | 285 | 238.25 | 345 | 288.25 | 395 | 329.92 | 445 | 371.59 | 495 | 413.25 |
| 46 | 39.09 | 106 | 89.09 | 166 | 139.09 | 226 | 189.09 | 286 | 239.09 | 346 | 289.09 | 396 | 330.75 | 446 | 372.42 | 496 | 414.09 |
| 47 | 39.92 | 107 | 89.92 | 167 | 139.92 | 227 | 189.92 | 287 | 239.92 | 347 | 289.92 | 397 | 331.59 | 447 | 373.25 | 497 | 414.92 |
| 48 | 40.75 | 108 | 90.75 | 168 | 140.75 | 228 | 190.75 | 288 | 240.75 | 348 | 290.75 | 398 | 332.42 | 448 | 374.09 | 498 | 415.75 |
| 49 | 41.59 | 109 | 91.59 | 169 | 141.59 | 229 | 191.59 | 289 | 241.59 | 349 | 291.59 | 399 | 333.25 | 449 | 374.92 | 499 | 416.59 |
| 50 | 42.42 | 110 | 92.42 | 170 | 142.42 | 230 | 192.42 | 290 | 242.42 | 350 | 292.42 | 400 | 334.09 | 450 | 375.75 | 500 | 417.42 |
| 51 | 43.25 | 111 | 93.25 | 171 | 143.25 | 231 | 193.25 | 291 | 243.25 | | | | | | | | |
| 52 | 44.09 | 112 | 94.09 | 172 | 144.09 | 232 | 194.09 | 292 | 244.09 | | | | | | | | |
| 53 | 44.92 | 113 | 94.92 | 173 | 144.92 | 233 | 194.92 | 293 | 244.92 | | | | | | | | |
| 54 | 45.75 | 114 | 95.75 | 174 | 145.75 | 234 | 195.75 | 294 | 245.75 | | | | | | | | |
| 55 | 46.59 | 115 | 96.59 | 175 | 146.59 | 235 | 196.59 | 295 | 246.59 | | | | | | | | |
| 56 | 47.42 | 116 | 97.42 | 176 | 147.42 | 236 | 197.42 | 296 | 247.42 | | | | | | | | |
| 57 | 48.25 | 117 | 98.25 | 177 | 148.25 | 237 | 198.25 | 297 | 248.25 | | | | | | | | |
| 58 | 49.09 | 118 | 99.09 | 178 | 149.09 | 238 | 199.09 | 298 | 249.09 | | | | | | | | |
| 59 | 49.92 | 119 | 99.92 | 179 | 149.92 | 239 | 199.92 | 299 | 249.92 | | | | | | | | |
| 60 | 50.75 | 120 | 100.75 | 180 | 150.75 | 240 | 200.75 | 300 | 250.75 | | | | | | | | |

**Code more than 500**
1 Where the code is in the range **501** to **1000** inclusive:
   a. Subtract **500** from the code and use the balance of the code to obtain a pay adjustment figure from the table above.
   b. Add this pay adjustment figure to the figure given in the box alongside to obtain the figure of total pay adjustment to date * **416.67**

2 Where the code **exceeds 1000** follow the instructions on **page 3**.

# TAX TABLES

**Month 2** May 6 to Jun 5        **Tables A** - Pay Adjustment Tables

| Code | Total pay adjustment to date £ | Code | Total pay adjustment to date £ | Code | Total pay adjustment to date £ | Code | Total pay adjustment to date £ | Code | Total pay adjustment to date £ | Code | Total pay adjustment to date £ | Code | Total pay adjustment to date £ | Code | Total pay adjustment to date £ | Code | Total pay adjustment to date £ |
|---|---|---|---|---|---|---|---|---|---|---|---|---|---|---|---|---|---|
| 0 | NIL | | | | | | | | | | | | | | | | |
| 1 | 3.18 | 61 | 103.18 | 121 | 203.18 | 181 | 303.18 | 241 | 403.18 | 301 | 503.18 | 351 | 586.50 | 401 | 669.84 | 451 | 753.18 |
| 2 | 4.84 | 62 | 104.84 | 122 | 204.84 | 182 | 304.84 | 242 | 404.84 | 302 | 504.84 | 352 | 588.18 | 402 | 671.50 | 452 | 754.84 |
| 3 | 6.50 | 63 | 106.50 | 123 | 206.50 | 183 | 306.50 | 243 | 406.50 | 303 | 506.50 | 353 | 589.84 | 403 | 673.18 | 453 | 756.50 |
| 4 | 8.18 | 64 | 108.18 | 124 | 208.18 | 184 | 308.18 | 244 | 408.18 | 304 | 508.18 | 354 | 591.50 | 404 | 674.84 | 454 | 758.18 |
| 5 | 9.84 | 65 | 109.84 | 125 | 209.84 | 185 | 309.84 | 245 | 409.84 | 305 | 509.84 | 355 | 593.18 | 405 | 676.50 | 455 | 759.84 |
| 6 | 11.50 | 66 | 111.50 | 126 | 211.50 | 186 | 311.50 | 246 | 411.50 | 306 | 511.50 | 356 | 594.84 | 406 | 678.18 | 456 | 761.50 |
| 7 | 13.18 | 67 | 113.18 | 127 | 213.18 | 187 | 313.18 | 247 | 413.18 | 307 | 513.18 | 357 | 596.50 | 407 | 679.84 | 457 | 763.18 |
| 8 | 14.84 | 68 | 114.84 | 128 | 214.84 | 188 | 314.84 | 248 | 414.84 | 308 | 514.84 | 358 | 598.18 | 408 | 681.50 | 458 | 764.84 |
| 9 | 16.50 | 69 | 116.50 | 129 | 216.50 | 189 | 316.50 | 249 | 416.50 | 309 | 516.50 | 359 | 599.84 | 409 | 683.18 | 459 | 766.50 |
| 10 | 18.18 | 70 | 118.18 | 130 | 218.18 | 190 | 318.18 | 250 | 418.18 | 310 | 518.18 | 360 | 601.50 | 410 | 684.84 | 460 | 768.18 |
| 11 | 19.84 | 71 | 119.84 | 131 | 219.84 | 191 | 319.84 | 251 | 419.84 | 311 | 519.84 | 361 | 603.18 | 411 | 686.50 | 461 | 769.84 |
| 12 | 21.50 | 72 | 121.50 | 132 | 221.50 | 192 | 321.50 | 252 | 421.50 | 312 | 521.50 | 362 | 604.84 | 412 | 688.18 | 462 | 771.50 |
| 13 | 23.18 | 73 | 123.18 | 133 | 223.18 | 193 | 323.18 | 253 | 423.18 | 313 | 523.18 | 363 | 606.50 | 413 | 689.84 | 463 | 773.18 |
| 14 | 24.84 | 74 | 124.84 | 134 | 224.84 | 194 | 324.84 | 254 | 424.84 | 314 | 524.84 | 364 | 608.18 | 414 | 691.50 | 464 | 774.84 |
| 15 | 26.50 | 75 | 126.50 | 135 | 226.50 | 195 | 326.50 | 255 | 426.50 | 315 | 526.50 | 365 | 609.84 | 415 | 693.18 | 465 | 776.50 |
| 16 | 28.18 | 76 | 128.18 | 136 | 228.18 | 196 | 328.18 | 256 | 428.18 | 316 | 528.18 | 366 | 611.50 | 416 | 694.84 | 466 | 778.18 |
| 17 | 29.84 | 77 | 129.84 | 137 | 229.84 | 197 | 329.84 | 257 | 429.84 | 317 | 529.84 | 367 | 613.18 | 417 | 696.50 | 467 | 779.84 |
| 18 | 31.50 | 78 | 131.50 | 138 | 231.50 | 198 | 331.50 | 258 | 431.50 | 318 | 531.50 | 368 | 614.84 | 418 | 698.18 | 468 | 781.50 |
| 19 | 33.18 | 79 | 133.18 | 139 | 233.18 | 199 | 333.18 | 259 | 433.18 | 319 | 533.18 | 369 | 616.50 | 419 | 699.84 | 469 | 783.18 |
| 20 | 34.84 | 80 | 134.84 | 140 | 234.84 | 200 | 334.84 | 260 | 434.84 | 320 | 534.84 | 370 | 618.18 | 420 | 701.50 | 470 | 784.84 |
| 21 | 36.50 | 81 | 136.50 | 141 | 236.50 | 201 | 336.50 | 261 | 436.50 | 321 | 536.50 | 371 | 619.84 | 421 | 703.18 | 471 | 786.50 |
| 22 | 38.18 | 82 | 138.18 | 142 | 238.18 | 202 | 338.18 | 262 | 438.18 | 322 | 538.18 | 372 | 621.50 | 422 | 704.84 | 472 | 788.18 |
| 23 | 39.84 | 83 | 139.84 | 143 | 239.84 | 203 | 339.84 | 263 | 439.84 | 323 | 539.84 | 373 | 623.18 | 423 | 706.50 | 473 | 789.84 |
| 24 | 41.50 | 84 | 141.50 | 144 | 241.50 | 204 | 341.50 | 264 | 441.50 | 324 | 541.50 | 374 | 624.84 | 424 | 708.18 | 474 | 791.50 |
| 25 | 43.18 | 85 | 143.18 | 145 | 243.18 | 205 | 343.18 | 265 | 443.18 | 325 | 543.18 | 375 | 626.50 | 425 | 709.84 | 475 | 793.18 |
| 26 | 44.84 | 86 | 144.84 | 146 | 244.84 | 206 | 344.84 | 266 | 444.84 | 326 | 544.84 | 376 | 628.18 | 426 | 711.50 | 476 | 794.84 |
| 27 | 46.50 | 87 | 146.50 | 147 | 246.50 | 207 | 346.50 | 267 | 446.50 | 327 | 546.50 | 377 | 629.84 | 427 | 713.18 | 477 | 796.50 |
| 28 | 48.18 | 88 | 148.18 | 148 | 248.18 | 208 | 348.18 | 268 | 448.18 | 328 | 548.18 | 378 | 631.50 | 428 | 714.84 | 478 | 798.18 |
| 29 | 49.84 | 89 | 149.84 | 149 | 249.84 | 209 | 349.84 | 269 | 449.84 | 329 | 549.84 | 379 | 633.18 | 429 | 716.50 | 479 | 799.84 |
| 30 | 51.50 | 90 | 151.50 | 150 | 251.50 | 210 | 351.50 | 270 | 451.50 | 330 | 551.50 | 380 | 634.84 | 430 | 718.18 | 480 | 801.50 |
| 31 | 53.18 | 91 | 153.18 | 151 | 253.18 | 211 | 353.18 | 271 | 453.18 | 331 | 553.18 | 381 | 636.50 | 431 | 719.84 | 481 | 803.18 |
| 32 | 54.84 | 92 | 154.84 | 152 | 254.84 | 212 | 354.84 | 272 | 454.84 | 332 | 554.84 | 382 | 638.18 | 432 | 721.50 | 482 | 804.84 |
| 33 | 56.50 | 93 | 156.50 | 153 | 256.50 | 213 | 356.50 | 273 | 456.50 | 333 | 556.50 | 383 | 639.84 | 433 | 723.18 | 483 | 806.50 |
| 34 | 58.18 | 94 | 158.18 | 154 | 258.18 | 214 | 358.18 | 274 | 458.18 | 334 | 558.18 | 384 | 641.50 | 434 | 724.84 | 484 | 808.18 |
| 35 | 59.84 | 95 | 159.84 | 155 | 259.84 | 215 | 359.84 | 275 | 459.84 | 335 | 559.84 | 385 | 643.18 | 435 | 726.50 | 485 | 809.84 |
| 36 | 61.50 | 96 | 161.50 | 156 | 261.50 | 216 | 361.50 | 276 | 461.50 | 336 | 561.50 | 386 | 644.84 | 436 | 728.18 | 486 | 811.50 |
| 37 | 63.18 | 97 | 163.18 | 157 | 263.18 | 217 | 363.18 | 277 | 463.18 | 337 | 563.18 | 387 | 646.50 | 437 | 729.84 | 487 | 813.18 |
| 38 | 64.84 | 98 | 164.84 | 158 | 264.84 | 218 | 364.84 | 278 | 464.84 | 338 | 564.84 | 388 | 648.18 | 438 | 731.50 | 488 | 814.84 |
| 39 | 66.50 | 99 | 166.50 | 159 | 266.50 | 219 | 366.50 | 279 | 466.50 | 339 | 566.50 | 389 | 649.84 | 439 | 733.18 | 489 | 816.50 |
| 40 | 68.18 | 100 | 168.18 | 160 | 268.18 | 220 | 368.18 | 280 | 468.18 | 340 | 568.18 | 390 | 651.50 | 440 | 734.84 | 490 | 818.18 |
| 41 | 69.84 | 101 | 169.84 | 161 | 269.84 | 221 | 369.84 | 281 | 469.84 | 341 | 569.84 | 391 | 653.18 | 441 | 736.50 | 491 | 819.84 |
| 42 | 71.50 | 102 | 171.50 | 162 | 271.50 | 222 | 371.50 | 282 | 471.50 | 342 | 571.50 | 392 | 654.84 | 442 | 738.18 | 492 | 821.50 |
| 43 | 73.18 | 103 | 173.18 | 163 | 273.18 | 223 | 373.18 | 283 | 473.18 | 343 | 573.18 | 393 | 656.50 | 443 | 739.84 | 493 | 823.18 |
| 44 | 74.84 | 104 | 174.84 | 164 | 274.84 | 224 | 374.84 | 284 | 474.84 | 344 | 574.84 | 394 | 658.18 | 444 | 741.50 | 494 | 824.84 |
| 45 | 76.50 | 105 | 176.50 | 165 | 276.50 | 225 | 376.50 | 285 | 476.50 | 345 | 576.50 | 395 | 659.84 | 445 | 743.18 | 495 | 826.50 |
| 46 | 78.18 | 106 | 178.18 | 166 | 278.18 | 226 | 378.18 | 286 | 478.18 | 346 | 578.18 | 396 | 661.50 | 446 | 744.84 | 496 | 828.18 |
| 47 | 79.84 | 107 | 179.84 | 167 | 279.84 | 227 | 379.84 | 287 | 479.84 | 347 | 579.84 | 397 | 663.18 | 447 | 746.50 | 497 | 829.84 |
| 48 | 81.50 | 108 | 181.50 | 168 | 281.50 | 228 | 381.50 | 288 | 481.50 | 348 | 581.50 | 398 | 664.84 | 448 | 748.18 | 498 | 831.50 |
| 49 | 83.18 | 109 | 183.18 | 169 | 283.18 | 229 | 383.18 | 289 | 483.18 | 349 | 583.18 | 399 | 666.50 | 449 | 749.84 | 499 | 833.18 |
| 50 | 84.84 | 110 | 184.84 | 170 | 284.84 | 230 | 384.84 | 290 | 484.84 | 350 | 584.84 | 400 | 668.18 | 450 | 751.50 | 500 | 834.84 |
| 51 | 86.50 | 111 | 186.50 | 171 | 286.50 | 231 | 386.50 | 291 | 486.50 | | | | | | | | |
| 52 | 88.18 | 112 | 188.18 | 172 | 288.18 | 232 | 388.18 | 292 | 488.18 | | | | | | | | |
| 53 | 89.84 | 113 | 189.84 | 173 | 289.84 | 233 | 389.84 | 293 | 489.84 | | | | | | | | |
| 54 | 91.50 | 114 | 191.50 | 174 | 291.50 | 234 | 391.50 | 294 | 491.50 | | | | | | | | |
| 55 | 93.18 | 115 | 193.18 | 175 | 293.18 | 235 | 393.18 | 295 | 493.18 | | | | | | | | |
| 56 | 94.84 | 116 | 194.84 | 176 | 294.84 | 236 | 394.84 | 296 | 494.84 | | | | | | | | |
| 57 | 96.50 | 117 | 196.50 | 177 | 296.50 | 237 | 396.50 | 297 | 496.50 | | | | | | | | |
| 58 | 98.18 | 118 | 198.18 | 178 | 298.18 | 238 | 398.18 | 298 | 498.18 | | | | | | | | |
| 59 | 99.84 | 119 | 199.84 | 179 | 299.84 | 239 | 399.84 | 299 | 499.84 | | | | | | | | |
| 60 | 101.50 | 120 | 201.50 | 180 | 301.50 | 240 | 401.50 | 300 | 501.50 | | | | | | | | |

**Code more than 500**

1. Where the code is in the range **501** to **1000** inclusive:
   a. Subtract **500** from the code and use the balance of the code to obtain a pay adjustment figure from the table above.
   b. Add this pay adjustment figure to the figure given in the box alongside to obtain the figure of total pay adjustment to date *    **833.34**

2. Where the code **exceeds 1000** follow the instructions on **page 3**.

# HM Revenue & Customs

# Taxable Pay Tables Manual Method

Tables B to D (April 2009)

Keep using Tables A 1993 issue – Pay Adjustment Tables

Use from 6 April 2009

# TAX TABLES

## Monthly paid

| Column A Month | Column B Use Table B on pages 7 and 8 |
|---|---|
| 1 | 3117 |
| 2 | 6234 |
| 3 | 9350 |
| 4 | 12467 |
| 5 | 15584 |
| 6 | 18700 |
| 7 | 21817 |
| 8 | 24934 |
| 9 | 28050 |
| 10 | 31167 |
| 11 | 34284 |
| 12 | 37400 |

If you do your payroll on a monthly basis use this table. If it's weekly use the table on page 6.
- Work out which month the pay is for – there is a chart on page 26 of the Helpbook E13 *Day-to-day payroll.*
- Pick the month you need from the month column in the table. Look at the figure in Column B.
- Is your employee's total taxable pay to date **less than or equal to** the figure in Column B? If so, use Table B on pages 7 and 8.
- If your employee's total taxable pay to date is **more than** the amount in Column B, use Tables C and D on pages 9 and 11.

**Example 3**
You are working out the tax due for Month 5. Your employee's total taxable pay to date is £1,200 which is **less than** £15,584 in Column B. So, use Tables B on pages 7 and 8.

**Example 4**
You are working out the tax due for Month 5. Your employee's total taxable pay to date is £17,500 which is **more than** £15,584 in Column B. So, use Tables C and D on pages 9 and 11.

# TAX TABLES

## Weekly paid

| Column A<br>Week | Column B<br>Use Table B on pages 7 and 8 |
|---|---|
| 1 | 720 |
| 2 | 1439 |
| 3 | 2158 |
| 4 | 2877 |
| 5 | 3597 |
| 6 | 4316 |
| 7 | 5035 |
| 8 | 5754 |
| 9 | 6474 |
| 10 | 7193 |
| 11 | 7912 |
| 12 | 8631 |
| 13 | 9350 |
| 14 | 10070 |
| 15 | 10789 |
| 16 | 11508 |
| 17 | 12227 |
| 18 | 12947 |
| 19 | 13666 |
| 20 | 14385 |
| 21 | 15104 |
| 22 | 15824 |
| 23 | 16543 |
| 24 | 17262 |
| 25 | 17981 |
| 26 | 18700 |
| 27 | 19420 |
| 28 | 20139 |
| 29 | 20858 |
| 30 | 21577 |
| 31 | 22297 |
| 32 | 23016 |
| 33 | 23735 |
| 34 | 24454 |
| 35 | 25174 |
| 36 | 25893 |
| 37 | 26612 |
| 38 | 27331 |
| 39 | 28050 |
| 40 | 28770 |
| 41 | 29489 |
| 42 | 30208 |
| 43 | 30927 |
| 44 | 31647 |
| 45 | 32366 |
| 46 | 33085 |
| 47 | 33804 |
| 48 | 34524 |
| 49 | 35243 |
| 50 | 35962 |
| 51 | 36681 |
| 52 | 37400 |

If you do your payroll on a weekly basis use this table. If it's monthly use the table on page 4.
- Work out which week the pay is for – there is a chart on page 26 of the Helpbook E13, *Day-to-day payroll*.
- Pick the week you need from the week column in the table. Look at the figure in Column B.
- Is your employee's total taxable pay to date **less than or equal to** the figure in Column B? If so, use Table B on pages 7 and 8.
- If your employee's total taxable pay to date is **more than** the amount in Column B, use Tables C and D on pages 10 and 11.

**Example 7**
You are working out the tax due for Week 22. Your employee's total taxable pay to date is £1,200 which is **less than** £15,824 in Column B. So, use Table B on pages 7 and 8.

**Example 8**
You are working out the tax due for Week 22. Your employee's total taxable pay to date is £17,500 which is **more than** £15,824 in Column B. So, use Tables C and D on pages 10 and 11.

# TAX TABLES

## Table B
To work out tax at 20%. Pages 3 and 5 tell you when to use this table.

### Table B
### Tax due on taxable pay from £1 to £15,000

| Total taxable pay to date | Total tax due to date | Total taxable pay to date | Total tax due to date | Total taxable pay to date | Total tax due to date | Total taxable pay to date | Total tax due to date | Total taxable pay to date | Total tax due to date |
|---|---|---|---|---|---|---|---|---|---|
| 1 | 0.20 | 51 | 10.20 | 100 | 20.00 | 5100 | 1020.00 | 10100 | 2020.00 |
| 2 | 0.40 | 52 | 10.40 | 200 | 40.00 | 5200 | 1040.00 | 10200 | 2040.00 |
| 3 | 0.60 | 53 | 10.60 | 300 | 60.00 | 5300 | 1060.00 | 10300 | 2060.00 |
| 4 | 0.80 | 54 | 10.80 | 400 | 80.00 | 5400 | 1080.00 | 10400 | 2080.00 |
| 5 | 1.00 | 55 | 11.00 | 500 | 100.00 | 5500 | 1100.00 | 10500 | 2100.00 |
| 6 | 1.20 | 56 | 11.20 | 600 | 120.00 | 5600 | 1120.00 | 10600 | 2120.00 |
| 7 | 1.40 | 57 | 11.40 | 700 | 140.00 | 5700 | 1140.00 | 10700 | 2140.00 |
| 8 | 1.60 | 58 | 11.60 | 800 | 160.00 | 5800 | 1160.00 | 10800 | 2160.00 |
| 9 | 1.80 | 59 | 11.80 | 900 | 180.00 | 5900 | 1180.00 | 10900 | 2180.00 |
| 10 | 2.00 | 60 | 12.00 | 1000 | 200.00 | 6000 | 1200.00 | 11000 | 2200.00 |
| 11 | 2.20 | 61 | 12.20 | 1100 | 220.00 | 6100 | 1220.00 | 11100 | 2220.00 |
| 12 | 2.40 | 62 | 12.40 | 1200 | 240.00 | 6200 | 1240.00 | 11200 | 2240.00 |
| 13 | 2.60 | 63 | 12.60 | 1300 | 260.00 | 6300 | 1260.00 | 11300 | 2260.00 |
| 14 | 2.80 | 64 | 12.80 | 1400 | 280.00 | 6400 | 1280.00 | 11400 | 2280.00 |
| 15 | 3.00 | 65 | 13.00 | 1500 | 300.00 | 6500 | 1300.00 | 11500 | 2300.00 |
| 16 | 3.20 | 66 | 13.20 | 1600 | 320.00 | 6600 | 1320.00 | 11600 | 2320.00 |
| 17 | 3.40 | 67 | 13.40 | 1700 | 340.00 | 6700 | 1340.00 | 11700 | 2340.00 |
| 18 | 3.60 | 68 | 13.60 | 1800 | 360.00 | 6800 | 1360.00 | 11800 | 2360.00 |
| 19 | 3.80 | 69 | 13.80 | 1900 | 380.00 | 6900 | 1380.00 | 11900 | 2380.00 |
| 20 | 4.00 | 70 | 14.00 | 2000 | 400.00 | 7000 | 1400.00 | 12000 | 2400.00 |
| 21 | 4.20 | 71 | 14.20 | 2100 | 420.00 | 7100 | 1420.00 | 12100 | 2420.00 |
| 22 | 4.40 | 72 | 14.40 | 2200 | 440.00 | 7200 | 1440.00 | 12200 | 2440.00 |
| 23 | 4.60 | 73 | 14.60 | 2300 | 460.00 | 7300 | 1460.00 | 12300 | 2460.00 |
| 24 | 4.80 | 74 | 14.80 | 2400 | 480.00 | 7400 | 1480.00 | 12400 | 2480.00 |
| 25 | 5.00 | 75 | 15.00 | 2500 | 500.00 | 7500 | 1500.00 | 12500 | 2500.00 |
| 26 | 5.20 | 76 | 15.20 | 2600 | 520.00 | 7600 | 1520.00 | 12600 | 2520.00 |
| 27 | 5.40 | 77 | 15.40 | 2700 | 540.00 | 7700 | 1540.00 | 12700 | 2540.00 |
| 28 | 5.60 | 78 | 15.60 | 2800 | 560.00 | 7800 | 1560.00 | 12800 | 2560.00 |
| 29 | 5.80 | 79 | 15.80 | 2900 | 580.00 | 7900 | 1580.00 | 12900 | 2580.00 |
| 30 | 6.00 | 80 | 16.00 | 3000 | 600.00 | 8000 | 1600.00 | 13000 | 2600.00 |
| 31 | 6.20 | 81 | 16.20 | 3100 | 620.00 | 8100 | 1620.00 | 13100 | 2620.00 |
| 32 | 6.40 | 82 | 16.40 | 3200 | 640.00 | 8200 | 1640.00 | 13200 | 2640.00 |
| 33 | 6.60 | 83 | 16.60 | 3300 | 660.00 | 8300 | 1660.00 | 13300 | 2660.00 |
| 34 | 6.80 | 84 | 16.80 | 3400 | 680.00 | 8400 | 1680.00 | 13400 | 2680.00 |
| 35 | 7.00 | 85 | 17.00 | 3500 | 700.00 | 8500 | 1700.00 | 13500 | 2700.00 |
| 36 | 7.20 | 86 | 17.20 | 3600 | 720.00 | 8600 | 1720.00 | 13600 | 2720.00 |
| 37 | 7.40 | 87 | 17.40 | 3700 | 740.00 | 8700 | 1740.00 | 13700 | 2740.00 |
| 38 | 7.60 | 88 | 17.60 | 3800 | 760.00 | 8800 | 1760.00 | 13800 | 2760.00 |
| 39 | 7.80 | 89 | 17.80 | 3900 | 780.00 | 8900 | 1780.00 | 13900 | 2780.00 |
| 40 | 8.00 | 90 | 18.00 | 4000 | 800.00 | 9000 | 1800.00 | 14000 | 2800.00 |
| 41 | 8.20 | 91 | 18.20 | 4100 | 820.00 | 9100 | 1820.00 | 14100 | 2820.00 |
| 42 | 8.40 | 92 | 18.40 | 4200 | 840.00 | 9200 | 1840.00 | 14200 | 2840.00 |
| 43 | 8.60 | 93 | 18.60 | 4300 | 860.00 | 9300 | 1860.00 | 14300 | 2860.00 |
| 44 | 8.80 | 94 | 18.80 | 4400 | 880.00 | 9400 | 1880.00 | 14400 | 2880.00 |
| 45 | 9.00 | 95 | 19.00 | 4500 | 900.00 | 9500 | 1900.00 | 14500 | 2900.00 |
| 46 | 9.20 | 96 | 19.20 | 4600 | 920.00 | 9600 | 1920.00 | 14600 | 2920.00 |
| 47 | 9.40 | 97 | 19.40 | 4700 | 940.00 | 9700 | 1940.00 | 14700 | 2940.00 |
| 48 | 9.60 | 98 | 19.60 | 4800 | 960.00 | 9800 | 1960.00 | 14800 | 2960.00 |
| 49 | 9.80 | 99 | 19.80 | 4900 | 980.00 | 9900 | 1980.00 | 14900 | 2980.00 |
| 50 | 10.00 | | | 5000 | 1000.00 | 10000 | 2000.00 | 15000 | 3000.00 |

## Table B – continued

To work out tax at 20%. Pages 3 and 5 tell you when to use this table.

### Table B
### Tax due on taxable pay from £15,100 to £37,400

| Total taxable pay to date | Total tax due to date | Total taxable pay to date | Total tax due to date | Total taxable pay to date | Total tax due to date | Total taxable pay to date | Total tax due to date | Total taxable pay to date | Total tax due to date |
|---|---|---|---|---|---|---|---|---|---|
| 15100 | 3020.00 | 20100 | 4020.00 | 25100 | 5020.00 | 30100 | 6020.00 | 35100 | 7020.00 |
| 15200 | 3040.00 | 20200 | 4040.00 | 25200 | 5040.00 | 30200 | 6040.00 | 35200 | 7040.00 |
| 15300 | 3060.00 | 20300 | 4060.00 | 25300 | 5060.00 | 30300 | 6060.00 | 35300 | 7060.00 |
| 15400 | 3080.00 | 20400 | 4080.00 | 25400 | 5080.00 | 30400 | 6080.00 | 35400 | 7080.00 |
| 15500 | 3100.00 | 20500 | 4100.00 | 25500 | 5100.00 | 30500 | 6100.00 | 35500 | 7100.00 |
| 15600 | 3120.00 | 20600 | 4120.00 | 25600 | 5120.00 | 30600 | 6120.00 | 35600 | 7120.00 |
| 15700 | 3140.00 | 20700 | 4140.00 | 25700 | 5140.00 | 30700 | 6140.00 | 35700 | 7140.00 |
| 15800 | 3160.00 | 20800 | 4160.00 | 25800 | 5160.00 | 30800 | 6160.00 | 35800 | 7160.00 |
| 15900 | 3180.00 | 20900 | 4180.00 | 25900 | 5180.00 | 30900 | 6180.00 | 35900 | 7180.00 |
| 16000 | 3200.00 | 21000 | 4200.00 | 26000 | 5200.00 | 31000 | 6200.00 | 36000 | 7200.00 |
| 16100 | 3220.00 | 21100 | 4220.00 | 26100 | 5220.00 | 31100 | 6220.00 | 36100 | 7220.00 |
| 16200 | 3240.00 | 21200 | 4240.00 | 26200 | 5240.00 | 31200 | 6240.00 | 36200 | 7240.00 |
| 16300 | 3260.00 | 21300 | 4260.00 | 26300 | 5260.00 | 31300 | 6260.00 | 36300 | 7260.00 |
| 16400 | 3280.00 | 21400 | 4280.00 | 26400 | 5280.00 | 31400 | 6280.00 | 36400 | 7280.00 |
| 16500 | 3300.00 | 21500 | 4300.00 | 26500 | 5300.00 | 31500 | 6300.00 | 36500 | 7300.00 |
| 16600 | 3320.00 | 21600 | 4320.00 | 26600 | 5320.00 | 31600 | 6320.00 | 36600 | 7320.00 |
| 16700 | 3340.00 | 21700 | 4340.00 | 26700 | 5340.00 | 31700 | 6340.00 | 36700 | 7340.00 |
| 16800 | 3360.00 | 21800 | 4360.00 | 26800 | 5360.00 | 31800 | 6360.00 | 36800 | 7360.00 |
| 16900 | 3380.00 | 21900 | 4380.00 | 26900 | 5380.00 | 31900 | 6380.00 | 36900 | 7380.00 |
| 17000 | 3400.00 | 22000 | 4400.00 | 27000 | 5400.00 | 32000 | 6400.00 | 37000 | 7400.00 |
| 17100 | 3420.00 | 22100 | 4420.00 | 27100 | 5420.00 | 32100 | 6420.00 | 37100 | 7420.00 |
| 17200 | 3440.00 | 22200 | 4440.00 | 27200 | 5440.00 | 32200 | 6440.00 | 37200 | 7440.00 |
| 17300 | 3460.00 | 22300 | 4460.00 | 27300 | 5460.00 | 32300 | 6460.00 | 37300 | 7460.00 |
| 17400 | 3480.00 | 22400 | 4480.00 | 27400 | 5480.00 | 32400 | 6480.00 | 37400 | 7480.00 |
| 17500 | 3500.00 | 22500 | 4500.00 | 27500 | 5500.00 | 32500 | 6500.00 | | |
| 17600 | 3520.00 | 22600 | 4520.00 | 27600 | 5520.00 | 32600 | 6520.00 | | |
| 17700 | 3540.00 | 22700 | 4540.00 | 27700 | 5540.00 | 32700 | 6540.00 | | |
| 17800 | 3560.00 | 22800 | 4560.00 | 27800 | 5560.00 | 32800 | 6560.00 | | |
| 17900 | 3580.00 | 22900 | 4580.00 | 27900 | 5580.00 | 32900 | 6580.00 | | |
| 18000 | 3600.00 | 23000 | 4600.00 | 28000 | 5600.00 | 33000 | 6600.00 | | |
| 18100 | 3620.00 | 23100 | 4620.00 | 28100 | 5620.00 | 33100 | 6620.00 | | |
| 18200 | 3640.00 | 23200 | 4640.00 | 28200 | 5640.00 | 33200 | 6640.00 | | |
| 18300 | 3660.00 | 23300 | 4660.00 | 28300 | 5660.00 | 33300 | 6660.00 | | |
| 18400 | 3680.00 | 23400 | 4680.00 | 28400 | 5680.00 | 33400 | 6680.00 | | |
| 18500 | 3700.00 | 23500 | 4700.00 | 28500 | 5700.00 | 33500 | 6700.00 | | |
| 18600 | 3720.00 | 23600 | 4720.00 | 28600 | 5720.00 | 33600 | 6720.00 | | |
| 18700 | 3740.00 | 23700 | 4740.00 | 28700 | 5740.00 | 33700 | 6740.00 | | |
| 18800 | 3760.00 | 23800 | 4760.00 | 28800 | 5760.00 | 33800 | 6760.00 | | |
| 18900 | 3780.00 | 23900 | 4780.00 | 28900 | 5780.00 | 33900 | 6780.00 | | |
| 19000 | 3800.00 | 24000 | 4800.00 | 29000 | 5800.00 | 34000 | 6800.00 | | |
| 19100 | 3820.00 | 24100 | 4820.00 | 29100 | 5820.00 | 34100 | 6820.00 | | |
| 19200 | 3840.00 | 24200 | 4840.00 | 29200 | 5840.00 | 34200 | 6840.00 | | |
| 19300 | 3860.00 | 24300 | 4860.00 | 29300 | 5860.00 | 34300 | 6860.00 | | |
| 19400 | 3880.00 | 24400 | 4880.00 | 29400 | 5880.00 | 34400 | 6880.00 | | |
| 19500 | 3900.00 | 24500 | 4900.00 | 29500 | 5900.00 | 34500 | 6900.00 | | |
| 19600 | 3920.00 | 24600 | 4920.00 | 29600 | 5920.00 | 34600 | 6920.00 | | |
| 19700 | 3940.00 | 24700 | 4940.00 | 29700 | 5940.00 | 34700 | 6940.00 | | |
| 19800 | 3960.00 | 24800 | 4960.00 | 29800 | 5960.00 | 34800 | 6960.00 | | |
| 19900 | 3980.00 | 24900 | 4980.00 | 29900 | 5980.00 | 34900 | 6980.00 | | |
| 20000 | 4000.00 | 25000 | 5000.00 | 30000 | 6000.00 | 35000 | 7000.00 | | |

Where the exact amount of taxable pay is not shown add together the figures for two (or more) entries that make up the amount of taxable pay to the nearest £1.

# TAX TABLES

## Table C – monthly paid
Page 4 tells you when to use this table.

### Table C
**Employee paid at monthly rates**

| Month | Column 1<br>If total taxable pay to date exceeds<br>£ | Column 2<br>Total tax due to date on pay in column 1<br>£ |
|---|---|---|
| 1 | 3117 | 623.46 |
| 2 | 6234 | 1246.93 |
| 3 | 9350 | 1870.00 |
| 4 | 12467 | 2493.46 |
| 5 | 15584 | 3116.93 |
| 6 | 18700 | 3740.00 |
| 7 | 21817 | 4363.46 |
| 8 | 24934 | 4986.93 |
| 9 | 28050 | 5610.00 |
| 10 | 31167 | 6233.46 |
| 11 | 34284 | 6856.93 |
| 12 | 37400 | 7480.00 |

Add tax at 40% as shown in Table D on the amount by which the total taxable pay to date exceeds the figure in column 1.

### Table C calculation

Employee's code is **431L**

The pay is in **month 4**

| | £ |
|---|---|
| Pay in the month | 5,800.80 |
| *Plus* previous pay to date | 9,332.64 |
| Total pay to date | 15,133.44 |
| *Minus* pay adjustment Table A figure at **month 4** code **431L** | 1,439.68 |
| Total taxable pay to date | 13,693.76 |
| *Round down* to the nearest pound | 13,693 |
| *Minus* amount in column 1 for **month 4** | 12,467 |
| Excess to be taxed at 40% | 1,226 |

**Tax due**

| | |
|---|---|
| Tax due on £12,467 from column 2 | 2,493.46 |
| Tax due on £1,226 from tables D | 490.40 |
| **Total tax due** | **2,983.86** |

# TAX TABLES

## Table C – weekly paid
Page 6 tells you when to use this table.

### Table C
**Employee paid at weekly rates**

| Week | Column 1<br>If total taxable pay to date exceeds<br>£ | Column 2<br>Total tax due to date on pay in column 1<br>£ |
|---|---|---|
| 1  | 720   | 144.15 |
| 2  | 1439  | 287.90 |
| 3  | 2158  | 431.66 |
| 4  | 2877  | 575.41 |
| 5  | 3597  | 719.56 |
| 6  | 4316  | 863.32 |
| 7  | 5035  | 1007.07 |
| 8  | 5754  | 1150.83 |
| 9  | 6474  | 1294.98 |
| 10 | 7193  | 1438.73 |
| 11 | 7912  | 1582.49 |
| 12 | 8631  | 1726.24 |
| 13 | 9350  | 1870.00 |
| 14 | 10070 | 2014.15 |
| 15 | 10789 | 2157.90 |
| 16 | 11508 | 2301.66 |
| 17 | 12227 | 2445.41 |
| 18 | 12947 | 2589.56 |
| 19 | 13666 | 2733.32 |
| 20 | 14385 | 2877.07 |
| 21 | 15104 | 3020.83 |
| 22 | 15824 | 3164.98 |
| 23 | 16543 | 3308.73 |
| 24 | 17262 | 3452.49 |
| 25 | 17981 | 3596.24 |
| 26 | 18700 | 3740.00 |
| 27 | 19420 | 3884.15 |
| 28 | 20139 | 4027.90 |
| 29 | 20858 | 4171.66 |
| 30 | 21577 | 4315.41 |
| 31 | 22297 | 4459.56 |
| 32 | 23016 | 4603.32 |
| 33 | 23735 | 4747.07 |
| 34 | 24454 | 4890.83 |
| 35 | 25174 | 5034.98 |
| 36 | 25893 | 5178.73 |
| 37 | 26612 | 5322.49 |
| 38 | 27331 | 5466.24 |
| 39 | 28050 | 5610.00 |
| 40 | 28770 | 5754.15 |
| 41 | 29489 | 5897.90 |
| 42 | 30208 | 6041.66 |
| 43 | 30927 | 6185.41 |
| 44 | 31647 | 6329.56 |
| 45 | 32366 | 6473.32 |
| 46 | 33085 | 6617.07 |
| 47 | 33804 | 6760.83 |
| 48 | 34524 | 6904.98 |
| 49 | 35243 | 7048.73 |
| 50 | 35962 | 7192.49 |
| 51 | 36681 | 7336.24 |
| 52 | 37400 | 7480.00 |

Add tax at 40% as shown in Table D on the amount by which the total taxable pay to date exceeds the figure in column 1.

### Table C calculation

Employee's code is **431L**

The pay is in **week 12**

|  | £ |
|---|---:|
| Pay in the week | 812.21 |
| *Plus* previous pay to date | 9,961.55 |
| Total pay to date | 10,773.76 |
| *Minus* pay adjustment Table A figure at **week 12** code **431L** | 996.72 |
| Total taxable pay to date | 9,777.04 |
| *Round down* to the nearest pound | 9,777 |
| *Minus* amount in column 1 for **week 12** | 8,631 |
| Excess to be taxed at 40% | 1,146 |

**Tax due**

|  | £ |
|---|---:|
| Tax due on £8,631 per column 2 | 1,726.24 |
| Tax due on £1,146 per tables D | 458.40 |
| **Total tax due** | **2,184.64** |

## TAX TABLES

### Table D – Tax at 40%

**Also to be used for Code D0.** Pages 3, 4 and 6 tell you when to use this table.

#### Table D

| Taxable Pay £ | Tax £ | Taxable Pay £ | Tax £ | Taxable Pay £ | Tax £ | Taxable Pay £ | Tax £ |
|---|---|---|---|---|---|---|---|
| 1 | 0.40 | 50 | 20.00 | 100 | 40.00 | 6100 | 2440.00 |
| 2 | 0.80 | 51 | 20.40 | 200 | 80.00 | 6200 | 2480.00 |
| 3 | 1.20 | 52 | 20.80 | 300 | 120.00 | 6300 | 2520.00 |
| 4 | 1.60 | 53 | 21.20 | 400 | 160.00 | 6400 | 2560.00 |
| 5 | 2.00 | 54 | 21.60 | 500 | 200.00 | 6500 | 2600.00 |
| 6 | 2.40 | 55 | 22.00 | 600 | 240.00 | 6600 | 2640.00 |
| 7 | 2.80 | 56 | 22.40 | 700 | 280.00 | 6700 | 2680.00 |
| 8 | 3.20 | 57 | 22.80 | 800 | 320.00 | 6800 | 2720.00 |
| 9 | 3.60 | 58 | 23.20 | 900 | 360.00 | 6900 | 2760.00 |
| 10 | 4.00 | 59 | 23.60 | 1000 | 400.00 | 7000 | 2800.00 |
| 11 | 4.40 | 60 | 24.00 | 1100 | 440.00 | 7100 | 2840.00 |
| 12 | 4.80 | 61 | 24.40 | 1200 | 480.00 | 7200 | 2880.00 |
| 13 | 5.20 | 62 | 24.80 | 1300 | 520.00 | 7300 | 2920.00 |
| 14 | 5.60 | 63 | 25.20 | 1400 | 560.00 | 7400 | 2960.00 |
| 15 | 6.00 | 64 | 25.60 | 1500 | 600.00 | 7500 | 3000.00 |
| 16 | 6.40 | 65 | 26.00 | 1600 | 640.00 | 7600 | 3040.00 |
| 17 | 6.80 | 66 | 26.40 | 1700 | 680.00 | 7700 | 3080.00 |
| 18 | 7.20 | 67 | 26.80 | 1800 | 720.00 | 7800 | 3120.00 |
| 19 | 7.60 | 68 | 27.20 | 1900 | 760.00 | 7900 | 3160.00 |
| 20 | 8.00 | 69 | 27.60 | 2000 | 800.00 | 8000 | 3200.00 |
| 21 | 8.40 | 70 | 28.00 | 2100 | 840.00 | 8100 | 3240.00 |
| 22 | 8.80 | 71 | 28.40 | 2200 | 880.00 | 8200 | 3280.00 |
| 23 | 9.20 | 72 | 28.80 | 2300 | 920.00 | 8300 | 3320.00 |
| 24 | 9.60 | 73 | 29.20 | 2400 | 960.00 | 8400 | 3360.00 |
| 25 | 10.00 | 74 | 29.60 | 2500 | 1000.00 | 8500 | 3400.00 |
| 26 | 10.40 | 75 | 30.00 | 2600 | 1040.00 | 8600 | 3440.00 |
| 27 | 10.80 | 76 | 30.40 | 2700 | 1080.00 | 8700 | 3480.00 |
| 28 | 11.20 | 77 | 30.80 | 2800 | 1120.00 | 8800 | 3520.00 |
| 29 | 11.60 | 78 | 31.20 | 2900 | 1160.00 | 8900 | 3560.00 |
| 30 | 12.00 | 79 | 31.60 | 3000 | 1200.00 | 9000 | 3600.00 |
| 31 | 12.40 | 80 | 32.00 | 3100 | 1240.00 | 9100 | 3640.00 |
| 32 | 12.80 | 81 | 32.40 | 3200 | 1280.00 | 9200 | 3680.00 |
| 33 | 13.20 | 82 | 32.80 | 3300 | 1320.00 | 9300 | 3720.00 |
| 34 | 13.60 | 83 | 33.20 | 3400 | 1360.00 | 9400 | 3760.00 |
| 35 | 14.00 | 84 | 33.60 | 3500 | 1400.00 | 9500 | 3800.00 |
| 36 | 14.40 | 85 | 34.00 | 3600 | 1440.00 | 9600 | 3840.00 |
| 37 | 14.80 | 86 | 34.40 | 3700 | 1480.00 | 9700 | 3880.00 |
| 38 | 15.20 | 87 | 34.80 | 3800 | 1520.00 | 9800 | 3920.00 |
| 39 | 15.60 | 88 | 35.20 | 3900 | 1560.00 | 9900 | 3960.00 |
| 40 | 16.00 | 89 | 35.60 | 4000 | 1600.00 | 10000 | 4000.00 |
| 41 | 16.40 | 90 | 36.00 | 4100 | 1640.00 | 20000 | 8000.00 |
| 42 | 16.80 | 91 | 36.40 | 4200 | 1680.00 | 30000 | 12000.00 |
| 43 | 17.20 | 92 | 36.80 | 4300 | 1720.00 | 40000 | 16000.00 |
| 44 | 17.60 | 93 | 37.20 | 4400 | 1760.00 | 50000 | 20000.00 |
| 45 | 18.00 | 94 | 37.60 | 4500 | 1800.00 | 60000 | 24000.00 |
| 46 | 18.40 | 95 | 38.00 | 4600 | 1840.00 | 70000 | 28000.00 |
| 47 | 18.80 | 96 | 38.40 | 4700 | 1880.00 | 80000 | 32000.00 |
| 48 | 19.20 | 97 | 38.80 | 4800 | 1920.00 | 90000 | 36000.00 |
| 49 | 19.60 | 98 | 39.20 | 4900 | 1960.00 | 100000 | 40000.00 |
|  |  | 99 | 39.60 | 5000 | 2000.00 | 200000 | 80000.00 |
|  |  |  |  | 5100 | 2040.00 | 300000 | 120000.00 |
|  |  |  |  | 5200 | 2080.00 | 400000 | 160000.00 |
|  |  |  |  | 5300 | 2120.00 | 500000 | 200000.00 |
|  |  |  |  | 5400 | 2160.00 | 600000 | 240000.00 |
|  |  |  |  | 5500 | 2200.00 | 700000 | 280000.00 |
|  |  |  |  | 5600 | 2240.00 | 800000 | 320000.00 |
|  |  |  |  | 5700 | 2280.00 | 900000 | 360000.00 |
|  |  |  |  | 5800 | 2320.00 | 1000000 | 400000.00 |
|  |  |  |  | 5900 | 2360.00 |  |  |
|  |  |  |  | 6000 | 2400.00 |  |  |

Where the exact amount of taxable pay is not shown, add together the figures for two (or more) entries to make up the amount of taxable pay to the nearest £1 below.

TAX TABLES

Student Loan Deduction Tables SL3

**HM Revenue & Customs**

# Student Loan Deduction Tables

Use from
6 April 2005

HMRC 03/06

# Student Loan Deduction Tables

## When to use these tables

- Use these tables for employees for whom you have received a Notice to Start Student Loan Deductions form SL1, or for new employees who have given you a form P45 with an entry in box 5 'Continue Student Loan Deductions'.
- If your employee doesn't give you a form P45 they should complete a form P46. If they have ticked the Student Loan section, box D on the P46, you should use these tables to start making Student Loan deductions.
- Before you can use these tables, you must work out the employee's earnings for the purposes of deducting Student Loans. Follow the instructions at Part 9 of the Employer's Helpbook E13, Day-to-day payroll.

## How to use these tables

- Decide which table to use:
  - For **weekly** paid employees use the table below
  - For **monthly** paid employees use the monthly table on page 3.
- Look up the amount of earnings in the week or month in the left hand column to find the corresponding Student Loan deduction. If the **exact** amount of earnings is not shown, look for the nearest figure **below** and use the amount of Student Loan deduction shown for that range of earnings.
- Turn to page 6 if:
  - earnings in the week or month **exceed** the highest amount of earnings shown in the table, or
  - you are making payment for a pay period other than a standard week or month.

If you need help using these tables, please call the Employer's Helpline on **0845 7 143 143** for advice.

### Weekly table

| Earnings in Week £ | Student Loan Deduction £ | Earnings in Week £ | Student Loan Deduction £ | Earnings in Week £ | Student Loan Deduction £ |
|---|---|---|---|---|---|
| 1 - 299 | Nil | 589 - 599 | 27 | 889 - 899 | 54 |
| 300 - 310 | 1 | 600 - 610 | 28 | 900 - 910 | 55 |
| 311 - 321 | 2 | 611 - 621 | 29 | 911 - 921 | 56 |
| 322 - 332 | 3 | 622 - 632 | 30 | 922 - 932 | 57 |
| 333 - 344 | 4 | 633 - 644 | 31 | 933 - 944 | 58 |
| 345 - 355 | 5 | 645 - 655 | 32 | 945 - 955 | 59 |
| 356 - 366 | 6 | 656 - 666 | 33 | 956 - 966 | 60 |
| 367 - 377 | 7 | 667 - 677 | 34 | 967 - 977 | 61 |
| 378 - 388 | 8 | 678 - 688 | 35 | 978 - 988 | 62 |
| 389 - 399 | 9 | 689 - 699 | 36 | 989 - 999 | 63 |
| 400 - 410 | 10 | 700 - 710 | 37 | 1000 - 1010 | 64 |
| 411 - 421 | 11 | 711 - 721 | 38 | 1011 - 1021 | 65 |
| 422 - 432 | 12 | 722 - 732 | 39 | 1022 - 1032 | 66 |
| 433 - 444 | 13 | 733 - 744 | 40 | 1033 - 1044 | 67 |
| 445 - 455 | 14 | 745 - 755 | 41 | 1045 - 1055 | 68 |
| 456 - 466 | 15 | 756 - 766 | 42 | 1056 - 1066 | 69 |
| 467 - 477 | 16 | 767 - 777 | 43 | 1067 - 1077 | 70 |
| 478 - 488 | 17 | 778 - 788 | 44 | 1078 - 1088 | 71 |
| 489 - 499 | 18 | 789 - 799 | 45 | 1089 - 1099 | 72 |
| 500 - 510 | 19 | 800 - 810 | 46 | 1100 - 1110 | 73 |
| 511 - 521 | 20 | 811 - 821 | 47 | 1111 - 1121 | 74 |
| 522 - 532 | 21 | 822 - 832 | 48 | 1122 - 1132 | 75 |
| 533 - 544 | 22 | 833 - 844 | 49 | 1133 - 1144 | 76 |
| 545 - 555 | 23 | 845 - 855 | 50 | 1145 - 1155 | 77 |
| 556 - 566 | 24 | 856 - 866 | 51 | | |
| 567 - 577 | 25 | 867 - 877 | 52 | | |
| 578 - 588 | 26 | 878 - 888 | 53 | | |

# TAX TABLES

## Student Loan Deduction Tables

### Monthly table

| Earnings in Month £ | Student Loan Deduction £ | Earnings in Month £ | Student Loan Deduction £ | Earnings in Month £ | Student Loan Deduction £ |
|---|---|---|---|---|---|
| 1 - 1261 | Nil | 1739 - 1749 | 44 | 2228 - 2238 | 88 |
| 1262 - 1272 | 1 | 1750 - 1761 | 45 | 2239 - 2249 | 89 |
| 1273 - 1283 | 2 | 1762 - 1772 | 46 | 2250 - 2261 | 90 |
| 1284 - 1294 | 3 | 1773 - 1783 | 47 | 2262 - 2272 | 91 |
| 1295 - 1305 | 4 | 1784 - 1794 | 48 | 2273 - 2283 | 92 |
| 1306 - 1316 | 5 | 1795 - 1805 | 49 | 2284 - 2294 | 93 |
| 1317 - 1327 | 6 | 1806 - 1816 | 50 | 2295 - 2305 | 94 |
| 1328 - 1338 | 7 | 1817 - 1827 | 51 | 2306 - 2316 | 95 |
| 1339 - 1349 | 8 | 1828 - 1838 | 52 | 2317 - 2327 | 96 |
| 1350 - 1361 | 9 | 1839 - 1849 | 53 | 2328 - 2338 | 97 |
| 1362 - 1372 | 10 | 1850 - 1861 | 54 | 2339 - 2349 | 98 |
| 1373 - 1383 | 11 | 1862 - 1872 | 55 | 2350 - 2361 | 99 |
| 1384 - 1394 | 12 | 1873 - 1883 | 56 | 2362 - 2372 | 100 |
| 1395 - 1405 | 13 | 1884 - 1894 | 57 | 2373 - 2383 | 101 |
| 1406 - 1416 | 14 | 1895 - 1905 | 58 | 2384 - 2394 | 102 |
| 1417 - 1427 | 15 | 1906 - 1916 | 59 | 2395 - 2405 | 103 |
| 1428 - 1438 | 16 | 1917 - 1927 | 60 | 2406 - 2416 | 104 |
| 1439 - 1449 | 17 | 1928 - 1938 | 61 | 2417 - 2427 | 105 |
| 1450 - 1461 | 18 | 1939 - 1949 | 62 | 2428 - 2438 | 106 |
| 1462 - 1472 | 19 | 1950 - 1961 | 63 | 2439 - 2449 | 107 |
| 1473 - 1483 | 20 | 1962 - 1972 | 64 | 2450 - 2461 | 108 |
| 1484 - 1494 | 21 | 1973 - 1983 | 65 | 2462 - 2472 | 109 |
| 1495 - 1505 | 22 | 1984 - 1994 | 66 | 2473 - 2483 | 110 |
| 1506 - 1516 | 23 | 1995 - 2005 | 67 | 2484 - 2494 | 111 |
| 1517 - 1527 | 24 | 2006 - 2016 | 68 | 2495 - 2505 | 112 |
| 1528 - 1538 | 25 | 2017 - 2027 | 69 | 2506 - 2516 | 113 |
| 1539 - 1549 | 26 | 2028 - 2038 | 70 | 2517 - 2527 | 114 |
| 1550 - 1561 | 27 | 2039 - 2049 | 71 | 2528 - 2538 | 115 |
| 1562 - 1572 | 28 | 2050 - 2061 | 72 | 2539 - 2549 | 116 |
| 1573 - 1583 | 29 | 2062 - 2072 | 73 | 2550 - 2561 | 117 |
| 1584 - 1594 | 30 | 2073 - 2083 | 74 | 2562 - 2572 | 118 |
| 1595 - 1605 | 31 | 2084 - 2094 | 75 | 2573 - 2583 | 119 |
| 1606 - 1616 | 32 | 2095 - 2105 | 76 | 2584 - 2594 | 120 |
| 1617 - 1627 | 33 | 2106 - 2116 | 77 | 2595 - 2605 | 121 |
| 1628 - 1638 | 34 | 2117 - 2127 | 78 | 2606 - 2616 | 122 |
| 1639 - 1649 | 35 | 2128 - 2138 | 79 | 2617 - 2627 | 123 |
| 1650 - 1661 | 36 | 2139 - 2149 | 80 | 2628 - 2638 | 124 |
| 1662 - 1672 | 37 | 2150 - 2161 | 81 | 2639 - 2649 | 125 |
| 1673 - 1683 | 38 | 2162 - 2172 | 82 | 2650 - 2661 | 126 |
| 1684 - 1694 | 39 | 2173 - 2183 | 83 | 2662 - 2672 | 127 |
| 1695 - 1705 | 40 | 2184 - 2194 | 84 | 2673 - 2683 | 128 |
| 1706 - 1716 | 41 | 2195 - 2205 | 85 | 2684 - 2694 | 129 |
| 1717 - 1727 | 42 | 2206 - 2216 | 86 | 2695 - 2705 | 130 |
| 1728 - 1738 | 43 | 2217 - 2227 | 87 | 2706 - 2716 | 131 |

# TAX TABLES

## Student Loan Deduction Tables
### Monthly table

| Earnings in Month £ | Student Loan Deduction £ | Earnings in Month £ | Student Loan Deduction £ | Earnings in Month £ | Student Loan Deduction £ |
|---|---|---|---|---|---|
| 2717 - 2727 | 132 | 3206 - 3216 | 176 | 3695 - 3705 | 220 |
| 2728 - 2738 | 133 | 3217 - 3227 | 177 | 3706 - 3716 | 221 |
| 2739 - 2749 | 134 | 3228 - 3238 | 178 | 3717 - 3727 | 222 |
| 2750 - 2761 | 135 | 3239 - 3249 | 179 | 3728 - 3738 | 223 |
| 2762 - 2772 | 136 | 3250 - 3261 | 180 | 3739 - 3749 | 224 |
| 2773 - 2783 | 137 | 3262 - 3272 | 181 | 3750 - 3761 | 225 |
| 2784 - 2794 | 138 | 3273 - 3283 | 182 | 3762 - 3772 | 226 |
| 2795 - 2805 | 139 | 3284 - 3294 | 183 | 3773 - 3783 | 227 |
| 2806 - 2816 | 140 | 3295 - 3305 | 184 | 3784 - 3794 | 228 |
| 2817 - 2827 | 141 | 3306 - 3316 | 185 | 3795 - 3805 | 229 |
| 2828 - 2838 | 142 | 3317 - 3327 | 186 | 3806 - 3816 | 230 |
| 2839 - 2849 | 143 | 3328 - 3338 | 187 | 3817 - 3827 | 231 |
| 2850 - 2861 | 144 | 3339 - 3349 | 188 | 3828 - 3838 | 232 |
| 2862 - 2872 | 145 | 3350 - 3361 | 189 | 3839 - 3849 | 233 |
| 2873 - 2883 | 146 | 3362 - 3372 | 190 | 3850 - 3861 | 234 |
| 2884 - 2894 | 147 | 3373 - 3383 | 191 | 3862 - 3872 | 235 |
| 2895 - 2905 | 148 | 3384 - 3394 | 192 | 3873 - 3883 | 236 |
| 2906 - 2916 | 149 | 3395 - 3405 | 193 | 3884 - 3894 | 237 |
| 2917 - 2927 | 150 | 3406 - 3416 | 194 | 3895 - 3905 | 238 |
| 2928 - 2938 | 151 | 3417 - 3427 | 195 | 3906 - 3916 | 239 |
| 2939 - 2949 | 152 | 3428 - 3438 | 196 | 3917 - 3927 | 240 |
| 2950 - 2961 | 153 | 3439 - 3449 | 197 | 3928 - 3938 | 241 |
| 2962 - 2972 | 154 | 3450 - 3461 | 198 | 3939 - 3949 | 242 |
| 2973 - 2983 | 155 | 3462 - 3472 | 199 | 3950 - 3961 | 243 |
| 2984 - 2994 | 156 | 3473 - 3483 | 200 | 3962 - 3972 | 244 |
| 2995 - 3005 | 157 | 3484 - 3494 | 201 | 3973 - 3983 | 245 |
| 3006 - 3016 | 158 | 3495 - 3505 | 202 | 3984 - 3994 | 246 |
| 3017 - 3027 | 159 | 3506 - 3516 | 203 | 3995 - 4005 | 247 |
| 3028 - 3038 | 160 | 3517 - 3527 | 204 | 4006 - 4016 | 248 |
| 3039 - 3049 | 161 | 3528 - 3538 | 205 | 4017 - 4027 | 249 |
| 3050 - 3061 | 162 | 3539 - 3549 | 206 | 4028 - 4038 | 250 |
| 3062 - 3072 | 163 | 3550 - 3561 | 207 | 4039 - 4049 | 251 |
| 3073 - 3083 | 164 | 3562 - 3572 | 208 | 4050 - 4061 | 252 |
| 3084 - 3094 | 165 | 3573 - 3583 | 209 | 4062 - 4072 | 253 |
| 3095 - 3105 | 166 | 3584 - 3594 | 210 | 4073 - 4083 | 254 |
| 3106 - 3116 | 167 | 3595 - 3605 | 211 | 4084 - 4094 | 255 |
| 3117 - 3127 | 168 | 3606 - 3616 | 212 | 4095 - 4105 | 256 |
| 3128 - 3138 | 169 | 3617 - 3627 | 213 | 4106 - 4116 | 257 |
| 3139 - 3149 | 170 | 3628 - 3638 | 214 | 4117 - 4127 | 258 |
| 3150 - 3161 | 171 | 3639 - 3649 | 215 | 4128 - 4138 | 259 |
| 3162 - 3172 | 172 | 3650 - 3661 | 216 | 4139 - 4149 | 260 |
| 3173 - 3183 | 173 | 3662 - 3672 | 217 | 4150 - 4161 | 261 |
| 3184 - 3194 | 174 | 3673 - 3683 | 218 | 4162 - 4172 | 262 |
| 3195 - 3205 | 175 | 3684 - 3694 | 219 | 4173 - 4183 | 263 |

4

## Student Loan Deduction Tables

### Earnings for Week or Month exceed highest amount of earnings shown in the tables

If earnings in the week or month exceed the highest amount of earnings shown in the table you will need to calculate the amount of deduction as follows:-

Step  Action

1  Deduct the 'pay period threshold' from **total** earnings in the week or month

  - deduct **£288.46** from earnings in the week for **weekly** paid employees, or,
  - deduct **£1,250.00** from earnings in the month for **monthly** paid employee.

2  Multiply the result of step 1 (the excess) by 9% (0.09).

3  If the result at step 2 includes an amount of pence, round the resulting figure to the nearest whole £ **below**.

4  Record the amount of Student Loan deduction on the employee's Deductions Working Sheet, form P11, in column 1j at the appropriate week or month.

#### Example

Weekly paid employee. Earnings in the week £1,200 rounded down to the nearest £ **below**. Amount of Student Loan deduction is £82 calculated as follows:

| | | |
|---|---|---|
| Earnings in the week | £1,200.00 | |
| Deduct **pay period threshold** | £   288.46 | |
| | £   911.54 | (Result Step 1) |
| Multiply excess £911.54 by 0.09 | £     82.03 | (Result Step 2) |
| Round result of step 2 to nearest £ **below** | £     82.00 | (Result Step 3) |

### Pay periods other than weekly or monthly

The pay period for Student Loan deductions is always exactly the same as the earnings period for National Insurance contributions.

If the pay period is a multiple of a week or a month:

Step  Action

1  Divide the earnings into equal weekly or monthly amounts to get an average weekly or monthly amount.

2  Find the amount of Student Loan deduction due for the average weekly or monthly amount.

3  Multiply the amount of Student Loan deduction by the number of weeks or months in the pay period.

4  Record the multiplied amounts on the employee's Deductions Working Sheet, form P11, in column 1j at the appropriate week or month.

If, exceptionally, the earnings period for National Insurance contributions is longer than one week, but not a multiple of a week or month (for earnings periods of less than 7 days, use one week):

Step  Action

1  Work out the number of days in the pay period.

2  Multiply the number of days by £15,000 (the annual threshold) and then divide the result by the number of days in the year to give you the **pay period threshold**. Round down the resulting figure to the nearest penny.

6

## Student Loan Deduction Tables

3. Deduct the 'pay period threshold' from the **total** earnings in the pay period.
4. Multiply the result of step 3 (the excess) by 9% (0.09).
5. If the result at step 4 includes an amount of pence, round the resulting figure to the nearest whole £ **below**.
6. Record the amount of Student Loan deduction on the employee's Deduction Working Sheet, form P11, in column 1j at the appropriate week or month.

### Example

Employee receives earnings of £1,100 for a pay period consisting of 25 days. Amount of Student Loan deduction is £6 calculated as follows:

| | | |
|---|---|---|
| Number of days in pay period is  25 | | (Result Step 1) |
| Calculate pay period threshold: $\frac{25 \times £15,000}{365}$ = £1,027.39 after rounding | | (Result Step 2) |
| Earnings in pay period | £1,100.00 | |
| Deduct **pay period threshold** | £1,027.39 | |
| | £   72.61 | (Result Step 3) |
| Multiply excess £72.61 by 0.09 | £     6.53 | (Result Step 4) |
| Round to nearest £ **below** | £     6.00 | (Result Step 5) |

## Suggestions

Any suggestions for improving these tables should be sent to
HM Revenue & Customs
PAYE Process Team
Crown House
Victoria Street
Shipley
West Yorkshire
BD17 7TW

**HM Revenue & Customs**

# National Insurance contributions Tables A and J

Use from 6 April 2009 to 5 April 2010 inclusive
Not Contracted-out Tables
CA38

## Earnings limits and NICs rates

| Earnings limits | Employee's contribution — Contribution Table letter A | Employee's contribution — Contribution Table letter J | Employer's contribution — Contribution Table letters A and J |
|---|---|---|---|
| Below £95 weekly, or below £412 monthly, or below £4,940 yearly | Nil | Nil | Nil |
| £95 to £110 weekly, or £412 to £476 monthly, or £4,940 to £5,715 yearly | 0% | 0% | 0% |
| £110.01 to £770 weekly, or £476.01 to £3,337 monthly, or £5,715.01 to £40,040 yearly | 11% on earnings above the ET | 1% on earnings above the ET | 12.8% on earnings above the ET |
| £770.01 to £844 weekly, or £3,337.01 to £3,656 monthly, or £40,040.01 to £43,875 yearly | 11% on earnings above the ET | 1% on earnings above the ET | 12.8% on earnings above the ET |
| Over £844 weekly, or over £3,656 monthly, or over £43,875 yearly | 11% on earnings above the ET, up to and including the UEL, then 1% on all earnings above the UEL | 1% on all earnings above the ET | 12.8% on all earnings above the ET |

# TAX TABLES

Table letter **A**  Weekly table

| Employee's earnings up to and including the UEL ▼ | Earnings at the LEL (where earnings are equal to or exceed the LEL) 1a | Earnings above the LEL, up to and including the ET 1b | Earnings above the ET, up to and including the UAP 1c | Earnings above the UAP, up to and including the UEL 1d | Total of employee's and employer's contributions 1e | Employee's contributions due on all earnings above the ET 1f | Employer's contributions ▼ |
|---|---|---|---|---|---|---|---|
| £ | £ | £ p | £ p | £ p | £ p | £ p | £ p |
| 180 | 95 | 15.00 | 70.00 | 0.00 | 16.77 | 7.75 | 9.02 |
| 181 | 95 | 15.00 | 71.00 | 0.00 | 17.01 | 7.86 | 9.15 |
| 182 | 95 | 15.00 | 72.00 | 0.00 | 17.25 | 7.97 | 9.28 |
| 183 | 95 | 15.00 | 73.00 | 0.00 | 17.49 | 8.08 | 9.41 |
| 184 | 95 | 15.00 | 74.00 | 0.00 | 17.73 | 8.19 | 9.54 |
| 185 | 95 | 15.00 | 75.00 | 0.00 | 17.96 | 8.30 | 9.66 |
| 186 | 95 | 15.00 | 76.00 | 0.00 | 18.20 | 8.41 | 9.79 |
| 187 | 95 | 15.00 | 77.00 | 0.00 | 18.44 | 8.52 | 9.92 |
| 188 | 95 | 15.00 | 78.00 | 0.00 | 18.68 | 8.63 | 10.05 |
| 189 | 95 | 15.00 | 79.00 | 0.00 | 18.92 | 8.74 | 10.18 |
| 190 | 95 | 15.00 | 80.00 | 0.00 | 19.15 | 8.85 | 10.30 |
| 191 | 95 | 15.00 | 81.00 | 0.00 | 19.39 | 8.96 | 10.43 |
| 192 | 95 | 15.00 | 82.00 | 0.00 | 19.63 | 9.07 | 10.56 |
| 193 | 95 | 15.00 | 83.00 | 0.00 | 19.87 | 9.18 | 10.69 |
| 194 | 95 | 15.00 | 84.00 | 0.00 | 20.11 | 9.29 | 10.82 |
| 195 | 95 | 15.00 | 85.00 | 0.00 | 20.34 | 9.40 | 10.94 |
| 196 | 95 | 15.00 | 86.00 | 0.00 | 20.58 | 9.51 | 11.07 |
| 197 | 95 | 15.00 | 87.00 | 0.00 | 20.82 | 9.62 | 11.20 |
| 198 | 95 | 15.00 | 88.00 | 0.00 | 21.06 | 9.73 | 11.33 |
| 199 | 95 | 15.00 | 89.00 | 0.00 | 21.30 | 9.84 | 11.46 |
| 200 | 95 | 15.00 | 90.00 | 0.00 | 21.53 | 9.95 | 11.58 |
| 201 | 95 | 15.00 | 91.00 | 0.00 | 21.77 | 10.06 | 11.71 |
| 202 | 95 | 15.00 | 92.00 | 0.00 | 22.01 | 10.17 | 11.84 |
| 203 | 95 | 15.00 | 93.00 | 0.00 | 22.25 | 10.28 | 11.97 |
| 204 | 95 | 15.00 | 94.00 | 0.00 | 22.49 | 10.39 | 12.10 |
| 205 | 95 | 15.00 | 95.00 | 0.00 | 22.72 | 10.50 | 12.22 |
| 206 | 95 | 15.00 | 96.00 | 0.00 | 22.96 | 10.61 | 12.35 |
| 207 | 95 | 15.00 | 97.00 | 0.00 | 23.20 | 10.72 | 12.48 |
| 208 | 95 | 15.00 | 98.00 | 0.00 | 23.44 | 10.83 | 12.61 |
| 209 | 95 | 15.00 | 99.00 | 0.00 | 23.68 | 10.94 | 12.74 |
| 210 | 95 | 15.00 | 100.00 | 0.00 | 23.91 | 11.05 | 12.86 |
| 211 | 95 | 15.00 | 101.00 | 0.00 | 24.15 | 11.16 | 12.99 |
| 212 | 95 | 15.00 | 102.00 | 0.00 | 24.39 | 11.27 | 13.12 |
| 213 | 95 | 15.00 | 103.00 | 0.00 | 24.63 | 11.38 | 13.25 |
| 214 | 95 | 15.00 | 104.00 | 0.00 | 24.87 | 11.49 | 13.38 |
| 215 | 95 | 15.00 | 105.00 | 0.00 | 25.10 | 11.60 | 13.50 |
| 216 | 95 | 15.00 | 106.00 | 0.00 | 25.34 | 11.71 | 13.63 |
| 217 | 95 | 15.00 | 107.00 | 0.00 | 25.58 | 11.82 | 13.76 |
| 218 | 95 | 15.00 | 108.00 | 0.00 | 25.82 | 11.93 | 13.89 |
| 219 | 95 | 15.00 | 109.00 | 0.00 | 26.06 | 12.04 | 14.02 |
| 220 | 95 | 15.00 | 110.00 | 0.00 | 26.29 | 12.15 | 14.14 |
| 221 | 95 | 15.00 | 111.00 | 0.00 | 26.53 | 12.26 | 14.27 |
| 222 | 95 | 15.00 | 112.00 | 0.00 | 26.77 | 12.37 | 14.40 |
| 223 | 95 | 15.00 | 113.00 | 0.00 | 27.01 | 12.48 | 14.53 |
| 224 | 95 | 15.00 | 114.00 | 0.00 | 27.25 | 12.59 | 14.66 |
| 225 | 95 | 15.00 | 115.00 | 0.00 | 27.48 | 12.70 | 14.78 |
| 226 | 95 | 15.00 | 116.00 | 0.00 | 27.72 | 12.81 | 14.91 |
| 227 | 95 | 15.00 | 117.00 | 0.00 | 27.96 | 12.92 | 15.04 |
| 228 | 95 | 15.00 | 118.00 | 0.00 | 28.20 | 13.03 | 15.17 |
| 229 | 95 | 15.00 | 119.00 | 0.00 | 28.44 | 13.14 | 15.30 |
| 230 | 95 | 15.00 | 120.00 | 0.00 | 28.67 | 13.25 | 15.42 |
| 231 | 95 | 15.00 | 121.00 | 0.00 | 28.91 | 13.36 | 15.55 |
| 232 | 95 | 15.00 | 122.00 | 0.00 | 29.15 | 13.47 | 15.68 |
| 233 | 95 | 15.00 | 123.00 | 0.00 | 29.39 | 13.58 | 15.81 |
| 234 | 95 | 15.00 | 124.00 | 0.00 | 29.63 | 13.69 | 15.94 |

▼ for information only - do not enter on form P11 *Deductions Working Sheet*

# TAX TABLES

Table letter **A**  Monthly table

| Employee's earnings up to and including the UEL | Earnings at the LEL (where earnings are equal to or exceed the LEL) | Earnings above the LEL, up to and including the ET | Earnings above the ET, up to and including the UAP | Earnings above the UAP, up to and including the UEL | Total of employee's and employer's contributions | Employee's contributions due on all earnings above the ET | Employer's contributions |
|---|---|---|---|---|---|---|---|
| 1a | 1b | 1c | 1d | 1e | 1f | | |
| £ | £ | £ p | £ p | £ p | £ p | £ p | £ p |
| 1412 | 412 | 64.00 | 936.00 | 0.00 | 223.24 | 103.18 | 120.06 |
| 1416 | 412 | 64.00 | 940.00 | 0.00 | 224.20 | 103.62 | 120.58 |
| 1420 | 412 | 64.00 | 944.00 | 0.00 | 225.15 | 104.06 | 121.09 |
| 1424 | 412 | 64.00 | 948.00 | 0.00 | 226.10 | 104.50 | 121.60 |
| 1428 | 412 | 64.00 | 952.00 | 0.00 | 227.05 | 104.94 | 122.11 |
| 1432 | 412 | 64.00 | 956.00 | 0.00 | 228.00 | 105.38 | 122.62 |
| 1436 | 412 | 64.00 | 960.00 | 0.00 | 228.96 | 105.82 | 123.14 |
| 1440 | 412 | 64.00 | 964.00 | 0.00 | 229.91 | 106.26 | 123.65 |
| 1444 | 412 | 64.00 | 968.00 | 0.00 | 230.86 | 106.70 | 124.16 |
| 1448 | 412 | 64.00 | 972.00 | 0.00 | 231.81 | 107.14 | 124.67 |
| 1452 | 412 | 64.00 | 976.00 | 0.00 | 232.76 | 107.58 | 125.18 |
| 1456 | 412 | 64.00 | 980.00 | 0.00 | 233.72 | 108.02 | 125.70 |
| 1460 | 412 | 64.00 | 984.00 | 0.00 | 234.67 | 108.46 | 126.21 |
| 1464 | 412 | 64.00 | 988.00 | 0.00 | 235.62 | 108.90 | 126.72 |
| 1468 | 412 | 64.00 | 992.00 | 0.00 | 236.57 | 109.34 | 127.23 |
| 1472 | 412 | 64.00 | 996.00 | 0.00 | 237.52 | 109.78 | 127.74 |
| 1476 | 412 | 64.00 | 1000.00 | 0.00 | 238.48 | 110.22 | 128.26 |
| 1480 | 412 | 64.00 | 1004.00 | 0.00 | 239.43 | 110.66 | 128.77 |
| 1484 | 412 | 64.00 | 1008.00 | 0.00 | 240.38 | 111.10 | 129.28 |
| 1488 | 412 | 64.00 | 1012.00 | 0.00 | 241.33 | 111.54 | 129.79 |
| 1492 | 412 | 64.00 | 1016.00 | 0.00 | 242.28 | 111.98 | 130.30 |
| 1496 | 412 | 64.00 | 1020.00 | 0.00 | 243.24 | 112.42 | 130.82 |
| 1500 | 412 | 64.00 | 1024.00 | 0.00 | 244.19 | 112.86 | 131.33 |
| 1504 | 412 | 64.00 | 1028.00 | 0.00 | 245.14 | 113.30 | 131.84 |
| 1508 | 412 | 64.00 | 1032.00 | 0.00 | 246.09 | 113.74 | 132.35 |
| 1512 | 412 | 64.00 | 1036.00 | 0.00 | 247.04 | 114.18 | 132.86 |
| 1516 | 412 | 64.00 | 1040.00 | 0.00 | 248.00 | 114.62 | 133.38 |
| 1520 | 412 | 64.00 | 1044.00 | 0.00 | 248.95 | 115.06 | 133.89 |
| 1524 | 412 | 64.00 | 1048.00 | 0.00 | 249.90 | 115.50 | 134.40 |
| 1528 | 412 | 64.00 | 1052.00 | 0.00 | 250.85 | 115.94 | 134.91 |
| 1532 | 412 | 64.00 | 1056.00 | 0.00 | 251.80 | 116.38 | 135.42 |
| 1536 | 412 | 64.00 | 1060.00 | 0.00 | 252.76 | 116.82 | 135.94 |
| 1540 | 412 | 64.00 | 1064.00 | 0.00 | 253.71 | 117.26 | 136.45 |
| 1544 | 412 | 64.00 | 1068.00 | 0.00 | 254.66 | 117.70 | 136.96 |
| 1548 | 412 | 64.00 | 1072.00 | 0.00 | 255.61 | 118.14 | 137.47 |
| 1552 | 412 | 64.00 | 1076.00 | 0.00 | 256.56 | 118.58 | 137.98 |
| 1556 | 412 | 64.00 | 1080.00 | 0.00 | 257.52 | 119.02 | 138.50 |
| 1560 | 412 | 64.00 | 1084.00 | 0.00 | 258.47 | 119.46 | 139.01 |
| 1564 | 412 | 64.00 | 1088.00 | 0.00 | 259.42 | 119.90 | 139.52 |
| 1568 | 412 | 64.00 | 1092.00 | 0.00 | 260.37 | 120.34 | 140.03 |
| 1572 | 412 | 64.00 | 1096.00 | 0.00 | 261.32 | 120.78 | 140.54 |
| 1576 | 412 | 64.00 | 1100.00 | 0.00 | 262.28 | 121.22 | 141.06 |
| 1580 | 412 | 64.00 | 1104.00 | 0.00 | 263.23 | 121.66 | 141.57 |
| 1584 | 412 | 64.00 | 1108.00 | 0.00 | 264.18 | 122.10 | 142.08 |
| 1588 | 412 | 64.00 | 1112.00 | 0.00 | 265.13 | 122.54 | 142.59 |
| 1592 | 412 | 64.00 | 1116.00 | 0.00 | 266.08 | 122.98 | 143.10 |
| 1596 | 412 | 64.00 | 1120.00 | 0.00 | 267.04 | 123.42 | 143.62 |
| 1600 | 412 | 64.00 | 1124.00 | 0.00 | 267.99 | 123.86 | 144.13 |
| 1604 | 412 | 64.00 | 1128.00 | 0.00 | 268.94 | 124.30 | 144.64 |
| 1608 | 412 | 64.00 | 1132.00 | 0.00 | 269.89 | 124.74 | 145.15 |
| 1612 | 412 | 64.00 | 1136.00 | 0.00 | 270.84 | 125.18 | 145.66 |
| 1616 | 412 | 64.00 | 1140.00 | 0.00 | 271.80 | 125.62 | 146.18 |
| 1620 | 412 | 64.00 | 1144.00 | 0.00 | 272.75 | 126.06 | 146.69 |
| 1624 | 412 | 64.00 | 1148.00 | 0.00 | 273.70 | 126.50 | 147.20 |
| 1628 | 412 | 64.00 | 1152.00 | 0.00 | 274.65 | 126.94 | 147.71 |

▼ for information only - do not enter on form P11 *Deductions Working Sheet*

## TAX TABLES

**Monthly table**

Table letter **A**

| Employee's earnings up to and including the UEL | Earnings at the LEL (where earnings are equal to or exceed the LEL) | Earnings above the LEL, up to and including the ET | Earnings above the ET, up to and including the UAP | Earnings above the UAP, up to and including the UEL | Total of employee's and employer's contributions | Employee's contributions due on all earnings above the ET | Employer's contributions |
|---|---|---|---|---|---|---|---|
| 1a | 1b | 1c | 1d | 1e | 1f | | |
| £ | £ | £ p | £ p | £ p | £ p | £ p | £ p |
| 2072 | 412 | 64.00 | 1596.00 | 0.00 | 380.32 | 175.78 | 204.54 |
| 2076 | 412 | 64.00 | 1600.00 | 0.00 | 381.28 | 176.22 | 205.06 |
| 2080 | 412 | 64.00 | 1604.00 | 0.00 | 382.23 | 176.66 | 205.57 |
| 2084 | 412 | 64.00 | 1608.00 | 0.00 | 383.18 | 177.10 | 206.08 |
| 2088 | 412 | 64.00 | 1612.00 | 0.00 | 384.13 | 177.54 | 206.59 |
| 2092 | 412 | 64.00 | 1616.00 | 0.00 | 385.08 | 177.98 | 207.10 |
| 2096 | 412 | 64.00 | 1620.00 | 0.00 | 386.04 | 178.42 | 207.62 |
| 2100 | 412 | 64.00 | 1624.00 | 0.00 | 386.99 | 178.86 | 208.13 |
| 2104 | 412 | 64.00 | 1628.00 | 0.00 | 387.94 | 179.30 | 208.64 |
| 2108 | 412 | 64.00 | 1632.00 | 0.00 | 388.89 | 179.74 | 209.15 |
| 2112 | 412 | 64.00 | 1636.00 | 0.00 | 389.84 | 180.18 | 209.66 |
| 2116 | 412 | 64.00 | 1640.00 | 0.00 | 390.80 | 180.62 | 210.18 |
| 2120 | 412 | 64.00 | 1644.00 | 0.00 | 391.75 | 181.06 | 210.69 |
| 2124 | 412 | 64.00 | 1648.00 | 0.00 | 392.70 | 181.50 | 211.20 |
| 2128 | 412 | 64.00 | 1652.00 | 0.00 | 393.65 | 181.94 | 211.71 |
| 2132 | 412 | 64.00 | 1656.00 | 0.00 | 394.60 | 182.38 | 212.22 |
| 2136 | 412 | 64.00 | 1660.00 | 0.00 | 395.56 | 182.82 | 212.74 |
| 2140 | 412 | 64.00 | 1664.00 | 0.00 | 396.51 | 183.26 | 213.25 |
| 2144 | 412 | 64.00 | 1668.00 | 0.00 | 397.46 | 183.70 | 213.76 |
| 2148 | 412 | 64.00 | 1672.00 | 0.00 | 398.41 | 184.14 | 214.27 |
| 2152 | 412 | 64.00 | 1676.00 | 0.00 | 399.36 | 184.58 | 214.78 |
| 2156 | 412 | 64.00 | 1680.00 | 0.00 | 400.32 | 185.02 | 215.30 |
| 2160 | 412 | 64.00 | 1684.00 | 0.00 | 401.27 | 185.46 | 215.81 |
| 2164 | 412 | 64.00 | 1688.00 | 0.00 | 402.22 | 185.90 | 216.32 |
| 2168 | 412 | 64.00 | 1692.00 | 0.00 | 403.17 | 186.34 | 216.83 |
| 2172 | 412 | 64.00 | 1696.00 | 0.00 | 404.12 | 186.78 | 217.34 |
| 2176 | 412 | 64.00 | 1700.00 | 0.00 | 405.08 | 187.22 | 217.86 |
| 2180 | 412 | 64.00 | 1704.00 | 0.00 | 406.03 | 187.66 | 218.37 |
| 2184 | 412 | 64.00 | 1708.00 | 0.00 | 406.98 | 188.10 | 218.88 |
| 2188 | 412 | 64.00 | 1712.00 | 0.00 | 407.93 | 188.54 | 219.39 |
| 2192 | 412 | 64.00 | 1716.00 | 0.00 | 408.88 | 188.98 | 219.90 |
| 2196 | 412 | 64.00 | 1720.00 | 0.00 | 409.84 | 189.42 | 220.42 |
| 2200 | 412 | 64.00 | 1724.00 | 0.00 | 410.79 | 189.86 | 220.93 |
| 2204 | 412 | 64.00 | 1728.00 | 0.00 | 411.74 | 190.30 | 221.44 |
| 2208 | 412 | 64.00 | 1732.00 | 0.00 | 412.69 | 190.74 | 221.95 |
| 2212 | 412 | 64.00 | 1736.00 | 0.00 | 413.64 | 191.18 | 222.46 |
| 2216 | 412 | 64.00 | 1740.00 | 0.00 | 414.60 | 191.62 | 222.98 |
| 2220 | 412 | 64.00 | 1744.00 | 0.00 | 415.55 | 192.06 | 223.49 |
| 2224 | 412 | 64.00 | 1748.00 | 0.00 | 416.50 | 192.50 | 224.00 |
| 2228 | 412 | 64.00 | 1752.00 | 0.00 | 417.45 | 192.94 | 224.51 |
| 2232 | 412 | 64.00 | 1756.00 | 0.00 | 418.40 | 193.38 | 225.02 |
| 2236 | 412 | 64.00 | 1760.00 | 0.00 | 419.36 | 193.82 | 225.54 |
| 2240 | 412 | 64.00 | 1764.00 | 0.00 | 420.31 | 194.26 | 226.05 |
| 2244 | 412 | 64.00 | 1768.00 | 0.00 | 421.26 | 194.70 | 226.56 |
| 2248 | 412 | 64.00 | 1772.00 | 0.00 | 422.21 | 195.14 | 227.07 |
| 2252 | 412 | 64.00 | 1776.00 | 0.00 | 423.16 | 195.58 | 227.58 |
| 2256 | 412 | 64.00 | 1780.00 | 0.00 | 424.12 | 196.02 | 228.10 |
| 2260 | 412 | 64.00 | 1784.00 | 0.00 | 425.07 | 196.46 | 228.61 |
| 2264 | 412 | 64.00 | 1788.00 | 0.00 | 426.02 | 196.90 | 229.12 |
| 2268 | 412 | 64.00 | 1792.00 | 0.00 | 426.97 | 197.34 | 229.63 |
| 2272 | 412 | 64.00 | 1796.00 | 0.00 | 427.92 | 197.78 | 230.14 |
| 2276 | 412 | 64.00 | 1800.00 | 0.00 | 428.88 | 198.22 | 230.66 |
| 2280 | 412 | 64.00 | 1804.00 | 0.00 | 429.83 | 198.66 | 231.17 |
| 2284 | 412 | 64.00 | 1808.00 | 0.00 | 430.78 | 199.10 | 231.68 |
| 2288 | 412 | 64.00 | 1812.00 | 0.00 | 431.73 | 199.54 | 232.19 |

▼ for information only - do not enter on form P11 *Deductions Working Sheet*

TAX TABLES

**HM Revenue & Customs**

**CA41**
National Insurance Contributions Tables

# National Insurance contributions Tables B and C

**Use from
6 April 2009 to
5 April 2010 inclusive**

TAX TABLES

## Earnings limits and NIC rates

| Earnings limits | Employee's contribution — Contribution table letter B | Employee's contribution — Contribution table letter C | Employer's contribution — Table letters B and C |
|---|---|---|---|
| Below £95 weekly, or below £412 monthly, or below £4,940 yearly | Nil | Nil | Nil |
| £95 to £110 weekly, or £412 to £476 monthly, or £4,940 to £5,715 yearly | 0% | Nil | 0% |
| £110.01 to £770 weekly, or £476.01 to £3,337 monthly, or £5,715.01 to £40,040 yearly | 4.85% on earnings above the ET | Nil | 12.8% on earnings above the ET |
| £770.01 to £844 weekly, or £3,337.01 to £3,656 monthly, or £40,040.01 to £43,875 yearly | 4.85% on earnings above the ET | Nil | 12.8% on earnings above the ET |
| Over £844 weekly, or over £3,656 monthly, or over £43,875 yearly | 4.85% on earnings above the ET, up to and including the UEL, then **1%** on all earnings above the UEL | Nil | 12.8% on earnings above the ET |

# TAX TABLES

**Weekly table**

Table letter **C**

| Employee's earnings up to and including the UEL ▼ £ | Earnings at the LEL (where earnings are equal to or exceed the LEL) 1a £ | Earnings above the LEL, up to and including the ET 1b £ p | Earnings above the ET, up to and including the UAP 1c £ p | Earnings above the UAP, up to and including the UEL 1d £ p | Total of employee's and employer's contributions 1e £ p | Employee's contributions due on all earnings above the ET 1f £ p |
|---|---|---|---|---|---|---|
| 130 | 95 | 15.00 | 20.00 | 0.00 | 2.62 | 0.00 |
| 131 | 95 | 15.00 | 21.00 | 0.00 | 2.75 | 0.00 |
| 132 | 95 | 15.00 | 22.00 | 0.00 | 2.88 | 0.00 |
| 133 | 95 | 15.00 | 23.00 | 0.00 | 3.01 | 0.00 |
| 134 | 95 | 15.00 | 24.00 | 0.00 | 3.14 | 0.00 |
| 135 | 95 | 15.00 | 25.00 | 0.00 | 3.26 | 0.00 |
| 136 | 95 | 15.00 | 26.00 | 0.00 | 3.39 | 0.00 |
| 137 | 95 | 15.00 | 27.00 | 0.00 | 3.52 | 0.00 |
| 138 | 95 | 15.00 | 28.00 | 0.00 | 3.65 | 0.00 |
| 139 | 95 | 15.00 | 29.00 | 0.00 | 3.78 | 0.00 |
| 140 | 95 | 15.00 | 30.00 | 0.00 | 3.90 | 0.00 |
| 141 | 95 | 15.00 | 31.00 | 0.00 | 4.03 | 0.00 |
| 142 | 95 | 15.00 | 32.00 | 0.00 | 4.16 | 0.00 |
| 143 | 95 | 15.00 | 33.00 | 0.00 | 4.29 | 0.00 |
| 144 | 95 | 15.00 | 34.00 | 0.00 | 4.42 | 0.00 |
| 145 | 95 | 15.00 | 35.00 | 0.00 | 4.54 | 0.00 |
| 146 | 95 | 15.00 | 36.00 | 0.00 | 4.67 | 0.00 |
| 147 | 95 | 15.00 | 37.00 | 0.00 | 4.80 | 0.00 |
| 148 | 95 | 15.00 | 38.00 | 0.00 | 4.93 | 0.00 |
| 149 | 95 | 15.00 | 39.00 | 0.00 | 5.06 | 0.00 |
| 150 | 95 | 15.00 | 40.00 | 0.00 | 5.18 | 0.00 |
| 151 | 95 | 15.00 | 41.00 | 0.00 | 5.31 | 0.00 |
| 152 | 95 | 15.00 | 42.00 | 0.00 | 5.44 | 0.00 |
| 153 | 95 | 15.00 | 43.00 | 0.00 | 5.57 | 0.00 |
| 154 | 95 | 15.00 | 44.00 | 0.00 | 5.70 | 0.00 |
| 155 | 95 | 15.00 | 45.00 | 0.00 | 5.82 | 0.00 |
| 156 | 95 | 15.00 | 46.00 | 0.00 | 5.95 | 0.00 |
| 157 | 95 | 15.00 | 47.00 | 0.00 | 6.08 | 0.00 |
| 158 | 95 | 15.00 | 48.00 | 0.00 | 6.21 | 0.00 |
| 159 | 95 | 15.00 | 49.00 | 0.00 | 6.34 | 0.00 |
| 160 | 95 | 15.00 | 50.00 | 0.00 | 6.46 | 0.00 |
| 161 | 95 | 15.00 | 51.00 | 0.00 | 6.59 | 0.00 |
| 162 | 95 | 15.00 | 52.00 | 0.00 | 6.72 | 0.00 |
| 163 | 95 | 15.00 | 53.00 | 0.00 | 6.85 | 0.00 |
| 164 | 95 | 15.00 | 54.00 | 0.00 | 6.98 | 0.00 |
| 165 | 95 | 15.00 | 55.00 | 0.00 | 7.10 | 0.00 |
| 166 | 95 | 15.00 | 56.00 | 0.00 | 7.23 | 0.00 |
| 167 | 95 | 15.00 | 57.00 | 0.00 | 7.36 | 0.00 |
| 168 | 95 | 15.00 | 58.00 | 0.00 | 7.49 | 0.00 |
| 169 | 95 | 15.00 | 59.00 | 0.00 | 7.62 | 0.00 |
| 170 | 95 | 15.00 | 60.00 | 0.00 | 7.74 | 0.00 |
| 171 | 95 | 15.00 | 61.00 | 0.00 | 7.87 | 0.00 |
| 172 | 95 | 15.00 | 62.00 | 0.00 | 8.00 | 0.00 |
| 173 | 95 | 15.00 | 63.00 | 0.00 | 8.13 | 0.00 |
| 174 | 95 | 15.00 | 64.00 | 0.00 | 8.26 | 0.00 |
| 175 | 95 | 15.00 | 65.00 | 0.00 | 8.38 | 0.00 |
| 176 | 95 | 15.00 | 66.00 | 0.00 | 8.51 | 0.00 |
| 177 | 95 | 15.00 | 67.00 | 0.00 | 8.64 | 0.00 |
| 178 | 95 | 15.00 | 68.00 | 0.00 | 8.77 | 0.00 |
| 179 | 95 | 15.00 | 69.00 | 0.00 | 8.90 | 0.00 |
| 180 | 95 | 15.00 | 70.00 | 0.00 | 9.02 | 0.00 |
| 181 | 95 | 15.00 | 71.00 | 0.00 | 9.15 | 0.00 |
| 182 | 95 | 15.00 | 72.00 | 0.00 | 9.28 | 0.00 |
| 183 | 95 | 15.00 | 73.00 | 0.00 | 9.41 | 0.00 |
| 184 | 95 | 15.00 | 74.00 | 0.00 | 9.54 | 0.00 |

▼ for information only - do not enter on form P11 *Deductions Working Sheet*

# TAX TABLES

**Monthly table**

Table letter **C**

| Employee's earnings up to and including the UEL ▼ | Earnings at the LEL (where earnings are equal to or exceed the LEL) | Earnings above the LEL, up to and including the ET | Earnings above the ET, up to and including the UAP | Earnings above the UAP, up to and including the UEL | Total of employee's and employer's contributions | Employee's contributions due on all earnings above the ET |
|---|---|---|---|---|---|---|
| | 1a | 1b | 1c | 1d | 1e | 1f |
| £ | £ | £ p | £ p | £ p | £ p | £ p |
| 1872 | 412 | 64.00 | 1396.00 | 0.00 | 178.94 | 0.00 |
| 1876 | 412 | 64.00 | 1400.00 | 0.00 | 179.46 | 0.00 |
| 1880 | 412 | 64.00 | 1404.00 | 0.00 | 179.97 | 0.00 |
| 1884 | 412 | 64.00 | 1408.00 | 0.00 | 180.48 | 0.00 |
| 1888 | 412 | 64.00 | 1412.00 | 0.00 | 180.99 | 0.00 |
| 1892 | 412 | 64.00 | 1416.00 | 0.00 | 181.50 | 0.00 |
| 1896 | 412 | 64.00 | 1420.00 | 0.00 | 182.02 | 0.00 |
| 1900 | 412 | 64.00 | 1424.00 | 0.00 | 182.53 | 0.00 |
| 1904 | 412 | 64.00 | 1428.00 | 0.00 | 183.04 | 0.00 |
| 1908 | 412 | 64.00 | 1432.00 | 0.00 | 183.55 | 0.00 |
| 1912 | 412 | 64.00 | 1436.00 | 0.00 | 184.06 | 0.00 |
| 1916 | 412 | 64.00 | 1440.00 | 0.00 | 184.58 | 0.00 |
| 1920 | 412 | 64.00 | 1444.00 | 0.00 | 185.09 | 0.00 |
| 1924 | 412 | 64.00 | 1448.00 | 0.00 | 185.60 | 0.00 |
| 1928 | 412 | 64.00 | 1452.00 | 0.00 | 186.11 | 0.00 |
| 1932 | 412 | 64.00 | 1456.00 | 0.00 | 186.62 | 0.00 |
| 1936 | 412 | 64.00 | 1460.00 | 0.00 | 187.14 | 0.00 |
| 1940 | 412 | 64.00 | 1464.00 | 0.00 | 187.65 | 0.00 |
| 1944 | 412 | 64.00 | 1468.00 | 0.00 | 188.16 | 0.00 |
| 1948 | 412 | 64.00 | 1472.00 | 0.00 | 188.67 | 0.00 |
| 1952 | 412 | 64.00 | 1476.00 | 0.00 | 189.18 | 0.00 |
| 1956 | 412 | 64.00 | 1480.00 | 0.00 | 189.70 | 0.00 |
| 1960 | 412 | 64.00 | 1484.00 | 0.00 | 190.21 | 0.00 |
| 1964 | 412 | 64.00 | 1488.00 | 0.00 | 190.72 | 0.00 |
| 1968 | 412 | 64.00 | 1492.00 | 0.00 | 191.23 | 0.00 |
| 1972 | 412 | 64.00 | 1496.00 | 0.00 | 191.74 | 0.00 |
| 1976 | 412 | 64.00 | 1500.00 | 0.00 | 192.26 | 0.00 |
| 1980 | 412 | 64.00 | 1504.00 | 0.00 | 192.77 | 0.00 |
| 1984 | 412 | 64.00 | 1508.00 | 0.00 | 193.28 | 0.00 |
| 1988 | 412 | 64.00 | 1512.00 | 0.00 | 193.79 | 0.00 |
| 1992 | 412 | 64.00 | 1516.00 | 0.00 | 194.30 | 0.00 |
| 1996 | 412 | 64.00 | 1520.00 | 0.00 | 194.82 | 0.00 |
| 2000 | 412 | 64.00 | 1524.00 | 0.00 | 195.33 | 0.00 |
| 2004 | 412 | 64.00 | 1528.00 | 0.00 | 195.84 | 0.00 |
| 2008 | 412 | 64.00 | 1532.00 | 0.00 | 196.35 | 0.00 |
| 2012 | 412 | 64.00 | 1536.00 | 0.00 | 196.86 | 0.00 |
| 2016 | 412 | 64.00 | 1540.00 | 0.00 | 197.38 | 0.00 |
| 2020 | 412 | 64.00 | 1544.00 | 0.00 | 197.89 | 0.00 |
| 2024 | 412 | 64.00 | 1548.00 | 0.00 | 198.40 | 0.00 |
| 2028 | 412 | 64.00 | 1552.00 | 0.00 | 198.91 | 0.00 |
| 2032 | 412 | 64.00 | 1556.00 | 0.00 | 199.42 | 0.00 |
| 2036 | 412 | 64.00 | 1560.00 | 0.00 | 199.94 | 0.00 |
| 2040 | 412 | 64.00 | 1564.00 | 0.00 | 200.45 | 0.00 |
| 2044 | 412 | 64.00 | 1568.00 | 0.00 | 200.96 | 0.00 |
| 2048 | 412 | 64.00 | 1572.00 | 0.00 | 201.47 | 0.00 |
| 2052 | 412 | 64.00 | 1576.00 | 0.00 | 201.98 | 0.00 |
| 2056 | 412 | 64.00 | 1580.00 | 0.00 | 202.50 | 0.00 |
| 2060 | 412 | 64.00 | 1584.00 | 0.00 | 203.01 | 0.00 |
| 2064 | 412 | 64.00 | 1588.00 | 0.00 | 203.52 | 0.00 |
| 2068 | 412 | 64.00 | 1592.00 | 0.00 | 204.03 | 0.00 |
| 2072 | 412 | 64.00 | 1596.00 | 0.00 | 204.54 | 0.00 |
| 2076 | 412 | 64.00 | 1600.00 | 0.00 | 205.06 | 0.00 |
| 2080 | 412 | 64.00 | 1604.00 | 0.00 | 205.57 | 0.00 |
| 2084 | 412 | 64.00 | 1608.00 | 0.00 | 206.08 | 0.00 |
| 2088 | 412 | 64.00 | 1612.00 | 0.00 | 206.59 | 0.00 |

▼ for information only - do not enter on form P11 *Deductions Working Sheet*

# TAX TABLES

Table letter **C**              **Monthly table**

| ▼ Employee's earnings up to and including the UEL | Earnings at the LEL (where earnings are equal to or exceed the LEL) 1a | Earnings above the LEL, up to and including the ET 1b | Earnings above the ET, up to and including the UAP 1c | Earnings above the UAP, up to and including the UEL 1d | Total of employee's and employer's contributions 1e | Employee's contributions due on all earnings above the ET 1f |
|---|---|---|---|---|---|---|
| £ | £ | £ p | £ p | £ p | £ p | £ p |
| 2092 | 412 | 64.00 | 1616.00 | 0.00 | 207.10 | 0.00 |
| 2096 | 412 | 64.00 | 1620.00 | 0.00 | 207.62 | 0.00 |
| 2100 | 412 | 64.00 | 1624.00 | 0.00 | 208.13 | 0.00 |
| 2104 | 412 | 64.00 | 1628.00 | 0.00 | 208.64 | 0.00 |
| 2108 | 412 | 64.00 | 1632.00 | 0.00 | 209.15 | 0.00 |
| 2112 | 412 | 64.00 | 1636.00 | 0.00 | 209.66 | 0.00 |
| 2116 | 412 | 64.00 | 1640.00 | 0.00 | 210.18 | 0.00 |
| 2120 | 412 | 64.00 | 1644.00 | 0.00 | 210.69 | 0.00 |
| 2124 | 412 | 64.00 | 1648.00 | 0.00 | 211.20 | 0.00 |
| 2128 | 412 | 64.00 | 1652.00 | 0.00 | 211.71 | 0.00 |
| 2132 | 412 | 64.00 | 1656.00 | 0.00 | 212.22 | 0.00 |
| 2136 | 412 | 64.00 | 1660.00 | 0.00 | 212.74 | 0.00 |
| 2140 | 412 | 64.00 | 1664.00 | 0.00 | 213.25 | 0.00 |
| 2144 | 412 | 64.00 | 1668.00 | 0.00 | 213.76 | 0.00 |
| 2148 | 412 | 64.00 | 1672.00 | 0.00 | 214.27 | 0.00 |
| 2152 | 412 | 64.00 | 1676.00 | 0.00 | 214.78 | 0.00 |
| 2156 | 412 | 64.00 | 1680.00 | 0.00 | 215.30 | 0.00 |
| 2160 | 412 | 64.00 | 1684.00 | 0.00 | 215.81 | 0.00 |
| 2164 | 412 | 64.00 | 1688.00 | 0.00 | 216.32 | 0.00 |
| 2168 | 412 | 64.00 | 1692.00 | 0.00 | 216.83 | 0.00 |
| 2172 | 412 | 64.00 | 1696.00 | 0.00 | 217.34 | 0.00 |
| 2176 | 412 | 64.00 | 1700.00 | 0.00 | 217.86 | 0.00 |
| 2180 | 412 | 64.00 | 1704.00 | 0.00 | 218.37 | 0.00 |
| 2184 | 412 | 64.00 | 1708.00 | 0.00 | 218.88 | 0.00 |
| 2188 | 412 | 64.00 | 1712.00 | 0.00 | 219.39 | 0.00 |
| 2192 | 412 | 64.00 | 1716.00 | 0.00 | 219.90 | 0.00 |
| 2196 | 412 | 64.00 | 1720.00 | 0.00 | 220.42 | 0.00 |
| 2200 | 412 | 64.00 | 1724.00 | 0.00 | 220.93 | 0.00 |
| 2204 | 412 | 64.00 | 1728.00 | 0.00 | 221.44 | 0.00 |
| 2208 | 412 | 64.00 | 1732.00 | 0.00 | 221.95 | 0.00 |
| 2212 | 412 | 64.00 | 1736.00 | 0.00 | 222.46 | 0.00 |
| 2216 | 412 | 64.00 | 1740.00 | 0.00 | 222.98 | 0.00 |
| 2220 | 412 | 64.00 | 1744.00 | 0.00 | 223.49 | 0.00 |
| 2224 | 412 | 64.00 | 1748.00 | 0.00 | 224.00 | 0.00 |
| 2228 | 412 | 64.00 | 1752.00 | 0.00 | 224.51 | 0.00 |
| 2232 | 412 | 64.00 | 1756.00 | 0.00 | 225.02 | 0.00 |
| 2236 | 412 | 64.00 | 1760.00 | 0.00 | 225.54 | 0.00 |
| 2240 | 412 | 64.00 | 1764.00 | 0.00 | 226.05 | 0.00 |
| 2244 | 412 | 64.00 | 1768.00 | 0.00 | 226.56 | 0.00 |
| 2248 | 412 | 64.00 | 1772.00 | 0.00 | 227.07 | 0.00 |
| 2252 | 412 | 64.00 | 1776.00 | 0.00 | 227.58 | 0.00 |
| 2256 | 412 | 64.00 | 1780.00 | 0.00 | 228.10 | 0.00 |
| 2260 | 412 | 64.00 | 1784.00 | 0.00 | 228.61 | 0.00 |
| 2264 | 412 | 64.00 | 1788.00 | 0.00 | 229.12 | 0.00 |
| 2268 | 412 | 64.00 | 1792.00 | 0.00 | 229.63 | 0.00 |
| 2272 | 412 | 64.00 | 1796.00 | 0.00 | 230.14 | 0.00 |
| 2276 | 412 | 64.00 | 1800.00 | 0.00 | 230.66 | 0.00 |
| 2280 | 412 | 64.00 | 1804.00 | 0.00 | 231.17 | 0.00 |
| 2284 | 412 | 64.00 | 1808.00 | 0.00 | 231.68 | 0.00 |
| 2288 | 412 | 64.00 | 1812.00 | 0.00 | 232.19 | 0.00 |
| 2292 | 412 | 64.00 | 1816.00 | 0.00 | 232.70 | 0.00 |
| 2296 | 412 | 64.00 | 1820.00 | 0.00 | 233.22 | 0.00 |
| 2300 | 412 | 64.00 | 1824.00 | 0.00 | 233.73 | 0.00 |
| 2304 | 412 | 64.00 | 1828.00 | 0.00 | 234.24 | 0.00 |
| 2308 | 412 | 64.00 | 1832.00 | 0.00 | 234.75 | 0.00 |

▼ for information only - do not enter on form P11 *Deductions Working Sheet*

# TAX TABLES

Table letter **C**

**Monthly table**

| Employee's earnings up to and including the UEL £ | Earnings at the LEL (where earnings are equal to or exceed the LEL) 1a £ | Earnings above the LEL, up to and including the ET 1b £ p | Earnings above the ET, up to and including the UAP 1c £ p | Earnings above the UAP, up to and including the UEL 1d £ p | Total of employee's and employer's contributions 1e £ p | Employee's contributions due on all earnings above the ET 1f £ p |
|---|---|---|---|---|---|---|
| 2532 | 412 | 64.00 | 2056.00 | 0.00 | 263.42 | 0.00 |
| 2536 | 412 | 64.00 | 2060.00 | 0.00 | 263.94 | 0.00 |
| 2540 | 412 | 64.00 | 2064.00 | 0.00 | 264.45 | 0.00 |
| 2544 | 412 | 64.00 | 2068.00 | 0.00 | 264.96 | 0.00 |
| 2548 | 412 | 64.00 | 2072.00 | 0.00 | 265.47 | 0.00 |
| 2552 | 412 | 64.00 | 2076.00 | 0.00 | 265.98 | 0.00 |
| 2556 | 412 | 64.00 | 2080.00 | 0.00 | 266.50 | 0.00 |
| 2560 | 412 | 64.00 | 2084.00 | 0.00 | 267.01 | 0.00 |
| 2564 | 412 | 64.00 | 2088.00 | 0.00 | 267.52 | 0.00 |
| 2568 | 412 | 64.00 | 2092.00 | 0.00 | 268.03 | 0.00 |
| 2572 | 412 | 64.00 | 2096.00 | 0.00 | 268.54 | 0.00 |
| 2576 | 412 | 64.00 | 2100.00 | 0.00 | 269.06 | 0.00 |
| 2580 | 412 | 64.00 | 2104.00 | 0.00 | 269.57 | 0.00 |
| 2584 | 412 | 64.00 | 2108.00 | 0.00 | 270.08 | 0.00 |
| 2588 | 412 | 64.00 | 2112.00 | 0.00 | 270.59 | 0.00 |
| 2592 | 412 | 64.00 | 2116.00 | 0.00 | 271.10 | 0.00 |
| 2596 | 412 | 64.00 | 2120.00 | 0.00 | 271.62 | 0.00 |
| 2600 | 412 | 64.00 | 2124.00 | 0.00 | 272.13 | 0.00 |
| 2604 | 412 | 64.00 | 2128.00 | 0.00 | 272.64 | 0.00 |
| 2608 | 412 | 64.00 | 2132.00 | 0.00 | 273.15 | 0.00 |
| 2612 | 412 | 64.00 | 2136.00 | 0.00 | 273.66 | 0.00 |
| 2616 | 412 | 64.00 | 2140.00 | 0.00 | 274.18 | 0.00 |
| 2620 | 412 | 64.00 | 2144.00 | 0.00 | 274.69 | 0.00 |
| 2624 | 412 | 64.00 | 2148.00 | 0.00 | 275.20 | 0.00 |
| 2628 | 412 | 64.00 | 2152.00 | 0.00 | 275.71 | 0.00 |
| 2632 | 412 | 64.00 | 2156.00 | 0.00 | 276.22 | 0.00 |
| 2636 | 412 | 64.00 | 2160.00 | 0.00 | 276.74 | 0.00 |
| 2640 | 412 | 64.00 | 2164.00 | 0.00 | 277.25 | 0.00 |
| 2644 | 412 | 64.00 | 2168.00 | 0.00 | 277.76 | 0.00 |
| 2648 | 412 | 64.00 | 2172.00 | 0.00 | 278.27 | 0.00 |
| 2652 | 412 | 64.00 | 2176.00 | 0.00 | 278.78 | 0.00 |
| 2656 | 412 | 64.00 | 2180.00 | 0.00 | 279.30 | 0.00 |
| 2660 | 412 | 64.00 | 2184.00 | 0.00 | 279.81 | 0.00 |
| 2664 | 412 | 64.00 | 2188.00 | 0.00 | 280.32 | 0.00 |
| 2668 | 412 | 64.00 | 2192.00 | 0.00 | 280.83 | 0.00 |
| 2672 | 412 | 64.00 | 2196.00 | 0.00 | 281.34 | 0.00 |
| 2676 | 412 | 64.00 | 2200.00 | 0.00 | 281.86 | 0.00 |
| 2680 | 412 | 64.00 | 2204.00 | 0.00 | 282.37 | 0.00 |
| 2684 | 412 | 64.00 | 2208.00 | 0.00 | 282.88 | 0.00 |
| 2688 | 412 | 64.00 | 2212.00 | 0.00 | 283.39 | 0.00 |
| 2692 | 412 | 64.00 | 2216.00 | 0.00 | 283.90 | 0.00 |
| 2696 | 412 | 64.00 | 2220.00 | 0.00 | 284.42 | 0.00 |
| 2700 | 412 | 64.00 | 2224.00 | 0.00 | 284.93 | 0.00 |
| 2704 | 412 | 64.00 | 2228.00 | 0.00 | 285.44 | 0.00 |
| 2708 | 412 | 64.00 | 2232.00 | 0.00 | 285.95 | 0.00 |
| 2712 | 412 | 64.00 | 2236.00 | 0.00 | 286.46 | 0.00 |
| 2716 | 412 | 64.00 | 2240.00 | 0.00 | 286.98 | 0.00 |
| 2720 | 412 | 64.00 | 2244.00 | 0.00 | 287.49 | 0.00 |
| 2724 | 412 | 64.00 | 2248.00 | 0.00 | 288.00 | 0.00 |
| 2728 | 412 | 64.00 | 2252.00 | 0.00 | 288.51 | 0.00 |
| 2732 | 412 | 64.00 | 2256.00 | 0.00 | 289.02 | 0.00 |
| 2736 | 412 | 64.00 | 2260.00 | 0.00 | 289.54 | 0.00 |
| 2740 | 412 | 64.00 | 2264.00 | 0.00 | 290.05 | 0.00 |
| 2744 | 412 | 64.00 | 2268.00 | 0.00 | 290.56 | 0.00 |
| 2748 | 412 | 64.00 | 2272.00 | 0.00 | 291.07 | 0.00 |

▼ for information only - do not enter on form P11 *Deductions Working Sheet*

TAX TABLES

**HM Revenue & Customs**

**CA39**
National Insurance Contributions Tables

# Contracted-out contributions for employers with Contracted-out Salary Related Schemes

Use from
6 April 2009 to
5 April 2010 inclusive

## Earnings limits and NICs rates

| Earnings limits | Employee's contribution — Contribution Table letter D | Contribution Table letter E | Contribution Table letter L | Employer's contribution — Table letters D, E and L | Employee's NICs rebate on earnings above the LEL, up to and including the ET (Applies to contribution category letters D and L only) | Employer's NICs rebate on earnings above the LEL, up to and including the ET |
|---|---|---|---|---|---|---|
| below £95 weekly, or below £412 monthly, or below £4,940 yearly | Nil | Nil | Nil | Nil | Nil | Nil |
| £95 to £110 weekly, or £412 to £476 monthly, or £4,940 to £5,715 yearly | 0% | 0% | 0% | 0% | | |
| £110.01 to £770 weekly, or £476.01 to £3,337 monthly, or £5,715.01 to £40,040 yearly | 9.4% on earnings above the ET | 4.85% on earnings above the ET | 1% on earnings above the ET | 9.1% on earnings above the ET | 1.6% on earnings from £95.01, up to and including £110.00 (or monthly or annual equivalents) | 3.7% on earnings from £95.01, up to and including £110.00 (or monthly or annual equivalents) |
| £770.01 to £844 weekly, or £3,337.01 to £3,656 monthly, or £40,040.01 to £43,875 yearly | 9.4% on earnings above the ET, up to and including the UAP, then 11% on earnings above the UAP | 4.85% on earnings above the ET | 1% on earnings above the ET | 9.1% on earnings above the ET, up to and including the UAP, then 12.8% on earnings above the UAP | | |
| Over £844 weekly, or over £3,656 monthly, or over £43,875 yearly | 9.4% on earnings above the ET, up to and including the UAP, then 11% on earnings above the UAP up to and including the UEL, then 1% on all earnings above the UEL | 4.85% on earnings above the ET, up to and including the UEL, then 1% on all earnings above the UEL | 1% on all earnings above the ET | 9.1% on earnings above the ET, up to and including the UAP, then 12.8% on all earnings above the UAP | | |

TAX TABLES

**HM Revenue & Customs**

**CA43**
National Insurance Contributions Tables

# Contracted-out contributions and minimum payments for employers with Contracted-out Money Purchase Schemes

**Use from
6 April 2009 to
5 April 2010 inclusive**

# TAX TABLES

## Earnings limits and NIC rates

| Earnings limits | Employee's contribution Contribution Table letter F | Employee's contribution Contribution Table letter G | Employee's contribution Contribution Table letter S | Employer's contribution Table letters F, G and S | Employee's NIC rebate on earnings above the LEL, up to and including the ET (Applies to contribution category letters F and S only) | Employer's NIC rebate on earnings above the LEL, up to and including the ET |
|---|---|---|---|---|---|---|
| Below £95 weekly, **or** Below £412 monthly, **or** Below £4,940 yearly | Nil | Nil | Nil | Nil | Nil | Nil |
| £95 to £110 weekly, **or** £412 to £476 monthly, **or** £4,940 to £5,715 yearly | 0% | 0% | 0% | 0% | 1.6% on earnings from £95.01, up to and including £110 (or monthly or annual equivalents) | 1.4% on earnings from £95.01, up to and including £110 (or monthly or annual equivalents) |
| £110.01 to £770 weekly, **or** £476.01 to £3337 monthly, **or** £5,715.01 to £40,040 yearly | **9.4%** on earnings above the ET | **4.85%** on earnings above the ET | **1%** on earnings above the ET | **11.4%** on earnings above the ET | | |
| £770.01 to £844 weekly, **or** £3,337.01 to £3,656 monthly, **or** £40,040.01 to £43,875 yearly | **9.4%** on earnings above the ET, up to and including the UAP, then **11%** on earnings above the UAP | **4.85%** on earnings above the ET | **1%** on earnings above the ET | **11.4%** on earnings above the ET, up to and including the UAP, then **12.8%** on earnings above the UAP | | |
| Over £844 weekly, **or** over £3,656 monthly, **or** over £43,875 yearly | **9.4%** on earnings above the ET, up to and including the UAP, then **11%** on all earnings above the UAP, up to and including the UEL, then **1%** on all earnings above the UEL | **4.85%** on earnings above the ET, up to and including the UEL, then **1%** on all earnings above the UEL | **1%** on all earnings above the ET | **11.4%** on earnings above the ET, up to and including the UAP, then **12.8%** on all earnings above the UAP | | |

437

# TAX TABLES

# Review Form & Free Prize Draw – Payroll Administration Level 2 Revision Companion (8/09)

All original review forms from the entire BPP range, completed with genuine comments, will be entered into one of two draws on 31 January 2010 and 31 July 2010. The names on the first four forms picked out on each occasion will be sent a cheque for £50.

Name: _____    Address: _____

**How have you used this Revision Companion?**
*(Tick one box only)*
☐ Home study (book only)
☐ On a course: college _____
☐ With 'correspondence' package
☐ Other _____

**Why did you decide to purchase this Revision Companion?** *(Tick one box only)*
☐ Have used BPP Texts in the past
☐ Recommendation by friend/colleague
☐ Recommendation by a lecturer at college
☐ Saw advertising
☐ Other _____

**During the past six months do you recall seeing/receiving any of the following?**
*(Tick as many boxes as are relevant)*
☐ Our advertisement in *Accounting Technician* magazine
☐ Our advertisement in *Pass*
☐ Our brochure with a letter through the post

**Which (if any) aspects of our advertising do you find useful?**
*(Tick as many boxes as are relevant)*
☐ Prices and publication dates of new editions
☐ Information on Revision Companion content
☐ Facility to order books off-the-page
☐ None of the above

Have you used the companion Course Companion for this subject?    ☐ Yes    ☐ No

Your ratings, comments and suggestions would be appreciated on the following areas

|  | Very useful | Useful | Not useful |
|---|---|---|---|
| Introduction | ☐ | ☐ | ☐ |
| Practice Activities | ☐ | ☐ | ☐ |
| Sample Simulations | ☐ | ☐ | ☐ |
| Exams | ☐ | ☐ | ☐ |
| Lecturers' Resource Section | ☐ | ☐ | ☐ |

|  | Excellent | Good | Adequate | Poor |
|---|---|---|---|---|
| Overall opinion of this Kit | ☐ | ☐ | ☐ | ☐ |

Do you intend to continue using BPP Course Companions/Revision Companions?    ☐ Yes    ☐ No

Please note any further comments and suggestions/errors on the reverse of this page.

The BPP author of this edition can be e-mailed at: janiceross@bpp.com

*Please return this form to: Janice Ross, BPP Learning Media, FREEPOST, London, W12 8BR*

**Review Form & Free Prize Draw (continued)**

Please note any further comments and suggestions/errors below

**Free Prize Draw Rules**

1. Closing date for 31 January 2010 draw is 31 December 2009. Closing date for 31 July 2010 draw is 30 June 2010.
2. Restricted to entries with UK and Eire addresses only. BPP employees, their families and business associates are excluded.
3. No purchase necessary. Entry forms are available upon request from BPP Learning Media. No more than one entry per title, per person. Draw restricted to persons aged 16 and over.
4. Winners will be notified by post and receive their cheques not later than 6 weeks after the relevant draw date.
5. The decision of the promoter in all matters is final and binding. No correspondence will be entered into.